10 STEPS TO HOME OWNERSHIP

10 STEPS TO HOME OWNERSHIP

A Workbook for First-Time Buyers

Ilyce R. Glink

TIMES BUSINESS

RANDOM HOUSE

Copyright © 1996 by Ilyce R. Glink

All rights reserved under International and Pan-American Copyright Conventions.
Published in the United States by Times Books, a division of Random House, Inc.,
New York, and simultaneously in Canada by Random House of Canada Limited,
Toronto.

Glink, Ilyce R.
    10 steps to home ownership : a workbook for first-time buyers /
Ilyce R. Glink. — 1st ed.
        p.   cm.
    ISBN 0-8129-2531-9 (trade pbk.)
    1. House buying—United States.   2. Home ownership—United States.
I. Title.
HD259.G53   1996
643′.12—dc20   95-44350
                                                             CIP

This book is intended as a general guide on the topics discussed and does not deliver
accounting or legal advice. It is not intended, and should not be used, as a substitute
for professional advice (legal or otherwise). The reader should consult a competent
attorney and/or other professional with specific issues, problems, or questions the
reader may have.

Random House website address: http://www.randomhouse.com/

Printed in the United States of America on acid-free paper

9 8 7 6 5 4 3 2

First Edition

*For Alexander, who makes me smile,
and Sam, who makes me laugh.*

*And in memory of Linda Levin Ragins,
whose radiant smiles and warm hugs
effortlessly brightened our lives.*

Contents

Preface

To the uninitiated, buying a home contains all the wonder and magic of, say, a ten-year-old's first trip to Walt Disney World, when you're old enough to know that life isn't really like AdventureLand, but young enough not to care. When we think about homeownership, it seems to be a place of mystery and contentment, a place where dreams come true and we all live happily ever after. It is a state of mind, being, and pocketbook we pine for, one enjoyed daily by millions. And those of us committed to the journey will do almost anything to get there, from pinching pennies to living with in-laws.

My grandfather used to say that the pre-engagement romance is the best part of any relationship. "After you get engaged," he'd say, "it's all business right up to the wedding." The same is true for wanna-be home buyers: The period of time before you start looking for a home may be, in retrospect, your favorite part of the process. There's time to analyze your finances, drool dreamily over newspaper ads, and think about what you really want and need in a home. There's also time to correct past financial mistakes and face important legal issues. Once you engage a real estate agent or broker, and begin looking for a home (at what often seems a frenzied pace), you may find yourself careening nearly out of control at times, hurtling toward the inevitable, wonderful conclusion: the closing.

10 Steps to Homeownership: A Workbook for First-Time Buyers is for people who believe the American dream of homeownership is within reach. It is for people who understand that homeownership has its advantages and disadvantages, and recognize that there are long-term responsibilities that cannot be ignored. It is a book designed to help all first-time buyers, but especially pre-buyers—those of you who are perhaps 3 months to 3 years out from being ready to look at homes listed for sale, but have already made the commitment to homeownership—figure out what needs to happen, when, and in what order, so that the path to homeownership is smoother.

10 Steps will help you sort out the financial and emotional issues of homeownership, from deciding whether you should rent or buy to dealing with any pressure you may feel from your real estate agent. It will help those of you facing credit problems learn how to solve them and those of you facing a credit crunch synch your finances with your homeownership goals. Use the charts, graphs, and worksheets to get your finances in ship-shape, then check out the legal issues that sometimes derail the best of intentions. Finally, *10 Steps* looks at the nuts and bolts of buyer/broker relationships, mortgage financing, and the closing, all from the perspective of someone who is not quite ready to visit that first open house.

One of the key points I've tried to bring to light in this book is that homeownership isn't for everyone. Some folks may find homeownership to be an expensive, time-consuming, and emotionally-draining experience. There are predictable expenses such as your monthly mortgage payments, property taxes, and insurance premiums. And there are your unpredictable expenses, like when the water heater blows and you've got to replace it immediately, often with money earmarked for vacation, camp, or a special gift. Homes, especially single-family houses, need regular, ongoing maintenance and upkeep. You've got to keep up with the landscaping, exterior and interior surfaces, and mechanical systems, all of which may need to be replaced or repaired during your tenure in the home.

Does it sound overwhelming? It doesn't have to be. Perhaps it will comfort you to know that roughly 66 million American families own their own homes. The federal government would like to see that number rise to 68 million homeowners by the year 2000, which would be the highest level of homeownership ever. That's 2 million additional homeowners by the turn of the century.

You could be one of them. It's never been easier for first-time home buyers to purchase their piece of the American Dream. Since the beginning of the 1990s, lenders have greatly reduced both the amount of cash needed for a down payment and the number of closing costs and fees you'll pay. Over the next few years, you'll see the price of loans fall as national lenders reach out directly to you, the consumer, through the Internet and through software that allows you to shop for homes and loans from the comfort of your kitchen.

Despite this good news and more, you must remember that the path to homeownership remains full of potholes. You'll have to work through the tough financial and emotional issues that are discussed in the book. Even an "easy" deal has its moments of instability and crisis. By assessing your personal financial and emotional resources (and those of your spouse or partner) before you even start looking for a home, you'll give yourself a chance to balance your needs and wants with your pocketbook. With preparation and a healthy dose of determination, you can overcome any obstacle that stands in your way.

Still, it helps to know what's coming. I've written this book to prepare you for what lies ahead. My 10 Steps take you from the day you decide that becoming a home buyer is a goal and not a dream, through the day you're actually ready to start looking for a home. When you're ready for the next step, I hope you'll find another book I've written, *100 Questions Every First-Time Home Buyer Should Ask*, an able guide. Together, these books should give you all the information you need about the process of buying a home.

Good luck, and happy house hunting!!

ILYCE R. GLINK
October 1996

P.S. If you have questions that aren't answered in this book, or if you just want to share your home-buying experiences, feel free to drop me a line. Write to: Ilyce Glink, P.O. Box 366, Glencoe, IL 60022. Those of you who are on the Internet may send e-mail to IlyceGlink@aol.com.

10 STEPS TO HOME OWNERSHIP

Introduction

In the hectic, rapidly changing world in which we live, there's something secure and old-fashioned about being a homeowner. Although people relocate more frequently today than in previous generations (Americans, on average, move every 5 to 7 years), the process of purchasing property indicates a decision to stay put, to plant roots and grow in one place for a while. Buying a home gives you a membership stake in a community and a sense of permanence.

Does the dream of owning a home seem out of reach for you, financially and emotionally? The shroud of mystery that still surrounds the home buying process often obscures the possible. Still, those who are ready to start looking for a home often say they can see the light at the end of the tunnel. Some of those who dream of buying don't even know how to find the entrance.

That's why I wrote this book. *10 Steps to Home Ownership: A Workbook for First-Time Buyers* should prove enormously useful, wherever you are on the path to homeownership. I hope it will especially help those of you who have made buying a home a goal but are months or even years away from going to your first open house.

Even if homeownership is years away, there are questions and issues that have to be dealt with: Am I better off renting or buying? How much does it cost each year to own and maintain a home? How do I clear up my credit history? How do I put together a down payment and a homeowner's budget? If you find yourself worrying about these and other issues and questions, you're not alone. All home buyers (particularly first-time buyers) have at some time stood in the same shoes.

3

No problem is insurmountable. For example, you can still buy a home *even* if you've declared bankruptcy, you owe a balance on your credit cards, you don't know where you want to live, or you hardly have any cash in the bank.

Start here and work your way through my sequence of the 10 Steps that can jump-start your homeownership plans. For each Step, the discussion of financial issues and emotional/family issues will help you deal with both your wallet and your worries. The worksheets, tables, and exercises I have provided should make it easier for you to understand how the numbers work. The amortization tables in Appendix II will help you figure out how much you'll pay monthly to a lender for your loan. And the resources listed in Appendix III include places where you can get a copy of your credit report, help on your credit issues, where to find an independent rating service for public schools, and more. The Glossary of Real Estate Terms will help you wade through the jargon you'll inevitably hear during your search for a home.

Most importantly, I wrote this book to reassure you that what you're facing has been faced successfully by millions of home buyers. Everyone has obstacles to overcome on the way to making this biggest, and often most long-term financial investment. And everyone, to a greater or lesser degree, overcomes them.

So will you.

Should I Rent or
Should I Buy?

**"Renting is the same as owning. Except you're paying some-
one else's mortgage."**

Anonymous Realtor

Are you a home buyer or a renter?

That question is easy enough to answer, especially if you take it literally:

A renter is someone who may someday want to own a home but for the moment is quite happy paying rent on a lease.

A home buyer is someone who has actively made the decision to buy a home, even if it means renting until he or she has saved up enough money.

Are you better off being a renter or a buyer? The answer to that question is more complicated. It depends on a wide variety of factors, including whether your job requires you to be transferred frequently, and where in the country you've chosen to live. Deciding whether you really want to buy a home means taking a long, hard look at both your finances and your feelings.

Financially, owning a home is often promoted as a better choice than renting. Currently, there are significant federal and state tax breaks: homeowners can claim deductions for real estate property taxes and for the interest paid on their mortgage each year. In

5

addition, long-term homeowners build *equity* (the financial stake or investment you have in a home)—and their personal wealth—both by *paying down* their mortgage and when their home appreciates in value. Many savvy home buyers increase their equity more quickly by buying homes that need cosmetic improvements (such as decorating) rather than structural renovation (walls need moving). These minor improvements can significantly increase the value of a home over a relatively short period of time with a modest investment.

Paying rent, the adage goes, is akin to throwing money out of the window. There is no long-term benefit financially. As a renter, you write a check each month to the landlord of your rental unit, and say good-bye to your money as you drop the envelope in the mail. A family living in Chicago has rented the same three-bedroom apartment for nearly 30 years. Figuring an average rent of $1,300 per month, these tenants have paid the landlord more than $450,000 in rent during the years they've lived there. If they had bought 30 years ago, they might have paid only $35,000 for a unit similar to the one they've occupied all these years. By now, not only would their home be paid off (they might have paid around $75,574 in principal and interest on a 30-year mortgage at 10 percent), but they would now own a home worth at least $300,000, and they would have been entitled to years of tax benefits.

Are there situations when renting makes better sense than buying? Definitely.

If you're going to be in one place for only a couple of years, buying a home can be a far more expensive choice than paying rent for the same period of time, even factoring in the tax breaks. For example, your home would have to be located in an area with extraordinary appreciation just to recoup your costs when you sell: a brokerage commission; city, county, and state transfer fees; title insurance; and a home warranty for the buyer, among other costs. If you buy and sell within a short period of time, you may well end up *losing* equity rather than building it.

Renting also makes good sense if you've identified the general area in which you want to live but haven't made a final decision as to the specific neighborhood. Buying a home in a neighborhood you don't know well is one of the top mistakes home buyers make. If you don't know whether you'll feel comfortable in a particular neighborhood, it may be better to rent a house or an apartment there for 6 months or a year, to get a feel for it. If you like living there and you like your neighbors, you'll feel much more comfortable signing a purchase contract and loan documents later on.

It's extremely important to review your personal finances and determine what you can afford comfortably. It's also worthwhile to explore your feelings about homeownership. There is a certain cachet to owning a home. It immediately connects you to the community in a permanent way. Unless you fail to pay your mortgage or your property taxes, you will be able to stay in that home for as long as you like—perhaps even for the rest of your life. And you, not a landlord, will benefit from any improvements you make to the home through its increased appreciation. You can paint your home any color you wish, expand or reconfigure it to better meet your needs, and add amenities to make yourself more comfortable.

Some renters, however, aren't quite ready to plant their roots. Single people in their 20s and early 30s may prefer to rent near other singles in a neighborhood that offers a more active lifestyle. People who are changing jobs or careers may not want the long-term financial responsibility that comes with a mortgage and property taxes. Some renters may prefer to have a landlord deal with maintenance problems.

If you're like most first-time home buyers, the home you ultimately purchase will likely be the biggest single investment you'll ever make. Before you make the decision to stay a renter or to start the home-buying process, you will need to deal with serious financial and emotional issues. Let's take a look at them.

FINANCIAL ISSUES

Your Financial Goals

FINANCIAL
ISSUE
1

When you're a first-time buyer, purchasing a home means putting most—if not all—of your capital toward your home purchase. But cleaning out a bank account may not suit everyone's personal financial goals. Think carefully about what your financial goals are, and about the order in which you hope to attain them. Then make your rent-or-buy decision.

What are some personal financial goals? For many people, they include owning or leasing a new car, buying stocks and bonds, starting a retirement account, or building up substantial savings. For your first goal, an excellent choice might be to pay off your credit cards and school loans and get yourself out of debt. (See Step 4, Building Credible Credit, for more information on debt and credit.)

There are many strategies for creating a successful financial portfolio, which likely will include owning a home. But unless you're extraordinarily lucky—or independently wealthy—you won't be able to do everything at once. You may be able to contribute to a retirement account and add a little to your savings, but will have to wait until another year to buy or lease a new car or pay off your car loan. Or, you may be able to pay off your personal debt in one or two years, and then concentrate on building up an account for a down payment on a home.

Most financial experts believe that owning your own home is a wonderful way to start building your personal wealth. They point to the principal portion of your monthly mortgage payment as enforced savings, and they extol the virtues of borrowing money that is subsidized (by the federal government, through the mortgage interest and real estate property tax deductions on your personal income tax return). Statistics show that the majority of the average American's personal wealth lies in his or her home equity.

On the other hand, some experts believe you'll build up wealth more quickly by living cheaply, calculating the money you would have spent each month as a homeowner (for a mortgage, maintenance and upkeep, and property taxes), and investing that amount in stocks, bonds, mutual funds, or certificates of deposit (CDs).

How does this strategy work? Let's say you have a wonderful deal on a cheap but pleasant apartment. Your rent is far less each month than you would have to pay to own your dream home in a great neighborhood. If you are paying $400 per month to rent that one-bedroom apartment rather than spend $1,000 per month to own your dream home, and you invest the savings of $600 per month in a stock mutual fund that grows at an average annual rate of 7 percent, in 30 years your $600 per month investment would be worth $732,000, perhaps far more than the unit you would have bought.

This scenario sounds wonderful, but it has some flaws. First, it's unlikely that you'll want to stay in a one-bedroom apartment for 30 years. If you're like most people, you'll get married or find a partner, and have children. Or perhaps you already have a spouse or partner and one child. That one-bedroom apartment will quickly become too small to accommodate you comfortably. Second, unless they've arranged for a direct deposit to a mutual fund account, most people aren't disciplined enough to take the $600 per month (or whatever it is) out of their paycheck. It's easier and more fun to buy CDs (the musical kind), clothes, and a car, go out to dinner, and take nice vacations. New studies show that generation X employees are more likely to save than their Baby Boomer parents, but almost no Americans put the majority of their paycheck into savings.

Whether the "living cheap" theory will work for you depends on your answers to the following questions: How cheap are you really willing to live, and for how long? Will you be diligent about socking away the "extra" cash each month? Will you carefully monitor your investments and switch if the rate of return goes down?

Ultimately, you have to assess your personal financial goals to find out whether homeownership will help you achieve them. Use the chart on page 10 to help you identify some of your personal financial goals. Put down *everything*, including the desire to be debt-free; the ability to put your kids through college; the cost of caring for an aging parent or relative; owning your own home, car, or sailboat; maintaining a portfolio of stocks and bonds; or being financially comfortable.

Most of us have fantasized about being rich and famous. Perhaps our lucky shot will come from winning the lottery. Perhaps a company we invest in will strike oil or create new must-have computer software. Theoretically, everyone has a chance to become rich, but relatively few people do. But that doesn't mean we can't be financially stable and even comfortable. Some of the financial goals on your personal list will move you well along the path to financial freedom—for example, owning your own home or owning a portfolio of stocks and bonds. Other goals, such as owning a sailboat, you may enjoy enormously but may drain your pocketbook rather than enhancing your wealth. That's not to say you should never own a stereo system or a home-theater television set. But you have choices. Prioritize your financial goals and then work toward the most important ones.

How Does the Potential Rise in Home Values Affect My Decision to Rent or to Buy?

FINANCIAL
ISSUE
2

Within every village, town, city, and metropolitan area, there are some neighborhoods where home prices rise and others where they fall. Even within a neighborhood where home values are generally appreciating, there will be homes whose values are flat or declining.

Why does this happen? Articulating the value of a home is an art, not a science. No two homes—even identically built homes in the same subdivision—are exactly the same. The homeowner's touches,

WORKSHEET
My Personal Financial Goals

Personal Financial Goals

Number of Years Estimated for Achievement

1. _____   _____
2. _____   _____
3. _____   _____
4. _____   _____
5. _____   _____
6. _____   _____
7. _____   _____
8. _____   _____
9. _____   _____
10. _____   _____
11. _____   _____
12. _____   _____
13. _____   _____
14. _____   _____
15. _____   _____
16. _____   _____
17. _____   _____
18. _____   _____
19. _____   _____
20. _____   _____

including decorating, upgrades, level of maintenance, amenities, and overall condition, contribute heavily to whether a home appreciates or depreciates in value. For example, if a neighborhood within an excellent school district has generally appreciated 5 percent per year for the past 10 years, but Mrs. Jones has failed to maintain her home at the level of other homes in the neighborhood, she might experience some appreciation—say, 1 to 2 percent per year—but it will be nowhere near the level enjoyed by her neighbors.

The way the tide is turning in a given neighborhood is important if you're considering buying a home there. Look for a neighborhood that has a good long-term potential but will also hold its value in the short term (just in case you have to sell quickly). In any neighborhood, look for the qualities that support home appreciation: excellent schools, neighbors who take an active interest in maintaining and upgrading their homes, and sound local economics. (For more information on finding good neighborhoods, see Step 6, Identifying Where You Want to Live.)

If a market is appreciating too quickly, watch out. Home buyers in the Northeast and in California got caught when, after a decade of double-digit appreciation, home values declined by as much as 50 percent. Home buyers who bought in 1988 or 1989, the peak years of the market, were, by the mid-1990s, stuck with homes worth half of what they paid for them. At the same time, some Rocky Mountain states—Montana, Nevada, and especially Colorado—have enjoyed several years of strong appreciation. These markets show no signs of slowing, but that kind of appreciation probably won't last forever.

Unless you're in an area with declining or flat appreciation, you'll likely do better owning than renting, because of the leverage you gain with your down payment. *Leverage* is a financial tool that enables you to spend a small amount of capital in order to control a larger amount of capital. In real estate, leverage comes into play when a small cash down payment allows you to buy a whole house using borrowed funds (your mortgage). Your house is valued in terms of its sales price, not on the basis of your down payment or how many mortgage payments you have made. If the property appreciates you'll make more money. Let's say your house costs $100,000, and you put down $10,000. If your home appreciates 5 percent, that is $5,000 you've "earned" on your $10,000 investment.

10 STEP
TIP

11

When deciding whether you're better off renting or buying, consider whether the neighborhood in which you're interested is going up in value, or down. If it's going up above the rate of inflation, your investment dollars will be working harder for you. If the neighborhood is declining in value, you may be better off renting, or looking for another neighborhood in which to buy.

FINANCIAL ISSUE 3

The Costs of Owning vs. Renting

The costs of homeownership are another important factor in deciding whether to rent or buy a home. Once you've found the place, renting is easy. You pay a fixed amount of money to your landlord each month, and you pay for your utilities. As a homeowner, you would also make a monthly payment—the mortgage payment to your lender—but your costs of homeownership go far beyond that monthly payment. And some of these costs may change, depending on the number of years you live in a home.

Homeownership involves *fixed* costs and *variable* costs. Fixed costs are stable from year to year, or may go up slightly. For example, if you buy a home with a 30-year fixed-rate mortgage, you will pay the same amount each month to your lender for 30 years (not including increases in your real estate taxes and property insurance premiums), regardless of what happens in the general economic climate. This is a fixed expense. But if you get an adjustable rate mortgage (ARM), where the interest rate adjusts at a preset interval to keep pace with a designated index, the amount you pay the lender will likely change every 6, 12, or 36 months. Your mortgage is then a variable cost.

Next to your mortgage and property insurance, your property taxes will be your biggest expense. In California, where Proposition 13 states that the property tax a homeowner pays will equal 1 percent of the purchase price of the home—forever, or until the law changes again—real estate property taxes are fixed costs. Almost everywhere else in the country, however, property taxes fluctuate every time they're reassessed, usually every couple of years. You can often count on paying around 1 to 3 percent (or more) of the purchase price of your home in real estate taxes.

A profusion of other quasi-fixed costs come along with homeownership: maintenance and upkeep of the property, landscaping, decorating (every home buyer wants to add his or her personal touches), water, sewage, trash removal, and utilities. Maintenance and upkeep can be big expenses, particularly if you're buying an older home.

Each month, you should put money into a maintenance fund in order to cover major capital expenses, like replacing the furnace or the roof. Then there are the occasional expenses. For example, if the house you buy has a fireplace, you might need to hire a chimney sweep every five years or so to keep the flue venting properly. And every year or two, you may have to hire someone to keep tree roots from clogging up your underground drain pipes.

The bottom line is this: Owning a home can be more expensive than renting, even with the current federal tax breaks figured in. But most homeowners hope to compensate for these additional costs by building equity (the enforced savings that accumulates with every mortgage payment) and by owning a home that appreciates in value.

Use the worksheet on page 14 to compare the costs of renting with the costs of owning a comparable home. If you don't feel ready to tackle this worksheet now, do it after you read through Step 2, How Much House Can I Afford?

The Tax Savings of Homeownership

FINANCIAL
ISSUE
4

In what year was the first mortgage interest deduction allowed? Most historians will tell you that when Congress passed the first U.S. income tax in 1913, it allowed a deduction for mortgage interest. An unconfirmed anecdote relates that, in 1863, a special tax was floated to fund the Union army during the Civil War; supposedly, that tax also included a mortgage interest deduction.

Whether the mortgage interest deduction first appeared in 1863 or fifty years later in 1913, it's pretty clear that the federal government has a long history of supporting homeownership. And that support comes in ways other than being able to deduct the mortgage interest you pay from your federal income taxes. For example, when you sell your home, Uncle Sam allows you 24 months to roll over into a new home any profits (capital gains) you may have realized on the sale. In most instances, there is no limit to the number of times you can use the "24-month rollover replacement rule." You can effectively postpone paying capital gains tax indefinitely.

Once you reach the age of 55, the federal government allows you a one-time perk: you can pocket tax-free the first $125,000 of capital gain on the sale of your home. Or, if you never sell your home but instead will it to your heirs after your death, your heirs benefit under current laws that permit them to inherit the home without paying taxes on any increase in the dollar value of the home.

WORKSHEET
The Costs of Owning vs. Renting a Home

Rental Costs	Amount/Month
Monthly Rent	_____
Electricity	_____
Gas (if applicable)	_____
Cable TV	_____
Other Costs	_____
Total Monthly Expenses	_____

Homeownership Costs	Amount/Month
Monthly Mortgage	_____
Property Tax Escrow*	_____
Property Hazard Insurance Escrow*	_____
Landscaping/Snow Removal	_____
Capital Maintenance Budget	_____
(An estimate of your yearly repairs on the home)	_____
Assessment for Condos and Co-ops	_____
Decorating	_____
(What you expect to spend on refurbishing your home from time to time)	
Gas	_____
Electricity	_____
Water	_____
Sewer	_____
Cable TV	_____
Other Utility	_____
Pest Control	_____
Other Costs	_____
Total per Month	_____

*The property tax escrow is equal to your property tax bill divided by 12. The hazard insurance escrow is equal to your annual insurance premium divided by 12.

Current laws and tax regulations are not set in stone, but the U.S. government has traditionally subsidized or promoted homeownership. Why? A research associate with the Urban Institute, a nonpartisan, nonprofit, Washington (DC) organization that conducts research on a host of contemporary public policy issues, points to a long-standing belief in this country that homeownership creates citizens who are more politically and socially active. This principle has been relatively unchallenged by scholarly research for generations. And, the vast majority of Americans buy the idea "It's good for me and good for the larger society."

Because of the public and private acceptance of the positive values of homeownership, the federal government has embarked on a whole series of policies to support it.

For more than two decades after the mortgage interest deduction was incorporated into the original federal income tax system in 1913, nothing changed for homeowners. Then, in 1937, when the U.S. economy was clawing its way out of the Great Depression, the Federal Housing Administration (FHA) was created. The FHA changed the way people bought homes. Formerly, home buyers bought their homes using short-term loans of only 1 to 5 years in length. Purchasers had to put down as much as 40 to 50 percent of the sales price *in cash*, and pay off the entire loan balance by the end of the short loan term. (Today, we call this a balloon loan.) The FHA offered the first 30-year mortgage, which for the first time made homeownership available to the vast majority of Americans. The 30-year mortgage caught on quickly, proving that millions of Americans had wanted to be homeowners and had been searching for a financial vehicle that would make it possible. The 30-year loan was the Model T of home financing. It made homes affordable for the masses.

A dozen years later, Congress passed the Housing Act of 1949. According to John Tuccillo, senior economist for the National Association of Realtors, the Housing Act of 1949 set as its goal a safe and livable home for all Americans. "This Act, and the updated Act in 1968, were used as justification for broader housing subsidies in the 1960s and 1970s," Tuccillo says.

Throughout the years, federal programs based on these Acts were developed to help more and more Americans become homeowners. In the 1980s, Jack Kemp, director of the Department of Housing and Urban Development (HUD) during the Reagan Administration, floated a pilot program to convert public housing to private ownership and give it to the residents. President Clinton has pushed HUD

Secretary Henry Cisneros to expand homeownership rates further by pressuring lenders to end discrimination in lending, liberalize underwriting terms, and create unusual packages of loans to attract a greater number of home buyers who otherwise could not afford to buy a home.

From this brief review of past efforts, it's easy to see why current tax law favors homeowners over renters. To summarize, today, as a homeowner, Uncle Sam lets you:

1. Deduct the interest on your mortgage, and your property taxes.
2. Use the "24-month rollover replacement rule" to defer your capital gain.
3. Use the $125,000 one-time tax-free capital gains exclusion after age 55, to avoid paying taxes on that portion of your capital gain.

As a renter, you get no federal tax breaks whatsoever (though in some states you receive some state tax benefits).

That's the good news for home buyers. But you have to be realistic. Not everyone who buys a home will be able to take full advantage of the mortgage interest deduction. Why? Because to take full advantage of the deduction, you have to itemize your deductions on your federal income tax form. The idea behind itemization is to lower the amount of income that can be taxed. To benefit from your payment of mortgage interest and real estate taxes, your itemized deductions must exceed the so-called standard deduction that the IRS allows everyone to take.

How do you figure out whether you'll be able to maximize your homeownership deductions? A lot of this depends on what tax bracket you're in and how big a mortgage you need. Folks in the higher tax brackets will be able to make the best use of tax deductions. However, most Americans (and many first-time home buyers) are in the bottom tax bracket. Some experts say that the break-even point is reached when you get a mortgage for around $60,000. At an 8 percent interest rate, you'll pay around $4,800 in interest per year. If you add in $2,000 in property taxes, that takes you to $6,800, or just about $250 more than the 1995 standard deduction for married couples filing jointly.

For more specific information about what your specific tax savings would be after you purchase a home, consult your tax adviser.

EMOTIONAL/FAMILY ISSUES

There's more to life than running the numbers. Before you make the decision to rent or to buy, consider the emotional and family issues that play directly into that decision.

When Renting May Be Better Than Buying

EMOTIONAL/
FAMILY ISSUE
1

Even when you know that you can live more cheaply in a home you own, renting may still be a better choice for you at a particular point in time. Here are some very solid reasons for deciding to rent rather than to buy a home.

"I Don't Know Where I Want to Live."   It isn't enough to like a particular house, townhouse, or condo. You have to know and like your neighborhood: you'll go through it several times a day, to get to and from your new home. If it isn't an area where you feel comfortable, you won't enjoy living there. Bottom line: If you don't know where you want to live, find a home to rent in the neighborhood you *think* you like, and try it out for six months or a year.

"I Might Be Transferred."   Being at high risk for transfer doesn't necessarily mean you shouldn't ever buy a home. But you should think carefully about the timetable for your prospective transfer. If you're going to be transferred within a year or two, it probably doesn't make financial or emotional sense for you to buy a home, unless your company is willing to pick up the costs of your purchase and sale. Keep in mind the substantial costs of selling a home: the broker's commission (a hefty 5 to 7 percent of the selling price), transfer taxes and fees (charged by the city, county, and state to transfer title into your buyer's name), and title insurance (which protects a buyer if a title problem surfaces), among others. Essentially, you'd have to buy a home in an area that's appreciating at least 5 percent annually to recoup all of those costs within two years.

Let's say you buy a home that costs $100,000 in an area that's appreciating at a rate of about 5 percent per year. After two years, the house has gone up about $10,000 in value. If you sell at the end of 2 years, your costs of sale might be as follows: broker's commission (6 percent), $6,600; transfer taxes and fees, $400; title insurance, survey, and attorney's fee, $1,000. They add up to about $8,000. In addition, you might need to spruce up your home a little before sale.

Looking at these numbers, it's easy to see how you might lose money if you sell within a short period of time, particularly in an area without substantial appreciation. (If you could sell your own home, you'd cut out a significant portion of the costs of sale. But 80 to 90 percent of all sellers in a given year will use a professional broker or agent to sell their home.)

If you think you might be transferred in 3 to 5 years, buying a home becomes a lot more feasible. If you buy carefully—or invest some hard-earned "sweat equity" in a fixer-upper—you should be able to recoup most, if not all, of the costs of purchase and sale, even within a 3- to 5-year time frame.

"I'm Not Sure I'll Have the Income to Support a Mortgage." There's nothing worse than being financially squeezed. If you're worried about whether you'll be able to pay the mortgage each month, you won't enjoy your life—or your new home. That's when you're better off renting. Although the actual monthly payments may be just as expensive as owning a home, at least you can get out of a lease in a relatively short period of time.

If you're planning to buy a home in the near future, try to get your landlord to allow you an *escape* clause before you sign a new lease. The escape clause permits you to end your lease early with, say, 3 months' notice or by paying an extra month's rent as a penalty, in case you sign an agreement to buy a home.

"I Have a Lot of Debt."   If you owe a lot of money on your credit cards, or if you've declared bankruptcy in the past 2 years, you may have a tough time getting approved for a loan to buy a home. When your personal debt is high, you may indeed be better off living as cheaply as possible and renting rather than buying. Living cheap will enable you to start paying off your debts and cleaning up your credit history. (For more information on credit problems, see Step 4, Building Credible Credit.)

"I Don't Have Enough Cash for a Down Payment."   Today's low-down-payment loans allow you to purchase a home with very little down (zero-down-payment loans require no down payment). Still, it's not a good idea to plunk every bit of spare cash you have into a down payment. First, you're going to need extra cash for closing costs, which can run an additional 2 to 3 percent of the selling price of the home. Second, it's a good idea to keep some cash readily available in case some hardship (such as a job layoff, or serious illness) occurs. If you're short on cash, it's probably a good idea to rent for a while and save up adequate funds for your move. (Endlessly saving for a down payment may mean you're committed to a lifetime of renting, however. See Step 3, Putting Together the Cash for Your Down Payment and Closing Costs.)

"The Neighborhood I Want Is Too Expensive." If you've already chosen the neighborhood in which you'd like to buy a home, but it's too expensive for you now, you have a couple of different options. You can rent, save your money, and hope that you'll be able to afford the home you want within a couple of years. Or, you can choose to buy a smaller house, a townhouse, a fixer-upper, or a condo in that neighborhood today.

"I Can't Afford the Size Home I'll Need Within Five Years." Buying the wrong size home is a common mistake among first-time buyers. They buy a studio or a one-bedroom condo, then immediately get married and decide to start a family. Within a year or two, their home is too small and they have to start looking all over again. This happened to one first-time buyer who bought a one-bedroom condo. Six months later, she decided she needed a second bedroom. So she sold her condo and bought a larger one in the same building. Within the year, she decided the two-bedroom condo was too big, so she sold it and bought another one-bedroom condo in the same building. A year later, she got engaged and put her one-bedroom condo on the market again.

If you know your family is going to grow, it may be in your best interest to continue to rent and save up for a home you'll be able to stay in for a minimum of 5 to 7 years.

There may be other reasons—both emotional and financial—why you'd prefer to rent rather than buy. It's good to get these reasons on paper. In the first column of the worksheet on page 20, list the reasons why you'd rather rent. In the second column, list all the reasons why you'd rather buy. Until you can articulate these feelings in writing, where they'll seem more real, it may be tough to know exactly which way you should go.

WORKSHEET
Reasons to Rent or to Buy

Rent	Buy
Financial	
_____	_____
_____	_____
_____	_____
_____	_____
_____	_____
_____	_____
_____	_____
_____	_____
Emotional	
_____	_____
_____	_____
_____	_____
_____	_____
_____	_____
_____	_____
_____	_____
_____	_____
Logistical	
_____	_____
_____	_____
_____	_____
_____	_____
_____	_____
_____	_____

The Risks Associated with Homeownership

Beyond the emotional or financial reasons why you may prefer to rent rather than buy, it's important to examine the real risks associated with homeownership. Personal challenges, such as divorce, a disabled child or spouse, death, or job loss, may mean you won't be able to afford the mortgage. If you can't make your payments, your lender will ultimately foreclose on your property, forcing you and your family out. Not only will the foreclosure be a black mark on your credit history, but you may also lose any cash you've put down and any equity you've built up in the property.

If your home burns down, floods, or is destroyed by earthquake, and you don't have adequate home insurance to cover these disasters, (above and beyond the hazard insurance your lender will require to cover the mortgage), you could lose a significant amount of money. Being adequately prepared for homeownership means understanding the risks associated with purchasing property.

On a more benign level, if you don't maintain your home, it could lose a substantial portion of its value. For example, if your roof leaks and you either give it a cheap patch or don't fix it, the roof could rot or the interior of the house could be damaged. If you don't regularly check your home for termites, mice, and other pests, they could eat away at your walls or floor joists. No one wants to buy a home that is infested with bugs, vermin, and the like.

Another risk you take as a homeowner is that your home may decrease in value simply because the neighborhood in which you live takes a turn for the worse. Perhaps gangs move in, the quality of many schools goes down slightly, or business development evaporates. If people in your neighborhood work for a single company and that company restructures or goes out of business and a lot of folks lose their jobs, your home could fall in value because there aren't enough people who can afford to move into your neighborhood. These, unfortunately, are circumstances over which you have no control.

If you're not inclined to take charge of the maintenance of your property, you may indeed be better off renting than buying. Brad and Debbie were renting a large apartment when their upstairs neighbor decided to play plumber and take a stab at fixing a leaky toilet. The only thing was, he forgot to turn off the water first. Gallons and gallons of water soaked through the ceiling. Brad and Debbie called the building engineers, who helped them haul all of their furniture, clothes, and artwork across the hall to an empty apartment. Brad said later that one of the reasons he rents instead of buys is that he prefers not to deal with maintenance issues. He and Debbie simply put away their things and left the building management to fix the problem and clean up the mess.

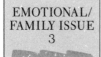

EMOTIONAL/
FAMILY ISSUE
3

Quality of Life

Think carefully about the quality of life you want, when deciding whether you should rent or buy. Where you live, and what you live in, are as important to the equation as the size of your bank account.

Most homes are nicer—or can be made nicer—than rental units. In homeownership, sweat equity counts. Over 5 years or more, home improvements generally return the cost of the investment and then some. Plus, you'll enjoy the renovations while you live there.

On the other hand, if you are renting an apartment that is a 5-minute walk to work, think carefully before you buy a home that requires a 45-minute commute each way to your job. That loss of personal time, and the pressures of commuting, may not be balanced by the additional wealth you're building through homeownership.

Finally, ask yourself whether your goal of homeownership is worth the disruption it may cause to your family or professional life. If your children are happy and successful in their schools, is it fair to switch them to a new school district, with new teachers and new friends, so that you can buy the house of your dreams?

How Much House
Can I Afford?

STEP
2

Not sure? You're not alone. Every home buyer spends a lot of time and energy wondering how much he or she can actually afford to spend on a piece of property. Here's how most home buyers do their estimating. First, they think about their gross income and the income of their spouse or partner. Some home buyers stop there, and apply the "2½ rule," which says that you can afford about 2 to 2½ times your income *if* interest rates are about 10 percent, you have 20 percent to put down in cash, and you have excellent credit with no debt. The problem is most home buyers who apply this rule forget (or don't know) everything except the 2½-times-your-income part of the equation.

More savvy home buyers know there is a lot more to the process. They start with income, but then they look at their debts and assets, and the stock that Grandma gave them 20 years ago. They count their pennies, raid their kids' piggy banks, and wonder whether they can borrow against their IRAs, Keoghs, and company retirement plans. Then, they make their best guess.

Really understanding how much you can afford to spend on a home will avoid a serious first-time-buyer mistake. Too many first-time buyers use an unscientific "eyeballing" approach to figure out how much they can afford to buy, and then they go out and look at property in that price range. Because they don't know how the numbers work, these buyers tour a class of expensive homes that they can't afford to buy, and are heartbroken when they see what their dollars will really buy. When you get used to imagining yourself in homes of a certain size, with desirable amenities, it's awfully difficult to settle for less.

Here's how the mistake happens. You and your spouse have a gross family income of, say, $60,000. Maybe you each earn $30,000 a year, or perhaps you earn $40,000 and your spouse earns $20,000. You're paying about $900 per month in rent. One Sunday morning, you decide that amount would be better spent on mortgage payments. Fair enough. How much can you afford to spend? Using the quick "eyeball" method, you figure that with a $60,000 joint income, and with a 30-year fixed-rate loan hovering around 10 percent, you can afford to spend between $120,000 and $150,000 on a home. Because you've heard that a seller's list price is negotiable, you open up the Sunday real estate ads and begin looking at the descriptions of homes priced between $150,000 and $200,000. And they sound marvelous—much nicer than the homes priced between $120,000 and $150,000.

But wait. Did you remember to factor in the years of car payments on that new Honda you bought 6 months ago? What about the school loan your spouse is paying off over the next 10 years? And the $4,500 of credit card debt that includes some of your honeymoon expenses? All of these debts can seriously affect how much house you can afford to buy. And if you've decided to buy a townhouse, condominium, or co-op, maintenance costs and the monthly or annual *assessments* (your share of the upkeep of the common areas of the property) may lower the range of the home price you can afford to pay.

In this Step, we're going to look at the emotional and financial issues that have an impact on the amount of money you can afford to pay for your new home. We'll analyze your assets, debts, income, the costs of homeownership and maintenance. We'll also look at how different types of homes, requiring different levels of upkeep or repair, and the rise and fall of interest rates can affect the amount you can afford to spend.

FINANCIAL ISSUES

FINANCIAL
ISSUE
1

Calculating How Much You Can Afford

Most real estate experts say that if you can afford to rent, you can afford to buy. Still, the question is often not "Can I afford to buy a home?" but "What home can I afford to buy?"

There are two good ways to figure out how much house you can afford to buy:

1. You can get yourself *prequalified* or *preapproved* by a local mortgage broker, mortgage banker, savings and loan, or credit union. In the real estate industry, companies that lend you money for a home are known as "lenders." Prequalification is a free service that lenders are happy to provide because it gives them an excellent opportunity to market their services to you. They take down your personal information (either over the telephone or in person), add up your assets and income, subtract your liabilities and debt, and then crank those numbers through a formula to determine how much you can afford to borrow. The principal difference between getting prequalified and getting preapproved by a lender is that, with preapproval, the lender commits in writing to funding the loan, pending a successful appraisal. Preapproval is therefore a much more thorough process than prequalification, which carries no commitment from the lender to fund your mortgage. With preapproval, you've actually applied for the loan. In effect, the lender looks at a few basic numbers and says, "If you can prove you make this much money and have these assets, and if the home appraises out in value, then we'll fund your loan." (For a more thorough discussion of preapproval and prequalification, see Step 9, Financing Your Home.)

2. You can read the rest of this Step and use the worksheets, which are based on the same calculations lenders use to prequalify and preapprove home buyers.

Although we'll go over this process in more detail in Step 9, Financing Your Home, it's important for you to know that although lenders appear to be acting independently, they in fact must follow very specific guidelines when they are approving mortgages. Almost all home loans are sold on the *secondary market*. That means the Federal National Mortgage Association ("Fannie Mae"), the Federal Home Loan Mortgage Corp. ("Freddie Mac"), or a private pension fund will likely purchase your loan from the lender who initially gave it to you. So even if you get a loan from Sunrise Mortgage Corporation, you will probably make out your monthly mortgage check to a mortgage services company that services home loans for Fannie Mae, Freddie Mac, or other institutions.

The secondary market sets the debt-to-income ratios that mortgage bankers and brokers must follow. *Debt-to-income* ratios are comparisons between how much debt you carry and how much income you earn. Through many years of trial and error, lenders have discovered that the average family can afford to pay only a certain percentage of its household income toward *debt service*, or the interest and principal paid each month on debts. The typical lending ratio is 28/36. Lenders have determined that home buyers can afford to spend no more than 28 percent of their gross income toward monthly mortgage payments on a home, and no more than 36 percent toward all debt service. In other words, the total of your mortgage principal and interest payments, real estate taxes, property or hazard insurance, car loan, credit card payments, and school loans should not exceed 36 percent of your gross income.

If you and your spouse earn a total of $60,000 per year, your gross monthly income is $5,000:

$$\$60,000 \text{ annual salary} \div 12 \text{ months} = \$5,000 \text{ per month}$$

To apply the 28/36 debt-to-income ratio, multiply your gross monthly income by .28 and then by .36:

$$\$5,000 \text{ monthly gross} \times .28 = \$1,400 \text{ (maximum monthly mortgage payments)}$$

$$\$5,000 \text{ monthly gross} \times .36 = \$1,800 \text{ (total monthly debt service)}$$

If your gross monthly income is $5,000, a conventional lender would allow you to pay a maximum of $1,400 toward your monthly mortgage payments, and a total of $1,800 toward your total debt service. (Payments on all your other personal debts, including your school and car loans and your credit card debt, could not exceed $400.) If you don't have any personal debt, a lender might allow your monthly mortgage obligation to go up to that $1,800 ceiling.

Do you feel you could afford to pay even more toward your total debt? You may be right on target. In the past few years, lenders (encouraged by Fannie Mae and by HUD) have been stretching their lending ratios for first-time and minority buyers. Special programs now allow some first-time buyers to stretch the 28/36 ratio to as high as 30/40, and sometimes higher. Instead of limiting your mortgage payment to 28 percent of your gross monthly income, and the payments on your total debt service (all your debt) to 36 percent of your gross monthly income, lenders will now allow you to put 30 percent of your gross monthly income toward your mortgage and 40 or 41 percent of your gross monthly income toward your total debt service. If you have no other debt (no car loan, school loan, and so on), your lender may allow you to use a full 40 or 41 percent of your gross monthly income for your mortgage payment.

A couple of percentage points may not seem like a big deal, but they can make the difference between being able to buy a home and staying a renter. Let's go back to our $60,000 annual/$5,000 gross monthly income example. This is how the percentage points translate to dollars:

$5,000 Gross Monthly Income

28/36 Debt-to-Income Ratio	*30/41 Debt-to-Income Ratio*
$1,400 for mortgage	$1,500 for mortgage
$1,800 for total debt service	$2,050 for total debt service

If you had a 30-year fixed-rate loan at 10 percent, you would be able to afford a loan amount of around $125,000 using the 28/36 ratio. However, you'd be able to get a loan of almost $135,000 using the higher ratio. That could be a big difference.

There are two key maxims in the lending industry:

1. The lower the down payment, the more risky the loan.
2. The higher the debt-to-income ratio, the more risky the loan.

Lenders have been surprised to find, however, that both low-down-payment and higher-ratio loans have proven somewhat less risky than they had originally imagined. Generally, only about 4 percent of all homeowners who have conventional mortgages are delinquent in paying them, and ultimately only 2 percent of the mortgages end in foreclosure. Lenders have seen that the delinquency and foreclosure rates for higher-ratio loans are about the same or just a little bit higher than for conventional loans.

The only time these ratios aren't followed is if you go to a *portfolio lender* to get your mortgage. A portfolio lender (it could be a bank, a savings and loan, or a credit union) keeps loans in-house instead of re-selling them on the secondary market. Sometimes, the loan rates on these portfolio loans are a little higher than on conventional loans, which will be sold to a Fannie Mae or Freddie Mac. But portfolio lenders play an important role in the home buying process because

1. Gross monthly income from all sources: _____

2. Multiply by

     .25 (25%)

     .33 (33%) or

     .36 (36%)

     (loan-to-income ratio):   × _____

3. Subtract your current monthly debt service:

     Credit cards   _____
        (enter your monthly minimum owed)

     Car loan(s)   _____

     Charge accounts   _____
        (from local merchants or
        department stores)

     School loans   _____

     Other personal debt   _____

     Total debt service   − _____

4. Subtract any assessments or homeowner
     fees you'll be charged   − _____
     (you'll have to guess, based on the types
     of condominium or co-op buildings you're
     thinking about buying into; or, find out
     what fees and assessments the present
     homeowners pay)

5. Maximum monthly mortgage payment   = _____ *

*Includes *PITI,* industry jargon for Principal, Interest, Taxes, and Insurance.

they make exceptions to the rules, and often flat-out break them if they deem a cause worthy enough. If you're recently self-employed, for example, or for some reason don't qualify for a loan that will ultimately be sold on the secondary market, you may be better off going to a portfolio lender.

To figure out how much house you can afford to buy, you must first figure out how much money you can afford to borrow. After you figure that out, you can add in the cash you will have available for the down payment and closing costs. I'll repeat one important caveat throughout this book: Just because a lender says you can afford to borrow a certain amount doesn't necessarily mean you'll feel comfortable borrowing that much cash. Real estate brokers often say that home buyers feel more comfortable if their mortgage payment represents only 25 to 33 percent of their gross monthly income. The preliminary worksheet on page 28 allows you to select whichever percentage you're most comfortable with. Test them all and compare them side-by-side, as in the example. (We'll discuss the comfort factor as one of the Emotional/Family Issues later in section of this Step.)

> You may not consider your monthly assessment or homeowner association fee important, but your lender will definitely count it when figuring out how much you can afford to spend on a home. Generally, you'll be able to spend less on a condominium or co-op unit than a single-family home (where there are no monthly assessments).

Here's how the numbers play out. Let's say your annual household income is $80,000 and your gross monthly income is $6,666.67 (rounded to $6,667 to make calculations easier). The dollar amounts of your loan-to-income ratios are: $1,667 (25% of $6,667); $2,200 (33% of $6,667); and $2,400 (36% of $6,667).

Let's assume you have some debt (most first-time buyers do, by the way), and your monthly payments are:

$220 car
100 school loan
<u>125</u> credit card
$445 total monthly debt service

Subtract your debt service from the percent of gross monthly income you've chosen. For the 33 percent ratio, the result would be:

$$\$2,200 - \$445 = \$1,775 \text{ maximum mortgage payment}$$

Your maximum mortgage payment includes money set aside for real estate taxes, hazard insurance premiums, and private mortgage insurance (PMI; your lender will require you to have this coverage if you put down less than 20 percent on your home). Unless you're planning a cash down payment of more than 35 percent on your home, your lender will likely require that you have a *property tax and insurance escrow.* This is the total cost of your annual property taxes and insurance premium, divided by 12 (to get the cost per month). Each month, $\frac{1}{12}$ of the cost of your property taxes and insurance premiums is tacked onto your mortgage payment. How much should you allow for real estate taxes and hazard insurance? Depending on where you live, real estate taxes will cost you 1 to 3 percent of the value of your home. Except in California, where real estate taxes are fixed at 1 percent of the sales price of your home, property taxes generally rise each year. Hazard insurance is also dependent on the value of your home. To insure your home, furnishings, clothes, and personal effects will probably cost you around $\frac{3}{10}$ to $\frac{8}{10}$ of one percent of the value of your home.

If you want to find out what your actual mortgage payment will be, you'll have to make a few guesses and subtract accordingly. For example, let's say you're looking at homes in the $125,000 price range. It's not unreasonable to assume that you'll face an annual property tax bill ranging from $1,250 (in California) to $3,750, and an annual insurance premium of around $500 to $1,000. (For more specific numbers, you may want to consult a friend or family member who lives in your area and is a homeowner.) Assuming a midrange of taxes and a high-coverage insurance premium, your costs would be:

$$\$2,500 \text{ (property taxes)} + \$1,000 \text{ (insurance)} = \$3,500$$

$$\$3,500 \div 12 = \$291.67 \text{ monthly tax and insurance escrow}$$

You then subtract your monthly tax and insurance escrow payment from your maximum monthly payment to find out the actual amount of the mortgage payment. Continuing the example from above, subtract $292 (rounded for the sake of clarity) from $1,775:

30

$$\$1,775 - \$292 = \$1,483$$

The comparison chart below uses the numbers that we've already calculated in our continuing example. Remember, we're assuming an annual income of $80,000, with a gross monthly income (GMI) of $6,667, and monthly debt of $445.

	25% of GMI	33% of GMI	36% of GMI
	$1,667	$2,220	$2,400
Less: Debt	− 445	− 445	− 445
Maximum mortgage payment	1,222	1,775	1,955
Less: Property taxes and insurance	− 292	− 292	− 292
Net mortgage payment	$ 930	$1,483	$1,663

As you can see, the spread between the financially conservative example (25 percent of GMI) and the maximum that conventional lenders will allow you to borrow (36 percent of GMI) is around $730. That $730 per month can make a significant difference when you're looking at homes.

Here's how to translate these numbers into the amount of loan you can carry. Multiply your net mortgage payment ($930, $1,483, or $1,663 in our example) by 12 to get the annual mortgage payment amount. Then divide that amount by the prevailing interest rate. (As the interest rate rises, you'll be able to afford a smaller mortgage. For comparison purposes, use a 30-year fixed-rate loan advertised in your local newspaper real estate section.) Here are two sample calculations:

1. 7.5 percent interest rate

   $930 × 12 (months) = $11,160 (annual payment)
   $11,160 ÷ .075 (7.5% interest) = $148,800 (total mortgage)

   $1,483 × 12 (months) = $17,796 (annual payment)
   $17,796 ÷ .075 (7.5% interest) = $237,289 (total mortgage)

   $1,663 × 12 (months) = $19,956 (annual payment)
   $19,956 ÷ .075 (7.5% interest) = $266,080 (total mortgage)

2. 10 percent interest rate

   $930 × 12 (months) = $11,160 (annual payment)
   $11,160 ÷ .10 (10% interest) = $111,600 (total mortgage)

$1,483 \times 12$ (months) = $17,796$ (annual payment)

$17,796 \div .10$ (10% interest) = $177,960$

$1,663 \times 12$ (months) = $19,956$ (annual payment)

$19,956 \div .10$ (10% interest) = $199,560$ (total mortgage)

The worksheet on page 33 takes you to the bottom line of what you can spend on your home.

Some loans will allow you to fold most of your closing costs into your mortgage, but you will need to have at least 1 to 2 percent of the purchase price in cash to cover the costs that must be paid at the closing, including the prepaid interest on the loan. That means:

For every $100,000 of the purchase price, you should have at least $1,000 to $2,000 in reserve for closing costs.

On a $200,000 home, you'll probably need at least $2,000 to $4,000 for closing costs.

If you target the barest minimum of cash needed for the down payment and closing costs, expect to have anywhere from 3 to 5 percent of the purchase price, in cash, ready to spend on the day your home closes (a little ahead of that date, you'll need to put up a cash deposit to show your good faith in the deal). Adding up all the extras:

For every $100,000 of the purchase price, you'll need $3,000 to $5,000 in cash.

For a $300,000 purchase, you'll need $9,000 to $15,000 in cash— as the bare minimum.

It's a good idea to have some extra cash in reserve, just in case you need more than the bare minimum, or to cover yourself in case of an emergency. We'll talk about this further in Step 3.

FINANCIAL
ISSUE
2

How Interest Rates Change What You Can Afford

Predicting the rise and fall of interest rates is one of the great pastimes of American economists. They sit at their desks and look at economic forecasts, corporate earnings, housing construction starts, and housing sales. Then they appear on talk shows, business analysis

1. Gross monthly income from all sources: _____

2. Multiply by
   25 (25%)
   33 (33%) or
   36 (36%)
   (loan-to-income ratio): × _____

3. Subtract your current monthly debt service:

   Credit cards _____

   Car loan(s) _____

   Charge accounts _____

   School loans _____

   Other personal debt _____

   Total debt service − _____

4. Subtract monthly or semimonthly condominium or co-op assessments, if applicable − _____

5. Maximum monthly mortgage payment = _____

6. Subtract real estate property and insurance tax escrow − _____

7. Net mortgage payment = _____

8. Multiply by 12 (months of the year) × _____ 12

9. Annual mortgage payment = _____

10. Divided by current interest rate ÷ _____

11. Total amount of mortgage = _____

12. Plus cash you have available for a down payment (save some for closing costs) + _____ *

13. Approximate amount you can spend on a home = _____

*In Step 3, Putting Together the Cash for Your Down Payment and Closing Costs, we'll talk more about how much cash you actually can put toward your down payment, and where you can find local sources of help. For now, these are the basic facts you need to know for these calculations: You can buy a home with as little as 2 to 3 percent of the sales price in cash. In other words, for every $100,000 of purchase price, you must have between $2,000 to $3,000 cash (as an absolute minimum) to put down on the home. For a $200,000 home, you should have between $4,000 and $6,000 available for a down payment.

programs, and comment spots on network and cable television, where they expound their views on where the bond market is headed and what that means for short- and long-term interest rates.

Home buyers play this game, too. They spend some time reading the financial and business sections of a few newspapers, listen to the economists and pundits, and try to decide when they should lock in their interest rates in order to get them at their nadir. Every home buyer wants to get the lowest rate. In 1993, when interest rates plummeted to around 6.75 percent for a 30-year fixed-rate mortgage (a 30-year low), a lot of wise homeowners refinanced their mortgages.

I know a few lucky folks who actually got one of those 6.75 percent, 30-year loans. And I know some folks who desperately wanted one of those mortgages with the super-low interest rate, but got so caught up in playing the wait-and-see-where-interest-rates-go game that they couldn't jump in when the market looked good. They forgot two of the simplest rules of finance:

1. You don't get the rate until you lock it in.
2. If the interest rate goes down, you can always refinance.

Sit on the fence and never jump off, and you might as well wave bye-bye to lower payments. In today's shifting markets, a low rate won't be around for too long—perhaps only a day or so.

But the big secret about interest rates is this: A quarter-point difference doesn't mean much, in either the short or the long run. It doesn't drastically change the amount of money you're paying each month in principal and interest. Here's how different interest rates work out for a $100,000, 30-year mortgage:

Interest Rate	Monthly Payment	Total Interest Paid
7.50%	$699.21	$151,721.99
7.75	716.41	157,910.79
8.00	733.76	164,160.47
8.25	751.27	170,451.76
8.50	768.91	176,813.51

For every $100,000 you borrow, the difference between getting a loan at 8 percent or 8.25 percent is $17.51 per month, or $210.12 per year. Over 30 years, the difference is only $6,291.29. The difference in the amount of interest paid in the short and long run is even smaller when you examine the effect various interest rates have on a 15-year mortgage for $100,000:

Interest Rate	Monthly Payment	Total Interest Paid
7.50%	$927.01	$66,862.61
7.75	941.28	69,428.76
8.00	955.65	72,017.71
8.25	970.14	74,625.31
8.50	984.74	77,253.05

(Monthly payments on a 15-year loan are much bigger than on a 30-year loan because you're paying off the principal in half the time. By paying off the principal faster, you're saving a lot on the interest payments over the life of the loan.)

As you can see, the difference in the monthly payment between a 15-year loan at 8 percent and the identical loan at 8.25 percent is only $14.49 per month. Over the life of the loan, you'll be paying only $2,607.60 more for your extra quarter-point in the interest rate. Even with a half-point spread, you're looking at a difference of about $30 per month, or $5,000 more in interest over the 15-year life of the loan.

Although the difference in payment is slight, lower mortgage interest rates can significantly alter the total amount of money that lenders will allow you to spend on a home. For example, if you and your spouse earn a combined gross income of $80,000 per year and have no debt, a lender would allow you to spend up to $2,400 per month (36 percent of your gross monthly income) on your mortgage payment, taxes, and insurance. For now, let's subtract $400 per month as your estimated monthly property taxes and insurance premium payment. At an interest rate of 10 percent, you'll be able to afford a maximum mortgage of $240,000:

$2,000 (net mortgage payment) $\times$ 12 (months) = $24,000 (annually)

$24,000 $\div$ .10 (10 percent) = $240,000 (maximum mortgage)

If interest rates fall to 9 percent, 8 percent, or 7 percent, you'll be able to afford a whole lot more:

35

Annual Mortgage Payment		Interest Rate		Total Mortgage
$24,000	÷	10.0%	=	$240,000
24,000	÷	9.5	=	252,632
24,000	÷	9.0	=	266,667
24,000	÷	8.5	=	282,353
24,000	÷	8.0	=	300,000
24,000	÷	7.5	=	320,000
24,000	÷	7.0	=	342,857

Let's look at another example. If your net monthly mortgage is $833 (after deducting taxes, insurance premiums, and PMI), and your annual mortgage payment is $10,000, here's how interest rates change what you can afford:

Annual Mortgage Payment		Interest Rate		Total Mortgage
$10,000	÷	10.0%	=	$100,000
10,000	÷	9.5	=	105,263
10,000	÷	9.0	=	111,111
10,000	÷	8.5	=	117,647
10,000	÷	8.0	=	125,000
10,000	÷	7.5	=	133,333
10,000	÷	7.0	=	142,857

The rise and fall in interest rates works exponentially for you. The difference in payments between a $100,000 loan at 8 percent and the identical loan at 8.5 percent is only $29.09 per month. The difference in total interest paid is only $5,200 over the life of the loan. And yet, that same half-point difference in the interest rate might mean you could qualify for a $125,000 loan instead of a $117,647 loan.

10 STEP TIP

Mortgage interest rates are a whole game unto themselves, and they have their own language to boot. As you move through the process of getting ready to look for a home, you will have to start to think about current interest rates and how they might affect you. I'm the first to admit that not everyone is a "numbers" person; don't let the math get to you. In fairly short order, you'll understand the lingo as well as if you were a longtime mortgage banker, and you'll be tossing off such jargon as "points," "junk fees," and "HUD-1 forms" with the best of them.

How the Choice of a Home, and Its Condition Affects How Much House You Can Afford

This is one of the great rules about real estate. No two houses are the same. When you first think about it, you might imagine that it can't possibly be true. After all, developers across the country have spent years building endless subdivisions of tract homes, each one identical to the next. How could all those homes *not* be the same?

In some cases, they are almost the same. More often than not—and this is true of subdivisions, particularly as they age—they are similar but not identical. What happens is that homeowners like to put their own touches on their home, usually through decorating but often through improvements and additions.

Some of the differences can't be seen from the outside. Gail's father is a developer. When she and her husband, Marty, bought a home in one of his new subdivisions in a northwest suburb of Chicago, her father added two feet to the floorplate of her house. That difference is not noticeable from the exterior, but buyers comparing the house with other homes within the subdivision will notice. Similarly, when a developer offers a basement as an option, some homeowners will opt to include one, some will choose a half-basement, and some will go with the standard crawl space. Just that one feature in a house can make a huge difference when the time comes to sell.

Similarly, how homeowners take care of their homes affects the price they receive when they decide to sell. Most home buyers want a house (when I use the term "house," I include condominiums, co-ops, and townhouses) that is in *mint condition*. When a house isn't new, mint condition or *blue ribbon condition* means that the house presents itself as being as close to brand-new as possible. For example, a home in mint condition might often have been freshly painted; old, worn-out carpeting has been replaced; hardwood floors have been polished; no windows are broken. The exterior has been taken care of as well: bricks have been tuckpointed, trim painted, siding and windows washed, landscape manicured. Everything has been given a facelift and looks fresh, clean, and inviting.

Many homeowners can't be bothered or can't afford to take such good care of their homes, even though a home is usually their biggest investment. Mechanical problems get patchy solutions, and interiors are left with peeling paint and bubbled wallpaper, stained carpets and floors, and dustballs the size of desert tumbleweeds.

Home buyers expect to pay more for a house in blue ribbon condition than for a house that needs a lot of work. "Existing" homes—the term brokers and agents use for all homes that are not newly constructed—tend to come in three varieties:

1. *Mint condition or blue ribbon.* These are homes on which the owners have lavished attention, money, time, and love. They are in perfect or nearly perfect condition, with fresh paint or wallpaper, polished hardware, and basement floors so clean you could eat off of them.

2. *Handyman's special or fixer-upper.* Fixer-uppers need work that can range from a lot of big things to an endless list of little annoying things that the owner didn't want to deal with. The best kind of fixer-upper homes involve plenty of cosmetic improvements (essentially decorating, which can be done inexpensively with paint, wallpaper, and carpet), but few structural faults (expensive, time-consuming renovations such as replacing the roof or a similar mechanical system, or moving walls). Ideally, you can do much of the work that's needed in this kind of home.

3. *A gut job or tear-down.* When developers refer to gut jobs, they mean houses that require removing the guts, or everything right down to the exterior surface. These are homes in such bad shape that they need everything: new mechanical and electrical systems, appliances, walls, windows, ceilings, and floors. If the buyer chooses to keep anything, it may be some structural detail that would be difficult, if not impossible, to replace. If the only redeeming feature of a house is the land on which it sits, the buyer may tear it down and start from scratch.

The quality of the home you choose—whether it is in mint condition, is a fixer-upper, or is a gut job—will have as much (or more) impact on how much house you can afford as interest rates. Because mint condition homes are so highly prized by home buyers, they are more, sometimes much more, expensive than homes that need a lot of cosmetic improvements.

For example, when my husband, Sam, and I bought our second home, it was a decorating disaster. The owners had lived there for twenty-five or thirty years, and hadn't touched the place in all that time. Avocado and gold velvet-flocked wallpaper was half peeling off the walls, and the green metallic wallpaper in the master bedroom had a pattern that looked like mold spores. The kitchen was brown, with yellow and brown wallpaper and plastic gray tiles that took hours and hours to scrape off. All of the windows were covered over with huge, heavy draperies. And the lovely hardwood floors had been either covered over in dark green or red-and-black shag carpeting, or, as in the living room, stained around a center throw rug! (Yes, you read that correctly. We believe the former owners didn't even bother to remove the rug before staining the floor.) In the third bedroom, the owner had put bookshelves over the fire escape door, blocking any exit. The shelves held a collection of elf and animal figurines he had made himself. But as we walked around inside, we tried to look past the decorating disasters so that we could examine the *bones* or structure of the home. We could see it had nine-foot ceilings, with lovely plaster mouldings and a huge marble-fronted wood-burning fireplace with a wood mantle. There were a good number of closets, and three full bathrooms (two of which were basically unusable). When we peeked around the curtains, we realized the home had southern exposure and beautiful views.

Because the owners were elderly and were unwilling or unable to make such simple changes as stripping off the wallpaper and painting the walls a nice, bright white, we were able to purchase the home for a lot less than if it had been in mint condition. Five years later, when we decided to sell, we had put the home in mint condition, and were able to reap a sizable profit from the sale.

What's the lesson here? You may be able to buy a bigger home in a better neighborhood if you're willing to take on a home that needs a considerable amount of cosmetic work. Avoid homes that require too much structural work, however, as that tends to be expensive and you may not be able to do it yourself.

If you are thinking about purchasing a fixer-upper, don't go into it with your eyes closed. The renovation will get done eventually, but it always costs more money and takes more time than you think it will. Here is a list of caveats for fixer-uppers:

- *Facelifts are more profitable than major surgery.* One of the best ways to ensure profits is to buy a home that needs cosmetic, rather than structural, work. Look for homes that need decorating but are structurally sound.

- *Don't guesstimate the cost of repairs.* Your broker can help you in some ways, but don't rely solely on his or her estimation of the costs of renovation work. Instead, hire a contractor or architect to tour the home with you before you make an offer.

39

- *Don't overpay for the home.* Once you have your estimate of renovation costs, subtract that amount from the price you think the house is worth. For example, if you decide that a property will be worth $100,000 fixed up but needs $10,000 of work, your maximum offer should be $90,000. Work out the numbers ahead of time. You should know approximately how much you will have to spend to renovate *before* you start negotiating. Then, stick to your budget.

- *Don't create a white elephant.* Look for a fixer-upper that is quite a bit less expensive than the rest of the neighborhood. Even if the home needs a substantial amount of renovation, you don't want to overimprove the property. If you do, you may ultimately have trouble selling the most expensive home on the block.

- *Expect to live there a while.* If your goal is to make big bucks by buying homes, renovating them, and selling them quickly, good luck! You'll need it because you'll probably have difficulty buying, renovating, and selling a property in less than 2 years. Plan to stay at least 3 to 5 years to maximize the value of your improvements.

The Neighborhood vs. Amenities Compromise. If you're not into fixing up homes, there are other ways to get more house for your money. When Karla decided to buy her first home, she knew she wanted a condominium with a security system, preferably a 24-hour doorman. But the neighborhood she wanted was prohibitively expensive for the two-bedroom, two-bath home she felt she needed. She ended up buying the size home she wanted, in her neighborhood of choice, by making another compromise. She picked a condo unit on a low floor that didn't offer quite the same views as the much more expensive condos located on higher floors in the same building. Brokers will tell you to always pick the "view" over the "nonview" because it's easier to sell, but that choice doesn't make sense in every case. Karla was able to purchase a wonderful unit with something of a view, in the right neighborhood, because she was willing to compromise on what she considered to be a less important feature: the view from the condo. Because of the tremendous price disparity between the view and nonview units in the building, and because of the building's excellent location and the unit's generous space, Karla's buyer broker felt that Karla would be able to attract someone like herself, someone who values location over view and doesn't have the means to afford both, whenever she decides to sell her home.

Different neighborhoods strongly affect how much house you'll be able to buy for the same amount of money. If you want to live in only the most expensive part of town, you may be able to afford only a studio or a one-bedroom condo. But if you're willing to move to the second, third, or fourth most expensive neighborhood, the same money may buy you a two- or three-bedroom condo or a townhouse, or even a small single-family home. If you're willing to move to the suburbs, you may be able to afford a four-bedroom newly constructed single-family house in an excellent school district.

Each neighborhood, within each town, village, city, or suburb, has homes that are more expensive and others that are less expensive. Each area develops its own pecking order of price and value. In a suburb near where I live, a five-bedroom, two-and-a-half-bath home with central air and a big backyard is on the market for around $300,000. The drawback of the house is that it is located a couple of houses away from the edge of the small downtown area. If that house could be moved another two blocks away from downtown, the price would likely rise to $400,000 or $500,000. If you wanted this particular suburb, with its fine schools, and didn't mind the close proximity to the downtown area—and could afford a $300,000 home—you might be willing to trade a not-as-good location for all the benefits that suburb has to offer, plus a huge home.

Remember, neighborhoods aren't static. Within even a good overall neighborhood, there will be better blocks and worse blocks, more desirable areas and less desirable areas. I don't advocate buying a home located across the street from a municipal dump, just to get into a particular neighborhood. (Why? Because if there is a toxic leak into your groundwater, the value of the home will plummet, and you may never be able to sell it.) But there's nothing wrong with buying a fixer-upper home on a busy street within a fine neighborhood. Location and condition will always affect the price of a home. If you're willing to make certain trade-offs, you may be able to buy the right size home in the right neighborhood.

Two Flats, Three Flats, and Home Sharing. Another way for first-time buyers to be able to afford more house than they otherwise could handle is to find a multifamily unit, move into one of the units, and rent out the other(s). Folks all over the country do this successfully. Steve and Sally bought a six-flat building in San Francisco, and the rent they collected for the other units allowed them to virtually live there for free. Mary Beth and her husband bought a two-flat house outside of New York City. They rent out one of the units, which helps pay a mortgage they couldn't otherwise afford when they bought the home. One day, they hope to be able to afford to convert the property back to a single-family home. Beth and her sister Sherri bought their father's two-flat and each moved into one of the units. In the Washington (DC) area, Robert bought a single-family house and rented out the two best bedrooms to friends. The income from their rooms pays the mortgage.

Playing landlord might not seem the best way to own property, but those who do it say it allows them to purchase property they could not otherwise afford. In the best situation, your tenants' monthly rents cover a good portion (or all) of your mortgage.

If you're going to look for a multifamily unit, or a single-family home in which you can rent out rooms, keep these tips in mind:

- Make sure the rental income you can get for the unit will cover a good portion of the expense of the mortgage. Do the numbers.
- Check whether local zoning ordinances limit the number of unrelated people who can live under the same roof. Some zoning ordinances only permit a maximum of four.
- Being a landlord means performing credit checks, screening applicants, and renting to financially responsible tenants. It also means you're responsible for fixing things like plumbing that may go wrong in their units.
- Find a broker who either specializes in this type of income property or can help you find it.

FINANCIAL ISSUE 4

How Maintenance Costs Affect How Much House You Can Afford

Old versus newer, or brand-new? An 1880s Victorian charmer versus prefab salt boxes, 1950s ranches, or a brand new colonial? Although many buyers may consider these concerns as housing *style* questions (and to some degree they are), there should be more to your final choice than a preference for an era. All homes require ongoing maintenance. Older or very old homes require lots of upkeep; newer and brand-new homes often require less. You've probably heard of or seen the movie *The Money Pit*, in which homeowner Tom Hanks throws piles of cash into fixing up and maintaining his home. Well, truth can be stranger than fiction. Home maintenance is an ongoing battle and it can get expensive, particularly if you let the important things slide.

Let's start with some definitions:

- *Old or very old.* This description is usually given to houses built before World War II. In most of the country, it refers to a home built at any time from the Civil War (mid-1860s) through the 1930s and even the early 1940s. In the Northeast, there are historic homes that date back to the early to mid-1700s, though this type of home generally attracts a specific audience and requires an extraordinary amount of maintenance and upkeep. On the plus side, if a house has been standing for 100 years, there's a good chance it will continue to do so if you keep it in good condition.

- *Newer.* Newer homes have a wide age span as well. They can date from the 1950s to 1960s, when developers began to fill the massive, pent-up demand for housing created by veterans of World War II, to the 1970s, or about 15 to 20 years ago. Homes in this age category were sometimes prefabricated, and many builders used lead-based paint and asbestos, a standard insulation material until the early 1980s.

  Real estate experts often say that 20- to 30-year-old homes have more problems than homes that are older. At around the 20-year mark, some of these homes need replacement of major mechanical or structural components—the roof, hot water heater, boiler or furnace, and sometimes the central air unit.

- *New.* New homes, or homes built within the past 10 years or so, are generally the easiest and cheapest to maintain. It's important to find one that was—or is—solidly built. Because of rising labor and materials costs, some developers today cut corners, leaving homes with sagging floors, cracked foundations, or roofs that go bad faster than they should, simply because they're not properly vented.

  If you purchase a brand-new home ("new construction," in real estate jargon), you shouldn't have to do much more than preventive maintenance. You may spend extra money, during the first few years, for flowers, shrubs, curtains, and other basics that generally aren't included in the purchase price of a new home.

43

Age Before Beauty. Old homes can be wonderfully charming residences, but they can be expensive to maintain. They often have boilers or furnaces that are 35–40 years old or older, hot water tanks that are 20–30 years old, and knob-and-tube wiring from the dawn of the age of electricity. If this stuff is working, you're OK, but it must be maintained carefully and can be expensive to replace or upgrade. For example, if you have a 40-year-old furnace, you'll need to have it cleaned and maintained annually, preferably by a professional who has had experience with a furnace of that age, make, and model. The yearly checkup can run anywhere from $100–$300 or more. Replacing the furnace could cost several thousand dollars. Windows of older or very old homes can leak air or have poor insulation. They may need recaulking from time to time (cost: a dollar or two for a tube of caulk) or a new sash (cost: several hundred dollars). Old bathroom tiles may need regrouting to keep water from seeping into the walls and floors.

If you live in a house that's surrounded by large, shady trees, it's likely that roots have found their way into your main underground drain and need to be pulled out. A company like Roto-Rooter® may charge as much as $200 to get all the roots out of your drainpipes, and you should probably have this done every year or so, depending on the number of trees on or near your property. Every 4 or 5 years, you may need to have the exterior of your home repainted. Depending on the size and finish, and how much scraping is involved, a professional may charge anywhere from $3,000 on up to paint the house and garage. If you have a brick home, you may need a mason to do some minor (or major) tuckpointing to keep the bricks in good shape. Cold-weather and warm-weather climates exact their own peculiar punishments. Severe winter weather can wreak havoc on driveways and gutters, not to mention the time spent shoveling. You may want to invest in a snowblower, or hire a local landscape company to shovel you out anytime it snows more than a couple of inches.

Your exterior landscaping is a three-season issue in cold-weather regions and a year-round concern in warm-weather areas. Lawns need mowing and fertilizing, leaves need raking, shrubbery needs trimming, sidewalks need edging, driveways (particularly blacktops) need a coat of sealant every couple of years. If you have a deck or wooden swingset, you'll need to apply a coat of stain or sealant from time to time, to protect it from the elements. In the first year of homeownership, you'll need to invest in some lawn care equipment; after that, your ongoing year-to-year expenses should be less.

In addition to the ongoing maintenance, it's important to plan ahead for the big expenses, even if they happen only once every few years. In cold-weather climates, replacing a roof, for example, can cost anywhere from $3,000 on up. You should have to do this only once every 15 to 30 years, but it might prove difficult to come up with the cash all at once. If you plan for maintenance issues and put some cash into a house maintenance fund each month, you'll have the necessary funds on hand when a major repair looms.

The chart on pages 46 and 47 shows you the types of basic maintenance issues you may expect in your future home and how often you'll need to address them. Some costs are too variable (V) to call. They depend on the type of home you buy single- or multifamily; stand-alone, co-op, or condominium; urban or rural; cold-weather or warm-weather climate. Take the time to do some research on the average costs of these variables in your area. They are important expenses of owning a home.

When you've estimated the variables for your home choice, calculate how much the *general* maintenance of the house is going to cost you on a monthly, semiannual, and annual basis. It could range from $500 per year to $5,000 or more. Whatever the amount, you'll also have to plan for the *one-time* or *scheduled* (every 5 to 10 years) expenses so that when the time comes to do them, you're prepared financially.

After you live in your home, or when you are touring a home with a professional house inspector or structural engineer, you may become aware of maintenance issues other than those we've already discussed. Your personal list may vary, depending on the climate, condition of the home, and quality of the terrain on which it stands. If you develop a good relationship with the sellers, ask about the way they've maintained the home, and whether there are things you should do regularly to keep it in excellent shape. Your home inspector or structural engineer should also be able to define the maintenance issues for the property and give you a ballpark figure for upkeep or replacement costs.

Think about setting up a maintenance schedule and budget for each home you're interested in. This is an area that a mortgage broker generally won't touch. You'll have to make these determinations yourself, preferably with the help of your broker or agent, a professional home inspector or structural engineer, friends who own homes, or a prospective seller with whom you may have become

Ownership/Maintenance Issues	Frequency	Approximate Cost
Ownership		
Mortgage payments (principal and interest)	Monthly	V
Private mortgage insurance (PMI)	Monthly	.004 to .006% of loan amount
Real estate taxes	Annually or in scheduled installments; or monthly escrow	1–3% of purchase price
Homeowner's insurance	Annually or monthly escrow	.03 to .08% of purchase price
Assessments	Monthly or annually	V
Homeowner association dues	Monthly or annually	V
Electricity	Monthly	V
Gas	Monthly	V
Water and sewer taxes (may be billed separately or together)	Monthly or semimonthly	V
Septic system	Annually or biannually	V
Garbage collection	Monthly or annually	V
Recycling (may be part of garbage collection bill)	Monthly or annually	V
Extermination services	As needed	V
Maintenance—Mechanicals		
Boiler and furnace upkeep	Annually	$100 to $500
Change filters in furnace	Semiannually	DIY $25+
Change filters in air-conditioning unit	Annually	DIY $15+
Rodding out sewer line	Annually or biannually	$80+
Change water/ice filters	Every 3 to 4 months	DIY $10 to $15
Change/add water softeners	As needed	DIY V

V = variable. Check the discussion in this step for further details.
DIY = do it yourself.
Note = The approximate costs for PMI, property taxes, and homeowner's insurance are the total annual cost, though you may pay them semi-annually or monthly.

Ownership/Maintenance Issues	Frequency	Approximate Cost
Fees for alarm company	Monthly or annually	$125+
Batteries in smoke detectors	As needed	DIY $5 to $10
Maintenance—Exterior		
Landscape	Minimum: three seasons	DIY $200+
Landscape—done by professional	Minimum: three seasons	$500+
Snow removal	As needed	DIY $50+
Snow removal—service	Per contract	$150+
Gutter cleaning	Annually or semiannually	$50–$100+
Window cleaning	As needed	$100+
Tuckpointing	Once every 10 to 15 years	$100+
House painting	3 to 5 years	$1,000+
Replacement of roof	Every 10 to 15 years	$1,500–$3,000+
Resurfacing or sealing driveway	Every 1 to 2 years	$500+
Water seal on deck	Every 1 to 2 years	DIY $25+
Maintenance—Interior		
Painting	Every 3 to 7 years	$500+
Replacing rugs or wall-to-wall carpeting	Every 10 to 15 years	$500–$2,000+
Buff and wax hardwood floors	Every 1 to 2 years	$100+
Polyurethane hardwood floors	Every 3 to 5 years	$100+
Recaulk or regrout bathroom tile	As needed	DIY $5+
Window caulk	As needed	DIY $5+
Replace major appliances	As needed	$400+ per appliance
Chimney sweep	As needed	$100+

V = variable.

DIY = do it yourself.

friendly. When you complete your basic annual budget, divide it into 12 equal parts. Treat this amount like a debt you *have* to repay each month, and make sure your net mortgage amount factors it in. After you move into your new home, set aside this amount of money into a *maintenance fund account.* Make sure you pay the account each month, so that you build up your targeted reserves. In that way, when you have a big expense, you'll be ready.

(Being aware of the costs of maintaining a home is one way to help determine the real cost of the home. We'll talk more about this in Step 8, Comparing Homes, Costs, and Finances.)

EMOTIONAL/FAMILY ISSUES

EMOTIONAL/
FAMILY ISSUE
1

Trade-Offs and Compromises

You're not going to get everything you want when you buy your first home, unless you've inherited lots of cash or recently won the lottery. Finding a home you and your family can live in comfortably may mean compromising on fundamental issues, such as which neighborhood you'll live in, or whether you really want to live through the mess of fixing up a dilapidated home.

It would be nice if all the issues were clear-cut. It would be easy to simply choose the cheaper neighborhood if some other important issues didn't come into play: your proximity to work, family, friends, and recreational activities you enjoy; the quality of local public schools; and the availability of services such as a grocery store, post office, dry cleaner, pharmacy, and houses of worship.

Thinking about how much house you can afford also means thinking about the quality and type of lifestyle you want, and what you're willing to do without. In my book, *100 Questions Every First-Time Home Buyer Should Ask*, I suggest that home buyers construct a wish list and then do a reality check. Essentially, a wish list contains everything you've ever wanted in a home, and a reality check is a list of everything you can't live without. For example, you may want a five-bedroom home, but can't live without three bedrooms. In Step 6, Identifying Where You Want to Live, you'll find worksheets and checklists that will help you create your own wish list and reality check. You're not at that point yet, but it's important to start thinking about the compromises and sacrifices you're willing to make in order to purchase your home.

Being Financially Comfortable vs. Owning a Home You Can't Really Afford

EMOTIONAL/
FAMILY ISSUE
2

Sometimes, I think the real estate industry is set up to get people to spend more money on a house than they should. Brokers are paid a percentage of the sales price of a home; if you buy a more expensive home, they make more money. Similarly, loan officers are paid a percentage of the loans they make. If you take a bigger loan to buy a bigger house, they'll make more money, too. But the main reason real estate brokers and agents like to push their clients into biting off a little more than they can comfortably chew is that they know home buyers generally make more money each year, and the payments—which originally seemed so uncomfortable—become manageable. And, if it means getting the right house for an extra $50 per month, brokers know that the stretch will ultimately be worth it.

Still, you may not be comfortable spending 36 percent of your gross monthly income (which works out to about 50 percent of your take-home pay if you work for an employer who withholds federal income taxes and social security payments) on your debts and mortgage. Forty percent of your gross income may seem even more ludicrous. You may be most comfortable spending only 30 percent of your gross monthly income on your mortgage, property taxes, insurance, and debts—and that's perfectly all right. But you have to be willing to sacrifice a little bit of house to achieve that kind of ratio.

The bottom line is this: If you don't feel comfortable spending as much money as the real estate or mortgage broker tells you that you can afford, don't make that kind of deal. Look for a cheaper home, and perhaps another neighborhood. If you can't sleep at night because you're feeling so financially stretched, if you have to count your pennies every time you go to the grocery store, if you can't give your children birthday gifts, your spouse anniversary gifts, or your family holiday presents, or buy a new T-shirt without first checking your checkbook, having a particular house may not be worth it. And, if you are stretched to the max and then have a financial crisis—a temporary job layoff or a job loss, the death of a spouse, or a major medical emergency—your stress level will increase exponentially. It's not a great way to live, though some do it better than others. Decide in advance how much you're willing to stretch financially in order to buy your first home.

Putting Together the Cash for Your Down Payment and Closing Costs

From time to time, the real estate industry, or the Department of Housing and Urban Development (HUD) surveys first-time buyers, and renters who would like to be first-time buyers. The pollsters ask the first-timers what kind of home they'd like to buy, how much they have to spend, and how much cash they have put aside for their down payment and closing costs. And then they ask what obstacles block their path to homeownership.

Throughout the years, in poll after poll, first-time home buyers have said that scraping together the cash for a down payment is far and away the most difficult hurdle to clear in buying a home.

Does that mean that most first-time buyers can't afford to pay the mortgage, property taxes, and insurance? Not at all. Studies have shown that, once they own a property, they have the means to pay for the costs of ownership and maintenance. But setting aside each month the extra cash that they'll need for the down payment and closing costs seems to be a challenge that many would-be homeowners can't manage.

Indeed, the mortgage industry—on both the primary and secondary levels—has recognized this problem and created a wide assortment of loan programs to tackle it head-on. Since the early 1990s, we've seen the introduction and widespread use of "no point, no fee" loans (a point is 1 percent of the loan amount), and low-down-payment loans that require as little as 3 percent of the purchase price in cash at the closing. More recently, the zero-down-payment loan has been introduced, to greater or lesser fanfare.

Twenty percent down in cash—for many years, that financial benchmark was the only game in town. If you didn't have 20 percent in cash to put down on a home, you weren't buying. Why 20 percent? It used to be a lot more. Prior to the invention of the modern mortgage, as much as 40 to 50 percent in cash was required. Lenders have long argued that the more cash a home buyer puts into a deal, the more stable and secure is the remaining amount that is financed. Few homeowners, the theory goes, are going to walk away from that much equity in a home. It represents too big a portion of their personal net worth; it's too much money to flush down the drain. Twenty percent in cash seemed to be the threshold; below that level, the number of defaults and foreclosures increased. Even now, the number of defaults and late payments on loans with a 15 percent cash down payment is significantly higher, compared to loans with a 20 percent cash down payment. As the down payment gets smaller, the number of late payments and defaults rises.

If low-down-payment loans are so risky, why do lenders make them at all? Good question. The answer is this: Although low-down-payment loans look risky when compared to conventional loans that are based on 20 percent cash, only a very small number of homeowners default on these loans. Currently, about 2 percent of homeowners with conventional loans (20 percent or more down, in cash) default. By comparison, the default rate for low-down-payment loans written by conventional lenders is around 4 percent, and the default rate for FHA (Federal Housing Authority, part of HUD) and VA (Veterans Administration) loans is between 6 to 7 percent. That means 96 percent of all conventional low-down-payment loans are good. In other words, the vast majority of individuals who put just a little bit of cash down on a home will not default. And, for the extra risk these loans entail, the lender requires the buyer to purchase extra insurance to cover what's known as the "top portion of the loan," or the first 20 percent of the purchase price (which would normally be paid in cash). If you default on your loan, and you put only 5 percent down in cash on the property, the lender has insurance that should protect its investment on that portion of the loan over 80 percent of the original value of the home.

Since their introduction, low-down-payment loans have grown into a significant portion of the market. According to the Federal Housing Finance Board, the share of mortgage loans made with less than 10 percent down in cash grew from 7 percent in 1989 to around 30 percent in 1995. Experts acknowledge that part of the increase in these loans is due to lenders' actively seeking new business to replace the rush of refinancings that dried up after interest rates rose again in the early 90s. Lenders, pushed by such secondary institutions as Fannie Mae and Freddie Mac, have been trying to reach out to the 9 million or so immigrant families who, the Census Board projects, will move to the United States during the 1990s. These families have stable incomes and want to buy homes, but don't have the necessary cash for large down payments. Another reason for the growing acceptance of low-down-payment loans is the realization that, as the appreciation of home values has stalled, move-up buyers have had less equity in their properties to roll over into new homes. If they want to trade up to more expensive homes, their equity represents a smaller portion of the purchase price. For example, if you sell a home for $100,000 and you have $20,000 in equity, you have a 20 percent cash down payment for a new home. But if you want to trade up to a $200,000 home, your $20,000 equity represents only a 10 percent cash down payment on the new purchase.

In this Step, which is a critical part of the home buying process, we'll talk about what a down payment is, how much cash you need, where to find it, how to save for it, how much cash you'll need for closing costs, and how to put yourself on a budget.

FINANCIAL ISSUES

FINANCIAL
ISSUE
1

Your Down Payment and How Big It Should Be

A *down payment* is simply the portion of the purchase price of a home that you choose to pay in cash. The down payment amount you choose usually depends on the amount of cash you have available, and how much of it you want to put into your home. There are no limitations—you could pay all cash for a property (a 100 percent down payment) or perhaps put nothing down—but there are financial benefits to be derived from making a down payment of at least 20 percent of the purchase price of a home. On the other hand, in some markets, it doesn't pay to put down as much as you can in cash.

Here are some down payment options to think about.

Zero Percent Down. There's nothing less than a zero-down-payment loan. But don't think a zero-down-payment loan means you're free from scraping together any cash for the deal. As you will discover, there are closing costs and fees that lenders will not let you fold back into the loan. However, zero percent down means you have no cash, or equity, in your deal. The mortgage package can be structured in one of three ways:

1. You get a mortgage for 100 percent of the purchase price from a lender. Today, these expensive loans are available through the VA to qualified veterans.
2. You get a mortgage for 80 to 90 percent of the purchase price of the home from a lender, and then the seller, your parents, or a nonprofit organization gives you a second loan, or a gift, for the remaining portion;
3. The seller offers to finance your entire purchase of his or her home.

Less Than Twenty Percent Down. If you're putting down less than 20 percent of the purchase price in cash, your loan will be lumped into the low-down-payment loan category.

The big difference among low-down-payment loans is the amount of private mortgage insurance (PMI) you pay the lender each month to cover the extra risk associated with this type of loan. Any loan that carries a loan-to-value ratio greater than 80 percent (which means you're borrowing more than 80 percent of the purchase price of the home and your down payment is less than 20 percent) usually has some form of PMI, which will add an extra $45 to $70 per month for every $100,000 you borrow. (Some lenders don't have PMI, per se; instead, they increase the interest rate to cover the increased risk of the loan.) But if you get one of the lowest low-down-payment loans (5 percent down or less), you'll pay for a higher-risk version of PMI, which is even more expensive.

Twenty Percent Down. Conventional mortgages are those that carry a loan-to-value ratio of at least 80 percent. In other words, you put down at least 20 percent of the purchase price in cash. Conventional loans allow for the best interest rates because they're less risky for lenders.

Real estate brokers generally believe that a buyer who puts down 20 percent of the purchase price in cash is a stronger buyer. This measure is not always accurate, however, because even wealthy purchasers sometimes prefer not to tie up all their funds in a down payment and may instead opt for a loan of more than 80 percent of the purchase price.

Thirty-Five Percent Down. If you, like most folks, think the world of residential real estate would be your oyster if you only had 20 percent to put down in cash, get ready for a rude awakening. Many lenders have the option of requiring you to have an escrow reserve for your hazard insurance premiums and real estate property taxes which the lender will then pay for you. You pay your lender $1/12$ of the insurance premium plus $1/12$ of your annual property taxes along with your mortgage each month. Lenders like the escrow requirement because it gives them security that your real estate taxes and property insurance will be paid on time. Plus, they gain free use of your money. Very few states require lenders to pay interest on escrow funds. But, in some states, if you put down 35 percent, you can request that the lender forgo the insurance and tax escrow.

Thirty to Forty Percent Down. Co-ops often stipulate the amount of cash required for a down payment. In a co-op (cooperative housing), you own shares in a corporation that owns the building or property where your unit is located. You pay rent each month in the form of an assessment, which entitles you to live in your unit. Ownership in co-ops is actually more like owning shares of stock in a publicly traded company than owning property. Co-ops often require a hefty cash down payment, sometimes as much as 30 to 40 percent of the purchase price, from prospective home buyers. Some co-ops do not allow financing; that means buyers are not allowed to get a mortgage to help pay for their purchase.

One Hundred Percent Down. If you've just won the lottery and you're swimming in cash, you may very well want to pay all cash for your first home. But if you're like most first-time buyers, paying all cash is out of your reach. Many financial experts advise their clients *not* to put too much down in cash. A smaller down payment allows you to put some of the extra cash into an emergency fund, and keep the rest available for various other investments. And, if you pay all cash for your home, you won't have a mortgage interest tax deduction on your federal income tax return.

How much cash do you need for a down payment? That depends on the purchase price of the home you're buying. If you want to buy a home that costs $100,000, you would need $20,000 for a 20 percent down payment, $15,000 for a 15 percent down payment, and so on.

How do you figure out the numbers? Multiply the purchase price by the percent down payment you'd like to make. Here are some examples for a home with a purchase price of $143,000:

$143,000 × .10 (10 percent) = $14,300 down payment

$143,000 × .15 (15 percent) = $21,450 down payment

$143,000 × .05 (5 percent) = $7,150 down payment

In addition to the cash for the down payment, you'll still need cash for closing costs (costs and fees charged by the lender and others involved in the closing process). For closing costs, depending on the number of loan origination points (again, a point is 1 percent of the loan amount) you choose, and what the closing costs are in the particular location in which you are buying a home, you should prepare to pay an *additional* 2 to 7 percent of the purchase price. Using our example above:

$143,000 × .02 (2 percent) = $2,860 in closing costs

$143,000 × .07 (7 percent) = $10,010 in closing costs

(For more details on closing costs, including a worksheet on how to estimate them, see Financial Issues 6 and 7, later in this Step.)

Figuring Out How Much Cash You Have for Your Down Payment and Closing Costs

FINANCIAL
ISSUE
2

How much cash do you have on hand? Some first-time buyers have only the cash in their pockets, plus a few dollars in the bank. Others have been saving for a home for years; they have stocks, bonds, money market accounts, and certificates of deposit, all waiting to be liquidated, consolidated, and applied to the purchase of the home.

Whether you have a lot of cash or no cash, or are somewhere in between, it's important to make an honest assessment of your financial net worth before you continue on the journey toward homeownership. If you, like many first-time buyers, don't have a lot of cash, that situation will affect your decision about how you finance your future home. Determining your financial net worth will also help you figure out whether you've got enough cash today to buy a home, or will have to step up your savings to reach your goal.

First, some definitions:

- *Assets* are things you own: cash, real estate, jewelry, stocks, certificates of deposit, furniture, artwork, clothing, money market accounts, mutual funds, and other financial investments.
- *Liquid assets* are either being held as cash or can be easily converted into cash. An example of a liquid investment is a savings account. All you have to do is walk into your bank and write out a withdrawal ticket. The teller will hand you cash from the account.
- *Illiquid* assets, also known as *investment assets*, may take some time (and may cost you some money) to convert into cash. Examples of illiquid or investment assets include stocks, certificates of deposit, real estate, some mutual fund shares, and some bonds.
- *Personal assets* refer to your personal belongings; such as furniture, artwork, jewelry, clothing, and your car.
- *Liabilities* are debts that you owe: credit card debt, school and auto loans, stocks you buy on margin accounts, money you owe to the IRS, and spousal or child support that you pay. Money you owe in your business (if self-employed) and department store items (like television sets and appliances) you bought on credit or on lay-away plans are also liabilities.
- Your *net worth* is the total of your assets minus your total liabilities.

Use the chart on pages 57–60 to calculate your present net worth.

Example of Net Worth Calculation.   Let's say Leonora and Gene have $5,000 in their checking and savings accounts. They own $3,000 worth of stock, two certificates of deposit (CDs) worth $2,500, and a mutual fund account with a $2,000 balance. Last year, Gene inherited a gold pocketwatch from his grandfather. A local jewelry store owner appraised the watch at $1,500 for insurance purposes and offered to buy it for $1,000.

If you add up their value, Leonora and Gene's assets are worth $13,500, which seems like enough to buy a home. But they've also got some debts to pay off: $2,000 in credit card bills, $7,000 in graduate school loans, and an $8,000 car loan that will be paid off in 3 years. Their liabilities total $17,000. Subtract Leonora and Gene's

WORKSHEET
Your Present Net Worth

What You Own (Assets)   **Approximate Cash Value**

Liquid Assets

Cash   _____

Checking account   _____
   Acct. no. _____

Passbook savings account   _____
   Acct. no. _____

Money market account   _____
   Acct. no. _____

Other accounts

   Acct. no. _____   _____

   Acct. no. _____   _____

   Acct. no. _____   _____

Treasury bills   _____

Cash value of life insurance   _____

Other liquid assets

_____   _____

_____   _____

_____   _____

Total Liquid Assets   _____

Investment Assets

All stocks—current value   _____

   Stock name _____

   Shares _____ Value per share _____

   Stock name _____

   Shares _____ Value per share _____

   Stock name _____

   Shares _____ Value per share _____

   Stock name _____

   Shares _____ Value per share _____

What You Own (Assets)   **Approximate Cash Value**

    Stock name _____

    Shares _____ Value per share _____

    Stock name _____

    Shares _____ Value per share _____

    Stock name _____

    Shares _____ Value per share _____

Certificates of deposit   _____

Bonds   _____

Mutual funds   _____

    Acct. no. _____

    Acct. no. _____

    Acct. no. _____

Limited partnerships shares, or investments   _____

    Name _____

    Share (%) _____ Value _____

    Name _____

    Share (%) _____ Value _____

Real estate investments   _____

Retirement accounts   _____

    Keogh Acct. no. _____

    401K Acct. no. _____

    Other Acct. no. _____

Other investment assets

_____   _____

_____   _____

_____   _____

_____   _____

Total Investment Assets   _____

What You Own (Assets)   **Approximate Cash Value**

Personal Assets

Automobile(s)   _____

Motorcycle(s)   _____

Boat   _____

Furniture/Appliances   _____

Artwork   _____

Jewelry   _____

Rare books/antiques   _____

Other   _____

Total Personal Assets   _____

What You Owe (Liabilities)   **Amount**

Credit card loans

    Acct. no. _____   _____

    Acct. no. _____   _____

    Acct. no. _____   _____

    Acct. no. _____   _____

School loans

Undergraduate loan   _____

    Interest rate _____

    Due _____

Graduate school loan   _____

    Interest rate _____

    Due _____

Spouse's school loan   _____

    Interest rate _____

    Due _____

WORKSHEET
Your Present Net Worth, *continued*

What You Owe (Liabilities)   **Amount**

Other school loan _____

   Interest rate _____

   Due _____

Automobile loan no. 1 _____

   Interest rate _____

   Due _____

Automobile loan no. 2 _____

   Interest rate _____

   Due _____

Personal loans _____

IRS debt _____

Amount borrowed against life insurance _____

Amount borrowed from 401k, Keogh, or other
   defined benefits plans _____

Loan from parents, relatives, or friends _____

Medical debts _____

Other debts

_____ _____

_____ _____

_____ _____

_____ _____

Total Liabilities _____

Liquid assets _____

Investment assets   + _____

Personal assets   + _____

Total assets   = _____

Less: Total liabilities   − _____

NET WORTH   = _____

out how much mortgage you can carry). It's OK to accept a cash gift from your parents or a relative, but it isn't such a good idea to take the money in the form of a loan, even a very-low-interest loan. If you obtain a loan, lenders will add the cost of that loan to your debt column, decreasing your chances of getting approved for a mortgage.

Some retirement plans allow you to withdraw money from your retirement account to buy a home. And some don't. Whether your plan will allow you to do this depends primarily on the plan managers who set it up. Other plans only permit you to borrow from the fund to cope with emergencies. Furthermore, if you don't pay the plan back—with interest—within a certain period of time, the "loan" is considered a distribution, and, if you're under 59½ years of age, you'll owe a steep penalty to the government, plus income taxes on the amount of the distribution. The advantage of using your retirement cash to buy a home is that you'll be paying back your own plan account, with interest, rather than paying interest to a mortgage company. That's why some home buyers would rather borrow from their parents or a relative than from a bank. To them, it makes more sense to keep the money in the family, and pay back their parents or relatives with a higher level of interest than their relatives would receive from a bank or even a money market account.

Add up your liquid and readily-available-but-illiquid assets. Determine how much you have in cash today, and how much you would have if you sold off some of your stocks and bonds. If you don't have many assets but want to purchase a home, consider selling your expensive motorcycle, your gold wristwatch, and any other items you own that may be worth cash. You may be able to hold a garage sale and raise additional funds by selling off items you no longer need.

FINANCIAL
ISSUE
3

Your Personal and Household Budget

After you add up the cash you have on hand for your down payment, you may quickly realize you don't have nearly enough to cover even a 3 percent down payment plus closing costs. In metropolitan areas like Los Angeles, San Francisco, or New York, first-time buyers commonly buy homes that cost as much as $200,000, or even $300,000. At that price level, you'd need $6,000 to $9,000 for a 3 percent down payment, plus another $5,000 to $8,000 for closing costs. That's a significant amount of cash.

Don't despair if you realize you're not quite there yet. Most first-time home buyers have to budget and save for their purchase. In a recent study on homeownership that included renters, a senior economist for the National Association of Realtors, discovered that 21 percent of all renters who turned into home buyers saved for a few months before they purchased a home; 22 percent saved for 6 months to a year; 26 percent saved for 1 to 2 years; 16 percent saved for 2 to 3 years; 5 percent saved for 3 to 5 years; and 9 percent saved for more than 5 years in order to have enough cash to cover the out-of-pocket costs associated with their purchase. Renters, on average, saved between $51 and $100 per month for their down payment, and about half of those polled said they'd have to save 3 years or longer before looking for a home.

The same survey found that would-be first-time home buyers expect to make some sacrifices in order to achieve their dream of homeownership. About half said they'd have to give up their vacation trips. Others said they'd have to give up buying new home furnishings, jewelry or clothing, appliances or electronics equipment, entertainment, sports, recreation, and a new car. A full 44 percent of those polled said they'd have to give up daily nonessentials and do some general "belt tightening."

How do you tighten your belt? The easiest way is to put yourself on a budget, and account for every dollar that comes in or goes out. For those of you who have a computer, personal financial software, like Quicken®, will help you keep track of your expenditures. For those of you who don't own a computer or who simply prefer to keep track of general expenses rather than itemize every cent, the budget worksheet on pages 65–72 should keep you on target.

Starting Out. Your first task is to come up with a budget that *works for you.* You need to know what you spend each month. Everything counts: the pair of shoes you bought last week, the cup of cappuccino you picked up on the way to the train, and the sports-extra edition of the local paper you read on the way home from work. If you drive, you should keep track of your gas expenditures, car payments, and the gallon of windshield washer fluid you picked up at the 24-hour superstore down the block. Big blocks of cash get frittered away almost thoughtlessly. How often do you buy lunch at work? If you spend an average of $5 per day (which is considered cheap in larger metropolitan areas), that's $25 per week, or around $1,300 per year—a nice chunk of down payment money. How often do you eat out in restaurants? If you're like most dual-income households, you're eating out, or ordering in, or picking up pre-prepared food a couple of nights a week. At a conservative $20 per dinner out, you're spending maybe $60 to $80 per week or up to $4,000 a year on convenience.

I'm not advocating that you give up all the frills, accommodations, and conveniences you've opted to use to make your busy life easier to manage. But when you start to see where the money goes, and when you can focus on the end goal, buying a home, you'll start making your own trade-offs.

Your Budget. The budget worksheet I've provided (pages 65–72) is divided into two sections: (1) income and (2) expenditures. The idea is to see the relationship between how much money comes in and how you spend it.

In the expenditures section of the worksheet, alongside the list of expense items, is a column where you enter the monthly cost of each item. Think about how many times during a year you purchase or spend money on that item. Then multiply your monthly cost by that number to come up with an annual cost.

Don't feel pressured to fill in every line item. Not every item on the list will apply to you. For example, if you are self-employed, you'll have to deduct your business expenses as well as your household expenses. Or, you may not have children, an aging parent, or a sick relative whom you support. The list is designed to get you thinking about details. If you're going to cut back and save money, you'll find a lot of it in the details.

Most people can't come up with every figure right off the top of their heads. Pull out the receipts you've stashed in your wallet, plus your checkbook, credit card statements, tax returns, and anything else you need to jog your memory. Make copies of the blank worksheet for future use. You'll want to revise your budget over and over again, as you continue to pare down your expenses and increase your savings.

If you run your finances the way major corporations do, your savings and debts match up on the bottom line, and your balance equals 0. Your goal in future budgets is to adjust your expenses so that you have extra cash (savings) to put into your house fund account.

WORKSHEET
Your Budget

INCOME

Sources	Amount Monthly	Amount Annually
Salary	_____	_____
Spouse's salary	_____	_____
Second job salary	_____	_____
Spouse's second job salary	_____	_____
Self-employed income	_____	_____
Business income	_____	_____
Investment income	_____	_____
Dividends (stock and mutual funds)	_____	_____
Cash gifts	_____	_____
Interest income (bank accounts and bonds)	_____	_____
Inheritances	_____	_____
Lottery winnings	_____	_____
Gambling winnings	_____	_____
Other	_____	_____
Subtotal—Income	_____	_____

EXPENDITURES

Item	Monthly Cost	Annual Cost
1. Household		
Rent	_____	_____
Utilities:		
Electricity	_____	_____
Telephone	_____	_____
Cellular telephone	_____	_____
Computer on-line services	_____	_____

Item	Monthly Cost	Annual Cost
Gas company	_____	_____
Cable TV	_____	_____
Other utilities	_____	_____
Groceries		
Food	_____	_____
Nonfood items	_____	_____
Insurance		
Health	_____	_____
Life	_____	_____
Renter's	_____	_____
Auto	_____	_____
Other	_____	_____
Alimony/Child support	_____	_____
Commuting expenses		
Train/Bus	_____	_____
Taxicabs	_____	_____
Tolls	_____	_____
Gas for car	_____	_____
Car pool contribution	_____	_____
Auto repair/Maintenance	_____	_____
Medical expenses		
Hospital	_____	_____
Doctors/Practitioners		
General	_____	_____
Ophthalmologist/Optometrist	_____	_____
Other specialist	_____	_____
Dentist	_____	_____

Item	Monthly Cost	Annual Cost
Chiropractor/Therapist	_____	_____
Other	_____	_____
Prescriptions/Over-the-counter drugs	_____	_____
Clothing		
Purchases	_____	_____
Dry cleaning	_____	_____
House of worship	_____	_____
Housecleaning service	_____	_____
Other	_____	_____
Subtotal: Household	_____	_____

2. Taxes

Item	Monthly Cost	Annual Cost
On income		
Federal	_____	_____
State	_____	_____
Other government	_____	_____
Social security (FICA)	_____	_____
Other	_____	_____
Subtotal: Taxes	_____	_____

3. Debt

Item	Monthly Cost	Annual Cost
Auto loan	_____	_____
School loan	_____	_____
Credit card debt	_____	_____
Loans from parents and friends	_____	_____
Other debt _____	_____	_____
_____	_____	_____
Subtotal: Debt	_____	_____

Item	Monthly Cost	Annual Cost
4. Money Put Aside*		
Savings	_____	_____
Retirement accounts		
401K	_____	_____
Keogh	_____	_____
Defined contribution	_____	_____
Other _____	_____	_____
House fund account	_____	_____
Stocks, bonds, mutual funds, investments	_____	_____
Other	_____	_____
Subtotal: Money Put Aside	_____	_____
5. Major Purchases		
Car	_____	_____
Boat	_____	_____
Motorcycle	_____	_____
Other vehicle	_____	_____
Computer	_____	_____
Furniture	_____	_____
Electronic equipment	_____	_____
Vacation timeshare	_____	_____
Continuing education		
Advanced degree tuition	_____	_____
Fees for classes	_____	_____
Other _____	_____	_____
_____	_____	_____
_____	_____	_____
Subtotal: Major Purchases	_____	_____

*The amount you're currently saving, or having withheld from your salary, in each category. If *none* in any category, enter a savings goal, in parentheses, so you are constantly reminded of what you'd like to be saving.

Item	Monthly Cost	Annual Cost
6. Children/Family		
Aging parent contribution		
Nursing home	_____	_____
Medical expenses	_____	_____
Other _____	_____	_____
Sibling/Relative contribution	_____	_____
Children	_____	_____
Diapers	_____	_____
Formula	_____	_____
Clothing	_____	_____
School tuition	_____	_____
Day care	_____	_____
Babysitters	_____	_____
Doctors	_____	_____
Prescription drugs	_____	_____
Games/Toys/Videos	_____	_____
Sporting equipment/Fees	_____	_____
Allowance	_____	_____
Furniture	_____	_____
Camp	_____	_____
Carpooling	_____	_____
Lessons	_____	_____
Other _____	_____	_____
_____	_____	_____
Other _____	_____	_____
_____	_____	_____
_____	_____	_____
Subtotal: Children/Family	_____	_____

Item	Monthly Cost	Annual Cost
7. Entertainment		
Movies	_____	_____
Books	_____	_____
Video rental	_____	_____
CDs/Tapes/Records	_____	_____
Restaurants		
Lunches out	_____	_____
Dinners out	_____	_____
Take-out food	_____	_____
Theater	_____	_____
Concerts	_____	_____
Subscriptions		
Newspapers	_____	_____
Magazines	_____	_____
Other _____	_____	_____
Other _____	_____	_____
_____	_____	_____
Subtotal: Entertainment	_____	_____
8. Recreation		
Sports events	_____	_____
Sports equipment	_____	_____
Other sports expenses	_____	_____
Club memberships	_____	_____
Lessons	_____	_____
Classes	_____	_____
Other _____	_____	_____
_____	_____	_____
_____	_____	_____
Subtotal: Recreation	_____	_____

Item	Monthly Cost	Annual Cost
9. Travel/Vacations		
Transportation	_____	_____
Airfare	_____	_____
Trains	_____	_____
Buses	_____	_____
Car rental	_____	_____
Boats	_____	_____
Other	_____	_____
Hotels	_____	_____
Tolls	_____	_____
Fees	_____	_____
Food	_____	_____
Gas	_____	_____
Recreation	_____	_____
Entertainment	_____	_____
Other _____	_____	_____
_____	_____	_____
Subtotal: Travel/Vacations	_____	_____
10. Miscellaneous		
Gifts	_____	_____
Postage	_____	_____
Bank account fees	_____	_____
Credit card fees	_____	_____
Other _____	_____	_____
_____	_____	_____
_____	_____	_____
_____	_____	_____
Subtotal: Miscellaneous	_____	_____

Item	Monthly Cost	Annual Cost
11. Self-Employed Business Expenses		
Self-Employed Expenses from Your Business	_____	_____

SUMMARY: ALL EXPENSES

Item	Monthly Cost	Annual Cost
1. Household	_____	_____
2. Taxes	_____	_____
3. Debt	_____	_____
4. Money Put Aside	_____	_____
5. Major Purchases	_____	_____
6. Children/Family	_____	_____
7. Entertainment	_____	_____
8. Recreation	_____	_____
9. Travel/Vacations	_____	_____
10. Miscellaneous	_____	_____
11. Self-Employed Business Expenses	_____	_____
Total Expenses	_____	_____
Total Income	_____	_____
Less: Total Expenses	− _____	_____
Net Savings (Debt)	= _____	_____

Creating a Budget. Once you know where all your money is going, you should be able to find ways to redirect some expenditures. Keep your eye on the bottom line of income. For every dollar you don't spend, you can make a significant contribution to a house fund (see Financial Issue 4). If you're serious about purchasing a home, you must prioritize your wants and your needs. You may want that new jazz CD, but if you buy two CDs per month, at a cost of about $10 each, that's $240 per year. For the same money, you could be a heck of a lot closer to your down payment and closing cost goals.

Something interesting happens when you start recording every dollar you spend. The whole process of finding less expensive ways to do things becomes second nature. You find yourself subconsciously making choices about spending that work within your large-scale plans. You become more focused, and more appreciative of the true luxuries that you allow yourself. It's the "leaner, meaner" and "no pain, no gain" concepts at work. But the rewards—in this case, paid-down debt and a fatter house fund account—are tangible and enormously satisfying.

It's not always easy to wean yourself away from conveniences. When Sam and I were first married, we both left jobs and decided to start our own businesses. We went from stable to unstable incomes. We didn't know how much our joint income would drop (it might have been 20 percent, 40 percent, or 60 percent less than the previous year), so we decided to cut back drastically on *all* of our spending. Instead of ordering in dinner twice a week, eating out twice a week, and buying our lunches every day, we cut back to eating out only once every two weeks, cooking at home, and taking our lunches to work. Instead of giving our family expensive holiday gifts, we made gifts, like seasoned olive oils and vinegars in fancy glass jars. When we had to travel, we used up our frequent flier coupons. After a while, we realized that we enjoyed watching our bank accounts grow more than we had enjoyed these conveniences.

No matter how much you cut back, you'll want to retain certain "luxuries." For example, if both of you work, you may consider having a housekeeper or maid service clean your home every week or two is a necessity rather than a luxury. That is your choice to make. By knowing where your money goes, you'll be able to make an informed decision.

If you've cut your budget to the bone and you feel you're still not saving enough money toward your down payment, you have another option: Take a second or a part-time job and apply the maximum amount of your earnings from this job toward your house fund. You might work as a sales clerk in a department store on the weekends, or sign on for the evening shift at a local supermarket. Or, if you or your spouse stays home with the kids, perhaps taking in an extra child or two during the week would provide the cash flow you seek. Kathy, a dental hygienist in Chicago, knits and sells sweaters for extra income. Whichever type of job you decide to take, don't fall for scams that advertise making quick money. Too many people have sent $500 or $1,000 to scam organizations and received nothing in return.

FINANCIAL
ISSUE
4

Creating a House Fund

After you've refocused and prioritized your budget, you should have some extra cash to plunk into your down payment and closing cost fund. Some people put all their cash into a general savings account. The problem with that approach is this: Funds that get commingled with your general savings tend to get spent. The idea behind creating a house fund is that this is untouchable money for your new home, and you're not going to lay a finger on it unless you're faced with a catastrophe. It's your proverbial nest egg.

The extra cash you're saving for investing in a home can be placed in a bank account, money market account, cash money market, mutual fund account, safety deposit box, large piggy bank, or hidden pocket in your mattress, though these last three suggestions won't pay you any interest. You'll be working hard to earn it and save it, so you should take advantage of financial institutions that will pay you for the privilege of holding it.

When will you have saved enough to buy your first home? That depends on how expensive your choice of a home is. Here's how the numbers work. Let's say you want to buy a home that costs $80,000. A 3 percent down payment (with a 97 percent loan from a conventional lender or FHA) comes to $2,400. You'll probably need another $1,600 for closing costs that can't be folded into the mortgage. That means you need to come up with at least $4,000 ($2,400 + $1,600 = $4,000) to close on the property.

How can you save $4,000? Believe it or not, you can accumulate that amount of money by saving $10.96 per day for a year:

$$\$4,000 \div 365 \text{ (days in a year)} = \$10.96 \text{ per day}$$

Put that much cash aside in a piggy bank (or better yet, a bank account), and you'll accumulate $76.71 each week and $328.80 each month. If you find a lender willing to fold all of your closing costs into your loan, you'll need to save only $6.58 per day:

$$\$2,400 \div 365 \text{ (days in a year)} = \$6.58 \text{ per day}$$

$$\$6.58 \times 7 \text{ (days in a week)} = \$46.03 \text{ per week}$$

With some discipline, you can easily add that much cash weekly to your house fund. Another way to make your savings grow is to gather up your daily pocket change. Everyone gets change—pennies you never seem to spend; nickels, dimes, and quarters that accumulate in large clumps all over the house. Perhaps you throw your spare change into a pot. If you don't, you should. Every day, empty out all your change (keep enough for a telephone call or a parking meter) into a jar, a pot, or your piggy bank. At the end of each week, add that amount to what you've already saved for your down payment that week. Deposit it all into your house fund, and watch it grow.

The keys to successfully saving up for your down payment and closing costs are vigilance and tenacity. Building your house fund must become your top priority—barring any medical emergencies, natural disasters, or job crises. Otherwise, you'll find yourself straying from the savings path and spending the money as quickly as you collect it. Resist the temptation to dip in for a special anniversary gift, or a new television set. Instead of exchanging expensive gifts with your spouse, buy a single rose (or the equivalent) and a nice card, and make a joint donation to your house fund. Years from now, as you and your spouse celebrate a milestone birthday or anniversary, and exchange gaily wrapped presents, you'll remember the time when you chose to give each other a house instead.

Saving money is a lot like dieting. If you're not careful—strict, even—it's easy to fall off the wagon and not save a dime. On the other hand, don't become an hour-by-hour money vigilante who becomes obsessed with the savings concept. Try not to miss a day of saving—or a week, or a month. Don't give yourself any basis for saying, "Well, I can't do this, so I might as well stop trying." Instead, get right back on track with your budget. Start putting your coins in the pot; start putting your $10 bills in the piggy bank. Don't let yourself get derailed by a missed day, week, or month of savings. This is not a race in which only the first person to save the down payment gets the house. There are millions of homes for sale each year in America and, when you're ready, one will become your new address.

liabilities from their assets, and you see their net worth is actually a negative amount of $3,500. That means, if they liquidated all of their assets and tried to pay off their debts today, they would still owe $3,500:

$13,500 (assets) − $17,000 (liabilities) = −$3,500* (net worth)

Don't Confuse Your Net Worth with Your Cash on Hand. Once you've calculated your entire net worth, it's time to examine your assets to see what kind of cash you actually have on hand to purchase a home. You may be able to liquidate most or all of your assets, but experts warn that it may not be prudent to do so. For example, you could borrow against the cash value of a life insurance policy, but you may not want to add that cost to your debts. Likewise, you may be able to withdraw some funds from an IRA or Keogh retirement plan, but the steep penalties and taxes you'll pay may make it not worth your while.

The best assets to include when figuring out how much money you have for your down payment and closing costs are those in cash—the money in your checking, savings, and cash money market accounts. Stocks and stocks-and-bonds mutual fund accounts (those not held within retirement accounts) are also good bets for liquidation, though you may risk cashing in at a time when the stocks have a lower value than when you bought them, or just before they go up substantially in value. If you have savings bonds (gifts from past events, like a graduation, birthday, or wedding) that have already come due, consider cashing them in. Just remember to set aside the cash to pay the IRS the taxes that will be due on the sale.

Another good source of money is the dividend accumulations that build up in whole-life insurance policies. According to Phil, an accountant in Chicago, some people who have invested in these whole-life insurance policies just let the tax-free dividends accumulate, gathering interest (which is taxable). If you need the cash, simply call your insurance agent and ask to have a check sent. Phil likes to call these dividends the "secret savings accounts."

The problem with borrowing against a whole-life policy, or any other insurance policy, is that you have to pay back the policy plus interest. That puts you deeper into debt at a time when you want to minimize your debt (lenders look up your total debt when they figure

---

*On financial statements, you'll frequently see a negative net worth expressed in parentheses. For example, −$3,500 might also be expressed as ($3,500).

WORKSHEET
Your House Fund: 24-Month Worksheet

Month	Amount Deposited	Interest	Total
1.			
2.			
3.			
4.			
5.			
6.			
7.			
8.			
9.			
10.			
11.			
12.			
13.			
14.			
15.			
16.			
17.			
18.			
19.			
20.			
21.			
22.			
23.			
24.			

Keeping Records.   Your bank should send you a monthly statement of your deposits into your house fund, but it's a good idea to keep your own record, in case the bank makes a mistake (banks do, from time to time). You can use detailed computer banking software, but the following worksheet should work nearly as well. (It assumes that you won't be making withdrawals.)

Closing Costs

FINANCIAL
ISSUE
5

First-time home buyers know they have to save up cash for their down payment. But they often don't realize that closing costs are another expensive part of the process. In fact, some buyers are so unaware of closing costs that they feel a bit overwhelmed—even betrayed—when they find out what costs and fees they'll have to pay in order to close title on their new home.

How much are closing costs? As we've seen, they can range from 2 percent to 7 percent of the purchase price of the home. On a $100,000 purchase, closing costs might be as little as $2,000 and as much as $7,000. To many first-time buyers, closing costs seem as insurmountable as the down payment.

Buyers (and sellers, for that matter) are encountering all kinds of closing costs—a term I'll use to define *all* the costs associated with closing on a piece of property, rather than just the lender's costs for closing on a loan. In general, closing costs can include everything from the lender's charge for preparing the closing documentation, to municipal, county, or state transfer taxes. You might pay $10 to get a certified copy of your paid water bill, and your new condominium association might exact a $250 move-in charge. As a home buyer, you may pay for as many as twenty different items.

Some of these costs are legitimate. Credit companies charge lenders for each credit check, so it's not surprising that the lenders pass along this cost (some lenders add a hefty surcharge) to home buyers. But some lenders, mortgage experts say, create "junk fees" purely to increase their profits.

Junk fees is a real estate industry term for lenders' fees that have glorified names but no substance. For example, a former loan officer for NBD Mortgage Company says that charging home buyers an "underwriting" or a "commitment" fee is nonsensical. Lenders, he argues, are being paid to underwrite loans, to commit to specific loans within specific parameters. Why should they get an additional fee for something they are already being paid to do? Junk fees are

77

often given legitimate-sounding names that simply confuse customers. To make it worse, not every lender gives every junk fee the same name, making it difficult for home buyers to compare fees directly with each other.

Lenders are supposed to make it easy for you to know and understand their closing costs. The federal government, under the Real Estate Settlement Procedures Act (RESPA) and the Truth in Lending Law, requires lenders to provide you with a written, good-faith estimate of all your closing costs within three days of applying for a loan. This good-faith estimate is supposed to accurately reflect your closing costs. (Before you formally apply for your loan, however, you should ask the lender to tell you what the closing costs are likely to be for your transaction.)

Despite the good-faith estimate, many home buyers are still surprised when they get to the closing, because the law doesn't require the lender to explain what the closing costs are for and who actually receives them. If your loan officer doesn't do a particularly good job of explaining the fees that will be attached to your loan, you may be unhappy on the day of the closing.

One thing to remember is that many closing costs charged by a lender are negotiable. Whether you can get the lender to back down from these closing costs depends on how good a negotiator you are. If you're tough, have done your homework, and have shopped around to find out what other lenders in your neighborhood or metro area are offering, then you may find a lender willing to negotiate on some—or all—of the closing costs. The time to negotiate, however, is *before* you complete your application. Once the lender has your money and a signed application, you've got your deal and you're done negotiating. Be aware of this basic trick: The lender may acquiesce easily to your request to eliminate the closing costs. If that happens, see whether he or she is trying to hike the interest rate you're paying. Lenders commonly agree to a "no point, no fee" loan that is above the going interest rate. Your goal in negotiation is to eliminate as many closing costs and fees as possible, while still getting the going interest rate.

Many of the items on the following list of closing costs are mortgage-related. If you don't need a mortgage, or think you'll end up with seller financing or a loan from a family member, then some of the listed closing costs won't apply. But others will, and you should be aware of them.

List of Closing Costs. The range of costs associated with each of the following items is simply an estimate. Actual costs will vary, based on local custom and competition in the marketplace.

- *Lender's points, loan origination, or loan service fees.* A point is 1 percent of the loan amount. Lenders often charge points in order to give you the lowest rate possible. Some lenders won't charge points for making the loan, but might charge loan origination or loan service fees. These fees range from 0 to 3 percent (or more) of the loan amount.
- *Loan application fee.* This fee, the lender's nonrefundable charge for taking your application, ranges from $0 to $500.
- *Lender's credit report.* The lender will hire a credit bureau to run a credit check on you. The lender is charged for the service and passes along that cost to you. This fee ranges anywhere from $40 to $150 or more.
- *Lender's processing fee.* This is a charge for pushing papers around the office. In this age of four-minute computer-assisted loan approvals, this fee of $75 to $150 may be negotiable.
- *Lender's document preparation fee.* Often considered a junk fee, especially since many of the forms are stored in the computer, this charge usually runs from $50 to $200.
- *Lender's appraisal fee.* Once you've applied for the loan, the lender has to make sure that your home is actually worth what you're paying for it, because you're using it as collateral for the loan. Lenders tend to charge you what they're charged by appraisers— usually $200 to $450 or more.
- *Prepaid interest on the loan.* This is the daily cost of your loan from the day of the closing through the end of the month in which the closing occurs. Although you usually pay your mortgage in arrears (say, on July 1 for the month of June), this cash is due up front at the closing.
- *Lender's insurance escrow.* Most lenders will want you to have an insurance escrow, in which they keep enough cash to pay your annual insurance premium plus a cushion of two months' worth of premiums. You usually pay the first year's premium up front at or before the closing, plus an additional amount to help build the escrow for the second year's premium.

79

- *Lender's real estate property tax escrow.* Alongside the insurance escrow, the lender collects from you, and then holds in your account, enough cash to pay your annual property tax bill, plus an extra ⅙ (or, two months' worth). Before the closing, you'll kick off the account by putting in anywhere from 33 percent to 50 percent of the next estimated tax bill, depending on when you expect to close and when the next tax payment is due. (After closing, you'll make monthly insurance and property tax escrow payments along with your monthly mortgage payment.)

- *Lender's tax escrow service fee.* This fee, to set up the escrow, can run anywhere from $40 to $80 or more.

- *Title insurance cost for the owner's and lender's policy.* Lenders want to be sure that their interest in your property is insured by the title insurance company. The cost for this coverage is based on the dollar amount of the mortgage you obtain from your lender.

- *Special endorsements to the title.* Depending on the type of property you pick, your lender may request that special endorsements be added when the lender's title policy becomes final. An endorsement is specific insurance coverage that the lender wants only for his or her benefit and protection. A location endorsement, which guarantees that the home is located as described in the loan, may cost $15. If you choose an adjustable rate mortgage (ARM), the variable rate endorsement may cost another $60, depending on the title company and the state in which you are located. For a townhouse, there may be a PUD (planned unit development) endorsement. At a cost of $15 to $50 each, endorsements can add a chunk of money to your closing costs. (These costs fluctuate from state to state and from title company to title company, and are subject to local custom.)

- *House inspection fees.* If you have your home inspected by a professional home inspector, he or she will probably insist on being paid when the work is completed. But if, for some reason, you haven't already paid this cost, it will be tacked on at the closing. These days, professional home inspectors and structural engineers often charge for their services based on the price of the home. Expect to pay $225 to $400 or more.

- *Title company or escrow company closing fee.* This fee can run anywhere from $150 to $400 and up. In states where escrow closings are more common, the cost can run up to $1,000. Depending on the custom in your state and county, the seller may split this cost with you.

- *Recording fees.* After you close on your home, your deed and your mortgage must be recorded with the county in which the home is located. This cost usually runs from $25 to $75.

- *Local (city, town, or village), county, and state property transfer taxes.* Also known as stamp taxes (because you're often given a stamp to paste on the deed), transfer taxes are another way for your town, county, and state to raise revenues. Essentially, you and the seller are being charged for buying and selling property. The charges that you, the buyer, will pay vary from city to city and from state to state. Sometimes the seller picks up the entire cost; sometimes the buyer does. In general, property transfer taxes can range from $0 to $5 per $1,000 of the purchase price, or more. In some areas, you may be assessed a flat fee of $25 or $50 per transaction.

- *Attorney's fee.* Whether you decide to get an attorney to help you through the home-buying process depends in large part on local custom. In Indiana and California, buyers and sellers are discouraged from using attorneys. In other parts of the Midwest, and in the Northeast, they're commonly used. If you need an attorney, you can often negotiate a flat fee, which might start at around $300 but will go up according to the experience of the attorney and how complicated your transaction is. In some places, it may be difficult to find an attorney who will charge only a flat fee. You'll then have to pay an hourly rate, which could run anywhere from $80 to $200 an hour, or more.

- *Condo move-in fee.* When it's imposed by an association, this charge can range from almost nothing to more than $400.

- *Co-op apartment fees.* Some co-op associations require a small fee for transferring shares of stock, for doing name searches, and/or for moving in. Each of these fees can range from $50 to more than $500. (For more information on co-ops, see Step 6, Identifying Where You Want to Live.)

- *Credit checks for condo and co-op buildings.* Some condos and co-ops will want to check your credit before they allow you to move into the building. If a fee is charged, it can range about $75 or more.

Even before you know what your actual closing costs are likely to be, you should start saving up for them. In Step 9, Financing Your Home, you'll find a detailed worksheet that will let you estimate your lender's closing costs, and will help you negotiate more easily with lenders. Step 10, The Closing, includes a worksheet on which you can enter all the details of your closing costs.

FINANCIAL
ISSUE
6

Getting Help in Building Your Down Payment

Malka had saved a lot of cash for her down payment. When the time came to purchase a home, she opted for a co-op in New York City. The co-op association required a 25 percent cash down payment, which was significantly more than she had saved. To make up the difference, she turned to her parents for help. Malka's not alone. According to a study published by the Federal Reserve Bank of Boston in 1994, nearly a quarter of all first-time buyers received from relatives some sort of financial assistance with their purchase. The study found that about 13 percent of the average down payment came from relatives. In cities where housing is expensive, first-time buyers got more help than buyers in cities where the cost of living is more moderate.

The current generation of first-time buyers isn't the first to look toward Mom and Dad for help. Your parents likely got some help from their parents or their aunts and uncles. My grandfather lent his nephew the cash he needed to buy his first home.

To a certain extent, the federal government makes it easy for parents to help out their children. Under current tax law, gifts of $10,000 a year or less can be made tax-free. That means a husband and wife can give each of their children (or anyone else) $20,000 a year tax-free ($10,000 from the father and $10,000 from the mother).

But what if your parents or relatives either don't have, or don't want to give or lend you, the money you need for your down payment? Fortunately, there are some other alternatives:

- *Seller financing.* Even if you can qualify for a standard 80 percent or 90 percent loan from a commercial lender, you might ask whether the seller will finance a second mortgage for the portion of the down payment you don't have.

- *Lease with an option to buy.* If you find a house you like, but haven't saved up enough of a down payment, ask whether the seller will allow you to lease the house with an option to buy it in the future.

If the seller agrees, negotiate to get some part of your monthly rent credited toward your down payment. The seller will want to have the least amount possible credited, and you will want to have all of it credited. Somewhere in the middle (perhaps 33 percent, 50 percent, or 66 percent rent credit), you'll come to an agreement. You'll need to put down some money as a nonrefundable *option fee;* that is, you pay a fee to have the option to purchase the property within a specific period of time. Have the seller credit the option money as part of your down payment as well.

- *Veterans Administration (VA) loans.* For qualified veterans who don't have enough cash for a down payment, a VA loan of up to $184,000 may be the solution. A VA loan is one of the true zero-down-payment loans, though there are extra points and fees (which can be folded back into the loan) for the privilege. The VA is also good about working with veterans who fall behind in their monthly payments. But there are strict eligibility requirements. If you served in the military and were honorably discharged, contact your local VA office for more information.

- *Government assistance.* Low-down-payment loans are one thing, but it's quite another to be given cash assistance or a below-market interest rate loan. Both of these options exist within the realm of a Community Development Block Grant (CDBG). Many communities use some of their CDBG funds to create special home buying opportunities for low- to moderate-income first-time buyers. Often, nonprofit housing agencies participate in these programs, offering free first-time homeowner education classes and financial counseling sessions. To find these programs, contact your local municipal housing agency, and read the real estate section of your local newspaper. Innovative programs for first-time buyers are often described in feature articles, as nonprofit agencies seek out home buyers who fit their desired financial profiles.

- *Co-signing loans.* If you have the amount needed for a down payment, but can't quite qualify for a loan on your own, you can ask your parents or friends to co-sign the loan with you. This means they, as well as you, are legally responsible for paying back the loan. There are other important issues as well. If your parents die while they are co-signers, the government may treat the co-signing of the loan as a gift to you, and you may owe inheritance or gift taxes on the "gift" of their signature. For more information, consult your accountant or real estate attorney.

- *Second jobs.* As we've already discussed, you or your spouse could take a second job and specifically earmark that income as cash for your down payment.

- *Buy with a partner.* If you have half the cash you need to purchase a home and you have a friend who also has half the cash he or she needs to buy a home, perhaps together you'd have enough to buy a house you could share. Earlier, we talked about how Mitch and Bob pooled their money and bought a four-flat on the northwest side of Chicago. Each buyer lived in one of the apartments, and they rented out the other two. Ultimately, the cash flow from the two rented units increased enough to more than pay the mortgage.

- *Foreclosure or property under distress.* One way to buy a home with little or no cash down is to find a property that is currently in foreclosure or is about to be put into foreclosure. When an owner doesn't pay his or her mortgage, the lender has the right to foreclose on the property, that is, take it over and try to sell it to recoup the amount of the loan that hasn't been paid back. You can sometimes negotiate with the lender to buy the home and have that lender finance the purchase; or, you can get your own financing. Sellers who are in default, but who haven't yet had their property foreclosed on by the lender, may be happy to sell their home to you at a deep discount. Before you do this, make sure you get the lender's permission. Then obtain the necessary title insurance. You'll probably want to have your real estate attorney draft the document and make sure you're getting what you bargained for.

- *Articles of agreement, installment land sale, land contract sale, or contract for deed sale.* Whichever name is used in your area for this type of sale, it is another way to buy a home with little or nothing down. Basically, you enter into an installment agreement to purchase the home over a specified period of time. The seller keeps legal title, and you receive equitable title, which means you receive an interest in the property but do not own it. The benefit to you, a first-time buyer, is that the seller will usually accommodate an extremely low down payment and still feel comfortable about it, because the seller retains title to the property until after you've paid off the loan. If you default on the loan, the seller will need to evict you to reclaim possession. All this may sound peachy, but if the seller has a mortgage on the property, he or she most likely has a "due on sale" clause in the terms of the mortgage agreement. If you buy the home on an installment contract, from a seller who hasn't obtained his or her lender's permission, and then the lender finds out, and forecloses on the home, you could lose all of the cash you've put into the home until that point. Ask your real estate attorney to advise you further and to write up the installment contract, before you proceed down this path.

EMOTIONAL/FAMILY ISSUES

Fighting the Savings Blues

EMOTIONAL/
FAMILY ISSUE
1

The hardest part about setting savings goals is getting started. Saving that initial $1,000, $5,000, or $10,000 can seem to take forever, as you scrimp and save and do without. However, you'll find that the emotional pain associated with "belt tightening" eventually fades as you get past your initial hurdles. If saving the first $1,000 is tough, the next $1,000 is easier. After a while, you'll be encouraged by how your down payment fund is growing, and you will be motivated to find ways of increasing it more quickly.

Still, on your 100th day of taking peanut butter and jelly sandwiches to the office, you may find yourself downright depressed. Or, a day may come when you frantically hunt through your closet for something fresh to wear and then realize that you haven't bought anything new in months (or years) and your clothing looks shabby (as opposed to "shabby chic").

If you reach an emotional pit where the fun has gone out of saving for your future home, treat yourself and your family to something new and different. Buy a new item of clothing for yourself or your children. Buy your spouse flowers. Plan a picnic or barbeque in the country. Plan an outing in the city. Find ways to inexpensively move your focus away from how much you're doing without.

Above all, keep your eye on the prize—your future home purchase. If all else fails, you may want to take a drive around some of the neighborhoods you like and visit a few open houses. Walking through a few homes that are for sale should quickly reignite your passion for growing your house fund account.

Building Credible Credit

These days, credit appears to be the "engine of our economy." Everyone has credit cards, and uses credit to buy cars, furniture, clothing, and even food. How much you're worth is often tied directly to how much you can borrow. Having a bad credit rating can hinder your goal of homeownership. In this Step, we'll talk about what credit is, how you get it, the problems you might encounter, and how to solve them. We'll also discuss how your job and work history can affect your credit, and how you might plan your career if you intend to buy a home within the next three years.

FINANCIAL ISSUES

FINANCIAL ISSUE 1

Your Credit History

If you don't have wads of cash stuffed in a mattress or locked away in a safety deposit box, you've probably used credit to buy some of the finer things in life—a college education, a car, a boat, or an engagement ring. Every purchase you make on credit and fail to repay in full within a stated time (or fail to repay at all) becomes part of your credit history. In the United States, there are companies that maintain enormous databases that contain detailed personal financial information, including debt and loan payments, residences, and whether a company has taken action to collect on a debt. If you ever purchased anything on credit, or were granted a loan, you are probably on file with one or more of these credit bureaus.

Among the largest credit bureaus (also known as credit reporting agencies) are TRW, Trans-Union, and Equifax. They gather credit information on a daily, weekly, and monthly, basis from credit card companies (American Express, Visa, MasterCard, Discover, and others), mortgage lenders, utility companies, department stores, and banks, and sell that information to companies that extend credit to consumers—mortgage brokers and lenders, finance companies, and department stores.

When they receive information, credit bureaus add it to the existing data in your file, which is continuously updated. If you pay off a loan, for example, or are late with a credit card payment, this information is entered in your file and becomes available to companies that may purchase a credit history to check on your financial health. If you take out a loan or fail to pay your federal income taxes, that information is reported and your file is updated. Credit reporting companies share their file information with each other, which would lead a reasonable person to believe that all credit bureaus are storing the same information. Sometimes, however, crucial data are overlooked or not transmitted to all companies. That's why it's important to check your credit at all of your local credit bureaus and compare who has what information and whether your data are correct. (This could cost you as much as $50 to $60, but one of the bureaus could reveal a credit mistake or inaccuracy that might trip up an otherwise successful loan application.)

The first step in identifying and solving credit problems is to ask to see what kind of personal and financial information credit bureaus have collected on you, your spouse or partner, and anyone else you might ask to co-sign your loan.

Conducting Your Own Credit Checkup. When you apply for a loan, one of the first things the lender will do is a *credit check*. A credit check allows the lender to scrutinize your credit history and see how you have handled past loans, whether you pay off your debts in a timely fashion, what credit cards you've been issued, what balances you carry on those credit cards, whether you've ever declared bankruptcy, and where you've lived.

As we've discussed, credit bureaus are in the business of selling your personal financial data. They usually sell it to companies that extend credit (like credit card companies and retail stores), but they'll also sell it to you. The time to check your credit is *before* you apply for a mortgage and the lender checks you out. It's like the adage trial attorneys live by: Never ask a question to which you don't already know

87

the answer. The same is true for credit. Unless you're sure you have good credit, don't apply for a loan. Being turned down for a loan application is a piece of personal financial information that could stand out like a headline on your credit history. It's a good idea to check your credit report for inaccuracies, inconsistencies, and omissions before you fill out any kind of loan application. In fact, some financial advisers recommend checking your credit every couple of years, just to make sure there are no surprises.

You can get a copy of your credit history by calling one of the credit bureaus and asking for it. The resources listed in Appendix III include the telephone numbers and addresses for TRW, Trans-Union, and Equifax. These companies will ask you some personal questions to verify your identity and will then send you your credit report. Some companies do this for free; others charge a small fee. You should know, however, that if you've ever applied for a loan and been rejected because of your credit history, you're entitled by law to get a free copy of your credit report from the credit bureau that furnished the report to the company that turned you down.

When Do I Need to Worry About My Credit History?   If you're in good financial shape—that is, you don't owe anything, you always pay on time, and you've never declared bankruptcy—you probably don't have to worry about your credit. If, however, you're paying off school loans over a long period of time, you've recently declared bankruptcy, or you have a history of paying bills late, then you could have some credit issues to clean up before a lender will approve your mortgage application.

What Credit Reports Cover.   Credit reports generally cover four basic categories of information:

1. *Personal identification and employment data.* Your name, birthdate, address, and social security number; your spouse's name and social security number; whether you rent or own your home—all these data are covered in a basic credit report. Other information that may be included is your employment history and any previous personal or business addresses.

2. *Payment history.* Every credit account that you have is listed in your credit report, along with your payment history—how much

credit has been extended, the balance you owe, and how quickly or slowly you have paid them. Related events, such as a referral of an overdue account to a collection agency, or a dispute with a credit card company over a charge, may also be reported.

3. *Inquiries.* Credit bureaus are required by law to keep a list of the sources of requests for your credit report for at least six months. Most credit companies keep these names for a longer period of time.

4. *Public record information.* Events that are a matter of public record and are related to your creditworthiness may also be included. These events might include bankruptcies, foreclosures, tax liens, mechanic's liens, and judgments against you.

When you actually receive a copy of your credit report for the first time, you may be surprised by how complicated it is and how difficult it is to understand. If you're confused, don't worry. You're not the first to be confounded by credit. It has happened to many others who have stood in your shoes. That's why I've included a copy of a real credit report on page 90.

Home Buyer X, as we'll call him, has more than a few credit problems. Although we've only included a piece of his credit history, you can see under the "Credit Summary" that he has a revolving credit balance of $2,035 and installment debt of $70,100. Under "Public Records" it's clear that he filed for Chapter 7 bankruptcy with $13,500 in liabilities and only $7,150 in assets. The bankruptcy was discharged in August, 1993.

Although I didn't include it here, the rest of Home Buyer X's credit history looks pretty bad. Most of his installment debt is in the form of credit cards (Discover, several Visas, and department store cards). Much of the debt has been written off, although it stays on your credit report for up to 7 years. In addition, between 1994 and 1996, there were 34 inquiries from various lenders, credit companies, and car dealers.

If you don't know how to read your credit history, you can pay a visit to a local mortgage broker, ask your real estate attorney, or make an appointment with a free or low-cost financial advisor from the Consumer Credit Counseling Service (see Appendix III, Resources for toll-free number and address). But if you look carefully at the entries, and then double check them with your credit card statements, you should quickly recognize where your credit problems are.

```
----------------------------------------------------------------------
C R E D I T   S U M M A R Y     * * *     T O T A L   F I L E   H I S T O R Y
PR=3   COL=3   NEG=5  HSTNEG=1-1   TRD=13 RVL=6  INST=7  MTG=0  OPN=0  INQ=35
               HIGH CRED   CRED LIM  BALANCE  PAST DUE  MNTHLY PAY AVAILABLE
REVOLVING:     $2035       $6300     $4260    $4048     $194        32%
INSTALLMENT:   $70.1K      $         $3792    $2717     $388
TOTALS:        $72.2K      $6300     $8052    $6765     $582
----------------------------------------------------------------------
P U B L I C   R E C O R D S
SOURCE      DATE      LIAB      ECOA          ASSETS        DOCKET#
TYPE                            COURT LOC                   PLAINTIFF/ATTORNEY
Z           8/93R     $13.5K    I             $7150
CHAPTER 7 BANKRUPTCY DISCH

Z           8/93R     $0        I             $7150
CHAPTER 7 BANKRUPTCY FILIN

Z           7/93R     $2537     I
CIVIL JUDGMENT
----------------------------------------------------------------------
C O L L E C T I O N S
SUBNAME         SUBCODE     ECOA OPENED   CLOSED $PLACED   CREDITOR          MOP
ACCOUNT#                         VERIFIED        BALANCE   REMARKS
```

FINANCIAL
ISSUE
2

Different Types of Credit Problems

Credit problems come in a variety of forms and amounts. Some are small and easily correctable, and some are large and will require a longer period to be resolved to a prospective lender's satisfaction. Here are the basic credit problems you might be facing.

1. *Debt.* Debt is the word the financial industry uses to describe any situation in which you borrow money. "Too much debt" is how the industry describes situations where people borrow more money than they can easily repay. There are a lot of different types of debt: credit card debt, retail store debt, charge accounts, auto loans, school loans, and money you owe to the Internal Revenue Service. You might also borrow from parents, relatives, and friends, although those debts may not be reflected in your credit report.

Lenders decide whether you're carrying too much debt by applying the debt-to-income ratio to the amount of money you owe to various companies (as we discussed in Step 2). For example, if you earn $50,000 a year but are paying back a $25,000 school loan, your true debt-to-income ratio is 1-to-2, or 50 percent. But that's not how lenders look at the numbers. (If they did, no one would ever qualify for a mortgage!) Most folks pay back their debts over time, with a payment that is a mix of principal and interest. If you're paying off your $25,000 school debt over, say, 10 years, at 6 percent interest, your monthly payment would only be around $278. Your $50,000 annual income translates into gross monthly income (GMI) of about $4,167, so the $278 payment represents only about 6 percent of your GMI. Because lenders will allow you to pay up to 33 percent (and sometimes more) of your GMI in debt service (including your mortgage, auto and school loans, and credit card debt), you'd be well below the automatic mortgage application rejection status if this were the only debt you owed. (You'll find a more detailed explanation of debt-to-income ratios in Step 2.)

2. *Late payments.* If you're chronically late in paying your bills, you've got a late payment problem. It can be a severe blight on your credit report because lenders like to lend money to people who repay it in a timely manner.

How late is late? Let's be clear here. If you don't pay your Visa bill by the due date, you're late, and it may show up on your credit history. If you've missed a payment completely, and the next one appears with a past-due notice and a finance charge, it's very likely that your tardiness has been noted on your credit report. If you're so late that your account has been referred to a collection agency, that will be reported on your credit history in addition to a late payment notice.

When does a late payment disappear from your credit history? Usually, late payments stay on your credit report for 2 years, though credit bureaus may legally keep them there for up to 7 years. But if you've missed only one payment in 2 years, and for the past 18 months you've paid on time, and if you have a good explanation for why you missed that payment, lenders won't usually deny your mortgage application based on that one piece of negative information. How you're coping with current credit issues is far more important to them.

3. *Bankruptcy.* When you don't have enough money (assets or income) to cover your liabilities (debts), you have the option of filing for bankruptcy. Once you've been declared bankrupt, a judge discharges your debts and, to a great degree, wipes your financial slate clean. Sounds easy, but it's not. Bankruptcy can be expensive and time-consuming, and may cast a long shadow over your credit. Most negative information may be kept on your credit history for up to 7 years; a bankruptcy can stain your credit report for as long as 10 years.

Bankruptcy is a significant credit hurdle, but it can be overcome, mortgage experts say. Five years ago, lenders wouldn't touch a recently bankrupt prospective borrower; today, lenders will grant a mortgage to an individual who went bankrupt just 2 years earlier but has established good credit since then.

4. *Errors.* Because of the volume of information being cataloged and entered daily into the credit database, errors have been known to creep in. A woman who shared the same name as her mother wound up being rejected for a mortgage because of an unpaid $78 hospital bill. As it turned out, that bill belonged to her mother and was miscoded in the computer. Even though she could prove the social security number on the bill was not hers, the woman's condo purchase was held up for 6 months while she cleared up the problem.

Often, errors are the result of a simple mix-up in names or social security numbers. But one good reason for checking up on your credit report is that someone else may be using your social security number or credit card numbers and playing havoc with your personal credit history.

5. *Repossessions.* If you buy a car, furniture, or appliances on the installment plan (you pay a little bit of interest and principal each month), and you fail to make a payment or two, the company that sold you the items may require you to give back the merchandise until it is paid for. If you refuse to give it back, the company may come by and take it (repossess it). Repossessions are usually noted in your credit report.

6. *Accounts turned over to a collection agency.* If you don't pay a bill, you may receive a threatening letter from a collection agency that has been hired by your creditor to collect on the overdue amount. If you receive such a letter, it should tip you off to a potential problem with your credit history. Collection agencies usually update credit reporting agencies on their efforts to collect on past-due bills.

7. *Too many credit inquiries.* It's perfectly normal to have prospective creditors checking your credit from time to time, but lenders get worried if you appear to be on a credit-gathering spree. It could mean that you're out to expand your credit quickly for a specific purchase, which, in the lenders' eyes, makes you a bigger risk. Credit inquiries stay on your credit report for 2 years, but lenders are particularly interested in the inquiry activity during the past 6 months.

8. *Too much available credit.* One of the easiest credit issues to fix is having too much available credit. Even if you've never carried a balance on any credit card, if you have a lot of cards, lenders simply add up the balance as potential debt you could take on at any moment. (A worksheet later in this Step will help you to catalog your credit cards and charge accounts and tally up your maximum available line of credit.)

One of the little known facts about the credit industry is that lenders look at your credit report as a running scorecard. When you apply for a credit card, auto loan, or mortgage, they tally up your current *credit score* and decide whether you're a good risk. What ingredients do lenders look at? Basically, everything we've just talked about. They look at the number of *tradelines,* a credit industry term for the number of individual listings on your credit report—mortgages, personal loans, student loans, auto loans, judgments, and credit card debt. Do you have too many credit cards, too much debt for your income level, too many delinquencies (late payments), or too many inquiries? Do you have a checking or savings account? (You should have both.)

How do you know when you've passed the "too many" mark? You don't, credit experts say. Credit scoring is a closely guarded industry secret, and each lender or creditor has its own formula. If you apply for a credit card and get turned down, don't imitate one unfortunate borrower who tried to get one of those "preapproved" credit cards that come in the mail. When he was rejected for that, he tried another. Each time, another credit inquiry was added to his credit report, which only worsened his credit history. What should he have done? Experts say he should have contacted one of the "big three" credit reporting agencies (TRW, Trans-Union, or Equifax) and asked to see a copy of his credit report. Using the lists and worksheets in this Step, he could have figured out what exactly was causing the problem, and then cleared up his credit report.

The Maximum Available Line of Credit

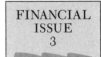

Although mortgage lenders are particularly interested in your debt, they're also interested in your untapped credit; they're going to be looking at how many credit cards you have, and the maximum credit limit on each one. For example, if your credit card has a $2,500 limit, even though you may not be carrying a balance on the account, mortgage lenders might treat that account as if you've borrowed to the maximum. The reason? At any moment, you can go into a store and charge up to your maximum credit limit. While you may not plan to do that (lenders will review the past year or two, to see whether you've carried any kind of a balance on the account), you still *could*, and that's what makes mortgage lenders nervous about lending. If you have a handful of charge accounts, it's easy to see how fast the numbers add up.

Use the worksheet on page 94 to assess your maximum available credit amount. When listing your different accounts, don't forget to

Credit Account Name	Account Number	Maximum Available Credit (Credit Limit − Current Charges)
1. _____	_____	_____
2. _____	_____	_____
3. _____	_____	_____
4. _____	_____	_____
5. _____	_____	_____
6. _____	_____	_____
7. _____	_____	_____
8. _____	_____	_____
9. _____	_____	_____
10. _____	_____	_____
11. _____	_____	_____
12. _____	_____	_____
13. _____	_____	_____
14. _____	_____	_____
15. _____	_____	_____
16. _____	_____	_____
17. _____	_____	_____
18. _____	_____	_____
19. _____	_____	_____
20. _____	_____	_____
Total Available Credit	_____	_____

include all your major national credit cards, your retail store charge accounts, your gas station accounts, your bank line of credit, your checking account line of credit, and any other charge accounts you may have.

Pruning Your Line of Credit. Don't be surprised if your total available credit is anywhere from several thousand dollars to more than $25,000. When I took stock of all my credit cards before we bought our first home, I was amazed to discover that I had 12 different accounts, including several department stores, several different Visas, and a Discover card. Credit cards are big business, and the average family receives offers of free credit cards each week. These companies are hoping you'll accept the ready cash they're offering and will then spend it. They make their money when you pay them the outrageously high interest rates they're charging.

Before you apply for a mortgage, you may need to prune your line of credit down to a manageable size in order to improve your credit-worthiness. You don't want lenders looking at your fifteen credit accounts, worrying that the day after you're approved for your mortgage you're going to go out and spend, *spend*, SPEND. Pick out your two or three most useful charge cards, and cancel all the rest. Call 800-555-1212 (the toll-free directory) and get the toll-free telephone numbers of your unwanted credit card companies. (Each company's contact number should also be listed on its most recent bill.) If you have an account at a local department store, call the customer service department and find out what kind of cancellation procedure the store requires. You may be able to cancel your account over the telephone, but you should follow up in writing. Ask for a letter stating that your account has been closed.

The bottom line is: It's good to have credit, but not so much credit that it makes lenders nervous.

Absence of Credit

Just a few years ago, lenders turned up their noses at consumers who were either shunned by the credit card industry, or who chose not to participate in the endless rounds of "Can I get approved and for how much?" Mortgage bankers and brokers wrongly believed that the only way to prove creditworthiness was by carefully managing the lines of credit extended by the likes of Visa, MasterCard, American Express, Discover, Diner's Club, and national or franchise retail stores.

FINANCIAL
ISSUE
4

All that changed when the Federal National Mortgage Association ("Fannie Mae"), the largest purchaser of mortgages on the secondary market, began looking toward the burgeoning immigrant population (predicted to be 9 million new families by 2000) as a new source of home buyers. After much research, Fannie Mae found that, as a group, this immigrant population was even more inclined toward homeownership than Americans who had been born in this country. However, Fannie Mae also discovered that the traditional means of certifying creditworthiness did not apply to them. These families did not, by and large, carry credit cards. They often bought homes together, pooling family money to help each person buy a home. Many immigrant groups were accustomed to a cash economy, and were unfamiliar with the idea of acceptable debt—so much so, they had to be educated about the benefits of a mortgage. Some families had wanted to save up to pay all cash for their homes.

If you don't have credit cards but are paying rent and utility bills (telephone, electricity, gas, and cable TV), you have established credit, even if you were not aware of it. Today, lenders will accept a history of on-time rent payments, long thought by some lenders to be indicative of the type of mortgage borrowers responsible renters will be, because many of them spend well in excess of the 28/36 debt-to-income ratio on their rent alone. If you have been paying your rent on time, think about having the lender contact your landlord to verify your timely payments.

If you don't have credit cards, it helps if you have savings and checking accounts at a local bank. If you don't have these accounts, open them up as quickly as possible so that the lender can see you know how to manage your money properly. The savings account can function as your house fund, or you can open up a new account specifically for that purpose.

10 STEP TIP

Let's say you're just out of college or graduate school and you don't have any credit cards but you've landed a job that pays well. You may still be able to convince a mortgage lender that you're an acceptable credit risk even though you haven't been on the job for at least two years. Another option: Ask your parents, a relative, or a friend to co-sign your loan. (But read about the important legal and financial ramifications to this solution, which are explained in Step 9, Financing Your Home.)

Figuring Out Your Current Debt

FINANCIAL ISSUE 5

If you have debt, it's probably a good idea to take stock of it up front, before you decide to buy a home. It's important to know exactly how much you owe, and to whom. Compare the interest rates you're paying, and look for a way to either pay down the accounts faster, or consolidate your debts under a less expensive umbrella.

The worksheet on page 98 will help you to identify your personal debt situation. You should include all debts that you owe, including school and auto loans, credit card accounts, overdue income taxes, and loans from family and friends.

Fixing Your Credit Problems

FINANCIAL ISSUE 6

If you want to buy a house, you're going to have to have at least fairly good credit. Having excellent (as opposed to fairly good) credit means you'll be able to get a mortgage with the least amount of trouble, at the most favorable terms and interest rates. Stabilizing your credit history at an excellent or good status should be one of your top priorities.

It may take some time to work out all the credit problems you have. As some credit counselors like to say, the road to credit heaven is paved with obstacles and frustrations. Here are some things you can do to improve your credit:

1. *Take stock of your current credit situation.* Start by ordering a copy of your credit report from TRW, Trans-Union, or Equifax. While you're waiting for it to arrive, use the budget worksheet in Step 3 page 65 to come up with how much you're spending on fixed living expenses and debt payments. Use the debt worksheet on page 98 to get a profile of how much debt you've got and what interest rates you're paying.

2. *Scrutinize your credit report.* It shouldn't take more than two weeks or so to receive your credit report by mail. When it arrives, look it over for errors such as someone else's debt posted to your account. If you are listed as delinquent on several accounts, and you're not, copies of your canceled checks may be accepted as proof that you paid on time. Look for other problems: too many credit inquiries, too much credit, or other inaccurate information. If you have a joint credit account and your partner has a credit problem, it could become

97

WORKSHEET
Debt

Creditor	Total Owed	Monthly Payment	Interest Rate
1. _____	_____	_____	_____
2. _____	_____	_____	_____
3. _____	_____	_____	_____
4. _____	_____	_____	_____
5. _____	_____	_____	_____
6. _____	_____	_____	_____
7. _____	_____	_____	_____
8. _____	_____	_____	_____
9. _____	_____	_____	_____
10. _____	_____	_____	_____
11. _____	_____	_____	_____
12. _____	_____	_____	_____
13. _____	_____	_____	_____
14. _____	_____	_____	_____
15. _____	_____	_____	_____
16. _____	_____	_____	_____
17. _____	_____	_____	_____
18. _____	_____	_____	_____
19. _____	_____	_____	_____
20. _____	_____	_____	_____
Total Owed	_____	_____	_____

your credit problem. If you lent your signature (co-signed a loan) to a friend or relative who has a late payment pattern or has used your name to apply for a line of credit, you could have a real problem on your hands.

3. *Fix credit report errors*. If you discover inaccuracies or errors in your credit report, write letters to your creditors (send copies to the credit reporting agency) and enclose documentation that supports your claims. To receive a brochure, and a sample letter, on how to dispute faulty credit bureau information, write to the Federal Trade Commission, Correspondence Branch, Washington, DC 20580. But be aware that this process could take some time, despite credit reporting agencies' claims that disputes are addressed within 30 days.

4. *Pay off your debt before you apply for a mortgage*. You don't need to be debt-free to get approved for a loan, but it certainly helps boost the amount lenders will allow you to borrow. Analyze your budget for ways to save additional money, then use that cash to pay down your debts faster. Cut out almost all luxuries. For you, that may mean cutting out your second daily newspaper, or eliminating your afternoon gourmet coffee habit (at $2.50 per cup). Maybe it means sharing rides, or taking public transportation to work instead of driving your car. (For more ideas on how to trim your budget, reread Step 3, Putting Together the Cash for Your Down Payment and Closing Costs.)

5. *Freeze your credit cards*. Many credit experts suggest that spendaholics literally freeze their credit cards in a container of water to make them difficult to get to at a moment's notice. If you have a safe deposit box, you may want to put them there. (That way, if you defrost the freezer, you won't be tempted to spend.)

6. *Cancel unused cards*. If you have too many credit cards on your credit report, cancel the accounts—in writing. A few months later, double-check to make sure the cards have actually been removed from your credit history and have not just been labeled "inactive."

7. *Know when you need professional help*. If you're finding it difficult to create a workable budget or put together a workout plan with your creditors, consider getting some free or low-cost professional help. The nonprofit Consumer Credit Counseling Service, which has 850 offices spread out over all 50 states, offers free or low-cost credit, debt, and budget counseling. Call the CCCS toll-free number (800-338-2227) for a referral to the office closest to you. One

caveat: CCCS is funded by credit card companies and institutional creditors and may have a slight bias in its counseling. For example, CCCS may urge you to settle on a workout plan rather than suggest bankruptcy, even if bankruptcy might be in your best interest. But a counselor will work with you to come up with a budget with which you can live, and may have some leverage in getting creditors to accept what you're offering.

8. *Beware credit repair companies.* There are companies out there that will charge you whatever arm and leg you have left to "clean up" your credit or "erase" a bad credit history. These companies can't do anything more for you than you can do for yourself. Before paying for their services (they'll charge anywhere from $50 to $1,000), remember that no one can simply erase a bad credit history, no matter how tempting that sounds. You can't change the past. And if you're offered a "money-back guarantee" for these services, take a hard look at the company offering that guarantee. Check for complaints with your local Better Business Bureau. If you find that a credit repair company has made false promises, contact your local consumer affairs office or the state attorney general's office. Don't get suckered in by promises that your credit slate will be wiped clean. The only way you can do that is by declaring bankruptcy, and your bankruptcy will stay on your credit history for 10 years.

9. *Make sure your workout payments are correctly reported.* After going through the hassle of setting up a workout payment with a creditor, it would be a shame to have that creditor report to the credit companies that you're not making the "minimum" payment. Be sure that your workout payments are correctly recorded as paid on time and in full, so that you start to improve your credit history.

10. *Consider consolidating your debt.* Some consumers continually consolidate their debt on new credit cards in order to take advantage of super-low "teaser" interest rates. ("Consolidating debt" is a phrase that applies to people who take out one large debt and pay off lots of little debts owed to a variety of creditors.) Like a 1-year adjustable mortgage, these credit card "teaser" rates are superficially low and short-term. But that small time frame may give you enough cash to pay down your largest bills. When the interest rate rises, you can either continue paying or switch cards again. As long as you use the cash savings to pay down what you owe, you're beating your debt.

Job or Career Issues and How They Affect Your Credit

When I graduated from college, my first impulse was to move away from home, rent an apartment, and buy a car. Then my grandfather stepped in and reminded me that, without a job, I didn't have the money for bus fare, let alone any big-ticket purchases. The lesson wasn't lost. Reality dictates that we first get jobs, then use our earnings to buy both the necessities and finer things in life.

Owning your own home is one of the finer things in life, and having a steady job—unless you are independently wealthy—is the necessary engine that fuels that purchase. That's why it's so important to match your career with your home buying time line. Mortgage lenders like to see prospective borrowers who have steady jobs that pay well. If you've held a job for a while—say, two years—lenders will feel that you'll be able to make regular mortgage payments. If you've skipped around a lot, working at several jobs within a short period of time, lenders will be very nervous, particularly if your job skipping has transcended career lines—from short-order cook to warehouse worker, messenger, and then secretary. Lenders look at a job history like that and wonder how you'll be stable enough to pay off a 30-year loan, even if each of your jobs paid better than the one before. On the other hand, if you've made several jumps within a single career path—or better yet, with a single employer—lenders consider that pattern favorably, particularly if you got a raise with each jump.

Lenders have other concerns about different types of jobs and how long you've stayed at each one. Here are some issues to think about.

1. *The 2-year rule.* Lenders like to see both financial stability and job stability when they look over a prospective borrower's mortgage application. To the vast majority of conventional lenders, job stability means you've held onto your present job for at least 2 years. Often, they won't lend money to an otherwise financially stable individual if he or she hasn't been at his or her job for at least 2 years. But, like all rules, there are exceptions. Lenders might consider approving your mortgage if you've been on the job for more than 1 year, but less than 2. Plus, if you're a professional (doctor, lawyer, accountant) just out of school, and you've begun a job that pays well and appears to be a long-lasting employment opportunity, you might find a mortgage banker willing to hold onto your loan (that is, put it in the bank's portfolio of loans that don't get resold to Fannie Mae). The bottom

line is: If you think you want to buy a home sometime within the near future, make sure your career path, and that of your spouse or partner, is as stable as possible.

2. *Career-to-career and lateral moves.* As we just noted, lenders like to see stability. They don't necessarily like applicants who continually jump from career to career, even if it means taking home a bigger paycheck. If you must make a move, do it either before you put in your loan application or after you close on your home. Don't decide to make a move 3 days before closing. Your lender may deny you the loan for your purchase.

3. *Double-income couples.* Although many couples would prefer to live off the salary of one spouse or partner, the reality is that, today, particularly for first-time buyers, it usually takes two incomes to qualify for your home purchase. In the not so distant past, in what some refer to as the "Dark Ages of lending," lenders refused to approve mortgages to couples who relied on both the husband's and the wife's salaries to pay the monthly living expenses. That's because lenders knew that many wives traditionally stopped working after having children. Today, such thinking is archaic, discriminatory, and thoroughly against the law. It's no one's business if you or your spouse plan to leave your job—after having children, to stay at home with them; or to tend a garden; or to start a company; or for any other reason. If you or your spouse is pregnant when you go to see the mortgage lender, and the lender asks you whether you plan to stop working after having children, simply say "My/Our child care issues have already been taken care of, thank you." Don't be dragged into a discussion of what those issues may be. It isn't the lenders job to pass judgment on whether you're going to be able to afford to pay for your home in 5 or 10 years. Mortgage lending is a little like taking a photograph: What matters is what appears in the photo the moment it is snapped. The day you apply for a loan is the day your financial "photo" gets taken and, aside from making sure nothing has changed before the closing, everything else is irrelevant.

4. *Self-employed home buyers.* If you work for yourself, or own more than 50 percent of the company you work for, lenders will consider you to be self-employed. To some lenders, being self-employed (even if you have been self-employed for years and years) ranks right up there with switching from career to career every 2 or 3 months: it's a strike against you. Self-employed people do buy homes every day, and although some lenders are skittish about working with those who are

self-employed, there are plenty of lenders who specialize in helping them complete loan transactions successfully.

If you are self-employed, expect lenders to have special requirements and conditions that you'll have to meet. First, they will most likely not budge on the 2-year rule. They will want to see that you've managed to run your business successfully for at least 2 years. They will ask for copies of your tax returns for the past 2 years and a year-to-date cash flow statement, and they will look carefully at your bank statements. If you provide them with the documents they need, and allay their concerns, lenders will work hard to get your mortgage approved.

5. *Cash businesses.* Lenders who have problems with self-employed individuals may also have problems with individuals who own cash businesses. What constitutes a cash business? Accountants say it's a business where it's difficult to verify what money comes in and what product or service goes out. Some examples are a dry cleaner, a tailor shop, or a mobile vegetable store—selling wholesale or retail off the back of a truck. In these businesses, the majority of customers pay in cash for the goods or services received. It's difficult to ascertain how much someone earns from a cash business, so it's tough to know whether a borrower is lying about his or her salary. Lenders don't like to loan money to owners of cash businesses because they worry that these applicants may be inflating their income in order to get the loan. If you own a cash business, try to find a mortgage broker or banker who specializes in certifying cash businesses.

6. *If you've been fired or laid off recently, or expect to be let go soon.* This is the classic "damned if you do, damned if you don't" nightmare of every home buyer. Sometime after you've applied for your loan and before you've closed on your home, you (or your spouse or partner) are fired or laid off from your job. Losing your job can derail your plans for a happily-ever-after purchase. Lenders can yank your loan approval on the basis that your financial "snapshot" has changed since the day you applied for your loan. If your lender asks whether you are still employed, you must disclose that you've been fired. If your lender doesn't ask, some attorneys believe that you don't have a duty to tell. If you do tell your lender, you will probably not get the financing you need for your purchase. What can you do? Not too much. If your prospects for a new job are excellent, and it appears you may be getting an offer for employment in the very near future, you can try to postpone your closing until after you've received a written offer from the new company or started work there. If it looks as if

you'll be unemployed for a while and you can't afford to purchase the home on your spouse's or partner's income alone, your smartest move may be to back out of your purchase. Even if it means losing a great interest rate, you're better off backing off than committing yourself to a home and a long-term mortgage that you may not ultimately be able to afford. *Consult with your attorney prior to making this decision. Your contractual obligation with the seller will be involved, and you may risk losing any amount already paid under the contract, or more.*

What should you do if you think you may lose your job after you close on your home? As long as you're employed through the date of closing, there's nothing that the lender can do to derail your purchase. After all, in the wacky world of corporate downsizing, your job might be spared after all. But if you know you're going to lose your job, think carefully before you close on your new home. You may pay less to live there than in a rental, but getting a new job may involve a transfer to a new city or state. You could end up losing heavily on your home if you have to sell quickly.

7. *Seasonal or migrant labor.* Lenders don't like to rely on seasonal or migrant labor income when qualifying you for a home purchase. If you work as a seasonal laborer during all four seasons, then you're viewed as self-employed in the seasonal laborer business. Again, try to find a lender who specializes in approving loans for people in your situation.

8. *Temporary disabilities.* If you are temporarily disabled and are receiving disability payments that are sufficient to cover your mortgage payments, your temporary disability shouldn't derail your plans to purchase a home, especially if you will be able to resume your regular job at your regular salary.

9. *Permanently disabled.* It is illegal for lenders to discriminate against disabled home buyers, either by rejecting their application for a loan or by charging them higher points and fees. If you suspect that this has happened to you, you can contact your state attorney general's office.

EMOTIONAL/
FAMILY ISSUE
1

EMOTIONAL/FAMILY ISSUES

Divorce, Debt, and Credit

Rarely does a divorce end happily for all; it's much more common for divorce to leave in its wake a collection of tattered emotions. And if there are financial problems—a likely scenario—a divorce can get downright treacherous.

Women and Divorce. Many studies have indicated that women often end up as the financial losers when they get divorced. They tend to get custody of the children, and although the husband/father pays child support and sometimes alimony, the amount often isn't enough to meet basic expenses. Women who have never before held jobs or had a credit card in their own name might find it difficult to get their personal lines of credit established. But credit card companies, which once discriminated against women, must now give a separate credit history for women showing credit cards held (or once held) jointly.

It's important for women to know how to establish their own line of credit. A woman can initiate her credit by getting a separate telephone line in her name and paying her own bills on time. (The telephone company may require the humiliating step of putting down a few hundred dollars up front, to cover the first few months' bills.) Signing up for a department store or gas company credit card also starts or expands a personal line of credit.

Spousal and Child Support. People paying spousal support (also known as alimony) and child support often wonder whether those payments, required by the divorce decree, go on their credit report. The answer is yes, they can. Judgments made against you and entered into the public record may be listed on your credit report. Spousal and child support are viewed by creditors as debts that must be paid regularly. They will be factored into your overall monthly debt, although lapses are not considered the same type of credit problem as when you pay your bills late. If you are late paying your spousal or child support, and your spouse goes back to court to order you to pay or to have your wages garnished, your default may then show up on your credit report.

Divorce and Credit Cards. When you and your spouse separate, you should immediately cancel all credit cards and accounts that you have jointly. If your spouse starts to spend and then refuses to pay, you will be held responsible for his or her debts. That's not a good way to clean up your credit history. Even if the courts mandate that your spouse must pay a certain amount or is responsible for particular bills, as long as your name is on the account, the creditors will look to you

105

for repayment. In desperate situations, you may be better off simply paying the debt and getting yourself out of the mess entirely.

EMOTIONAL/
FAMILY ISSUE
2

Debt and Self-Esteem

Being in debt is like having a huge weight slung around your shoulders at all times. It may depress you, interfere with your sleep (you lie awake wondering how you're going to pay off the debt), and deplete your self-esteem. You may feel that you're a failure, or that you've somehow crossed a line and become a bad person.

What you've crossed is the boundary into dangerous financial territory. There's nothing criminal about being in debt. Debtors only become criminals when they intentionally rack up thousands of dollars of credit card bills and then refuse to pay them off.

If you're finding yourself resistant to the idea of paying off your debts, you should explore these feelings with a trusted friend, family member, or religious adviser. Try to think about what payments you fell behind on, and why. One young woman had been regularly making on-time payments on her school loan. When her father died, she suddenly found herself with a $3,000 funeral bill. All her school loan cash went to bury her father. When she explained that to the creditor holding her school loan, her payments were temporarily suspended until she was able to pay off the funeral bill. If you have a sudden and legitimate expense, such as a funeral or a medical emergency, lenders are more likely to be understanding than if you fall behind because you bought a new car or stereo.

If you feel as though you'll never get out of debt, you may be trying to take too many steps at once. Consolidate your bills under the lowest interest rate you can get, then start paying them off slowly and methodically. Give yourself a gold star on your weekly calendar every time you make an on-time payment. If you make these payments one by one, and put any extra cash into paying down the principal, you'll soon find you're paying off your balance far faster than if you simply paid the minimum each month. (You'll also be saving hundreds or even thousands of dollars in the process.)

EMOTIONAL/
FAMILY ISSUE
3

Kids and Credit Cards

Who is actually running up the debt in your family? If you've given a credit card to your high school-age or college-age child and, instead of using it for emergency purposes only, he or she is paying for pizza parties and the latest CDs, you may have a problem.

Explain to your children that credit cards aren't free money; they are for emergency use only. Involve your entire family in your quest to fix your credit history, and explain how it affects them all. Spend some time showing them how credit cards work and how finance charges are assessed. Explain how long it will take you to pay off your debt if you only make the minimum payments and make no more purchases on that card.

If none of these tactics works, either take away the card or have the creditor put a limit on how much your children can charge on their accounts. Then put them on a repayment plan so they begin to understand the long-term implications of charging.

Losing Your Job

EMOTIONAL/ FAMILY ISSUE 4

Often, our self-esteem gets wrapped up in the jobs we hold and the salary we take home. If you get a promotion, you feel great. If you lose your job, you feel awful. If you spend years planning and saving for the purchase of your first home, and you lose your job just as you've signed the offer to purchase, you may feel you're letting down your family as well as yourself. Remember, even if you lose one home while you reestablish yourself financially, there will be others to buy. Rather than trying to stretch yourself financially to the point where you can't sleep at night, take a more conservative approach and back away from the deal. You may have to cope with your family's—and your own—disappointment initially, but you'll be better off in the long run.

Mismatched Careers

EMOTIONAL/ FAMILY ISSUE 5

In the real world, two spouses or partners in a dual-income family rarely bring in exactly the same amount of money. If a family grosses $80,000 annually, one spouse may make $55,000 or $60,000, and the other spouse will earn $20,000 to $25,000. Rarely will each person earn $40,000.

Again, our self-esteem often gets caught up in the job we hold and the salary we earn. If a first-time buyer couple is purchasing a home, the spouse who makes less money may feel as though he or she isn't entitled to have his or her name on the deed. Or, if the first-time buyers are engaged, but not married, and one person is bringing a lot of cash to the deal and the other person has nothing to contribute except time, energy, and "sweat equity," the person who doesn't have any cash for, say, the down payment, may feel less of a homeowner than his or her partner.

Don't let these emotional and family issues cloud your home purchase. Even if you have almost no cash to contribute to a down payment, your income will help pay the maintenance expenses of the home. If you contribute your "sweat equity"—that is, you work hard to do things that will increase the value of the property—then you've earned your rightful title as homeowner. If you always count how many pennies are being contributed, and try to make certain that you and your spouse or partner are contributing an exactly equal share, you'll drive yourself crazy and could seriously damage your relationship.

There is an appropriate time, however, to count pennies. If you and a partner (who is not a spouse) are purchasing property together, and each of you has agreed to put the same amount of money into the deal, then you should be tallying up each expense and dividing it in half. When purchasing property with a partner, it's a good idea to spell out this kind of arrangement in writing. In that way, each of you knows up front (because it's on a piece of paper that each of you will sign) what is expected of him or her. (For more information, see Step 5, Legal Issues and Their Consequences.)

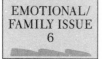

EMOTIONAL/
FAMILY ISSUE
6

Mismatched Credit Histories

These days, both you and your spouse are likely to have credit reports that need some attention. There may be blemishes from late payments, or an overabundance of credit cards, or an unpaid bill lurking around.

It can happen that one spouse or partner's credit history is a complete washout while the other person's credit is terrific. If the spouse or partner with the good credit history also has enough income to support the entire mortgage amount, the pair are in luck. It will be a lot easier to qualify for a loan using one good credit history than two mediocre credit histories.

The way to fix this situation is to work diligently at cleaning up both credit histories as much as possible before you purchase your home. Pay down your debt and resolve any issues that could stand in the way of your being approved for your loan. It's best if you both have a minimum of weak links. You'll qualify for a cheaper mortgage that can be approved more quickly.

Legal Problems and Issues

Real estate professionals try to make everything easy for home buyers and sellers today. The language in their fancy-looking contracts seems almost understandable. Your real estate broker may even be your loan officer; many real estate brokers also own mortgage companies. Across the country, brokers will try to tell you that buying a home is such an easy process that you don't even need an attorney to check over your documents before you sign them. You don't understand something? The broker will readily step in and explain it to you.

All that service is well and good, but it doesn't replace having a real, live, experienced real estate attorney checking to make sure you don't sign away crucial rights and interests in your purchase contract. And it doesn't take into account folks who have some legal problems and issues that should be resolved before they ever start looking for a home.

Whether you're 3 months or 3 years away from buying a home, think now about some legal problems you might face, because legal problems tend to take more time than others to resolve. Legal problems might interfere with your purchase if:

- You can't afford to buy on your own and require a co-signer for your loan.
- You purchase a home with partners.
- You attempt to purchase a home before your divorce is finalized.
- You're involved in an ongoing lawsuit.

These are just some of the major legal issues that may have consequences for your home purchase. Some, or all, may pertain to your current situation. Others may surface just before closing. Even if you're not currently facing one of the problems described in this Step, it's a good idea to familiarize yourself with what may crop up.

LEGAL ISSUES

LEGAL
ISSUE
1

Borrowing a Signature

Recently, in Chicago, several family members offered to help a brother buy homes to rehab and resell. Ted used his mother's equity from her present residence as a down payment on several properties. Ted's brother, Tom, co-signed the loan (also called "lending a signature") to assure the lender that Ted could afford the monthly mortgage payments. It all went fairly well, except Ted neglected to tell his mother and Tom that he planned to skip town and leave them holding the bag. Tom's mother will lose all the equity she had in her home, and Tom may end up in bankruptcy.

How much is a signature worth? If it's John Hancock's and it is on the original Declaration of Independence, it could be worth millions of dollars. If it's yours, and you co-sign a loan for a friend or relative, your signature could be worth everything you own—your home, bank accounts, stocks, possessions, and good credit history.

Many first-time home buyers ask parents, siblings, relatives, and friends to co-sign loans for them (it's also known as *borrowing a signature*). And more often than not, the arrangement goes well. When Rosa wanted to buy her first home, a $60,000 bungalow, she asked her brother and a friend to both co-sign the loan. Her brother and his family would share the house with Rosa and her family; the friend would continue to live in her own home. Two years later, Rosa and her family are happy homeowners.

But there are pitfalls in the co-signing process that you should recognize and try to avoid. What many home buyers and their co-signers often don't realize is that putting their signature on the loan documents makes them entirely responsible for paying off the debt, should the lender not be paid. In other words, if your best friend co-signs your loan and you fail to make the mortgage payments, the lender will turn to your friend and demand those payments. If your house burns down, and you don't have enough homeowner's insurance to repay the mortgage, your friend's pockets had better be plenty deep.

The bottom line is: Borrowing a signature can have serious consequences. The person who co-signs your loan will go on the title as an owner of the property. His or her credit report will list the mortgage as a debt, and should your co-signer get into financial trouble, his or her creditors could come after a piece of your home.

Choose Your Co-Signer Carefully. Don't ask just anyone to co-sign your loan. When making this important decision, choose someone whom you know well and who is financially stable. You and your co-signer must mutually understand how your personal finances and credit histories will be bound together, and what could happen to both of you if something goes wrong. For example, once your friend or relative co-signs your loan, it may be much more difficult for him or her to get another loan or refinance his or her own home loan.

Most importantly, don't choose someone who will worry incessantly about whether you've paid your mortgage and taxes, and kept up your insurance premiums. That kind of constant pressure and questioning could affect your relationship with your co-signer.

Buying with Partners

LEGAL ISSUE 2

As homes get more expensive, more first-time buyers are purchasing homes with the help of friends or relatives. That help sometimes comes in the form of a gift of cash, which is used to defray down payment and closing costs. Or, it may come in the form of lending a signature, which we discussed above. But often, two families, two friends, nonmarried couples, or parents and children will purchase a home together. There are numerous types of partnerships. Parents may purchase a condominium with their child in the town where their son or daughter will be attending college. Or, a family might purchase a single-family home with an "in-law" apartment, which will house an aging parent or relative. Nonmarried couples might purchase a home together. Two families may join financial forces and purchase a two-family home (also called a two-flat home in some parts of the country) where they can live separately while enjoying the benefits of a larger, more expensive piece of property. Two friends might purchase a single-family home or a multifamily building and rent out several apartments.

111

Buying a home with a partner offers some benefits, including an expansion of your homebuying opportunities, but it puts you in a smaller enclosure, legally and emotionally, compared to having someone co-sign your loan. Because the relationship is more intimate—that is, you will be constantly dealing with your partner—there are more questions to ask and answer before you proceed with your purchase. The most obvious questions are listed here, but you would be wise to consult an attorney, who may have others involving legal issues.

- *Where should the property be located?* It's important that you and your partner agree on the location of your future home. As we discussed earlier, think about location in terms of city or suburb, neighborhood, and place on the individual block.

- *Is your partner going to live on the property, either with you or in another apartment?* What kind of space do you want, and what type of property are you interested in? Do you want absolute privacy? Living in a two-family home might not provide enough privacy for you. Would sharing a common wall suffice? If so, a double-sided townhouse might work out. Do you want to live vertically (on multiple levels) or horizontally (on a single level)? Do both you and your partner want a porch, or patio, or garden?

- *What will happen if you get into a disagreement about the property?* Disagreements are inevitable in a partnership. At some point in time, hopefully not too often, you and your partner will disagree on something—noise issues; deciding when to sell; whether to pave the backyard; whether to build a new garage; or some other decision or expenditure. What is important is how you handle that test of your relationship.

- *What if one of you wants to sell but the other doesn't?* If fortunes change for either of you, or if one of you gets transferred to another city or state, one of you may want to get out of the property. If this happens several years down the line, and the person who is staying can afford to own and maintain the property alone, then the problem is much less serious. If, however, neither of you can afford to maintain the property individually, you'll have some tough decisions to make. It's a good idea to talk about this possibility in advance, even if neither of you can foresee leaving at any time in the future.

- *What if repairs must be made but your partner doesn't want to pay up?* Almost all homes need constant attention and maintenance. It's a good idea to decide in advance of looking for a home how much each of you can afford to spend on maintenance and repairs each year (use the worksheet on pages 46–47 in Step 2 as a guide). Then find a home whose maintenance schedule fits your budget. Inevitably, you'll need to do some repairs, especially if you stay a long time. Decide in advance how the repair bills will be split and what will happen if one of you doesn't want to, or can't, pay a fair share.

- *Who will collect the rent and be responsible for tenants and repairs if you buy a multifamily building?* Being a landlord can be tough. There's rent to collect, tenants to find, and a property to maintain. If you and your partner purchase a four-family home, for example, you'll have to decide in advance who will be responsible for working with the tenants. If you have complementing strengths, you may want to divide the job into more manageable parts. For example, perhaps you'll find the tenants, negotiate the leases, and collect the rent, and your partner will be responsible for maintaining the property.

- *How will you hold title?* Among the several different ways in which you can hold title are: joint tenancy with rights of survivorship (each person is on the title, and, at the death of one, his or her interest in the property automatically passes to the other owner); and tenancy in common (each owner can own a specific percentage of the property). Each type of tenancy has certain benefits. Investigate these options thoroughly with your attorney.

- *How will any profits or losses from selling the property be shared between you?* If you've done it right, there may be some profits to share between you when you eventually sell the property. If you're unlucky and the value of your property falls, you should decide in advance how you will handle the extra payments required.

Choose a partner with whom your relationship is comfortable and on an even keel. There will be difficult issues to discuss and you want the playing field to be level. Ideally, neither of you should overwhelm the other, though, at times, one of you may hold the upper hand. If you can't discuss these issues in a sensible, reasonable manner, it should clue you in to the possibility that there may be rocky times ahead.

10 STEP TIP

LEGAL
ISSUE
3

Divorce

Most of the issues surrounding divorce and the home buying process arise in the area of credit. When you're married, you and your spouse can have joint and individual credit. When you separate, you'd be wise to immediately cancel all of your joint credit accounts, to eliminate the possibility that your soon-to-be ex-spouse will ruin your credit. As we've discussed, nothing will derail your opportunity to secure a home loan faster than bad credit.

If you purchase property by yourself while still married, your spouse may have to sign a document waiving any right he or she may have in the property you are buying. Most states provide spouses with certain rights (called homestead rights) to property bought during the marriage, particularly the marital home. If you're in the filing process but your divorce hasn't yet been finalized, and you wish to purchase property, you may have to ask your soon-to-be ex-spouse to sign a document in which he or she waives any rights he or she may have in the home you're buying.

If it is uncomfortable to ask your departing spouse for his or her signature, you may wish to postpone closing on your new home until after your divorce has been finalized.

LEGAL
ISSUE
4

Lawsuits and Judgments

Ahmed owned several fast-food franchises. In one of them, he was being sued for $100,000. At the same time, Ahmed and his wife were trying to buy their first home. Although he had plenty of assets, and the income to cover the mortgage, he was turned down for the loan. Why? Because the lender wasn't sure what would happen with the lawsuit. If Ahmed lost the suit and had to pay $100,000 plus other fees and costs, and perhaps the plaintiff's court costs, it might have thrown his debt-to-income ratio out of whack. After the suit was settled, Ahmed reapplied for his loan and was approved.

Lenders have always been leery about approving loans to people who are in the middle of a lawsuit. And with good reason. As the trial of the elderly woman who spilled McDonald's hot coffee while riding in her son's sports car have taught us, it's difficult to predict the outcome of any case. Lenders have tremendous discretion when asked to approve loans to folks who are involved in any kind of litigation.

114

On the application for your loan, you will be asked whether you are currently a plaintiff or defendant in any litigation. You must answer truthfully. If you don't, and the lender finds out later, you may be in a lot of trouble. To the federal government, home buyers who lie in their mortgage applications have committed fraud. However, if you inform a lender that you are involved in litigation, you should expect to face a barrage of questions concerning the case. If you are being sued for a lot of cash, don't be surprised if you are turned down for a loan.

Some lenders do make loans to folks whose credit histories are blemished or who have other problems (like pending lawsuits) that disqualify them for a conventional loan. These lenders, sometimes referred to as "hard money lenders," typically lend cash at higher interest rates. If you have to purchase your home while a lawsuit is pending (some cases go on for years), a hard money lender might be an option. But you should expect to pay sky-high interest rates (5 to 10 points above prime is considered normal for hard money lenders), which may make owning a home too expensive for you.

Your other option is to wait until the case is settled or a judgment has been reached. Once a settlement is reached and entered into the court record, it may become part of your credit history. If a judgment against you is large and will drag down your debt-to-income ratio, consider living cheaply for a while and plowing every dime you can into paying off the judgment as quickly as possible. If the judgment is small, or is in your favor, consider paying another visit to your local mortgage broker to assess where you stand for getting your mortgage approved.

Rules to Live by When Purchasing Community Property

LEGAL
ISSUE
5

Whether you choose to live in a single-family house or in a condominium or cooperative housing building, you are going to face certain rules that may limit your full enjoyment of your property.

Condo, Co-op, and Townhouse Associations. If you plan to purchase a condominium, co-op, or townhouse, you will likely have to agree to live by a set of predetermined rules. Some of these rules govern the times you may use the sunroom, or the barbecue grills, or the laundry room. They may stipulate that all residents must recycle.

Some rules may make perfect sense and some may be nonsensical. One co-op has a rule that prohibits grown men and women from wearing shorts in the lobby.

Some of the most important rules and regulations are those that govern which pets, if any, may live on the property, what size they can be, and how you must care for them. Pet rules generally raise the hackles on owners' and would-be owners' necks. Some folks have strong feelings, pro and con, about animals. It's common for condos and co-ops to exclude pets altogether. Or, residents may be allowed to have cats, but only if they install wall-to-wall carpeting, so that the noise doesn't disturb the neighbors downstairs. You may be permitted to have a very small dog, perhaps under 25 pounds. Some multifamily buildings allow almost any kind of animal you'd want—except Vietnamese pot-bellied pigs.

In addition to dictating what kind of pets residents may have and how much they can weigh, condos and co-ops often have rules governing pets' behavior. Many associations prohibit pets from being taken out through the front elevator or lobby. Others insist that all pets (usually cats or dogs) be on a short leash when taken through public spaces in the building. And owners must always clean up after a pet that makes a mess.

Whether or not you're a pet owner, you should think about the types of rules condos, co-ops, and townhouses may have and decide whether you want to abide by them. Community living requires compromises, and you may not want to make those compromises. If you ignore the rules, you may face penalties and fines set by the association board. You can try to change the rules, but it may be difficult, unpleasant, and time-consuming. Often, there is little respect for people's feelings. In one building, a large majority of the tenants wanted to permit cats, in part because allowing cats would help the co-op units sell faster. But one tenant wrote a scathing five-page report on the dangers of having cats in the building. When the votes to change the building policy were counted, the motion failed, largely because of this report.

Village Ordinances.   If you choose to live in a single-family home, there may be village or city ordinances that could limit your ability to fully enjoy your future property. For example, some municipalities limit the number of unrelated people who can live in a single-family home. If you and a friend buy a home together, and then plan to rent out the extra bedrooms to other friends who are unrelated to you, you may run afoul of a village ordinance.

Another common ordinance is a prohibition against running a business from your home or even having a home office. In some cities, local officials are beginning to realize how outdated these ordinances are, particularly in light of the advanced technology (computers, modems, and fax machines) that makes working at home a silent, yet productive endeavor. Still, in many places it is against the law to conduct *any* business from a home. If you plan to operate a home-based business, check out the local ordinances in the villages or towns you are considering. There are often other niggling ordinances, regulating, for example, when you may water your lawn, what size and type of fencing can be installed, or at what hour visitors' cars must be removed from street parking areas.

Finally, when checking out homes and neighborhoods, pay a visit to the local municipal planning office. Be sure there are no plans for a municipal dump or an extension of the tollway anywhere near your future home. Don't count on the seller or broker to give you this kind of information (even if they are required by law to do so).

If any of these laws, ordinances, or rules are going to bother you, look elsewhere for a home. Fighting them down the road will only bring you headaches, and a much lighter wallet.

FINANCIAL ISSUES

FINANCIAL ISSUE 1

Hiring an Attorney

With more than a million lawyers currently practicing in the United States, and with extravagant judgments and settlements reported daily in the media, it must seem as if everyone has—or should have—a lawyer in his or her pocket. But the reality is that attorneys are expensive and you need to use them judiciously. Besides, not every attorney can help you fix every problem you have.

The world of attorneys is divided into specialties and subspecialties, just the way the world of medicine is. There are general practitioners, but you wouldn't go to an ear-nose-and-throat doctor if you had a broken leg. Similarly, there are general practitioners in the law, and these attorneys can help you do a variety of things. Then there are the specialists: bankruptcy attorneys, divorce lawyers, litigation

117

attorneys, patent lawyers, insurance defense lawyers, and real estate attorneys, among others.

When purchasing property, it's always a good idea to retain a real estate attorney, to make sure that your interests are being protected. In several states around the country, attorneys are not routinely involved in house closings. Instead, escrow companies perform certain functions that permit home buyers and home sellers to close on their deals, and the real estate brokers give home buyers and sellers assistance in "interpreting" what the language on the contracts actually means. Even if this is the common way of approaching a home purchase in your area, this assistance falls far short of having a real estate attorney, or any other kind of attorney, representing your interests exclusively.

When do you need an attorney? If you are facing some of the legal issues discussed in this Step, you may want to hire an attorney to help you work them out. Here are the different types of attorneys who may be able to help you.

Real Estate Attorney. If you're planning to have someone co-sign your loan, or to buy a home with a partner or partners, you'd be wise to find a real estate attorney who can walk you through the potential pitfalls that might accompany a complicated purchase. A good real estate attorney should be able to draft a partnership agreement and explain the intricate details of sharing in a purchase of property. If you're getting a loan from a family member or friend, ask a real estate attorney to draft the loan agreement so that it meets with IRS standards for an "arm's length transaction." If you work with a buyer's broker (see Step 7, Choosing the Right Broker), your attorney can look over and explain the buyer brokerage agreement and agency disclosure agreement, if there is one. He or she can coach you in preparing your offer, negotiating the details, and assisting in the closing of the property. If you're in the process of getting divorced and need your soon-to-be ex-spouse's waiver of his or her homestead rights, your real estate attorney may be able to help. Here are the most frequently asked questions about hiring attorneys.

- *How do I find one?* The best real estate attorneys come recommended by real estate agents and brokers who use them, or by friends and relatives who have recently had a good experience. If you don't know anyone who recently used a real estate attorney they liked, you can call the American Bar Association or your local bar association and ask for a referral. Once you have a couple of names, spend some time thoroughly interviewing each attorney. Ask about a schedule of fees and what they cover, a policy on when fees must be paid, how long the attorney has been practicing, whether that entire time was spent in this particular locale and specialty, and so on.

- *How do attorneys charge?* Like most lawyers, real estate attorneys generally come in two varieties: (1) they work for a law firm or (2) they are solo practitioners. Attorneys who work for law firms generally charge by the hour. Solo practitioners often charge flat fees for doing house closings. For any additional work, or for a house closing that includes more work than is standard, you may be billed at an hourly rate, or you may be able to negotiate an expanded flat fee. The general range for a house closing is anywhere from $300 to $600 and up. Beware of attorneys who offer to charge you less than $300 for your house closing. The fee may be too good to be true, or they may want you to use a title company that pays them a substantial fee to do title work rather than legal work.

Be sure to ask what your attorney's fee includes. Ask how much time he or she will spend with you. Ask whether the attorney, or his or her secretary, will be answering your questions. Finally, be sure to question the attorney thoroughly on his or her experience with residential house closings.

- *Is there anything else I should know?* Don't allow the attorney (or anyone else, for that matter) to pressure you into doing something you don't feel comfortable doing or ready to do. If you feel the attorney is taking advantage of you, or is not doing what he or she promised to do, you can report the attorney to the department that regulates attorneys in your state.

Bankruptcy Attorneys and Litigators. Some attorneys specialize in working with individuals who are in a financial crisis. These attorneys, called bankruptcy attorneys, can help in sorting through legal options and deciding what to do if bankruptcy looms. Lawyers who specialize in courtroom appearances are called litigators. They work with plaintiffs and defendants who are involved in lawsuits.

- *How do I find one?* As with a real estate attorney, the best way to find a bankruptcy attorney or litigator is by word of mouth. Some firms specialize in these fields. If you're working with the Consumer Credit Counseling Service (CCCS) or another non-profit financial counseling service, your counselor may have a list of bankruptcy attorneys to recommend to you. A tax adviser or accountant may also have a list of names, or you can call your local bar association for recommendations.

- *How much do they charge?* Most attorneys in this type of practice charge an hourly fee. Sometimes you can negotiate a flat fee for a specific service.

FINANCIAL
ISSUE
2

Resolving Your Legal Issues

Whether or not you use an attorney, it's important to resolve any legal issues you face *before* you start the prequalification process. As we've discussed, most lenders won't look kindly on an unresolved lawsuit. They recognize that even if you win the case, your legal fees might eat into your down payment or your ability to make your monthly mortgage payments.

Make paying off your legal obligations and judgments a top priority. If you can't pay them off immediately, try to establish a payment plan with your creditor. Then work hard to pay off the judgment.

EMOTIONAL/FAMILY ISSUES

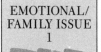

EMOTIONAL/
FAMILY ISSUE
1

Approaching Your Partner About a Partnership Agreement

Sometimes, home buyers are a little overwhelmed by any talk about money. At the first mention of debt and obligations, they clam up, hoping the situation will go away on its own. But when you're going into a major financial investment (like buying a house) with another person or with your family, you must face all the tough financial issues up front. If you don't, they could come back to haunt you.

If you think you and your partner ought to have a partnership agreement in place before you purchase property together, you should discuss the issue with your partner. Together, you should then find and meet with a real estate attorney who can review your various options and help you outline the goals of the partnership.

Your partnership agreement should detail and assign the responsibilities you're sharing. If the situation gets emotional or sticky, slow down and try to work out the problems together. If you can't face discussing some of the tougher financial issues with your partner, or you're having trouble confronting him or her over a particular problem, you may want to rethink your choice of a home buying partner.

STEP
6

Identifying Where
You Want to Live

Where do you want to live? Most first-time home buyers have either a very narrow, specific idea of the community, the neighborhood, or even the block where they want to live, or they have absolutely no idea at all. Paul, a Washington (DC) attorney, using the "shoe leather" method of house hunting, managed to narrow his search to two townhouses located within the same development. Sherry and Ken, however, couldn't decide among six different suburbs of San Francisco. As is true with most extremes, neither is a particularly good way to begin your search for a home.

Where you ultimately choose to settle down will make a big difference to your family, both financially and emotionally. In some ways, correctly identifying where you want to live and choosing the type of home you want to live in are the most important decisions you'll make in the process of planning to purchase a home. Why? Because if you buy the right home at the right price in the right place, and everything else goes wrong with the transaction, you'll probably still feel good about your purchase.

You must be able to identify what kind of home, what kind of community, neighborhood, suburb, or city, what geographic region, and what state is right for you. In this Step, we'll talk about the different options that are available to home buyers, and how you can identify which ones are right, or will be right, for you. We'll talk about wish lists and reality checks, trade-offs, and changing neighborhoods. As you'll see, even the small details count.

FINANCIAL ISSUES

Finding the Right Community

FINANCIAL
ISSUE
1

For some home buyers, finding the right community revolves around where they and/or their spouses work. A lot of people like to live close to where they work. A short commute time allows a more leisurely lifestyle. But for some folks, living close to work simply isn't an option; housing may be too expensive, or not available. Or perhaps the school district doesn't meet the needs of their children.

The majority of first-time home buyers have a tough time deciding where they want to live. Recently, one young doctor couldn't figure out whether she wanted to live in Oregon, Illinois, Indiana, or Ohio. When she stopped to think about why she was having so much trouble getting started down the home buying path, she realized that the states she had identified contained hospitals where she would like to practice, and until she received a job offer, she couldn't move forward with selecting a state, let alone a neighborhood.

If, as a first-time buyer, you limit your scope too much, you may miss out on a wonderful opportunity that falls slightly outside the geographical, financial, stylistic, or architectural boundaries you've set for yourself. On the other hand, if you've set the world (or an entire metropolitan area) as your oyster, you may be overwhelmed by the myriad choices available to you, and may find it difficult to limit your focus enough to thoroughly explore realistic possibilities.

Different Options Mean Different Costs.   City, suburbs, small town, rural land. Established communities and neighborhoods, or a brand new subdivision. The cost of where you live changes relative to: age and level of establishment of the neighborhood; quality of housing; location within a metro area; proximity to major work centers, services, and shopping; quality of schools, parks, and local government; and recreational opportunities. Balancing your budget against the amenities you hope to get when you buy your home boils down to *compromise.* As we've already discussed, you're probably not going to get everything you want the first time out. You may have to amend your primary choice of neighborhood, school district, and size or style of home.

Still, you're bound to get something you want. How do you know when you've found the right community? Here are some realities to think about when deciding where you want to live:

- *Homes in the best school districts appreciate faster than homes in mediocre school districts.* This truism is worth remembering when looking for a community or neighborhood. By limiting your search to those communities that include good or excellent school districts, you may be doing yourself a better favor financially than you realize. Homes in excellent school districts go up in value faster—sometimes twice as fast—than homes in fair or poor school districts. Families are generally far more concerned about their children's education than about anything else on their wish list.

  When choosing a school district, be sure to spend some time investigating not only the examination rankings, but who attends the school and who teaches there. Drop by for a visit and ask to meet with the principal or to sit in on a class. Go through the local newspaper and watch for school buzzwords. You want a district that is well-funded and has a tax base that can adequately support its future development. Watch out for schools that are on the decline, have installed metal detectors, or have gang or drug problems. (See the resources in Appendix III for additional information on SchoolMatch, a national company that helps home buyers find out detailed information about various schools and school districts.)

- *Amenities count.* A good school district can be considered an amenity, but there are others you should search for as well: a well-maintained, well-funded park district that offers ample recreational opportunities for you and your family; a good public library; a community with a diverse tax base (look for commercial buildings, retail stores, and self-contained light industrial parks) so that the entire tax burden of supporting the community is not carried on your shoulders and those of your future neighbors; excellent access to public transportation, roads, and highways; nearby shopping and what the industry calls "service retail" (grocery stores, dry cleaners, veterinarian, bakery) and so on.

- *Environmental hazards.* As you search for a good community, bear in mind these environmental hazards that you should try to avoid:

  —A nearby municipal dump. If something toxic leaches into the soil, you may never be able to resell your home.

  —Overhead high-power electrical wires. Some studies have linked these "power towers" to cancer and other diseases, but many other studies have failed to prove any direct connection.

Still, home buyers are generally frightened of this issue, thanks to scary reports on national television magazine shows.

—A site that is not sufficiently far downstream from a major chemical or industrial plant. (The plant may not currently be releasing chemicals into the water, but it may have done so years ago, and the water may not be truly safe.)

—High levels of radon, an odorless gas that can cause brain defects and lung damage, particularly in young children. A radon problem in a single-family home may be easily and cheaply fixed, but you should check for high radon levels in an area. Your broker should know whether an area has high levels of radon, or you can check with the local municipal planning department. Radon is generally not a problem in high-rise condominium or co-op buildings.

—Unwrappable, unremovable asbestos. A popular fire retardation material used extensively through the late 1970s and early 1980s, asbestos has been known to cause lung cancer. It is usually harmful only when in a "fryable" state (small bits and dust are breaking off and blowing around in the air), and can often be remedied by a professional wrapping of the material, or by removing it entirely.

—Leaded paint and water. Watch out for these toxic concerns, especially in older homes. They can, however, be easily and safely dealt with once you've purchased a home.

• *The road well traveled makes the driver weary.* Finding a home that's relatively close to your job and/or your spouse's job should be a top priority. Although that's the road (or public transportation line) you'll travel most frequently, you should also consider how far away from your family, friends, and house of worship you want to be. If you live in one community, and your parents live 45 minutes away, you may not see them as often as if they lived only 5 minutes away. Similarly, if you spend 30 to 45 minutes, each way, driving out to visit friends, you may not get to see them as often as you like. One solution is to find a middle point, a community that's perhaps only 20 minutes away from your friends and family. Or, choose a location that's closer to one group of people than the other.

• *Location, location, location.* Real estate professionals often use the cliché "Location, location, location" to describe the most important asset of a home. What they're saying is that where a home is geographically located is important on three different levels:

125

(1) the community you select, (2) the neighborhood you select within that community, and (3) where on the specific block the home is located. If you're buying in a multi-story building, location also refers to where in the building you're located.

When thinking about where you want to live, it's best to start with the general and work your way to the specific. First, choose a state, then a metropolitan area, then a city. Then start driving around different neighborhoods, examining them for school districts, amenities, parks, services, retail shopping, where your house of worship is located, and so on. Finally, after much research, you'll settle on a neighborhood that seems to fit what you want, need, and can afford. Walk around that neighborhood's different blocks, identifying which are the nicest, which have the best homes, which have the biggest setbacks (distances from the street), the largest lots, the best access. Are the corner lots the most desirable or the least? Is being across from the park the best location or the worst? "Location, location, location" is ultimately a maxim about choosing the one thing that is almost impossible to change about your new home: the land on which it is situated.

After you've picked out a particular metropolitan area or some specific cities or suburbs within that area, purchase two large maps of each area. The maps should show major parks and landmarks, and legible street names. As you begin narrowing your search, use one map as a guide. Use several transparent colored markers to indicate the neighborhoods you've explored and the streets you particularly like. For example, yellow might indicate the route you've driven through a neighborhood. When you find a street you like, use orange (over the yellow) so that you remember you like it. For each school you locate, put a blue "X" on the map. Green might indicate highways, railroads, and public transportation routes. If you have an extra color, like purple, you might use it to highlight retail shopping, grocery stores, and other amenities. When you're done, you should be able to tell at a glance which neighborhoods have the amenities you prefer. Once you've narrowed down your choices of neighborhoods, take the second map and make enlarged photocopies of those sections. Or, go to the local village or city hall and ask for a map that specifically shows the school districts and the amenities available in the community. Carefully highlight (with your transparent colored markers) the streets you like. When you start your house-by-house exploration, you can put a small orange "X" at the specific location of each home you like. You'll begin to develop a true understanding of the housing stock of a particular neighborhood, and will learn what the neighborhood is all about (and, perhaps, whether you can be happy there).

Deciding What You Want to Live In

Once you've decided generally where you want to live, it's time to figure out what you want to live in. Part of this decision will fall under the heading of compromise: In a top school district, the homes may be too expensive for you to purchase the house of your dreams. Or, the house you've envisioned in your mind's eye may not exist in that area, and you'll have to settle for a townhouse, a condominium, or a co-op. You'll also need to figure out whether you want (or can afford) a home in move-in condition (where nearly everything has been renovated) or new construction, or whether you'll have to make do with a smaller fixer-upper in which lots of projects await a handy homeowner.

Here's a rundown of the different housing options you may have in a particular neighborhood:

- *Single-family home.* The single-family home, the most popular and most expensive type of housing, forms the basis of the American dream of homeownership. And, it generally appreciates faster than other types of homes. But if you are looking to move into an established, expensive neighborhood with a great school district, you may have to compromise and buy a single-family home that is smaller than you'd like, or one that needs fixing up.

  Another option is to buy a single-family home at a slightly less desirable location within the same overall excellent area. For example, if corner lots are less desirable and therefore less expensive, consider buying one in your favorite neighborhood. Is a bigger home on a smaller lot available to you, or a smaller home on a larger lot? (You would have room for expansion, when your budget permits.) If Colonials or Victorians are prized in your favorite neighborhood, consider purchasing a newer, more modern home whose price may be deeply discounted. Just remember, if there are too many other negatives to the house and its location, you won't see the same kind of appreciation (and may ultimately have trouble selling it) as you might if you pick a single-family home in the best location within the second-best neighborhood.

- *Condominium, co-op, townhouse.* If a single-family home in the neighborhood of your choice is out of your price range, you might want to consider purchasing a condominium, co-op, or townhouse. These alternatives to single-family housing offer renters a lower-cost opportunity to become home buyers. A townhouse, especially if it is multilevel, ought to give you the most single-family-home feeling. But remember that condos, co-ops, and townhouses usually have monthly or annual assessments. Those assessments may eat into your total purchasing power by reducing the amount you can qualify to borrow from a lender.

- *Multifamily home.* We've discussed how purchasing a multifamily home might be a way for you to become a home buyer in a neighborhood where a single-family home is too expensive for you. By living in one unit and renting the others, you gain income that helps you pay your mortgage—or pays the mortgage entirely. Another option is to purchase a multifamily building with a friend or relative. Still another option, if permitted in your area, is to buy a single-family home and rent out the extra bedrooms. Judy, a homeowner in Massachusetts, rents out several bedrooms each year to college students.

- *Existing home vs. new construction.* If you've got your heart set on buying new construction, you may have to trade your dream neighborhood for it. It is generally more expensive to buy a newly built home than to buy one that has been around for a while and needs fixing up. Plus, existing homes are the major portion of the housing in older, more established neighborhoods. Often, bargains can be found among existing homes that have been let go or are located in neighborhoods that are changing. (See the 10 Steps Tip at the end of this section for more information on being an urban pioneer.)

- *Fixer-upper vs. move-in condition.* Even if you don't buy a brand-new home, it will cost you substantially more to purchase a home that's in "move-in" condition than one that needs fixing up. Most home buyers don't have the will or the way (i.e., the cash) to fix up their new home; that makes them more willing to pay up front for a home that's already redone. Many excellent values can be found in fixer-upper homes, however, particularly if you're at all handy. In fact, fixer-uppers may be the best bargain left. In the 1970s and 1980s, homes doubled, tripled, and quadrupled in value, simply because of rising Baby Boomer demand. In the 1990s and into the 21st century, real value must be created, or added, to the property. Doing much of the work yourself will return the greatest profit. But remember to allow yourself time to realize the appreciation. It won't happen overnight, and, generally, if you try to sell your home within a year of completing major repairs or renovations, you may not get all of your money out of a big project. Give yourself 3 to 5 years there, and you'll likely get to enjoy the fruits of your labors, plus the added appreciation in your home's value.

Being a pioneer means being the first to do something. In the middle of the 19th century in America, the word referred to people who, in the name of manifest destiny, pushed westward and settled in the country's undeveloped regions. Today, being a pioneer in real estate means being among the first to settle in neighborhoods that are changing or gentrifying. Those who are first to enter a neighborhood that is somewhat rundown or forgotten usually end up getting the biggest return on their money when they sell the property (assuming the neighborhood eventually turns around). But while you're living in a neighborhood, waiting for it to turn into a hot commodity, you may have to put up with neighbors who let their property get rundown, or who don't care about cleaning the neighborhood up or making sure it's safe. Not every home buyer is cut out to be an urban pioneer. It takes an individual who isn't dependent on neighborhood services, who doesn't require much of a neighborhood, or who believes in the rejuvenation of a neighborhood. If you decide to investigate this route, beware. Brokers will often tell you, "This is going to be the next hot neighborhood." They might be right or they might be wrong. What's worth remembering is that *they simply don't know.* A recession can capsize the beginning of the rejuvenation of a neighborhood, and it may never recover. Julie and Jacob paid around $350,000 for a new house in a neighborhood that seemed to be getting hot. Then they got hit by the recession of the early 1990s, and interest in their neighborhood simply dried up. Five years later, when they tried to sell their home, they got less than $325,000. Your best bet: Buy the property because you love it and because you feel the neighborhood is livable as it is today.

10 STEP TIP

FINANCIAL
ISSUE
3

How Long You Want to Live There

Part of identifying where you want to live is knowing how long you plan to be there. According to some studies, Americans move an average of every 5 to 7 years, though the latest figures on home buyers show they tend to stay in their homes as long as 7 to 15 years. The time track on which homeowners seem to buy and sell homes corresponds loosely to what I refer to as the cycle of life. If you're single, in your early 20s, and you want to be a homeowner, you'll probably be looking for a one- or two-bedroom condominium in a part of town that has a lot of other young singles and offers plenty of recreational opportunities and an active nightlife. You'll probably stay there 5 to 7 years, or until you meet the right person, fall in love, and establish a long-term relationship. Once you marry, or consent to this long-term relationship, you'll realize that your condo is too small for your joint lifestyle. So you'll sell and move to a larger home. You'll then decide whether you want children. If you do, you'll probably have them within the next 5 to 10 years. Because raising children brings an exponential need for more space, you may quickly outgrow your second home.

So you'll sell and move again. This time, however, you may try to find a home in a school district that will accommodate your children's needs. And you may stay there 10 to 15 years, or until your children are through with school. Or, if you are fortunate, and do well in business, you may opt to trade up to a larger, nicer home in the same neighborhood. Once your children are grown and out of the house, you may feel that it's too big to handle, so you'll sell it and move to a smaller home, or perhaps a townhouse or a condominium, which offers additional amenities and services. If you live in a cold-weather climate, you may decide to purchase a second home somewhere warm, to which you will ultimately retire.

But What About You?   It's all well and good to talk about patterns, and averages, and what's typically going to happen. However, you need to take a long, hard look at where you are in the cycle of life and where you hope to be 3 to 7 years *after buying your first home*. If you're in the planning stages, and you don't expect to start looking for a home to buy for another year or 2 (or 3 or 4), you'll have to set your sights to 6 to 10 (or 11) years out (the number of years until you buy a home, plus another 3 to 7 years of living there) to help you choose the right location and the right size home.

You have to think about other issues as well, beginning with work. If your job requires frequent transfers to different cities, it may be difficult for you to become a homeowner and truly reap the benefits of homeownership. Selling your home and moving is costly, especially if you have to do it every 3 years. You'd have to be extremely lucky—and savvy—to make money on a home if you move every 3 years or sooner. If you want to take a stab at it, your best bet is to find a house that needs cosmetic work (decorating), rather than structural repairs (such as replacing the roof or the furnace). The value you add to your home may help offset the costs of paying the broker's commission (usually 5 to 7 percent of the selling price). Also, pick an excellent school district, where demand for homes tends to stay fairly strong, even during a recession.

Another circumstance with which you may have to deal is care of your aging parents. If you think your parents may need some assistance within the next 5 to 7 years, and may even need to live with you, choose a home and a location that will make it easy to help them. If you're going to purchase a house and have the option of having a bedroom and bath on the first floor, that arrangement may be easier for your parents than having them climb stairs every day. A disability or illness could also seriously affect what type of home you purchase.

Examining these and other issues closely will help you figure out what home buying time line you're on, and what kind of house you should be thinking about. I can't stress this often enough: How long you plan to live in a home should be one of the most crucial factors in your decision to buy property. It affects every part of the home buying process, from where you live to what kind of home you purchase and what type of financing you use. Not accurately gauging your short- and long-term time line can cost you dearly, especially when your mortgage payments are due or it's time to sell your home.

Constructing Your Wish List and Reality Check

FINANCIAL
ISSUE
4

Would you drive across the United States without a roadmap? Even if geography was your favorite subject in school, you might not know which roads cut the most direct route between New York City and San Diego. So you'd start off heading west, hoping you wouldn't get sidetracked and end up in Canada or Mexico.

Buying a home without constructing a wish list and a reality check is like driving cross-country without a roadmap. Wish lists and reality checks tell you a lot about the kind of home buyer you are and the things that are really important to you and your family. They help you plan your purchase, learn the value of compromise, and trade off what's not important for amenities you can't live without.

Let's start at the top. A *wish list* is a list of everything you might ever want in your home. It includes basics like the number of bedrooms and bathrooms, your first-choice neighborhood and school district, and your ideal distance from work, house of worship, friends, and family. Beyond the basics, a wish list includes your fantasies. The latest models of kitchen appliances and conveniences. A three-car garage. An attic you can build out later. A marble master bathroom with a jacuzzi. All of the things you've always wanted to have in your dream home should be included on your wish list.

A *reality check* is everything you can't live without. For example, you may want a five-bedroom, four-bath single-family colonial house. Who wouldn't like to have all that extra space? But when you look at the size of your family, and your true needs, you realize that you absolutely have to have three bedrooms and at least one and a half baths. What's the difference between five bedrooms and three bedrooms in your preferred neighborhood? Maybe a couple of hundred thousand dollars. What else can you not live without? Some folks living in cold-weather climates absolutely have to have a garage for their car. Perhaps you'd like a two- or three-car attached garage that's heated, but you absolutely must have a one-car garage.

Your wish list and reality check give you the building blocks to figure out exactly what you want and need in a home. They also help you prioritize the items on your list, identifying those that are truly vital to your ability to live comfortably in your affordable house, and those that can be set aside until you trade your first home for one that's bigger and better.

The worksheets that begin on page 133 will help you identify the items that should be included in your wish list and reality check. Don't worry if it takes you a few times to get the matchup right. The process of paring down a wish list and building up a reality check can take weeks, months, or even years. When my husband, Sam, and I started searching for a single-family home, we were looking on the north side of Chicago. We ended up, 3 years and 150 homes later, in a suburb 20 miles from the city. Throughout the years, we've written several wish lists and reality checks, some together and some separately. Each time we realized our tastes or priorities had changed, we rewrote the lists again.

10 STEP TIP

132

It's important that you actually put pen to paper when constructing your wish lists and reality checks. As you will see in the worksheets that follow, there are dozens of items you may want to include, chosen from literally hundreds of options. If you don't write down everything, you may find yourself forgetting some of the basics. Also, by putting your list in black and white, you'll more readily focus on the issues initiated by the wish list and the reality check. You and your spouse or partner, wish lists and reality checks in hand, should then review them, issue by issue. Discuss them; decide which items are paramount to you both. After you've worked together on your lists, you should have a good idea of what your spouse or partner considers important in a home.

City, Suburb, or Neighborhood

What is your ideal neighborhood? _____

_____

What are the blocks you'd like to live on? _____

_____

What are your preferred school districts? _____

_____

Do you want to live close to your children's future school? Within walking distance?_____
How far exactly? _____

_____

How far from work do you want to be? _____

_____

Does the community have a park district? Is there a park nearby? Is that important?_____

_____

Is safety important? What kind of crime statistics should your new neighborhood have?

_____

Do you want a neighborhood that has a mixture of young and old people? Do you want a
place where nearly everyone is the same age and has children? _____

_____

What kinds of services do you want in your neighborhood (dry cleaners, laundromat,
grocery store, superstores, etc.)? _____

_____

_____

_____

What kinds of stores do you want near you (gift store, bookstore, children's clothing,
outdoor equipment, major shopping mall)? _____

_____

_____

_____

How many miles do you want to be from these services? Stores? House of worship? Family and friends? _____

_____

Are there any clubs nearby that you already belong to or would want to join? _____

_____

How do you plan to get to work? If you will take public transportation, do you want to be within walking distance of the train or bus? _____

_____

How far from the nearest airport do you want to be? _____

_____

How far from your favorite recreational activities do you want to be? _____

_____

Building Exterior

Do you prefer a single-family, condominium, co-op, or townhouse development? _____

_____

What style of house do you prefer? Colonial? Farmhouse? Contemporary? Ranch? Victorian? Cape Cod? Should it have one story or two? _____

_____

Do you prefer brick, stone, aluminum or vinyl siding, or stucco as an exterior? _____

_____

Do you want a bright house with a lot of windows? _____

_____

Should the house have a north, south, east, or west exposure? _____

_____

Do you want a lot of land? A big or small yard? Wooded or sunny area? _____

_____

_____

Do you want a pool? Tennis court? Other recreational amenity? _____

_____

_____

_____

What kind of parking accommodations do you want (indoor, outdoor, covered, uncovered, parking for guests)? Do you prefer an attached garage? For how many cars? _____

_____

Do you want to have a deck? A patio? A sundeck? _____

_____

Building Interior

What kind of condition should the house be in? Would you prefer a fixer-upper or gut job? Or do you want a house that is in move-in condition? _____

_____

How many bedrooms would you like to have? _____

_____

How many bathrooms? _____

Do you want a great room? Family room? Game room? Media room? Home office? Library? Den? Billiard room? _____

_____

_____

Do you want all these rooms separate from or attached to the kitchen? Attached to any other room? _____

_____

Do you want a separate guest room with private bath, which might later house an aging parent? _____

_____

Do you want a fireplace? Wood-burning or gas? In more than one room? _____

_____

Would you prefer an attic that could be built out for later expansion? _____

Do you want a full or partial basement? One that is build out or buildable? _____

_____

What kind of closets and storage should the home have? _____

_____

What kinds of appliances would you like? _____

_____

Do you prefer hardwood floors, tile, or carpet? _____

_____

What kind of bathroom and kitchen finishes do you prefer? _____

_____

_____

Will you have the cash to make decorating changes after you purchase the home, or should you find something you can live with for a few years? _____

Mechanicals

Do you want central air and central heat? _____

_____

Do you prefer radiators, forced-air heat, baseboard electric heat, or gas heat? _____

_____

Should the rooms all have ceiling fans? _____

Do you prefer a slab foundation, crawl space, or basement (if terrain permits)? _____

_____

Condominiums and Co-ops

If you prefer a condo or co-op, do you want a small, medium, or large development? High-rise or low-rise? _____

_____

_____

What kind of security system do you prefer? Gated community? Doorman? Electronic locking system? _____

_____

_____

What percent of the owners should also live there? Should it be primarily owner-occupied, with some rentals? _____

_____

Do you prefer neighbors who move frequently or who live there for a long time? _____

_____

What kind of amenities would you like? Pool? Tennis courts? Exercise facility? Storage lockers? Party room? Sun deck? Backyard? Place for a barbecue? _____

_____

_____

What is your preferred parking situation? Do you want an attached garage? Assigned parking space? Deeded parking space? _____

_____

Building a Wish List. The Dream House Wish List Worksheet (pages 133-137) will help you to construct your own wish list. On page 139, I've provided a Dream House Priorities Worksheet you can use to record the key items on your checklist in their descending order of importance. I intended the questions in these worksheets to be fairly complete, but don't limit yourself. Everyone wants different amenities in a home. Feel free to add any items you can think of. If your mind is a blank, think about homes you've been in that had features you liked. Think about the home you grew up in. What did you like and dislike about it?

When you have filled in all the answers that apply to your dream house on the Dream House Wish List Worksheet, read them over and try to prioritize your dream home's features. Which characteristic is *most important* to you? Put that down first on the Dream House Priorities Worksheet that follows. Then enter the second most important feature, the third, and so on. Have your spouse or partner prepare a separate priorities worksheet. When you both have finished, compare your priorities. You may have very different concepts about the most basic features of your future home. Identify the joint priorities, review the individual priorities (those that are on only one worksheet), and discuss in detail the reasons for your choices. Your spouse or partner may have concerns you hadn't thought of. Listen carefully and consider what you should negotiate and where you should yield.

Don't feel you have to limit yourself to the 20 spaces allowed here. Use a separate piece of paper if necessary. Photocopy this blank worksheet and use it when you are considering a real home and need to prioritize what it offers.

Creating Your Reality Check. As we've discussed, a reality check is everything you cannot live without. It's the backbone of your search for a home, the basics that meet your minimum needs. For example, you may want to live in the very best school district in your state. But if that's 100 miles from your job, you'll have to settle for the best school district that's geographically convenient. You might want an attached garage in which you also have storage space. But, for safety and security reasons, you have to have a deeded parking strip that is close to the door of your home.

Does the gap between your wants and your needs remind you of the Grand Canyon? You're not alone. Except for the very few for whom money is an unlimited commodity, almost no one gets

Spouse/Partner 1	Spouse/Partner 2
1. _____	_____
2. _____	_____
3. _____	_____
4. _____	_____
5. _____	_____
6. _____	_____
7. _____	_____
8. _____	_____
9. _____	_____
10. _____	_____
11. _____	_____
12. _____	_____
13. _____	_____
14. _____	_____
15. _____	_____
16. _____	_____
17. _____	_____
18. _____	_____
19. _____	_____
20. _____	_____

everything that's wished for in a first home. As you trade up, move from home to home, and become wealthier and more established in life, your wish list will expand to encompass things you may not even be able to conceive of today. Your reality check will change as well. One day, when you find your third, fourth, or fifth home, it may even resemble today's wish list.

Your reality check will keep you sane throughout the home buying process. As you tour dozens (or hundreds, as in our case) of homes, you may become swayed by amenities you can't afford to buy. Relying on your reality check will allow you to keep emotion out of the equation. At a glance, you'll be able to check off your bare necessities. If a home doesn't meet those, you'll know immediately it isn't the right property for you.

Creating your reality check is easier than drawing up your wish list. Five major topics form your guidelines:

1. *Size.* How many people will live in your new home? You, your spouse or partner, and your two children? You may need at least three bedrooms. If that's the minimum you absolutely must have to make life comfortable, then put that at the top of your reality check. Even if you're single and want to buy a condominium, you may still need two bedrooms for resale purposes.

2. *School district.* Homes in the best school districts sell faster and for more money than homes in mediocre school districts. It's smart to purchase a home in the best school district you can afford, but that school district might not offer special programs tailored to the physical and mental challenges facing your child. You can afford to buy a home in almost every school district in America, but it may mean sacrificing some of your other needs. Still, if getting into a particular school district is vital, then put that down as a necessity on your reality check.

3. *Work, transportation, and commuting.* Unless you've won the lottery lately, you're going to have to work to pay the mortgage, insurance premiums, and property taxes for your new home. Think carefully about the maximum amount of time you want to spend commuting. If you're going to drive to work, what roads and highways will you have to take? If you'll be taking a train or bus, decide whether you want to be close enough to walk to the station, or will be content to drive there (and pay a parking fee). When Sam and I bought our most recent home,

he put "Walk to the train station" at the top of our reality check.

4. *Amenities.* Amenities refer to more than having a wood-burning fireplace or an attached garage. Amenities are also the recreational and educational opportunities in your neighborhood—a public library, or a park district that offers free ice skating in winter and free concerts in summer. From your wish list, choose the amenities you cannot live without, both in your home and in your neighborhood.

5. *Services.* More than ten years ago, Judy and Philip moved into a Chicago neighborhood that was changing from abandoned commercial and warehouse buildings to rebuilt loft condominiums. They were urban pioneers. But when they moved in, the services city dwellers normally expect weren't available. For example, there were no grocery stores, no dry cleaners, no cafés. They had to drive everywhere. If you and your spouse or partner don't have a lot of extra time, you should think twice about buying a home in an area that is miles from the basic services and retail shopping you'll need every day.

The Reality Check Worksheet on pages 142–143 organizes basic needs under these five headings—and allows space for you to add some others.

> The Reality Check Worksheet is meant to be a portable tool. After you've filled it out, bring it along when you begin touring homes, or when you're working with your broker in his or her office. Compare the size, shape, and amenities of various homes with the bare minimums on your list. Keeping your Reality Check Worksheet handy will help establish some valuable emotional distance between you and a home, a seller, or a broker.

10 STEP TIP

Trade-Offs: Learning to Prioritize

During your search for a home, you may hear brokers talk about *trade-offs.* Purchasing real estate is a lesson in compromise. You often will have to give up something in order to get something that's more valuable to you. When is the best time to make your trade-offs? It's not a one-time activity. You'll be doing it throughout the home buying process.

FINANCIAL ISSUE 5

141

	WORKSHEET	
	Reality Check	

Item	Spouse/Partner 1	Spouse/Partner 2
1. Size		
Bedrooms	_____	_____
Bathrooms	_____	_____
Family room	_____	_____
Extra rooms	_____	_____
Expandable	_____	_____
Other	_____	_____
2. School District		
Top choice	_____	_____
Second choice	_____	_____
3. Work, Transportation, and Commuting		
Distance acceptable	_____	_____
Public transportation	_____	_____
Walking distance?	_____	_____
Other	_____	_____
4. Amenities		
Property and Structure		
Property condition	_____	_____
Yard	_____	_____
Garage/Parking	_____	_____
Other	_____	_____
Other	_____	_____
Other	_____	_____

Item	Spouse/Partner 1	Spouse/Partner 2
Neighborhood		
Library	_____	_____
Park district	_____	_____
Playground	_____	_____
Programs for children	_____	_____
Recreational opportunities	_____	_____
Other	_____	_____
Other	_____	_____
Other	_____	_____
Other	_____	_____

5. Services

Item	Spouse/Partner 1	Spouse/Partner 2
House of worship	_____	_____
Grocery store	_____	_____
Dry cleaners	_____	_____
Specialty foods	_____	_____
Mechanic	_____	_____
Other	_____	_____
Other	_____	_____
Other	_____	_____
Other	_____	_____

Trade-offs start immediately. When you begin to create your reality check, you're subconsciously making a determination that, among the many items you want in a home, there are definite things you can't live without. Your reality check contains (or should contain) your highest priorities, the elements of your lifestyle that are so important that you might turn down a home or its location if they're not there. Depending on your priorities, you might trade off, say, a school district for an extra bedroom.

When you begin combining your wish list and reality check with those of your spouse or partner, your discussion should lead you to add and subtract some items and to do further prioritizing. You might have a two-car garage as the third item on your wish list when your spouse or partner has placed it sixth. His or her third item might be a wood-burning fireplace, which is twentieth on your list. Each of you will eventually have to compromise on items and priorities. The final list should represent fairly your spouse or partner's lists and yours, assuming you both put serious thought into your reality check.

Prioritizing the items on your wish list and reality check can take a lot of time and be emotionally draining. It might help if you buy a packet of 3″ × 5″ index cards. On each one, write one item on your wish list and reality check. Put them in order on the floor or on a large table top. As you and your partner or spouse start your prioritizing, move the cards around in various sequences. You'll avoid ripping up pieces of paper and rewriting your lists.

When you start shopping around for agents and homes, beware of brokers or agents who promise to get you everything on your wish list and reality check. Unless you are extremely lucky or possess incredible wealth, it's unlikely you'll be able to get everything you want. Concentrate on getting what you need.

EMOTIONAL/
FAMILY ISSUE
1

EMOTIONAL/FAMILY ISSUES

When You and Your Spouse Can't Agree on Your Wish List and Reality Check

144

Next to the death of a spouse or child, or loss of a job, buying a home ranks as one of the most stressful situations you'll encounter. Homes represent so much to us emotionally and financially that we often pour equal parts of emotion and logic into the decision-making process. That can be a big mistake, especially if you allow all that emotion to get in the way of your primary relationships.

It's important that you and your spouse or partner agree on the items in your reality check. As we've already discussed, the reality check is your basic roadmap to buying *the house you need*. (Think of the wish list as a map that includes all the wonderful sights along the way.) If you and your spouse disagree irreconcilably on some of the major points, that may be a loud and clear signal that you aren't ready to buy a home. For instance, if one of you feels that a two-bedroom condo is the right choice, and the other is fixed on buying a three-bedroom single-family house, its not the time to be looking for a home. Slow down and spend whatever time it takes to reach a meeting of the minds with your spouse or partner.

It's important for you and your spouse or partner to be in sync before you approach a broker. If you convey mixed signals to the broker you ultimately choose to work with, you can wreak havoc with your home search. Neither you nor your spouse or partner will be completely happy with the houses you see. In the end, you'll just waste everyone's time.

What should you do if the disagreement persist? Go down your wish list and reality check item by item, and try to figure out why you and your spouse or partner have arrived at those orders of priorities. Are both of you being a little unrealistic about the items on your wish lists that you'll be able to get in your price range? The only cure for that impasse is to start reading the "for sale" ads in the newspaper and touring open houses on the weekends. After several weeks or months, you'll develop a solid concept of the amenities you can afford.

Safety

EMOTIONAL/
FAMILY ISSUE
2

If you decide to buy a home in a high-crime area, you must confront some additional concerns about safety. It's all well and good to be an urban pioneer, especially if the neighborhood eventually turns and you sell your home for a fat profit, but no amount of money is worth feeling constantly insecure and unsafe in the very place that's supposed to shield you from the outside world's threats. You need to be comfortable within your home, and that means picking a neighborhood where your home doesn't have to be a fortress just to survive. Be realistic: You're not going to find a community like Andy Griffith's

Mayberry, where the crime of the week is an unpaid $2 parking ticket. The 1950s are gone and, in some areas, safety is a daily life-or-death issue. If you find a neighborhood where you feel safe and secure, where you don't have to worry about allowing your children to play in your own backyard, your peace of mind and quality of life will far exceed any profit you might make in another location.

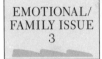

EMOTIONAL/
FAMILY ISSUE
3

Satisfying the Whole Family

When some parents make a decision about what kind of home they should buy, they exclude the opinions of their children, aging parents, or other family members who may live with them. I don't think your children's or parents' opinions are more important than yours, but they may offer an insight that, for one reason or another, escaped you.

How do you find out what your older children or aging parents want in your next home? Ask for their opinions and consider their suggestions, but make it clear that you have the final say. Even your 3-year old can be invited to express small preferences. Just don't be surprised if some ideas that are proffered make a lot of sense.

EMOTIONAL/
FAMILY ISSUE
4

The Flexibility Factor

Experts say we live in the time of the "flex-family." Children are returning to the nest in droves because they can't afford a nest of their own. Seniors are living longer and healthier than ever before. They, too, are moving in with their children. To accommodate these societal changes, families are looking at homes differently than they did before.

Today, it is not unusual to find houses that have home offices, secondary master suites, and "great rooms" (a term used for combined kitchen and family areas) instead of living rooms. If you are a single parent and your grown children or aging parents are living with you, your needs and wants are different from those of a two-parent family with 2.3 kids, two cars, and a dog.

It's important to recognize where you fit into the marketplace and to choose a home that will allow your family the flexibility it needs as it grows and changes. For example, while your children are still young, you may not mind sharing a single full bath. As they get older—and spend more time in there—the flexibility of a second full bath will be welcome. If an older, ill parent moves in with you, you may want to convert the storeroom next to that second full bath into a bedroom that offers your parent extra privacy.

Choosing the
Right Broker

Every once in a while, I get this question from a first-time home buyer: Is it all right to look for a home without using a real estate agent or broker? Or, I'll get a letter from someone who has a problem down the line, perhaps discovered by a professional home inspector or by a lender during the process of trying to secure a mortgage. Many of these folks indicate that they have gone down the path to homeownership solo, without the aid of a real estate agent or broker.

I'm not sure I understand why some buyers fail to avail themselves of the professionals whose whole career is spent helping people turn a dream of homeownership to reality, especially when using a real estate broker doesn't cost the buyer anything. In almost every case, the seller pays the listing agent a commission in a range of between 5 and 7 percent of the selling price of the home. The seller isn't going to raise the price you agree on by 2.5 to 3 percent to cover your "share" of the commission. He or she is already committed to paying that fee. Except for the "commitment fee" that some buyer's brokers charge (which we'll discuss later in this Step), buyers usually don't pay for broker representation.

Some home buyers think that if they don't use a real estate agent, the seller will be more amenable to lowering the price of the home. These home buyers mistakenly think that if the seller has the opportunity to pay less in commission, he or she will share the "savings" with the buyer. Fair is fair, right? This line of thinking seems logical, but it doesn't work in residential real estate. The seller is obligated to pay a certain percentage of the selling price of the home as a commission or fee to the broker who lists the home. Whether a buyer's

147

broker is assisting you or you use the listing broker to complete your offer, the seller usually pays the same commission to the listing broker. (The listing broker then splits the commission—usually 5 to 7 percent of the sales price for full-service brokers—with the buyer's broker. The two brokers then split their halves of the commission with the agents who actually represented the buyer and seller during the transaction. So if you use the listing agent as your agent—which would be a dual agency situation—he or she gets all of the commission.) Even if you find a home that is "for sale by owner" (called FSBO in the industry, and pronounced "fizz-bo"), it's possible that the home is wildly overpriced to begin with. Assuming you succeed in knocking down the seller's price somewhat, you won't necessarily be paying less than you would have, and you might pay a lot more than you should.

So, if the issue isn't really cash out-of-pocket, and you're not going to get the seller to split the "savings," why do some buyers insist on plowing through the complicated maze of residential real estate alone?

Ultimately, I think, their motivation boils down to control. Some buyers want to be in complete control of what is probably the largest purchase they're ever going to make. They decide that the best way to control the situation is to shop by themselves. There are several problems to this "solution." Buyers can look at the FSBOs that are available and negotiate directly with the sellers. But FSBOs are only a small percentage of the vast number of homes that are for sale in any area. If you go to homes that are listed but you're not represented by a buyer's broker, the seller's listing broker will, in almost every case, take on the role of a dual agent and represent you as well—even if you don't want to be represented.

The bottom line is: It's important for you to find a good agent to help guide you through the home buying process. A good agent or broker can open your mind to new neighborhoods and areas you might not have otherwise considered. He or she can show you homes you might not have otherwise seen. And, he or she can help you avoid the potholes that plague the road to homeownership.

Do you absolutely *need* a broker to buy a home? There's no law that says you can't go it alone. You can look through open house listings in the paper. You can drive through the streets looking for FSBOs. If you're hooked up to the Internet, you can surf through various websites and home pages and review the different properties that are listed. But unless you're buying the home you're renting, or the house next door to the one you're renting, you'll probably do better if you work with a competent real estate agent.

In this Step, I describe the different types of brokers. You'll learn how they function in the purchase of real estate, how much they cost, what your broker should do for you, and when you should start to contact prospective brokers.

BROKERAGE ISSUES

The Different Types of Real Estate Brokers and Agents

BROKERAGE ISSUE 1

There are five basic categories of brokers, including conventional brokers, buyer's brokers, single agents, dual agents, and nonagents or facilitators.

Conventional Brokers. It used to be easy: All real estate brokers practiced conventional brokerage (also known as seller or listing or subagency brokerage). Today, there are other options. But conventional brokers have always represented the interests of the seller, and they continue to do so, even if they shepherd you, the buyer, from house to house to house. The concept of conventional brokerage is this: The broker (also known as the *subagent to the seller*) represents the interests of whichever seller owns the house being shown to the buyer. If you, as a prospective buyer, see five different homes on a single day, "your" broker has actually represented five different sellers on that day.

The problem with conventional brokerage is that there really is no one to help you, the buyer, make such important decisions as which home to buy and how much to pay. Because they represent sellers, conventional brokers or subagents are often precluded from discussing with you the shortcomings of a particular piece of property. They cannot point out its flaws, tell you whether it is overpriced, or discuss the reasons why the seller is trying to sell it. I once went with my sister-in-law to look at some property in Boston. We went to see several condominiums. Each had several obvious flaws. In one, a particularly noticeable water stain covered most of the ceiling in the bedroom. The agent never said a word as he showed us the space. Finally, I asked him about the water stain. "I'm not sure what that is," he said. I asked him what price he would pay for the property. "Full price," he said. By the book. Conventional brokers are obligated to get the best

149

price and deal possible for the seller. They are not necessarily required to tell you about any defects you can see with the naked eye, and they may only have to disclose structural defects if you ask about them.

Why do buyers still use conventional brokers? Some home buyers don't realize that other options are available. They may believe that all brokers are created equal and that there are no discernible differences. Remember: You do have other choices.

Buyer's Brokers. In many areas, conventional brokerage is still the name of the game. Buyers are shown properties by agents representing the interests of the seller rather than by agents who represent the buyer's best interests. At the end of the 1980s, a new form of brokerage began to emerge. Called *buyer's brokerage*, it is based on the principle that buyers are entitled to equal representation in real estate transactions.

When a buyer's broker takes you around, he or she is supposed to have your best interests at heart: to find you the best possible house and help you purchase it at the best possible price and on the best possible terms. Buyer's brokers should be happy to give you *comps* (the sales price of homes that are similar to the one you're looking at and have recently sold in your neighborhood) so that you can get a pretty good idea of how much a prospective home is worth. They should also use all reasonable (and legal) means to probe the seller's motivations for selling. By knowing a seller's motives (a death, divorce, job loss, job promotion, new baby, live-in help, live-in aging parent), you can guess how flexible he or she might be on price, terms, and closing date.

When buyer's brokerage first emerged, many conventional brokers were skeptical. But buyers who used buyer's brokerage liked it and talked about it. They were able to buy their homes for less money, and they had a better understanding of the process of purchasing a home. One study showed that home buyers who used buyer's brokers paid about 5 percent less for their homes than those who used conventional brokers or subagents.

Single Agents. After buyer's brokerage became a popular component of real estate brokerage, a host of conventional brokers decided that they, too, should be buyer's brokers when working with home buyers, even though they continued to represent sellers when taking listings. As separate representation became more mainstream, some brokers felt that even though they represented the best interests of buyers when working with buyers and the best interests of sellers when working with sellers, there was a risk of having a conflict of interest. Gradually, the concept of a *single agent* became popular.

Single agents represent *either* buyers or sellers in residential real estate. They do not trade off their loyalty, depending on whom they represent in a transaction. *Exclusive buyer's brokers* represent only the interests of buyers. They never take listings, and they never represent both sides in a single transaction. *Exclusive seller's agents* never represent buyers, nor will they represent both sides in a single transaction. They only take listings and work for sellers.

Single agents feel that their continuous representation of one side keeps them focused on their clients and their clients' best interests. If a conflict arises, they diffuse it by referring away the business. For example, if an exclusive buyer's broker represents two clients, both of whom are interested in the same property, the situation will be disclosed to the two clients and, if they prefer, one buyer will be referred to another buyer's broker, who will then represent his or her best interests. If an exclusive seller's broker holds an open house at a listing and is approached by a buyer to put together an offer, he or she will refer the buyer to a buyer's broker.

Dual Agents.   It's not always possible to use a single agent (they do not exist in some market areas). Nor is it illegal to represent both sides in a single transaction, which is what *dual agents* do: they represent both the buyer and the seller on a particular purchase/sale. They must help both sides work toward a compromise in which everyone is happy and no one feels cheated.

Dual agency generally isn't planned. Some home buyers start looking at open houses before they have signed on to work with a particular broker. Because they're technically not represented, the listing agent can claim them as his or her clients. If they like the home and decide to make an offer, they might decide to use the listing agent, concluding that he or she knows the seller better than anyone else would. In that regard, the home buyers are right. But no home buyers should forget where a broker's loyalties lie. First and foremost, the broker still represents the seller. If, by state law, the agent representing the buyer must give his or her full allegiance to the buyer, then the dual agent may end up representing no one. The dual agent cannot give his or her complete loyalty to both the buyer and seller in the same transaction.

A dual agency situation can occur in another way. The buyer's broker and seller's broker may work for the same company. This

151

kind of transaction is often referred to as an "in-house" deal (because it happens within one firm). Some brokerage companies give brokers and agents who complete in-house deals additional compensation.

A dual agency situation makes many brokers nervous. In recent years, there have been court cases in which judges ruled that the buyer's or seller's confidentiality was compromised by dual agency, and that both parties were hurt. Many larger real estate companies have taken steps to ensure that problems don't happen and confidential information isn't compromised.

Nonagents or Facilitators. Dual agents have tried to limit their liability by changing the way dual agency is performed. Because it's extremely difficult to represent both sides fairly in the same transaction, and impossible to represent each side's best interests (imagine hiring the seller's attorney to represent you at the closing), some real estate brokers have decided it's best to represent neither side.

These days, you might hear a lot about *nonagents, facilitators, designated agency,* or *transactional brokerage*. As nonagents, dual agents represent neither party's best interests and do not discuss or divulge either side's confidential information. Instead, brokers act as facilitators to get the deal done as expediently and fairly as possible. With designated or transactional agency, a dual agency brokerage firm will designate one agent to act as the buyer's agent and a different agent to act as the seller's agent. The big problem with nonagency or facilitators is that no one really represents you. There is no one protecting you or advising you who has only your interests in mind.

It's important to remember that dual agents have divided loyalties. Whether you've worked with your dual agent as a buyer's agent for a long time or not, a dual agent faces a tough conflict involving people's emotions and lots of money. If you have worked with your agent as a buyer's broker, you may have divulged confidential information about your finances and how much you can afford to pay for a home. To protect yourself against this predicament, play your financial cards close to your vest from the outset of your relationship with the broker. It's none of his or her business how much you can afford to spend on a home. He or she should advise you how much a home is worth. But if you tell a conventional broker or a dual agent how much you'd be willing to pay for a home, that effectively becomes your offer. You can pretty much count on the broker to slip this vital piece of information to the seller. Even if that doesn't happen, you should still protect yourself against the possibility.

The Cost of Working with a Real Estate Broker or Agent

BROKERAGE
ISSUE
2

As brokers have begun to assume less fiduciary responsibility (to lessen their liability) in a deal, there has been talk about changing the way they are compensated. But before we explore possible changes, let's talk about the way real estate professionals are currently compensated.

When sellers hire a broker to list their property, they agree to pay a commission on the sale. The commission is based on the final sales price of the property. A standard commission (all commissions are fully negotiable) generally ranges from 5 to 7 percent of the sales price of the home. For example, if a home sells for $100,000 and the agreed-on commission is 6 percent of the sales price, the seller ends up paying the listing broker $6,000.

Continuing the example, that $6,000 is split between the brokerage company the buyer's agent works for and the brokerage company the seller's agent works for. Each side usually receives 50 percent of the commission—in this case, $3,000. The brokerage firm splits its share of the commission, usually 50/50, with the agent who actually represented the buyer or the seller. The buyer's agent—the person who actually helps the buyer throughout the transaction—and the listing agent would each receive $1,500.

This form of commission sharing was developed when everyone worked for the seller. The theory behind this commission structure was that all the money came from the seller, so everyone owed the seller his or her fiduciary duty. Now that buyer's brokerage has become an important component, the rules and rationalizations about commissions and how they're paid has changed somewhat.

When buyer's brokerage first emerged, buyer's brokers began asking home buyers to sign an exclusivity agreement. Essentially, the agreement said that the buyer would pay the agent a commission, stated as a flat fee, an hourly fee, or a percentage of the sales price of the home. Home buyers balked at having to shell out more cash. Most buyers need every available cent to pay for their new homes. To respond to that concern, buyer's brokers either got sellers to reduce the sales price of the home by the amount the buyer would need to pay as the commission, or got the listing brokers to agree to split their commission with a buyer's broker.

Today, most *multiple listing services* (MLSs are companies that physically list properties for sale and publish them on a private

153

on-line system and in books for brokers) have brokerage companies sign an agreement, up front, in which they agree to split commissions with buyer's brokers. Some buyers are still confused by "how the seller can pay the buyer's agent's commission," but most accept it as a fact of life. By stating openly whom they represent, buyer's agents put listing agents on notice as to where their loyalties lie. Single agents (including both exclusive buyer's brokers and exclusive seller's brokers) get compensated in the same way.

If you use a buyer's agent and end up purchasing a home that is for sale by the owner (often called a *FSBO* in real estate jargon and pronounced "fizz-bo"), you will likely be responsible for paying the agent the commission you agreed to in your exclusivity agreement. If you agreed to pay 3 percent of the sales price of the home, that's what the agent will be expecting. In most cases, however, the agent will be able to negotiate his or her fee into the final price of the home.

Should You Pay an Up-Front Fee to a Buyer's Agent?   Some buyer's brokers (particularly exclusive buyer's brokers) ask home buyers to pay an up-front fee of $500 or $1,000. Brokers use the fee to extract a little loyalty from their home buyers, because buyers have traditionally been able to switch agents at will. The brokers' reasoning is: "If buyers have $500 or $1,000 into the search before it even begins, they'll stay with me until they've closed on a home." The fee goes toward paying the commission; or, if the seller pays the buyer's agent's fee, the original fee is returned to the home buyer at the closing. If the buyer decides not to use the broker to purchase a home, the fee is kept as payment for services rendered.

Personally, I'm not in favor of home buyers paying up front for brokerage services. If a buyer's agent is good, he or she should be able to keep clients without requiring an up-front fee. A lot of buyer's brokers, however, disagree with this thinking. They say a fee helps them know whether a home buyer is committed, and it reminds the home buyer that a commitment is involved. Several buyer's brokers have said that if a home buyer balked at paying the fee, they would either reduce it or eliminate it. The bottom line is: If the buyer's agent you think you want to work with charges an up-front fee, ask him or her whether the fee can be waived. If the agent says no, ask whether the fee can be reduced. If the agent insists on a fee and you still want to work with that person, then pay it. But be wary of real estate professionals who are inflexible. That kind of inflexibility can cause other kinds of problems down the road.

What Your Broker Should Do for You

Brokers come in all shapes, sizes, religions, races, and personalities. When the time comes to find one, concentrate on finding a real estate professional who has had plenty of experience in helping first-time buyers find, and close on, the right home. Experience alone, however, does not make a real estate broker a good choice. Here are some characteristics of a good broker. A good broker:

1. *Listens carefully.* One of the most important things a real estate agent can do is *listen to you*—and not simply for the things you say you want in a home and neighborhood. A good agent should be able to read between the lines and be intuitive about amenities you don't even know you need.

2. *Explains thoroughly.* An agent needs to be able to communicate effectively with first-time home buyers who may be unfamiliar with the process of buying a home. When your agent explains a difficult term or concept, you should be able to understand him or her well enough to explain it to someone else.

3. *Answers readily.* A good real estate agent can be a fabulous source of information about both the housing stock and the communities in which available homes are located. He or she should also be an expert in getting you from point A (when you start to look for homes) to point Z (when you shake hands after the closing). You shouldn't have to tell your agent to check up on the sellers or that the next portion of earnest money is due. The agent should be guiding you. If you want to know more, ask! (But ask during business hours and not at 3:00 A.M.)

4. *Communicates frequently.* Your agent should talk to you at least several times a week, from the day you agree to work together to find a home. On that day, you should set aside an hour or two just to talk about what you want and need in a home, and to either look through the listing book or scan current computer listings of homes within your price range. Your broker should contact you when there is a site to show you, and set up days on which you visit several homes. The agent should also follow up and ask which homes did you like, and what didn't you like about those you rejected?

5. *Learns easily.* The process of buying a home is a learning process for everyone. As you see more homes, you'll reprioritize your

155

wish list and reality check items. As your broker gets to know you better and observes how you react to different homes, he or she should be able to show you homes that better meet your wants and needs.

6. *Is flexible and lets you be flexible.* Flexibility is key in finding and closing on the right home. Brokers often say that "buyers are liars" because home buyers (particularly first-time home buyers) change their minds so frequently. It's not uncommon for a first-time home buyer to start off wanting a single-family home in one community and end up purchasing a condo or townhouse on the other side of town. Home buyers don't intentionally mislead brokers; everyone changes during the process of buying a home. A good broker will allow you to explore several communities and will take the time to show you different types of homes, to help you expand your housing horizons. If you change your mind too often and ultimately can't commit to any property, you will likely drive your real estate agent crazy. But if you find someone who has had a lot of experience with first-time buyers, he or she should know how to help you become selective when choosing a home.

BROKERAGE
ISSUE
4

Finding a Good Broker

There are more than a million licensed real estate agents in the United States. Many work for small mom-and-pop shops. Some are affiliated with large national chains like Century 21, Coldwell Banker, Prudential Preferred, Red Carpet, and ERA. Others work for large local firms, like Chicago's Baird & Warner, Los Angeles's Jon Douglas, and Dallas/Ft. Worth's Ebbie Halliday. Of the million-plus real estate agents, around 700,000 belong to the National Association of Realtors (NAR).

The NAR is a nonprofit trade organization, based in Chicago, that offers Realtors® (a designation reserved for members of the NAR) educational materials, a library, and a stalwart lobbying effort on Capitol Hill. The NAR also has an ethics code governing how Realtors work with the public. To retain their membership, all Realtors must adhere to the NAR code of ethics. Most of the real estate agents you'll come across are Realtors. Those who are not must still be licensed by your state to help you buy or sell property, and all must display their licenses in their offices and show them to you upon request. You can verify that a real estate agent or broker is licensed by contacting the department that regulates real estate licenses in your state.

With all these individuals holding licenses enabling them to help people purchase and sell real estate, it isn't too difficult to find a real estate agent who can help you buy a home. The trick is to find a very good agent, one who is right for you and your family.

There are several ways to do this:

1. Open your local newspaper to the real estate section, and see who runs the biggest ads.

2. Find the "Real Estate" heading in your local yellow pages, and see who runs the biggest ads.

3. Ask friends and family who recently bought or sold a home whether they liked the person who worked with them. If they were satisfied with his or her performance, write down the contact data. (The "liked" and "satisfied" parts may seem obvious, but a California first-time buyer recently ran into trouble because the attorney she used didn't follow through the way he was supposed to. Where did she find this fellow? Her brother had used him to buy his house, and he hadn't done a good job for him either!)

4. Visit open houses and spend some time talking to the real estate agents about homes in the neighborhood. Ask these listing brokers what they think is a good definition of a buyer's agent. Ask them what kind of agent they'd want their own children to use.

5. Call your local board of Realtors and ask for the names of the agents who sold the most property last year. Usually, the local boards give out awards based on the dollar volume of sales and the number of transactions.

The point is, there are plenty of ways to get together a short list of names of brokers. The next step is to interview these brokers. Feel free to ask the brokers or agents questions that will allow you to get to know them better. Remember, you'll be hiring an agent for an important job—to help you find a home. Make sure he or she is qualified by conducting a kind of job interview. Feel free to ask the broker for a resume. (Some may not have a formal resume prepared. If not, then ask them about their past work experiences.) Find out how long he or she has been a real estate broker or agent, and whether all of that time was spent in your area.

The worksheet on page 159 will help you remember what to ask brokers and how to compare various brokers side-by-side. Beyond these items and concerns, there's always a "chemistry" factor, which can't be quantified in black and white. You'll know when the chemistry is right.

It's a good idea to ask a broker for a few recent references you can call. Make sure they're current. Try to find someone who is a first-time buyer and is in the process of working with the broker. Ask your broker for the name of a first-time buyer who closed on his or her home within the past few months. When you call the reference, ask how it was to work with the broker day in, day out. Working with a real estate broker or agent is a little like setting up a temporary partnership. You'll get to know each other *very* well in the short period of time you work together, and you want the experience to be pleasant. (See Emotional/Family Issue 1 for more details on personality clashes.)

When Should You Hire a Broker?   The time to hire a broker is when you're really ready to buy a home. The timing is important. After you've contacted several brokers and decided which one you're going to use, you can expect a good broker to be all over you like a bad haircut. The broker will want to get you up and running as an official home buyer by showing you homes that are for sale. When you first start working with an agent, all this attention can feel like pressure to quickly identify, negotiate for, and purchase the home of your dreams. That pressure is a killer for many first-time home buyers who are at a very early stage in the process. It can extinguish your interest in the search, and the time you spend looking for a home will then seem to drag rather than fly.

Before you officially "hire" your broker, make sure you've interviewed several and have had some informal chats with seller's brokers hosting open houses. Wait until you feel comfortable with many of the issues we've discussed so far in this book. You're not going to be ready to work with a broker until you feel confident that your finances and credit are in order, that you've saved enough for your down payment, and that you know deep in your heart that you're ready to make the sacrifices required to achieve your dream of home-ownership.

Here are some questions to ask real estate agents you might like to work with. See Emotional/Family Issue 1 on page 160 for ideas on other questions to ask.

Item/Concern	Broker 1	Broker 2
Years in real estate business		
Years with present firm		
Homes sold last year ($ volume)		
Homes sold last year (number of transactions)		
Price range of homes sold		
Clients		
First-timers (%)		
Move-up (%)		
Sellers (%)		
Are you an exclusive buyer's broker?		
Do you charge an up-front fee?		
What are the primary neighborhoods or communities you work in?		
Are you a smoker or non-smoker?		

No one can tell you when it's the right time to hire a broker. A comfortable, breezy beginning with your broker can quickly become a whirlwind of activity. If you start to feel like you're suffocating under all this new information and pressure, take a step back. Call your broker or agent and tell him or her that you'd like to take things a little more slowly. You're well within your rights to slow down or even to stop the process all together. No one—not the broker, your spouse or partner, your friends, or your parents—can force you to buy a home before you're ready. How will you know when you're ready? You won't feel as though you're fighting a tidal wave, and you'll begin to enjoy the process more.

EMOTIONAL/FAMILY ISSUES

Personality Clashes

Finding the right real estate broker is a little like going on a blind date. Your friends give you some phone numbers and you start calling around to find someone you like. You may even try one of the mini dates that have become fashionable. Before committing to one individual, you may schedule a couple of coffee meetings at which you discuss your needs and wants and what the agent or broker may be able to do for you.

Like a blind date, your first encounter with a real estate agent may end with some sort of personal connection or with nothing at all. Sensing a personal connection is good; it means that you've found in this individual someone you feel you can trust. But don't get discouraged if that spark is missing. You may simply need more time and another meeting to decide whether you want to spend the next several months working in close proximity with this person or would be better off working with someone else.

The failure rate for real estate relationships is probably a lot lower than for romantic alliances, but the personality clashes can be just as traumatic. Buying a home is one of the most emotion-filled things you'll do in life, and when emotions are involved, even the smallest problem can flare up into a major confrontation. The relationship between a buyer and broker depends a lot on chemistry. And, although real estate agents may be reluctant to admit it, there are times when brokers and their clients just don't get along.

Brokers say the best way to prevent problems is to thoroughly interview several brokers before agreeing to work with one. Get to know each broker or agent. Ask him or her personal questions. What are his or her likes and dislikes? Is the agent organized or disorganized, a smoker or a nonsmoker, an early bird or someone who is habitually late? Is the agent the type of person who is constantly losing keys or knows where everything is all the time? Is he or she flexible or rigid?

Sometimes, it's helpful to work with a person whose personal life mirror your own. If, for example, yours is a young family with small children, it may help to work with someone who either has small children now or whose children are a bit older than your own. Or, if you're a single woman looking for a particular kind of condominium, a single female broker may identify more closely with some of your concerns about safety.

It's helpful when buyers and brokers can establish a common ground, but experts say a good broker is a professional who should be able to help anyone find the right home. "I don't think it's necessarily true that older buyers work better with older brokers, or that a buyer with children will do better with a broker with children. A good broker doesn't have to exactly mirror his clients' lives," says Jim, a broker in Chicago.

Often, if a personality clash is going to happen at all, it will begin at the get-go, brokers say. And if the clash goes unchecked, it can escalate into what one broker calls a "living hell." If you find yourself in this situation, contact the managing broker of the real estate firm that employs your agent and ask for a three-way meeting. With the managing broker, you, and your broker or agent present, you can air grievances in a controlled setting. If there is no way of reaching a compromise, many managing brokers will simply reassign a buyer (or a seller, for that matter) to another agent in the firm. As a buyer, however, you have the right to terminate your relationship with the broker and the firm.

If the buyer's broker you choose to work with asks you to sign an exclusivity agreement, make sure it provides for an easy and cost-free termination if things don't work out. The possibility of a personality clash so severe that you'd want to sever your buyer's broker agreement is, I think, one reason why home buyers should not pay nonrefundable up-front exclusivity agreement fees. Regardless of whether you're going to pay a fee, make sure your contract gives you, in writing, the ability to sever your buyer's brokerage agreement at any time.

10 STEP TIP

EMOTIONAL/
FAMILY ISSUE
2

Should Your Family Help You Choose Your Broker?

Some experts believe that every member of a family should have an equal voice in making major decisions. That method may work when deciding where to go for dinner on Sunday night, but it doesn't work so well when deciding which real estate agent to use when looking for a home.

Ultimately, you and your spouse or partner should decide which broker or agent will guide your search for a new residence. Your children, unhampered by certain pressures, may have valuable insights to share. Introduce your children to prospective brokers, particularly if they will be accompanying you occasionally to showings. Watch how the broker reacts to your children (who, we will assume for the sake of discussion, are impeccably behaved). Does he or she treat them with respect or ignore them completely? If you have aging parents who will be living with you, it may help to have them meet your prospective broker as well. Again, watch how the broker treats your relatives and responds to their input.

Be aware that your children or relatives may have hidden biases against the process, and that these might surface as reasons why you shouldn't use a particular agent. If your children fear a move, and worry that they won't like their new home, they may resent anyone who is facilitating that change. After everyone has had a chance to meet a prospective agent, discuss their reactions to him or her. Then, after all the votes are in, you and your spouse or partner should decide which broker you feel will work best for you and your family.

Comparing Homes, Costs, and Finances

STEP
8

In the real estate industry, the concept of value is amorphous. The value of a house (or condo, or co-op, or townhouse) fluctuates yearly—sometimes monthly, or even weekly—based on ever-changing market conditions, the condition of the home, and the costs associated with owning it. For that reason, it's difficult to answer the question, "How much is it worth?" There is one certainty, however. The answer to true value does not lie in how much the seller wants for his or her home (though that is what the seller and the listing broker want you to believe). In fact, the listing price of a home sometimes has nothing to do with its market value.

Figuring out how much a home is actually worth is a tricky process. You'll have to do your homework, pull out your calculator, and spend some time learning to recognize certain "value markers." Once you've figured out what a property is worth relative to others that are similar in the area, you can begin to compare various homes.

FINANCIAL ISSUES

The Costs of Homeownership

As we discussed in Step 2, How Much House Can I Afford?, a variety of issues come into play when calculating how much you can spend on a home. How much you earn, and the sum total of your cash on hand and your liquid investments are important. But there are other ongoing considerations that may affect the price you can afford to

FINANCIAL
ISSUE
1

163

pay for your home. They include property taxes, home maintenance, and assessments.

Property Taxes. You've probably heard this dinosaur of a one-liner: The only two things you can count on are death and taxes. As a homeowner, you'll be paying property taxes until you sell your property. If you don't pay your taxes, your property will be sold at auction to satisfy your tax bill.

Let's start at the top. Most local governments tax property owners on the current market value of property to help pay for basic services, such as police and fire protection, municipal or county government salaries and expenses, and the cost of keeping local schools open.

The property tax you will pay is based on a rate determined by the county tax collector and on what the county says your home is worth. The tax collector bases the rate on several factors, including how much it will cost to run the local government, what percentage of that budget must come from property owners, and how many property owners there are. Once the tax collector sets the rate, it is usually the same for every residential property owner in the municipality. The reasons taxes vary from city to city, and even from neighborhood to neighborhood, include the imposition of each municipality's fees and the varying value of each individual piece of property.

As a property owner, you can expect to pay property taxes that range from less than 1 percent to 3 percent of your property's assessed market value. If your property is estimated to be worth $100,000 and the tax rate is 2 percent, you'll pay $2,000 in property taxes:

$100,000 (market value) $\times$ .02 (tax rate) = $2,000 (tax bill)

In some parts of the country, citizens have voted for property tax relief, which essentially has capped property taxes at a fixed point. In California, for example, Proposition 13 capped property taxes at 1 percent of the purchase price of the home. So, if you were to pay $300,000 for a home in Oakland, California, this year, your annual property taxes would be $3,000. No matter how long you own your home, you'll pay $3,000. If you sell your home in ten years for $400,000, your buyer will pay $4,000 in property taxes.

Compare California's Proposition 13 with Illinois's property tax system. The average Cook County, Illinois resident pays in real estate property taxes approximately 2 percent of the purchase price of a home. On a $300,000 house, an Illinois resident would pay approximately

$6,000 in real estate property taxes. (Ask your broker or real estate attorney for the going real estate tax rates in your area.)

Property taxes are calculated differently, depending on whether you live in a single-family house, a condominium (including town-house developments), or a co-op. For a single-family home, you pay taxes on the entire property.

When you purchase a condominium, however, you are responsible for paying property taxes not only on your condo unit, but on your proportionate share of the common elements—the garage, backyard, lobby, and hallways. The condominium property is viewed as a single entity. In many instances, once the value of the property is assigned, individual tax bills are created using the formula of ownership that the original developer created and wrote into the condominium declaration. If you own 4.5 percent of a condominium complex estimated to be worth $1 million, your condo is estimated to be worth $45,000. If you are in a state where you pay approximately 2 percent of the value in taxes, you'll be writing a $900 check for your taxes.

Co-op properties are taxed in a similar way. As you will recall from previous Steps, when you purchase a co-op, you're actually purchasing shares in a corporation that owns your building. You pay rent each month in the form of an assessment. The co-op corporation is taxed on the total value of the property, and each owner pays his or her proportion of the tax, measured on the basis of the number of shares he or she owns. If your co-op building is worth $10 million and the current property tax rate is 2 percent of the market value of the building, your co-op's tax bill would be $200,000. If your shares equal 2.5 percent of the co-op building, your taxes would be approximately $5,000.

$$\$10,000,000 \text{ (property value)} \times .02 \text{ (state tax rate)} = \$200,000$$

$$\$200,000 \text{ (co-op tax bill)} \times .025 \text{ (your ownership share)} = \$5,000 \text{ (your tax bill)}$$

In a co-op, you pay $1/12$ of your share of the tax bill each month as part of your assessment. (It's a co-op's equivalent of the real estate property tax escrow that lenders often require of home buyers.) In our example, approximately $417 of your monthly assessment would go toward your share of the co-op property tax bill:

$$\frac{\$5,000 \text{ (your tax bill)}}{12 \text{ months}} = \$416.67 \text{ (monthly installment of property taxes)}$$

165

Because the co-op is taxed as a single corporate entity, you will not receive a separate real estate property tax bill from your local assessor.

> Some first-time buyers don't understand that *paying your property taxes on time is as important as paying your mortgage on time.* If you don't pay your property taxes, your home will be sold at auction to satisfy the debt on your property taxes. This is so important, I'm going to say it again: *Paying your property taxes isn't an option. If you don't pay your taxes on time, your property could be sold at auction.*

Because property taxes are an integral part of homeownership, you must consider them when comparing the costs of owning and maintaining different homes. If two homes are comparable but one has an annual property tax bill of $3,500 and the other has a tax bill of $2,500, you may be willing to pay more for the home with the lower tax bill. Over time, almost all tax bills rise, but lower ones tend to rise more slowly.

It's also important to realize that each city and county charges its residents a different amount for the specialized local services it provides. For example, one city may require its residents to recycle and charge all residents a fee for that service. Or, a local government may provide a leaf, tree, and grass clippings recycling service and offer free compost and mulch to residents. When you analyze your estimated property taxes, be sure to research the services you're getting for that money. If you're in a top school district, you may pay higher real estate taxes than residents in lower-quality school districts. The bottom line is: Consider the size of a property's real estate taxes, but remember that sometimes paying a little more gets you a lot more service.

Annual Maintenance Costs.   Along with property taxes, the costs of maintaining a home are one of your most important considerations when you're determining a correct valuation for a piece of property. In other words, the more expensive a home is to maintain, the less money you should pay for it. For example, say you're considering two homes, one with a slate roof that will last for 100 years and one with an asphalt shingle roof that will need replacing in less than 7 years. Assuming everything else is the same, which house would you choose to buy? All things are never quite equal in real estate, but you might choose the slate-roof house, knowing that, at most, you'll have to pay $1,000 or so over the years to repair it, but you won't have to pump in the $5,000 to $10,000 you would need for a new roof for the other house.

When you look at homes, consider whether they are high-maintenance or low-maintenance. Obviously, a high-maintenance home will be more costly to own. As you're touring homes, ask yourself the following questions:

1. *What is the age of the property?* Very old homes that haven't been well taken care of can be expensive to own and maintain. In newer homes (10 to 50 years old), maintenance may be easier, especially if some ongoing upkeep has been done. It may seem that brand-new homes would have the fewest maintenance problems, but this isn't always the case. Some developers use cheap appliances or mechanical systems that will need replacement within a short time.

2. *How old are the mechanicals and are they in good shape?* The mechanical systems of a house include the water heater, furnace, and sump pump, and the air conditioning/heat, plumbing, and electrical systems. If the boiler is 40 years old or older, chances are it will last a while with proper cleaning and servicing. If you have a new furnace, it may not last much beyond the time covered by its warranty, but it might be fine for 5 or 10 years. Check out the plumbing. Lead pipes could mean you'll have to install a water purification system. Sump pumps can break. And if there are trees on the property, their roots may have clogged the sewer pipes. Has anything been replaced recently?

3. *Can you see any potential structural defects or problems?* Though you're not trained as a professional home inspector, you *can* and *should* look for obvious flaws: water stains on ceilings or walls; dampness or standing water in the basement; rat droppings or piles of sawdust that might be evidence of a pest problem; roof shingles that appear to be peeling off the roof or are bumpy or wavy; several layers of roof shingles applied on top of each other—a clue that when you need a new roof, you might have to do a "tear off" (stripping the entire roof off, down to the boards, which is a much more costly replacement); large cracks (more than ⅛ inch wide) in the foundation walls; or walls and door frames that don't meet in 90-degree angles. Any of these problems could be costly to repair or resolve.

4. *What kind of interior and exterior finishes does the home have?* If the exterior is brick or vinyl siding, it will need only the most

167

moderate maintenance, including the occasional tuckpointing or washing. If, however, the house has wood siding or wood trim, you'll need to paint it every few years. Wood floors may need to be waxed every year to maintain their finish. Carpet will need to be cleaned occasionally.

5. *What kind of landscaping does the home have?* A large yard with many trees could mean several hours of care each weekend.

6. *Are there any potential environmental problems on the property or in the neighborhood?* Ask the seller and the broker these important questions: Is there lead paint in the house? Is the plumbing of an age where it might possibly have been soldered together with lead (causing a potential lead problem with the water)? Is an underground storage tank buried on the property? Is the area known to have a radon problem? How close is the nearest municipal dump, commercial area, or gas station? Do high-powered electric tension wires cross through the area? (Some of these questions don't have anything to do with whether your home is high-maintenance or low-maintenance, but they raise issues that could cause you a lot of problems as a homeowner and future home seller.)

Some folks enjoy spending hours taking care of their gardens. Others prefer to spend the time doing other things. Knowing whether you're a person who prefers a high-maintenance or low-maintenance home is key to enjoying your new home. Condos and co-ops are relatively low-maintenance. Often, with a condo building, there isn't any outdoor space to worry about; the condo or co-op association takes care of the exterior maintenance. Even some new townhouse developments are "maintenance-free": the association handles landscaping and the repair and replacement of common-area items and exterior areas, such as the roof. Living in a maintenance-free community may be easier, but it may not be cheaper than living in a single-family home because the fee for these services is paid as part of your monthly assessment. Read on for more details.

Assessments. For condo or co-op dwellers, a monthly or annual assessment is a fact of life. As we discussed earlier, an assessment is your share of the cost of maintaining and operating the common elements of a condominium or co-op building or development. The assessments are usually calculated according to your percentage share of ownership. For example, if you own 5 percent of your townhouse or condominium or co-op development, your assessment should be 5 percent of the cost of owning and operating the property.

But when you buy a home that comes with an assessment, the assessment changes the home's value. A three-bedroom, two-bath condominium that carries a $500 monthly assessment should carry a lower price tag than a same-size condominium that has only a $200 monthly assessment.

That's how lenders think through affordability. If you can afford to spend a total of $1,000 per month on the mortgage and property taxes for a single-family home, it stands to reason that, if you decide instead to buy a condo with a $200 monthly assessment, you'll be able to spend only $800 on your mortgage.

$1,000 (total available for monthly mortgage/
　　　　property tax payment)
　−200 (assessment)
$　800 (net available for monthly mortgage payment)

As we've already discussed, lenders will include the amount of your monthly assessment when calculating your debt-to-income ratio. The assessment is a monthly obligation you must meet. *The net effect is to reduce the amount you can spend on a home.*

If you don't pay your assessment, condo and co-op associations generally have the right to levy late payment fees, sue you for back assessments, or foreclose on your home.

FINANCIAL
ISSUE
2

Location, Location, Location

As we've already discussed, where a home is located (within a city, within a neighborhood, on a particular street, within a single building) is crucial to determining its value. When you begin to compare homes, it's important to factor location into your house valuation formula.

- *Single-family house.* First, think about where the house is located in relation to the entire neighborhood. Are shops and various

169

services within walking distance? Is the house close to major forms of transportation and to the schools your children will be attending? Is it too close to any of these amenities? Many families want to be within a few blocks of the local public school, but they prefer not to have their backyards adjacent to the school playground. Next, think about where the house is located on its block. Is it on a corner, or on the interior row? Is it next to a high-rise building or a three- or six-flat building? Are there many homes just like it on the block? Does the block have a nice residential feel or is it mixed residential–commercial?

- *Townhouse.* If you're considering a townhouse, start by asking yourself about the townhouse's location in relation to shopping and service retailers, such as a dry cleaner. If the townhouse is located within a subdivision, compare its location with the premium location within that subdivision. For example, is it better to be located on the perimeter, or is an interior location better? Are end units more prized, or are middle units preferred? Are you close to the entrance of the subdivision, or do you have to drive several blocks to get there? Do you have to walk far to the garbage drop-off or mail pick-up spot?

- *Condominium or Co-op.* The location questions for a townhouse apply here as well. If your condo or co-op is located in a high-rise building you also need to consider where the unit is located in the building. If one side of the building has a fabulous view and another faces a windowless brick wall, you can bet that units with the full view will be more prized than units with a peek-around or no view. Which is more important to you, the lower cost or the better view? If there are two views—say, a water view vs. an urban view, an east view (sunrise) vs. a west view (sunset), or a high-floor vs. a low-floor perspective—remember that a unit with the best view in a building will generally appreciate faster than a unit with only a so-so view, even if the so-so has more amenities.

As you begin to compare different houses, condos, co-ops, or townhouses, continue to ask yourself: What is the premier location for this neighborhood, subdivision, or building, and how do the homes I'm seeing compare with it?

Market Forces

When comparing one home to another, it's important to know what kind of market forces are shaping their value. When real estate agents and brokers talk about "markets," they mean how quickly real estate is being bought and sold. There are three kinds of markets:

FINANCIAL
ISSUE
3

1. *Buyer's market.* A buyer's market occurs when there are too many homes for sale and too few qualified buyers to purchase them. In terms of supply and demand, a buyer's market means there is too much supply and too little demand. Prices tend to come down because homes are taking a long time to sell. The market favors the buyer.

2. *Seller's market.* In this type of market, there are too few homes and too many qualified buyers who want them. In other words, demand exceeds supply. Prices tend to go up, and homes tend to sell quickly. The market favors the seller. Real estate agents like this kind of market because properties will turn over very quickly.

3. *Neutral or balanced market.* In a neutral or balanced market, the numbers of homes for sale and home buyers to purchase them are about equal. Homes sell steadily, and for reasonable prices.

As you begin to compare properties in different neighborhoods, it's important to know what kind of market forces exist in each neighborhood, because they will affect the value of the properties. For example, if you like a home and it is in a seller's market, you may offer more for the home than you would if it had been in a buyer's market. Conversely, if the home is in a buyer's market, you may offer less.

How do you know which market you're in? One of the ways to find out is to ask your broker how quickly homes are being sold in your neighborhood. If homes sell in less than 45 days, you're probably in a seller's market. If homes take longer than 4 to 6 months to sell, you're probably in a buyer's market. If you see a lot of "For Sale" signs posted in your neighborhood and homes appear to be taking a long time to sell, you may be in a buyer's market. Most multiple-listing services (MLSs) keep track of how long it takes for homes to sell. Ask your broker about the average number of days a home is listed.

Although bidding wars are rare, they do occur. They are more common in seller's markets, where buyers can get into a tizzy trying to snap up homes before someone else gets to them. Though sellers love a bidding war, they are almost always bad news for home buyers. The increased competition means you'll pay more than you want to—or more than you should—for a home. Also, there is increased stress about getting the deal done. If you find yourself in a bidding war, consider stepping out of the deal and allowing the other home buyer to proceed. If you lose that home, there will always be another. But if you get that home and pay too much for it, you may have a problem on your hands when the time comes to sell it, especially if you plan to stay only a short period of time.

FINANCIAL
ISSUE
4

The Costs of Renovation

When determining the value of a home, it's important to consider its actual condition versus the condition in which you'd like it to be. For example, a house that has been freshly painted inside and out, and has new carpeting, is going to sell for more money than a similar house with peeling paint and wallpaper, and worn-out carpeting. Conversely, if you are looking at two similar homes and one needs a lot of renovation to bring it up to the neighborhood standard, you should pay less for that home than for one that meets or exceeds the neighborhood standard.

How much less? Well, there's the rub. There are different ways to estimate how much more or less to offer for a home that needs work. One of the best ways is to first determine how much the home would be worth if it met the neighborhood standard. Then, add up the cost of doing the needed repair or renovation. Finally, subtract the cost of the repairs from the maximum amount you're willing to pay for the home.

As an example, let's say there are two houses for sale in the same neighborhood. Both have three bedrooms, two baths, an attached garage, and a nice garden. One is in perfect, move-in condition. The other has 20-year old kitchen appliances, worn-out carpeting, and peeling wallpaper in the upstairs bathroom. How do you value these homes based on their condition?

Let's assume that the value of the home in mint condition is $100,000 and that, if the fixer-upper were in mint condition, it might also sell for $100,000. To get it in that shape, you'd have to spend

$2,000 on new carpeting, $500 to repaper the bathroom, and another $2,500 to replace the stove, oven, dishwasher, and refrigerator.

> $100,000 (house in mint condition)
> − 5,000 (upgrades)
> $ 95,000 (maximum price you should pay)

Pricing Repairs and Renovations. Unless you're a contractor with extensive experience in repairing or renovating homes, you probably won't know exactly what it will cost to get something done. And there may be hidden costs beneath the moldy-looking wallpaper that you're not aware of. Your broker may be able to suggest a ball-park estimate of how much the repairs will cost. But beware if he or she gives you an "off-the-top-of-my-head" amount. If your bid will be based on the renovation information, get an estimate from a reliable source. You can call various construction companies and find out how much it would be to, say, renovate a kitchen. Or, call or visit a local home improvement store, and ask how much certain items cost. There is a myriad of choices, but a salesperson at a Home Depot or Builders Square might be able to tell you that replacing your front door will cost you anywhere from $200 to $1,000, depending on the door choice and the cost of installation.

> If you or your spouse can do repairs and renovations on your own, you will save cash in the long run. But when comparing homes for their costs, get an estimate from a professional contractor. Don't try to accurately estimate the costs on your own.

FINANCIAL
ISSUE
5

The Square-Foot Approach

Real estate brokers often calculate the number of square feet within a house to help them assess its value. A square foot is a two-dimensional square measuring one foot on each side. Brokers usually measure a home by its inside (room) dimensions. (Developers usually measure the exterior of the home.) Here's how real estate brokers determine size. Let's say you're looking at a house that has a living room that's 14' × 18', a dining room that's 16' × 12', a kitchen that's 12' × 12', and three bedrooms, measuring 15' × 18', 12' ×

12′, and 10′ × 10′. In addition, the house has an entry hallway, measuring 6′ × 9′, and two bathrooms, measuring 5′ × 9′ and 10′ × 9′. How many square feet are in this home? To find out, multiply each room's dimensions, then add up the number of square feet:

Room	Dimensions (Feet)	Area (Square Feet)
Living room	14′ × 18′	252
Dining room	16′ × 12′	192
Kitchen	12′ × 12′	144
Bedroom 1	15′ × 18′	270
Bedroom 2	12′ × 12′	144
Bedroom 3	10′ × 10′	100
Entry hallway	6′ × 9′	54
Bathroom 1	5′ × 9′	45
Bathroom 2	10′ × 9′	90
Total		1,291 square feet

Together, all of the rooms in this house have a total of 1,291 square feet, which we'll round up to 1,300. Some space in a hallway and in closets is lost space, and basements are not usually calculated into square footage totals even if they're finished. If we add in another 100 square feet to cover the extra space, there is a total of 1,400 square feet in this house.

After you've calculated how many square feet are in the home, it's time to figure out how much per square foot the owner is asking you to pay. The math is fairly straightforward. Simply divide the listing price of the home by the number of square feet it contains. If the house is listed for $100,000, divide that number by 1,400 square feet to come up with a price per square foot (psf):

$$\frac{\$100,000 \text{ (list price)}}{1,400 \text{ (square feet)}} = \$71.43 \text{ psf}$$

Most listing sheets give the number of square feet in a house or the land on which it sits. For example, an acre of land is equal to 43,560 square feet. If one acre of land is selling for $50,000, that land is worth about $1.15 per square foot. When using square feet to compare the cost of each home, compare the size of the home separately from the size of the property. That's because the price of land differs from neighborhood to neighborhood. Also when calculating the price per square foot, be sure to measure accurately. If you miss a room, or if the listing broker gives you an incorrect number, it could throw off your comparisons.

The price per square foot is an excellent baseline to use when comparing *similar* homes. It is less useful if one of the homes you like has been completely renovated and the other needs a significant amount of work. Still, figuring out the price per square foot should give you a range of value you can work with.

FINANCIAL
ISSUE
6

Household Amenities

No two homes are exactly alike. Even if you look at two houses built at the same time in a single subdivision, or two condominiums in the same building, each will have been maintained to a different standard by its owner. And even if the level of maintenance is the same, the different amenities or decorating that may have been added to the home over the years will affect the value. For example, if a single-family house has an attached garage, it will certainly be worth more than the same style of house with a detached garage, or a covered carport, or no parking space at all. A house with a two- or three-car attached garage will be more valuable than a house with an attached one-car garage. Depending on where you live in the United States, an in-ground swimming pool can be an asset or an albatross. In a community where the four-bedroom home is standard, a three- or five-bedroom home can be a tough sell. Similarly, a house with a brand-new kitchen/family room addition may be overpriced for a community where those amenities aren't coveted by a majority of the residents.

When comparing homes, it's important to look objectively at a home's amenities and to think about the price tag homeowners in your community put on these amenities. Once you get an idea of what these amenities are worth (their value usually has nothing to do with how much they cost to install), you can do some addition and subtraction based on the number of amenities a prospective home has or doesn't have.

For example, if most of the single-family homes in your community have a wood-burning fireplace and the home you're looking at doesn't, you may want to subtract $1,000 (or $2,500, or whatever amount your agent tells you a fireplace is worth to a home's value in your neighborhood) from the maximum amount you're willing to pay for the home. If the home you like has an in-ground swimming pool, perhaps you'll add $5,000 (or whatever that amenity is worth in that community) to the price you're willing to pay.

If you're not sure how to value an amenity, ask your real estate broker. He or she should be able to guide you as to its worth relative to the community.

FINANCIAL ISSUE 7

The Value of a Home's Amenities

Now that you've looked at comps, the cost of living in a home, the neighborhood, location, and square footage, and the amenities of a property, it's time to put all your data together and come up with a total value for the home. Use the worksheet on pages 177–178 to help you itemize how much amenities contribute to a home's value. Characteristics that detract from a home's overall value should be entered in parentheses, indicating their negative effect.

10 STEP TIP

Although it may seem unnatural at first, after a while you'll begin to think about a home as being the sum of its parts. It's a good idea to look closely at all the pieces you'll be buying, but don't forget that this is one whole piece of property. At the end of the day, you're not going to be able to do a cost analysis of every individual piece. No one is going to buy one fireplace or one swimming pool. You're looking to buy a *home*. A prospective home may indeed have all of the desired parts, but if they don't work together, you may be better off buying a home that has a sense of unity rather than one that offers an extra half-bath.

FINANCIAL ISSUE 8

Maximizing Your Investment

It's difficult to know where home prices will go in a given year. Unless you're in a highly overvalued market (one that resembles southern California and the Northeast during the early 1990s), your area will likely continue to appreciate. But real estate is really a local issue, and it's important to remember that, even in the best of times, there will be homes that fail to appreciate in value and may even depreciate.

What can you do to protect your investment? Sometimes nothing and sometimes a lot. The following suggestions may enhance your ability to purchase a home that will continue to go up in value:

1. *Buy in the best neighborhood you can afford.* Buying in the most desirable neighborhoods gives you a leg up during recessions, when less

Item	Value (+/−)

Cost of Living

Property taxes   _____

Maintenance   _____

Assessments   _____

Other   _____

Location

Within neighborhood   _____

On block   _____

Within subdivision   _____

Within building   _____

View   _____

Other   _____

Market Forces

Buyer's market   _____

Seller's market   _____

Neutral market   _____

Other   _____

Condition Issues

Move-in condition   _____

Fixer-upper   _____

Gut job   _____

Other   _____

Square Footage

Total for dwelling   _____

Total for land area   _____

Item	Value (+/−)
Amenities	
Garage	_____
Garden	_____
Swimming pool	_____
Tennis court	_____
Size of lot	_____
Extra bedroom(s)	_____
Extra bathroom(s)	_____
Additional room(s)	_____
Ceiling height	_____
Basement finished	_____
Basement unfinished	_____
Sunroom/Den/Library	_____
Fireplace(s) (gas or wood-burning)	_____
Stained glass window(s)/door(s)	_____
Appliances (new, used, or broken)	_____
Central air conditioning	_____
Brick, vinyl or aluminum siding, or stucco	_____
Slate roof	_____
High-efficiency storm windows	_____
View (desirable, so-so, or none)	_____
Exposure (north, south, east, west)	_____
Single-story, two-story or higher, or split level	_____
Other	_____

popular neighborhoods may decline in value. Usually, the best neighborhoods surround the best school districts. They also offer a wide variety of shopping, services, and transportation options. You may also be close to recreational activities, such as a lakefront, park district, or local swimming club.

If you have to choose between buying a bigger home in a less desirable neighborhood or buying a smaller home in a better neighborhood, it's a choice worth weighing carefully. Homes located in better neighborhoods appreciate at a greater rate than homes in just-OK neighborhoods. But a lot will depend on what you find and how much you can afford to spend.

2. *Buy a fixer-upper.* One of the best ways to ensure that your home will appreciate or at least maintain its present value is to purchase a home that isn't up to the neighborhood standard in terms of upkeep and amenities. For example, if every home on the block offers a new eat-in kitchen and the house you're considering doesn't, it may be an opportunity for you to buy the home at a reasonable price, and, over the years, when you have additional cash, put in that new kitchen. Generally, homeowners who make such improvements get all of their money out of the improvement and more. Plus, they get the use of their renovations.

3. *Buy a home with expansion possibilities.* If you can't afford a bigger home in the best neighborhood, consider buying a smaller home that offers room for expansion. You may be able to afford a small home on a big lot, and you can add onto it when you have the money. Again, there are many smaller gems (or diamonds in the rough) that offer a lot of potential.

4. *Don't buy (or build) a white elephant.* Here's how most homes tend to appreciate. Someone on the block thinks about selling and decides to try and push the price ceiling for homes in the neighborhood up a notch or two. So the seller lists the property for a bit more than the sales price of the most recently sold property. Once the home sells, it's usually at the peak of its value. It won't appreciate further until all the other homes on the block start selling for amounts higher than its sales price.

In places like Los Angeles, San Francisco, and New York, homes topped out in price during 1988 and 1989. If you bought then, you bought at the peak. During the recession of the early 1990s, those homes fell in value by a third or even a half. Home values have begun to come back, but most are gaining at a much slower rate.

179

Homeowners who bought in the late 1980s must wait for other homes in their neighborhood to start selling for more than they paid. Only then will they see any appreciation.

When it comes time to buy a home, do your homework. Find out how much homes similar to the one you're considering sold for in the past. Try to avoid paying more for your home than any home in the area has ever sold for. The homes may continue to appreciate, so if you pay the most you might still make money. But generally, keep this rule of thumb in mind: Never buy the most expensive home on the block.

That goes for building a new home as well. Never build the most expensive home on your block. If you're buying in a subdivision, don't put in a marble jacuzzi if no one else has it. Don't build a five-bedroom home if four-bedrooms are standard. No one wants to be stuck with a white elephant.

5. *Before you buy a home, think about how easy or difficult it will be to sell it.* Before you sign on the dotted line, reexamine all the details about your future home. Think about its location, relative to the neighborhood and block. Think about why you like the home. Think about what you don't like and what others may not like. Consider where are the nearest environmental concerns, like municipal dumps, existing and past gas stations, possible sources of water contamination. Make sure a new recycling center isn't going in behind you, that your street isn't going to be widened, and that your property isn't about to be condemned for a new highway exit ramp. These are possibilities that can make your home fall in value. Even if they don't actually bring harm to you or the property, they can cause your home to depreciate in value. Future home buyers have to be alert to noticing potential dangers (such as nearby electromagnetic power towers). Also, don't forget that perceived dangers can be as damaging to a home's value as real ones.

EMOTIONAL/FAMILY ISSUES

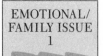

EMOTIONAL/
FAMILY ISSUE
1

Underbuying: Spending Less Than You Can

It often doesn't occur to home buyers that less can be more. However, some buyers, particularly some first-time buyers, have discovered that paying less than they can for a home has a decidedly positive effect on both their financial and emotional lives.

The concept of *underbuying* simply means that you spend less on a home than you can actually afford. As an example, let's assume you have the cash on hand and the income to support the purchase of a $150,000 home. Just because you can afford to buy it doesn't mean you should. By purchasing a less expensive home, you not only save on the mortgage payments each month (which could be a considerable savings), but you can also budget lower amounts for your PMI (private mortgage insurance) or perhaps even do away with it altogether, home insurance, and real estate property taxes. That should free up some extra cash each month and year for home improvements and maintenance.

Underbuying goes against a long-held principle in real estate, which states that you should buy the most house you can afford (some call it "overbuying"). Let's examine why real estate agents have been pushing home buyers to spend as much as or more than they actually can comfortably afford.

Real estate agents work on commission. Until the beginning of the 1990s, just about all agents, even those who worked with buyers, worked for the seller. Even though they took the buyer around, they owed their loyalty to the seller. Their first obligation was to get the seller as much money as possible, even at the expense of the home buyer's financial health. Today, home buyers have buyer's brokers to guard against overbuying. And, home buyers have become increasingly sophisticated about the home buying process. Most now realize that just because the broker may be pushing them to spend a lot of money on a home doesn't mean they have to do it.

Home buyers are being more conservative today because corporate America no longer offers its employees the same type of job security it once did. Corporations no longer keep employees around to wait out the slow periods. Instead they fire them. Since the recession of the early 1990s, many hundreds of thousands of people have lost their jobs. Economists will argue that about the same number of jobs were created just after the recession, and that in fact the United States has been creating jobs, but many Americans don't perceive it to be true. That's because new jobs are generally created in dribs and drabs while folks seem to get fired in a big lump.

The bottom line is: Perception is often more powerful than reality. If you don't think you're going to be able to keep your job, move up, and prosper, don't buy as big a home as you might in other circumstances.

181

Another reason many home buyers choose to underbuy these days is that, in most places, homes no longer appreciate at the same pace they did during the 1970s and 1980s. In those decades, double-digit appreciation wasn't unheard of—in fact, it was the norm. With that kind of scenario, it made sense to buy more home than one could realistically afford. In some parts of the country (particularly Los Angeles and the Northeast), home buyers were doubling their investment every two to three years. Today, except in a few parts of the country, that kind of appreciation doesn't exist, and stretching one's pocketbook makes less sense.

Underbuying is a conservative way of purchasing property, but it can ease your mind, which counts for a lot. It also gives you an opportunity to do two things: (1) take the additional cash you would have spent paying down a bigger mortgage each month and put it into stocks, savings, or a college fund; or (2) use the overage to pay down your mortgage each month, effectively saving thousands of dollars in interest. (See Step 9, Financing Your New Home, for more details.)

EMOTIONAL/
FAMILY ISSUE
2

Lifestyle vs. Investment

One of the nice things about the 1990s is that folks have rediscovered a basic fact about real estate: It's not always about making money. When you buy a home, you're not just buying an investment. A house isn't like a stack of perfect, never-opened baseball cards, or a flawless diamond, or even a sheaf of stocks sitting in a safe deposit box. It's about life and living and about feeling that you have a safe haven. When you shop for a home, buy one that makes you feel comfortable and safe, a place where you and your family will be happy. If the house you buy doesn't appreciate as much as a house in a "hot" neighborhood, that's OK. If you buy in an established neighborhood, rather than one where you'll be a pioneer breaking ground in an area that won't heat up for five years, you may get more enjoyment out of your purchase.

Money isn't everything. It's not nearly as important as the sense of satisfaction you'll get from knowing that your house is truly your castle and the neighborhood in which you reside makes you feel safe and secure.

Financing
Your Home

Although you may be months (or years) away from even looking for a home to buy, it's never too early to start thinking about financing your purchase. I say that because many first-time buyers (and repeat buyers, too) find that looking for the right lender and choosing the right mortgage can be an overwhelming experience.

This Step isn't meant to be the end-all guide to getting your financing. Rather, it is a short summary of some of the options you will have and the decisions you'll have to make. More complete information can be found in my book, *100 Questions Every First-Time Home Buyer Should Ask*.

As you go through this Step, if you feel that you don't quite have a grip on some of the concepts we've already discussed, such as loan-to-value ratios, you can find a more thorough explanation in Step 2, How Much House Can I Afford? Specific topics can be reviewed by tracking them down via the index.

Lenders will look at four major issues when deciding whether to loan you the cash you need to purchase a home: your job, your credit, your assets, and your liabilities.

FINANCIAL ISSUES

Prequalification vs. Preapproval

Mortgage brokers and bankers—called "lenders" in real estate jargon—can be enormously useful to home buyers. Not only do they lend the money to buy a home, but they also work with buyers well ahead of the purchase, helping them to get their credit in shape and figuring out how much they can afford to spend on a home.

In addition, lenders can either prequalify or preapprove buyers for a home purchase. If you become *prequalified* for a loan, it means that the lender has taken a look at your annual income, your assets, and your liabilities, and has crunched those numbers through a series of formulas (you'll find them in Step 2, How Much House Can I Afford?). When you're prequalified for your home loan, the lender will have told you that you can qualify for a certain amount of a mortgage. Armed with that knowledge, you can start your house hunt knowing what size loan you can afford.

Preapproval takes the prequalification process one step further. When you get preapproved for a loan, your credit has been reviewed and the lender has committed to provide you with a specific loan amount, not tied to any specific property. The only catch is that the house (or townhouse, condominium, or co-op unit) you ultimately choose must appraise at an acceptable value; that is, the lender's appraisers must certify that the home is actually worth at least what you're paying for it. You will probably pay an application fee, an appraisal fee, and a credit check fee when you apply for preapproval, but these fees vary and some lenders waive them.

According to listing brokers, the prequalification and preapproval processes turn you into a more substantial buyer because one of a seller's biggest worries—that you, the buyer, either aren't qualified to get a loan or won't get approved for a loan—is removed. Almost every home purchase/sale contract is contingent on getting financing, and, of all the components of the process, financing generally takes the longest time to get in place. A seller could lose a month or more waiting for a buyer to be qualified and approved for a home loan (though the process is much faster today than it once was). By getting prequalified or preapproved for your loan up front, even if you keep the financing contingency in the contract, the seller should feel more confident about your ability to actually purchase the home.

Preapproval is a stronger endorsement than prequalification. But if there are up-front costs that may tie you into using that lender, prequalification may be sufficient.

(For more information on shopping for a lender, see Financial Issue 8, later in this Step.)

Lending Ratios

As we discussed in Step 2, lenders will only approve a loan amount that allows you to *comfortably* meet the monthly mortgage payments, home insurance and private mortgage insurance premiums, and any assessments. To quickly review, the 28/36 ratio means that lenders will allow you to spend 28 percent of your gross monthly income (GMI) on your mortgage payment, and up to 36 percent of your GMI on your total debt payments. Some lenders will expand these ratios to 30/40 or 30/41, allowing you to spend up to 41 percent of your GMI on your total debt.

> Today's permissiveness in lending can lead to *overborrowing,* a situation similar to overbuying, which we discussed in Step 8. Sometimes, the heady feeling that accompanies finding out exactly how much loan they can carry overtakes reason, and home buyers who are normally cautious and conservative individuals find themselves running out and borrowing to their limit. Remember, just because a lender will allow you to dig yourself deep into debt doesn't mean you have to pick up the shovel. Lenders are counting on your being upwardly mobile and well able to afford the loan in the future. That may be the case, but you don't want to spend the first 10 years of your loan term in unnecessary misery.
>
> Here's my suggestion: Consider spending only 25 percent of your gross monthly income on your mortgage, and no more than 30 percent on your total debt. Although not significantly less than the 28/36 ratio normally suggested by lenders, the lower ratio might be the difference that allows you a few luxuries (like decorating your new home, or ordering in dinner when your kitchen stuff is still in packing boxes).

Although 28 percent of your gross monthly income doesn't sound like a lot, remember that this cut is from your *gross* income, not your *take-home pay.* The difference, once you deduct taxes, can be staggering. For example, if your gross monthly income is $3,000 (which translates into a $36,000 annual salary), 28 percent is $840 per month, all of which can be put toward a mortgage payment. Thirty-six percent, or $1,080, can be put toward your total debt service. If you don't have any other debt, the entire amount can go toward a mortgage, property taxes, and insurance premiums. If $1,080 doesn't sound like a big chunk of $3,000, remember that, with a gross salary of $36,000, you may be in the 28 percent tax bracket. That means you're only taking home about $28,000, or $2,400 a month. Suddenly, that $1,080 jumps up to 40 percent of your take-home pay. Before you commit to spending 40 percent of your take-home pay on a mortgage and debt service, be sure to think about whether that kind of commitment will leave you feeling pinched.

FINANCIAL
ISSUE
3

Property Tax, Hazard Insurance Escrows, and Private Mortgage Insurance

Real estate tax and insurance escrows have been a part of homeownership since the 1930s, when the Great Depression made it next to impossible for people to scrape together the money to pay their property tax. The cash in a real estate tax or insurance escrow assures the lender that the loan's collateral (your home) will not be sold or seized for nonpayment of property taxes, nor lost to a fire or other catastrophe for lack of insurance.

Protecting their investment is so important to lenders that they are legally entitled to demand that you open an escrow account when they give you the loan. They are also empowered to collect enough to pay your annual premiums *plus* two months' cushion. In other words, you pay more than the amount needed to meet your tax and insurance premium obligations. The money generally goes into a non-interest-bearing account (only a small handful of states require lenders to pay homeowners interest on their escrow accounts).

Several years ago, an investigation of escrows by 26 state attorneys general found that some 6 million homeowners were being overcharged annually, from $100 to $900 each. The total amount of overcharging was put as high as $50 billion. Since then, lenders have changed the way they structure escrows. If the escrow account has more than two months' worth of extra payments (amounts above those needed to pay the annual taxes and insurance premiums), the mortgage servicer must return the difference within a specified period of time.

Is there any way to get out of having an escrow account? I know of only two. First, some lenders will allow you to pledge an account. That is, you may put enough cash into an account to cover a little more than one year's worth of property taxes and insurance premiums. You then pay the ongoing taxes and insurance premiums from other funds. The lender (or bank where the account is pledged) pays you interest on the account but, if you don't pay your taxes and insurance premiums, your mortgage lender has the right to withdraw the sums in the pledged accounts to pay the taxes and premiums. A lender may also charge you a setup fee, which could range from $40 to 3 percent of the loan amount. The second way to get out of an escrow account is to put down more than 35 percent, in cash, on your home. The line of thinking is this: If you've got that much down on your property, your equity in it is high, and you won't risk it by not paying your taxes and insurance premiums.

Down Payment Options. It's unlikely you'll put down 35 percent in cash on a home the first time out. (Don't worry, that day will come.) Instead, private mortgage insurance (PMI) premiums and real estate property tax and insurance will be a fact of life for you. As we've discussed, your PMI premiums will vary, depending on how much you've put down.

Here's how the down payment–PMI relationship works:

1. *20 percent down payment.* A home loan with an 80 percent loan-to-value ratio (you must put down 20 percent, in cash, on your home) or less (you put down more than 20 percent in cash— perhaps 25, 30, or 40 percent) is considered a conventional loan. The best part about putting down at least 20 percent of your home's purchase price in cash is that you don't need to take out (and pay for) private mortgage insurance, and you usually get the best loan terms.

2. *Low down payment (below 20 percent).* If you put down, in cash, between 5 percent and 19 percent of your home's purchase price, your loan falls into a lending category called "low down payment." Generally, the smaller the down payment, the higher the interest rate, because the PMI premiums are higher. If you have a loan-to-value ratio of 85 percent (15 percent down payment), your loan will carry a lower interest rate (including PMI) than if your loan-to-value ratio had been 90 percent (10 percent down payment). A 95 percent loan-to-value ratio will carry an even higher interest rate (including PMI).

3. *FHA and 3/2 loans.* What can you do if you don't have even 5 percent to put down in cash on a home? You might want to contact your local Federal Housing Authority (FHA) office. The FHA is a division of the Department of Housing and Urban Development (HUD). One of its purposes is to help people who can't otherwise qualify for a loan. There's a problem with FHA loans, however: They generally are more expensive than other loans because they carry higher up-front fees and costs.

Also, the property must be inspected by an FHA inspector, who will evaluate whether the home meets minimum housing and safety standards. (If the house fails to pass the inspection, the FHA will not fund a loan unless the repairs required by the inspector are made prior to the closing. Depending on what the purchase contract states, you or the seller would have to make and pay for those repairs.)

Several years ago, the FHA introduced a 3/2 loan. It allows the home buyer to put down, in cash, 3 percent of the price of the home, and receive an additional 2 percent as a gift from a nonprofit organization, a state or local agency, or friends and relatives. With this lowest of low-down-payment loans, however, comes an education requirement. The home buyers who choose a 3/2 loan must attend homeownership classes at which they learn about the costs of homeownership and how to budget for them.

4. *97 percent loan packages.* After the FHA came out with the 3/2 loan, non-FHA lenders saw how many people came knocking on the FHA's door. They also saw that the loans were profitable and, despite conventional wisdom, relatively few people defaulted on their mortgage obligations. So, non-FHA lenders created loan packages in which buyers have to scrape together only 3 percent of the purchase price.

In the few years since these loans were introduced, lenders have confirmed that the default rate does not go up significantly between loans that carry a 95 percent loan-to-value ratio and those that have a 97 percent loan-to-value ratio. That's good news for consumers, because it means that these loans are widely available. On the other hand, this type of loan often carries a higher interest rate.

5. *Zero down payment.* Except for VA loans (which are available to qualified veterans only), there is not a national mortgage program (as this book went to press) that allows a buyer to buy a home without investing a penny. But there are ways to buy a home with nothing down. Under a certain FHA program, you can finance 97 percent of your purchase and receive the other 3 percent as a gift. Or, lenders will give you an 80 percent first loan at normal interest rates, and then issue a second mortgage on the remaining 20 percent at a substantially higher interest rate. A third option is to get an 80 percent loan and have the

seller take back a second mortgage. With each of these options, you're not putting anything down, yet you are able to purchase your home. Remember that you'll still have some closing costs and fees that have to be paid in cash.

Mortgages That Lenders Offer

FINANCIAL
ISSUE
4

Shopping for a loan has become a little like shopping for apples. You may find ten varieties of apples at your local fruit market. Some are yellow, some green, some pink, some red. Some are organic, some are not. Some are grown in northern Michigan, others are grown in Oregon, Washington State, or southern California. Which apple do you choose? Your choice may depend entirely on which is the cheapest, how they taste, or, on which variety you need for a particular recipe.

The key difference between apples and mortgages is that if you're unhappy with your apple selection, you can buy different apples the next day. You're going to be paying off this mortgage, however, for a long while. If interest rates drop, perhaps you'll refinance within 6 months or a year. But, more than likely, you'll have your loan for 5 to 7 years, or until you sell your home.

Because you'll be investing a sizable amount of money in your choice of a loan, it's a good idea to start learning what your options are even before you look at homes to buy. In this Financial Issue, you won't learn every detail about every type of mortgage offered in the marketplace, but you will learn what choices exist, and why choosing one type of loan over another might help you buy a more substantial home or save thousands of dollars in interest payments.

One person who can help you sort through the myriad choices available is your local mortgage broker or banker. Also, the real estate section of your local newspaper will likely have a mortgage table featuring loans (and the interest rates they carry) that are readily available in your marketplace.

Let's look at the basic loan types you're likely to run across when it's time to search for your home loan.

Fixed-Rate Mortgages. Fixed-rate loans have long been the most popular type of loan in the real estate market. One of the reasons for this popularity is that the loan is stable. Buyers who choose a fixed-rate loan product will know exactly how much they owe each month

189

over the life of the loan. Their monthly mortgage payment will never change.

Of the fixed-rate loans, the most popular is the 30-year fixed-rate mortgage (which means that the loan lasts for 30 years). But other lengths have gained popularity as lenders seek to make loans even more affordable and as home buyers have come to realize that they probably won't live the rest of their lives in the first home they buy. You can now get a 15-year fixed-rate loan (which effectively cuts your interest rate payment almost in half), a 20-year fixed-rate loan (which will save you thousands over a 30-year loan), and a 40-year fixed-rate loan. The 40-year variety is being pushed by some lenders as a wonderful new product for first-time buyers. True, it puts your monthly payment amount somewhat below that of a 30-year loan, but it adds so much interest onto the back of your loan that you might never pay it off. And if you do, you'll have paid more than three times the original loan amount in interest, an outrageous waste of money.

Adjustable Rate Mortgages (ARMs). These mortgages have a variable interest rate that fluctuates according to the financial index (or benchmark) they are tied to and the type of ARM obtained. Some indexes move slowly; others move quickly. Some ARMs may adjust annually, some monthly, or every 3 years, or every 6 months.

ARMs have some nice features that make them desirable in some situations, even when the fixed-rate-loan interest rate is low:

1. The first-year rate of an ARM is generally a point or two below the market rate. This first-year rate is called the *teaser* rate.

2. The interest rate on many, but not all, ARMs is capped. Usually, it can rise only 5 or 6 points (depending on the ARM type) over the life of the loan, starting from the teaser rate. If your starting interest rate (the teaser rate) on an ARM is 5 percent, and you have a 5-point cap, the highest possible interest rate on your loan is 10 percent.

3. The rise of the interest rate on ARMs is limited to either one or two percentage points per year. Your rate could never rise from 5 percent to 10 percent overnight. It would take several years to go that high, assuming that the loan rose to its maximum limit each year (a worst-case scenario).

Over the years, research has shown that folks who got ARMs tended to pay less in interest than buyers who chose 30-year fixed-rate loans. ARMs are, however, a little riskier. After all, the interest rate could shoot up again, and although your ARM rate would be capped, you could end up paying an interest rate that is two or three percentage points higher than a fixed-rate loan.

ARMs are most useful to home buyers who plan to stay in their homes only 5 to 7 years. If you compare a worst-case scenario ARM (where the interest rate rises to its cap each year) with a fixed-rate loan, you'll usually do as well or better with an ARM over the short run.

Like fixed-rate loans, ARMs offer a variety of terms. Consumers can negotiate for a 1-year, 3-year, 5-year, 7-year, or even a 10-year ARM. The rates are locked in for the length of the agreed-on opening period (with a 5-year ARM, for example, the initial rate is locked in for the first 5 years), after which the loan's rate adjusts.

Different lenders have different terms for their loans. In other words, one lender's ARM may differ significantly from another lender's, though on the surface the loans may seem similar. Make sure you ask specifically how each loan works before you sign on the dotted line.

Two-Step Loans. Several years ago, Fannie Mae introduced a new type of loan called a "two-step loan." The goal was to combine the stability of a fixed-rate loan with the lower rates of an ARM.

Generally, two-step loans offer two options. The most common forms of the loans are a 5/25 ("five-twenty-five") and a 7/23 ("seven-twenty-three"). These loans carry an interest rate that is fixed for the first 5 or 7 years. Then the loan adjusts once; it converts into either a 1-year ARM (meaning that it adjusts annually) or a fixed-rate loan. The starting interest rate on a 5/25 or 7/23 is lower than on a standard 30-year fixed-rate loan. On any of these loans, the amortization is over a 30-year period. In other words, at the end of 30 years, you will have paid off the loan in full.

When its 10/1 ("ten-one") loan was introduced, Fannie Mae referred to it as an ARM because, at the end of 10 years, it converts into a 1-year adjustable loan. But you likely won't stay in your home

191

for 10 years, so the loan will feel like a 30-year fixed-rate loan, but will carry a lower interest rate.

Balloon.   If you have a balloon loan, the interest you pay during the term of the loan will not fully pay off your debt. At the end of a balloon loan term, you'll owe the remaining principal in one lump sum. Usually, balloon loans are short in length, perhaps 3 to 7 years, although they are often amortized as if they were 30 years in length. In other words, you're paying down some of the principal of the loan as if you were holding a 30-year loan, but the loan ends after 3 to 7 years. At that time you owe a lump sum to the bank. Balloon loans are sometimes (but infrequently) arranged as "interest-only" loans: You pay only the interest on the loan, and you owe the entire principal at the end of the loan term.

Balloon loans were actually the original form of the home mortgage in this country. They were more common before Fannie Mae introduced the two-step loan. Why would anyone want a balloon loan today? It tends to carry lower interest rates than a 30-year fixed-rate loan. Ellyn recently took out a 7-year balloon loan on her condo. She doesn't plan to stay in her home for 7 years, and she pays an interest rate that's 1¼ percent less than a 30-year fixed rate loan. By choosing a balloon loan, she will save thousands of dollars over the life of her loan.

Negative Equity.   These loans aren't terribly popular anymore, mostly because home buyers have realized what a lousy deal they can be. A negative equity loan means that your mortgage and interest payments are fixed at a dollar amount that doesn't equal all the interest you owe on your loan. The interest that you don't pay is added to the back end of your loan, and could significantly add to the amount you owe.

People originally liked negative equity loans because they enabled them to buy property at a lower payment than was available with a 30-year fixed loan. The introduction of the 5/25s and 7/23s has made negative equity loans virtually obsolete.

Graduated Payment.   With the introduction of other mortgage products, the graduated payment mortgage has essentially evaporated. But you may run across this loan under different names. A graduated payment loan is a stepped-payment mortgage that starts out with a below-market interest rate, but the rate increases a certain number of percentage points each year until the loan levels out at a higher interest rate. The loan is calculated on a 30-year amortization schedule, so that it is paid off in 30 years. Graduated payment mortgages require a tremendous number of individual calculations. Mountains of paperwork make these loans difficult and expensive.

FHA Loans. Government-backed Federal Housing Administration (FHA) loans, often called the "first-time buyer's mortgage," have long been available to buyers who have only a tiny amount of cash for a down payment or whose credit and finances were deemed too risky by conventional lenders. Most conventional lenders can do FHA loans.

VA Loans. Veterans of the United States armed forces are entitled to a wide variety of benefits, including the opportunity to get a zero-down-payment home loan backed by the Department of Veterans Affairs. The VA started the program at the end of World War II; since 1945, more than 13 million veterans have obtained loans worth more than $360 billion.

Not having to put down any cash on a new home is worth thinking about, but VA loans, like FHA loans, can be more expensive than their conventional counterparts. The veteran mortgagee is required to pay some closing costs, including a VA appraisal, credit report, survey, recording fees, a 1 percent loan origination fee, and a VA funding fee. Some of these fees shrink if the veteran makes a cash down payment on the home.

Probably the biggest drawback to a VA loan is that only veterans may apply. The VA has strict limitations on who qualifies for a VA loan. You are eligible if you served 90 days of wartime service in World War II, the Korean Conflict, the Vietnam War, or the Persian Gulf War, and were not dishonorably discharged. You are also eligible if you served between 6 and 24 months of continuous active duty from 1981 through today and were not dishonorably discharged. Check with your local VA office for more details on eligibility.

Biweekly Mortgage. With a regular mortgage, you make 12 monthly payments per year. With a biweekly mortgage, you make 26 payments each year (one every other week). Some folks like this arrangement because, by paying down the principal faster, they save thousands of dollars on their loans. A 30-year mortgage is paid off in about 15 or 16 years.

193

The quick-pay advantage sounds nice, but a biweekly mortgage isn't everyone's cup of tea. First, lenders often charge a nonrefundable fee of $400 to $800 for setting up a biweekly mortgage. Second, a biweekly loan ties you into making a heavy schedule of payments each year. The amount of each payment is much less than a monthly payment, but you have to remember to make more than twice as many payments. And if you have a bad month financially, it's that much easier to fall behind in your payments.

If you want to reduce the effort and still derive the financial benefits of biweekly loan payments, all you have to do is write another check (for $1/12$ of your average mortgage payment), and enclose it with your monthly mortgage payment. Enclose a note to the lender asking that the second check be applied toward the principal. If you make one extra mortgage payment per year, you'll effectively cut a 30-year loan almost in half.

Shared-Appreciation Mortgage.   A shared-appreciation mortgage is a financial concept borrowed from commercial property transfers. The lender will offer you a below-market rate in exchange for a share of the profits when you sell the home. There are significant benefits to doing this: You get all the tax benefits (including all deductions), and the lender doesn't make any money unless you do. On the other hand, if the home appreciates, you could end up paying a lot of that profit to the lender.

Shared-appreciation mortgages are most commonly coordinated by nonprofit associations seeking to help low-income first-time buyers become home owners. They use Community Development Block Grants (CDBG) money to help make up the difference between what low- to moderate-income families can afford and what the competitively priced conventional lenders want to see on their borrower's balance sheet.

You may encounter variations on the loan types we've discussed. Borrowers want their home loans custom-tailored to meet their personal financial needs. By customizing loans, lenders keep consumers from comparing and contrasting loans directly. A lender who has customized his or her portfolio can honestly tell you, "My loan is different from any other out there," but don't let that dissuade you from doing your research on how the fees and costs of each loan stack up.

Special Financing Options

FINANCIAL
ISSUE
5

Almost all first-time buyers purchase homes using some sort of financing. Most will go through commercial lenders: a bank, credit union, or savings and loan, or a mortgage broker who deals directly with institutional investors.

There are other ways to finance your purchase: seller financing, family financing, a buy-down mortgage, articles of agreement, and leasing the home with an option to purchase it down the line. Here's a brief rundown on these alternative financing options.

Seller Financing. In the right circumstances, seller financing may be the hidden gem of real estate finance: It's good for the buyer *and* the seller. To start at the beginning, seller financing means the seller takes on the role of the lender and gives you a loan to purchase his or her property. You might put down 5 or 10 percent on the home, and the seller finances the remaining 90 to 95 percent of the purchase price. Every month, you'll pay the seller the principal and interest amount you've agreed to.

> If you want to buy a home using seller financing, look for a home owned by folks who probably won't need the cash from the sale to finance the purchase of their next home. Best bets: elderly homeowners who are moving to a rental apartment or a retirement home they already own. Or, a seller who does not currently live on the property, or someone who has already paid off his or her mortgage. Young families who are trading up to a larger home generally need all the cash they can get their hands on. Be sure to tell your real estate agent you're interested in seller financing. He or she may know of some sellers who are willing to finance the buyer simply for the regular monthly income. Also, it doesn't hurt to propose that arrangement. Sellers who hadn't considered taking back a mortgage, or had thought they wouldn't want to, might be persuaded of the benefits to both parties. You won't know until you ask.

Why is seller financing such a good deal for everyone? Buyers like seller financing because they can get the prevailing interest rate and not pay points or other junk fees. It's also generally easier, less frustrating, and less time-consuming to work with a seller rather than with a commercial lender. Sellers like it because they generally can get a higher return on their money from the sale, and it arrives as a nice monthly stream of income. Furthermore, the loan is secured by a property they know well. If you, the buyer, stop paying on the loan, the seller will have to start foreclosure proceedings, and can ultimately take back the house.

Seller financing can come in any shape or size or length, but the most common loans are either fixed-rate or balloon loans. Some sellers prefer a 30-year loan, and some prefer a 7-year loan. Make sure, however, that your note is drafted properly. If you're getting seller financing, invest a couple of hundred dollars to have an attorney prepare the proper documents. You want to make sure your rights are protected.

Sellers can "take back" a first or a second mortgage. A first mortgage, also called a *purchase money mortgage,* is usually the largest loan (and often, the only loan) against a property. A bank might finance 80 percent of the purchase price, with a seller giving you a second mortgage for the remaining 20 percent. With that strategy, and your 5% down in cash, you can avoid paying for private mortgage insurance (PMI).

Family Financing.   Instead of working with a commercial lender or using seller financing, some home buyers prefer to use family money to finance their purchase. Family financing can be a terrific alternative, if your family is in a position to help out.

The first thing you have to determine is whether your relatives are giving you a gift or offering you a loan. Sometimes, family members will offer to finance your loan for you. They act as your bank, putting up even the cash for the closing costs. You then repay them with principal-and-interest payments as you would any commercial lender. Some parents lend their children money interest-free, or at a super-low interest rate. But if you want to be able to claim the mortgage interest deduction on your personal income tax return, the Internal Revenue Service (IRS) requires that your family financing be an "arm's length transaction." That's IRS-speak for a loan that more or less conforms to what you'd be able to get in the open marketplace. As an example, let's say that the weekly mortgage tables show that a 30-year fixed-rate loan is available on the market for 7.5 percent with zero points. Your parents offer you the same loan with an interest rate of only 2 percent. That may result in an objection from the IRS. The IRS would like to see your parents give you a loan that reasonably conforms to the loans available in the open market. The IRS understands that most parents and relatives won't make their loved ones pay points and fees, and might give them an interest rate that is a little below the going rate, but the rate has to be in the ballpark.

The nice thing about financing from relatives is that the money stays in the family. You're still paying your mortgage each month, but the interest—a substantial amount that adds up quickly—goes right back into your family's pockets. And because the interest rate you'll be paying is probably higher than the rate your family could get in a savings account or even a money market—and, for better or worse, you're a known credit risk—it's a good deal for everyone.

It's important that any loan you get from a family member be documented in writing. This is for your protection as well as your parents' or relatives'. Should something happen to your family or relative, you're going to want to be able to prove that the loan was a loan, and not a gift. It's a good idea to hire an attorney to draft up a formal loan document (this shouldn't cost more than a couple of hundred dollars). The document should spell out the exact terms of the loan and how it will be repaid. You should sign the loan document, as should your co-borrower and any family members or relatives who are giving you the loan. Then each person involved in the agreement should keep a copy of the loan document somewhere safe—perhaps in a safe deposit box in your local bank.

10 STEP
TIP

Buy-Down Mortgages.   If your family members or the seller want to give you a helping hand but can't afford to either float the entire loan or give you a substantial gift, it may be possible for them to participate in a buy-down mortgage. "Buy down" means that the interest rate steps up during the first few years of the loan, before leveling off.

Let's say the prevailing interest rate on a 30-year fixed-rate loan is 8 percent. You can't quite qualify today for that 8 percent loan, but you believe in the power of upward mobility and feel that, in a couple of years, paying that interest rate won't be a problem. If your seller agrees to help you with a 3-2-1 buy-down loan, the interest rate you pay the first year would be 3 points less than the prevailing rate—in this case, 5 percent. The second year, the interest rate would rise to two points below the prevailing rate, or 6 percent. The third year, the interest rate would rise to 1 point below the prevailing rate, or 7 percent. In

197

the fourth year of the loan, the interest rate would stabilize at the prevailing loan (or note) rate, which, in our example, is 8 percent.

The seller—or whoever is giving you the loan—makes up the difference between the real interest rate (the hypothetical 8 percent) and the interest rate that has been bought down. The seller would give your lender an amount of money that covers the difference, and the lender would keep that money in an escrow account. Each month, when you pay your mortgage, the lender takes out from the account the amount of money that is needed to make the mortgage payment whole.

Let's assume the loan is a 30-year fixed-rate loan of $100,000 with the 8 percent interest rate we've discussed. The seller would buy down the rate to 5 percent in the first year. The interest rate would step up by one point each year. Here's how it looks:

	Monthly Payments		
Year	_Loan at 8 Percent_	_Buy-Down Loan_	_Difference per Month/Year_
1	$733.76	$536.82 (5%)	$196.94/$2,363.28
2	733.76	599.55 (6%)	$134.21/$1,610.52
3	733.76	665.30 (7%)	$ 68.46/$ 821.52
4	733.76	733.76 (8%)	-0-
	⋮	⋮	⋮
30	Difference over life of loan		$4,795.32

For approximately $5,000, a gift to you, the person who buys down your loan is giving you very solid support toward buying a home. The seller, on the other hand, has been able to successfully sell his or her property for the buy-down amount. To work out your own calculations, use the amortization tables in Appendix II.

10 STEP TIP

Although lenders can set up a buy-down loan, you may have trouble finding one that will agree to do it simply because it requires more work than other types of loans. Look for a lender that portfolios loans. Portfolio lenders keep a percentage (or all) of the loans they make in-house and do not resell them on the secondary market to investors like Fannie Mae and Freddie Mac. Because they keep their own loans, portfolio lenders write their own lending rules and are usually more flexible than other types of commercial lenders.

Articles of Agreement.   With written articles of agreement, you enter into an installment payment agreement to buy a home over a specified period of time. The seller keeps legal title to the home, and you receive equitable title. That means you receive a legal interest in the property but do not own it. The benefit to you, the buyer, is that the seller will usually accept a much smaller down payment (perhaps 5 percent of the sales price of the home). You will still feel comfortable with the arrangement because the seller retains title to the property until you've paid off the loan in full.

> Purchasing a home through an articles of agreement can work very well for some home buyers. But it is extremely important that you consult with an attorney who understands the ins and outs of these types of transactions. They can get very complicated, and you will want to make sure your rights are protected.

Lease with an Option to Buy.   If you have the income to make regular monthly mortgage payments, but don't have a drop of cash for a down payment, you may want to consider a lease with an option to buy, also known simply as a lease/option. A lease/option allows buyers to build up a down payment while they're living in their prospective home. The concept has a lot of pluses for home buyers and home sellers.

How does it work? First, you purchase a 1-year (or multiyear) option on a home by giving the seller a nonrefundable option fee, which is usually a small percentage of the price of the house. Then, you move into the home and pay rent each month, a portion of which the seller should credit back to you as the down payment for the home.

For example, if you were to pay $1,000 per month in rent, with 33 percent of the rent credited toward the down payment, you'd accumulate $333 each month, or nearly $4,000 per year, toward a down payment for the home. In addition, your nonrefundable option fee may be credited toward the down payment.

There are no hard and fast rules about how much of the rent should be credited toward the down payment. The credit fluctuates anywhere from zero percent to 100 percent. It's up to you and the seller to negotiate how much of the rent should be credited. You should aim for 100 percent credit, but the seller will naturally want as little as possible credited toward the down payment. It's not uncommon to see rent credits of 33 percent or 50 percent.

199

Before you negotiate the rent credit, however, you and the seller should negotiate the price and terms of the sale of the home, just as if you were buying it outright. Once you and the seller have reached an agreement, the price of the home can never vary, even if it appreciates in value.

Buyers should remember that even though they essentially have an option to purchase the home at a later date, the seller remains the sole owner of the property until a buyer exercises an option and closes on the home. That also means that sellers retain the tax benefits of homeownership and can deduct mortgage interest and property taxes from their federal income taxes.

Let's say you're happily ensconced in your lease/option, but at the end of the year, you find you still don't have enough of a down payment to purchase the home. What can you do? Usually, lease/options are renewable (though you may be asked to pay another nonrefundable fee, which may also be applied toward the down payment). You may renew your option when your current option expires, and renew it each year if you so desire. A home investor at a California home buyers' fair once told me she had been renewing her option on a particular home for 23 years. During that time, the house tripled in value. Now she knows what she is buying. And, she has nearly paid off the house in rent credits.

On the other hand, if you decide, at the end of the year, that you don't like the home or the neighborhood, you can pay your last month's rent and walk away.

How can you find a lease with an option to buy? Some sellers advertise their homes as lease/options. The rest of the time, it's up to you to ask. Good bets are sellers who have had their home on the market for a long time, or who have already purchased another home and are paying two mortgages. Try to find someone who doesn't need the cash from the sale of the home to purchase his or her next residence. Once you've targeted a seller, approach him or her about the possibility of a lease/option. But don't expect the seller's broker to be thrilled. The broker will still get a commission, but not until you actually purchase the property. And, if you're like that California investor, the real estate agent might retire before the commission check shows up in the mail. You may want to reach an understanding with the buyer's agent who is representing you during the transaction: You will pay him or her a flat fee when you sign the lease/option, on its renewal date, or when you close on the home.

It's a good idea to hire a real estate attorney to draw up your lease/option for you. This is a relatively complicated transaction, and you want to make sure your rights are protected. When interviewing attorneys, make sure they've had plenty of experience doing lease/options for residential purchases.

FINANCIAL
ISSUE
6

Other Sources of Help for First-Time Buyers

For a lot of reasons, nonprofit agencies and federal, state, and local municipalities like to support homeownership. First, homeownership promotes social stability. If all the residents of a neighborhood own their homes, they're more likely to take care of that neighborhood and try to increase the value of their homes. They're also likely to stay in their homes longer than they would stay in a rental unit. Second, homeownership adds revenue to city and state coffers. Home buyers and seller pay transfer taxes (sometimes called transfer stamps; a fee charged per dollar of the selling price of the home) to the local city, county, and state governments. Homeowners pay real estate taxes. They spend money to fix up their homes, contributing additional sales tax dollars to the income side of the public budget.

With so many pluses to homeownership, it's no wonder that a panoply of opportunities has opened up for first-time home buyers across the country. These homeownership opportunities come in many forms and are offered by a variety of local and state housing agencies. They're also offered by local nonprofit housing agencies.

These programs tend to limit participation to home buyers who meet certain income requirements or whose homes meet certain price limits. In other words, they're designed for home buyers who fall into the lower- to middle-income range. These numbers change frequently (and are often based on the median income of your city, county, or state), so it wouldn't be helpful to list them here. But don't think it's unusual if a first-time home buyer program limits participation to individuals who earn no more than 85 percent of the annual median income for their city.

Many of these first-time home buyer programs have built-in educational components. Studies have shown that first-time home buyers become more successful homeowners (that is, they don't default on their loans) if they've attended classes on the costs associated with homeownership. In these classes, they learn how much it will cost to

201

own and maintain a home, and how to budget for homeownership expenses. Although you may feel you have a handle on these issues, attending the homeowner education class is usually a requirement for getting the nonprofit's or housing agency's help.

Finding First-Time Buyer Help.   Help for first-time buyers exists, but finding it can be a little tricky. Usually, programs are introduced in waves, so if you start hearing about one program, there may be others nearby.

Start by checking out your local and state housing agencies. They may offer first-time buyer programs or can refer you to nonprofit agencies that do. Scour the local newspapers for stories about these programs. Do some research in past issues of your local papers, or call the real estate section and query the editors about available help. (Members of the press sometimes get the early word on these programs.) Also, check out local banks and savings and loans. Banks sometimes offer special loans with below-market interest rates for the early years of first-time buyers' loans. You may also want to check with local houses of worship. Occasionally, they will sponsor first-time buyer programs for their own members or for a community at large. At a minimum, they may be able to refer you to other nonprofits that act as sponsors.

First-time buyer assistance comes in several varieties. There are agencies that offer help in putting together a down payment. They may give you a portion of your down payment as an outright grant, or allow you to work for it, or make it possible to borrow it at a reduced rate. Other programs are similar to the shared appreciation mortgage we talked about earlier in this Step. The nonprofit will provide you with the down payment on your home, but you're responsible for making all the mortgage payments. When you sell the home, you and the nonprofit split any profits realized on the sale. You may also encounter programs that provide you with the cash and expertise to help bring your new home up to code. Programs like Habitat for Humanity, which is identified with former U.S. President Jimmy Carter and his wife, Rosalyn, build or renovate low-cost homes for first-time home buyers. Finally, you may come across some programs that will buy down your mortgage interest rate for the first few years of your loan. Be flexible about the kind of help you're seeking, and ask a lot of questions. Make sure there are no long-term strings attached to a program before you sign up for it, and be aware of any rules or qualification limitations that might jeopardize your participation.

Finding the Right Lender

At the beginning of 1996, there were approximately 50,000 mortgage brokers in the United States. In addition, thousands of institutions were lending money to home buyers and to homeowners looking to refinance. In other words, when you're looking for a home loan, there are a lot of options.

Let's start with some basic distinctions.

- *Mortgage brokers* are involved with the origination side of the real estate business. They take loan applications, process the forms, and then submit the files to an institutional investor—typically a savings and loan, a bank, or a mortgage banker—who underwrites and closes the loans. Mortgage brokers usually work with a wide variety of investors who buy loans on the secondary market, providing mortgage brokers with an almost inexhaustible supply of money with which to make new mortgages. Mortgage brokers are, then, in the middle between you and the secondary-market lenders (like institutions or pension funds) who buy huge volumes of home loans and either keep them or repackage them for other investors. The brokers' fee for their services may come in the form of origination points, an application fee, a document preparation fee, and other fees.

- *Mortgage bankers* go a step further. They, too, work within the origination side of the real estate business; they take loan applications from home buyers and from home owners looking to refinance. But they also get involved with servicing the loan and closing the loan in their own name and with their own funds. If you were to go to a bank for a loan, for example, the mortgage banker (also called your *loan officer*) would take your application and lend you money from the bank's own coffers. After you close on your loan, the same bank might service your account, collect payments, and make sure your real estate taxes were being paid. Or, it might sell your loan on the secondary market.

As we've discussed, mortgage brokers and mortgage bankers make their money from points and fees. They also make money on the spread between the rate on your loan and the going rate on loans in the secondary market. For example, if your loan has an interest rate of

8 percent, and loans are sold to the secondary market with an interest rate of 7.5 percent, the mortgage broker or mortgage banker would earn a fee based on the half-point difference between the loan you have and the interest rate on loans in the open market. In the lending industry, these are often referred to as *premiums*.

How should you choose your lender? Don't base your decision solely on the rate a lender is offering. The mortgage business is extremely competitive in most areas. If a lender appears to be offering a deal that's too good to pass up, chances are you should do just that. That's not to say some lenders won't try to undercut others in price and fees. They will, and you should encourage that by negotiating the fees and interest rate associated with your loan. That's how you get a good deal.

There has always been some concern in the lending industry about conflicts of interest that mortgage brokers face. When you go to a mortgage broker, the broker sorts through the loan packages offered by various lenders and helps you choose the one that's right for you. For this you pay a fee, usually known as discount points or loan origination points. What may not be clear is that the mortgage broker often receives *premiums* from the lender. A premium is a fee based on the difference between the rate that the mortgage broker gets for you and the going rate of the loan. The spread between those two numbers determines how much of a premium the broker will get from the lender. There are those in the industry who believe that the mortgage broker has an incentive to find you a higher interest rate simply because that will increase his or her fee. Worse, few mortgage brokers openly disclose the premiums they receive to their customer, the borrower. A non-profit organization called the National Association of Mortgage Planners aims to cut the conflict of interest by taking only a fixed fee of 1.5 percent of the loan amount from the borrower. Any premiums given on the loan will be disclosed and returned to the borrower to help defray expenses. While the NAMP's ethics haven't yet caught on nationwide, their following can only grow. See the Resources section information on how to contact NAMP's members.

To find a good lender, start by soliciting recommendations and referrals from anyone who has recently bought a home using financing, or has recently refinanced. Ask your real estate broker for the names of two or three of the best mortgage brokers he or she has worked with recently (within the past 3 months). Call these companies and speak to the loan officers. Try to find someone who appears knowledgeable about the local real estate market and can communicate financial and loan information in a way you understand and with which you feel comfortable. Check your local newspaper's real estate section. There may be a weekly mortgage column that monitors a handful of the local mortgage brokers and bankers and compares the interest rates and points each is offering for certain types of loans. The lenders' addresses and telephone numbers are usually provided. Finally, search the ads in the real estate section. Some lenders have toll-free telephone numbers and offer free loan counseling by telephone.

Above all, be sure you find a lender who offers you exemplary service and complete information about each loan program, and responds directly to your questions. Don't wait around for a loan officer who is too busy to tend to your needs or answer your questions. Find someone who is willing to sit down with you, run through the numbers, and explain which loan options might work best for your family. All lenders should offer to prequalify you for free. After all, this is an easy way for them to market their services to you.

Getting a Loan Through Your Real Estate Broker. There are other places to find financing. Your real estate broker's office may be one of them. Real estate firms, especially large ones intent on increasing their profits, may offer additional services to home buyers whom real estate brokers see as captive audiences. Many real estate firms have either hooked up with local mortgage companies, or have bought or started mortgage companies and brought them inside their offices. Once you're on the premises, the reasoning goes, you'll like walking across the office to the mortgage desk to get your loan. No shopping around; just sit down and do it.

The mortgage option at your local real estate broker's office may come in a couple of different forms. First, there are *computerized loan originations* (CLOs): computer terminals that feature the mortgage products of local mortgage brokers. As many as 25 different mortgage brokerage companies may be listed; or, a couple of different companies may be listed, but each offers about 50 products, so there is the appearance of choice but no tough competition. With CLOs, the real estate brokerage firm usually gets a fee when a home buyer closes on a loan. The mortgage brokers call it a referral fee. Others call it a conflict of interest because you're being steered toward a particular lender with whom the real estate firm has a financial relationship. (You may still get a great loan at a great price, but you'll have to do some research to find that out.)

205

Another, better computerized version offers the loan products from 25 national lenders. This version also has a camera that allows you to see the mortgage broker who is assisting you. You can choose the loans on screen, compare the fees and costs, and decide which one you'd like to hear more about. In this version, the real estate broker gets no fee for providing this service, which eliminates any conflict of interest. However, the mortgage broker you see takes a half-point fee for his or her services, which is comparatively low. Technically, the mortgage broker's fee is paid by the lender, but it's charged back to you in the form of higher fees and interest rates.

You may also see a mortgage company, owned by the real estate brokerage firm, offering loans (or discounted loans) to the real estate company's home buyer clients. If you see a setup like this, you should know that your real estate broker receives a fee for steering home buyers like you to the mortgage side of the company. That's not to say that the loans may not be competitive and good, but you won't know until you start to do your homework. Research what local mortgage brokers and bankers are offering before you allow yourself to be pigeonholed into one loan officer's office.

10 STEP TIP

Many real estate experts question whether it's in a home buyer's best interest to work with a real estate broker to get a loan. First, it may not be a good idea to let the real estate broker see all your financial cards. If your broker wants to sit down with you and help you figure out exactly how much you can afford, then he or she is privy to your personal financial information. Your real estate broker will then be in a position to tell other people (especially home sellers) that you can afford to go higher. Buyer's brokers (especially exclusive buyer's brokers) will say they hold such information confidential. But there's always a possibility that something will slip out. If you're working with a traditional agent or conventional agent, he or she is a seller's broker who is obligated to tell the seller everything discovered about you—including information on your personal finances.

The real estate industry is moving toward more consolidation, and real estate firms are expanding the scope of their operations. In the next few years, you can expect to see real estate brokerages offering other services, including mortgage, title insurance, escrow, relocation, and moving. Whether you choose to use the services offered by your real estate agent is up to you. But before you agree to anything, be sure you review your options thoroughly, to make sure you get the best service at the best price.

Getting a Loan Through the Internet. If you're wired, that is, if you've got access to the Internet and are considering either searching for a home or applying for a loan electronically, you may find the following information useful.

In the early 1990s, most folks still didn't know about the Internet and World Wide Web (WWW). America Online, one of the largest online services for consumers, had several hundred thousand customers in 1993. Today, it has more than 6 million. The boom in Internet and computer-to-computer communication seems likely to continue through the end of the millennium and beyond.

In the real estate industry, computers have been particularly helpful. There are computer software packages that can help you calculate how much you can afford to pay for a home, and what your monthly mortgage payment schedule will look like throughout the entire loan term. You can do these calculations with a pencil and paper, but a computer can do them in the blink of an eye.

In the mid 1990s, the real estate industry suddenly discovered the Internet's possibilities for increasing sales. Thousands of websites sprang up overnight. Most of these sites, sponsored by various real estate brokerage firms, advertised different homes for sale. Information about homes listed for sale was previously considered private information, and was given only to other real estate brokers and agents. Today, real estate brokers realize they can attract home buyers to websites with free information about communities (demographics, education, and crime statistics), and then give the prospective buyers the opportunity to scan listings and ask for more information.

What the industry has discovered is that many home buyers like to do a lot of their own digging. They prefer to use their computers to browse through the Internet searching for real estate listings in their neighborhood of choice, or for information on mortgage types and interest rates. There's nothing wrong with doing this, although some real estate agents would prefer to sit by your side as you do it. But the Internet isn't always a bed of roses, either. Here are some things to keep in mind.

1. The listings on the Internet represent only a very small sample of all the homes that are for sale in your neighborhood. Right now, only a tiny percentage of real estate brokers put their listings on line. And most of them are scattered over tiny websites. In the fall of 1995, I spent some time pretending to look for a home in Chicago.

On one site, I found only six listings in Cary, Illinois, a distant sub-urb. That site was run by a major newspaper in town and purported to feature all kinds of listings from the entire metro area. Were that so, there should have been thousands of listings. By the summer of 1996, the paper had put up a new web site featuring hundreds of list-ings. Even if you tap into a brokerage firm's site, it will display only the homes for sale through that brokerage firm, and maybe not even all of those. When you work with a real estate broker who taps into the local multiple listing service (MLS; by computer), you will be able to get a list of all the homes that are for sale by all brokers who are members of the local MLS. That should be a very high percentage of all the homes that are available, though it won't include local FSBOs.

2. Almost all of the listings on the Internet are sponsored by real estate brokers. In other words, very few of these homes are for sale by their owners. If you're looking through the Internet, you'll see what local real estate brokers have paid to have you see. Be aware that you're looking for a home through rose-colored glasses. A real estate brokerage site features listings of that firm only. Savvy home buyers will consider each home page nothing more than an advertisement from the listing agent.

3. When you send an e-mail about a property to the broker who lists it, you may be engaging in a dual-agency relationship; that is, you're asking the seller's broker questions about the property. If you end up buying that home, the seller's broker may either represent only the seller or try to represent both of you. If he or she represents both sides of the transaction, then you have a dual-agency relation-ship and your interests are not being exclusively represented, and may in fact not be represented at all. You may end up paying too much for the property and will never know because you have not had any independent representation. (For more information on buyer's broker relationships, see Step 7, Choosing the Right Broker.)

4. The Internet does not distinguish among websites, nor does it police them. In other words, crooks could be putting up home pages and advertising nonexisting homes for sale, and you'd never know. Don't buy a home you see on the Internet without going through all the normal channels we've discussed in this book.

5. Few mortgage brokers and banks are wired, but their numbers are growing. Lenders can do loans quite cheaply over the Internet; however, federal law requires them to offer the same loan price to every borrower, so you may or may not save money by online borrowing. It's

good to use the Internet if you're curious about mortgage prices (if you can find them), but it's best to do this information gathering by telephone and actually speak with the lenders themselves. In the near future, there will be software products and Internet sites that will allow you to quickly and easily search the Net for a loan or home.

Some lenders claim to be able to process your loan entirely through the Internet. Currently, the technology exists to keep financial information safe, but it's unclear who is actually using it. When you're sending such detailed personal financial information through a network that isn't secure, your credit information could be stolen or tampered with. The risks right now are high.

Still, the Internet is an excellent place to look for information on mortgage rates. You may not get information on mortgages that are directly available in your neighborhood, but if you can find a mortgage calculator, it will help you run the numbers using a formula similar to the one in this book.

Finally, remember that the Internet isn't free. Every hour you spend searching (you could spend hundreds of hours browsing from site to site) will cost you money.

Comparing the Costs of Loans

Once you've begun scouring the newspapers (and the Internet) for different rates, it's time to call various lenders and ask them specific questions about how their loan programs work, and what fees and points are attached to them.

It helps to compare the loans side by side (apples to apples). Lenders, however, would prefer that you didn't. When you compare loans side by side, it's easy to see which is the best deal. Lenders try to confuse the issue and may change the name of a loan in order to muddy its true nature. Nevertheless, you must persevere. Ask how long the loan term is. Ask how the loan is amortized. Ask what index an adjustable rate mortgage (ARM) is tied to. Ask when the loan rate rises and what the annual and "life of the loan" caps are. Then, start asking about fees.

Use the worksheet on page 210 to help you compare the cost of each loan.

It's important to remember that different lenders may call their fees different names. If you don't recognize the name of the fee, ask what it is for—and keep asking until you understand. Make sure you

FINANCIAL
ISSUE
8

209

WORKSHEET
Comparing Loans

Issue/Fee	Loan A	Loan B	Loan C	Loan D
Loan type				
Interest rate				
Loan term				
APR				
Monthly payment				
ARM index				
Interest rate caps				
Each adjustment period				
Lifetime				
Origination points				
Application fee				
Credit report				
Processing fee				
Document preparation fee				
Appraisal fee				
Tax service fee				
Flood insurance certification				
Underwriting fee				
Courier charges				
Title insurance				
For lender's policy				
Special endorsements				
Recording assignment of mortgage				
Other fees				

list all the fees for each lender, and each loan type. Either photocopy the worksheet, or create another just like it for each loan type. Compare the same loan types with each other. You should compare all 30-year fixed-rate loans side by side, for example. You may not get an accurate comparison if you compare an ARM from one mortgage broker with a fixed-rate loan from another.

Unless a lender's fee covers something tangible (such as the cost of the appraisal), it may be used to pad the lender's bottom line. For example, lenders pay only $2 to $15 for each credit check. But they may charge you $30 to $80, and will say the extra charge is to cover office expenses. Or, they may say the document preparation fee pays for processing the necessary papers. Well, many lenders now do paperless loans via their computers, and they get an approval within minutes. Remember, fees are negotiable, and you should try to get the lender to get rid of them all *without raising the interest rate.* If you spend enough time on the telephone with a handful of lenders, each will understand that you're serious and that your business is up for bids. They should then be more open to negotiating with you. Remember, the time to negotiate fees is *before you apply for your loan.* Once you've applied, you've struck the deal and it's too late to negotiate. Be certain that everything you and the lender agreed to is written into the final application. Otherwise, you're out of luck.

Documentation You'll Need to Get Your Loan Started

One of the smartest things you can do before you ever apply for a loan is *get your paperwork in order.* Lenders will want to see a mountain of paperwork: old tax returns, paycheck stubs, and checking and savings account statements. Use the checklist on pages 212–213 as a guide to the items lenders may ask for.

EMOTIONAL/FAMILY ISSUES

Discrimination in Housing and Lending

One Sunday, a mixed-race couple visited an open house. They toured the first floor and liked it very much. They had their broker call on Monday to make an appointment to see the rest of the house. The listing broker, after confirming that this was the same couple who

211

_____ All W2 forms for the past 2 years for each person who will be a co-signer on the loan.

_____ Copies of completed tax forms, including any schedules or attachments, for the past 2 years.

_____ Copies of 1 month's worth of pay stubs.

_____ Copies of the three most recent bank statements for every bank account, IRA, 401K, Keogh, or stock account that you have. Bring a copy of your most recent statement of valuation for any other assets you have.

_____ If gift funds are involved, the giver must provide a canceled check, copies of the giver's recent bank statements, or other proof that he or she had that money to give. You may be asked to show the deposit slip for the gift. The giver will have to fill out a gift letter affidavit (available from the loan officer), indicating that the funds were a gift and that the gift giver does not expect repayment.

_____ Complete copies of all divorce decrees.

_____ If you are self-employed, complete copies of the past 2 years' business tax returns, and a year-to-date profit and loss statement and balance sheet, with original signatures.

_____ A list of your addresses for the past 7 years.

_____ If you have made any large deposits (i.e., larger than your monthly income) into your bank accounts in the past 3 months, an explanation as to where the funds came from, with proof.

_____ If you have opened a new bank account in the past 6 months, a letter explaining the source of the money to open this new account.

_____ Addresses and account numbers for every form of credit you have.

_____ Documentation to verify additional income, such as from social security, child support, and alimony.

_____ If you have had a previous bankruptcy, a complete copy of the bankruptcy proceedings, including all schedules, and a letter explaining the circumstances for the bankruptcy.

_____ If you're applying for a Federal Housing Administration (FHA) or Veterans Administration (VA) loan, a photocopy of a picture ID and a copy of your social security card; and, for a VA loan, proof of induction or enlistment and honorable discharge.

_____ If you have had any judgments against you, a copy of the recorded satisfaction of judgment; also, copies of documents describing any lawsuits with which you are currently involved.

_____ Proof of payment of any outstanding collections against you or against anyone who will be applying with you for a loan.

When you've actually signed a contract for a home and begun the mortgage approval process in earnest:

_____ A copy of the back and front of the canceled check for your earnest money. (You won't have this until you've written your earnest money check as the good-faith deposit you attach to your offer for purchase.)

_____ Copy of the sales contract and all riders. You'll also need names, addresses, and phone numbers of both brokers and both attorneys. If you are using an escrow officer, you may have to provide his or her information also.

_____ Copies of a survey or title policy for the home you are buying, if available when you apply for the mortgage, or when it becomes available during the purchase process. (You get these from the seller.)

_____ Copies of condominium, townhouse, or co-op association documents (if applicable), including a current and prior year's budget for the association.

had visited the house the day before, made a big fuss about how the couple couldn't see the house and she didn't want to deal with them.

Considering that the house had been on the market for over a year without stirring a tremendous amount of interest, the buyer's broker representing the couple thought this reaction was rather strange. The broker pursued it but none of his calls were returned.

"What do we have here?" wondered the buyer's broker. Possibly, the listing broker is simply stupid and doesn't know how to sell a home. Perhaps this is why the house has been on the market for so long. Or is the broker lazy? She may not want to bother putting in the work to sell her listing. The third possibility is the ugliest: The broker doesn't want a mixed-race couple buying this particular home and moving into the neighborhood.

No matter where you live in this country, racial discrimination raises its heinous head from time to time. There are White folks who don't want Blacks moving into their neighborhoods; Black folks who don't want Asians; Asians who don't want Hispanics; and so on. On the mortgage side, there are lenders who find it "unprofitable" to lend to Blacks, Hispanics, Asians, and other minority or immigrant groups. Some lenders keep their operations out of cities (so they can avoid inner-city clients) and concentrate their lending activities in largely White, middle-class, or affluent suburban neighborhoods. Other lenders, despite increased pressure from both the Justice Department and the Department of Housing and Urban Development (HUD), continue to reject Black applicants twice as often as White applicants.

It's disheartening enough to confront the dense forest of racial discrimination, but imagine how this barrier affects individuals: A young couple looking to buy a home and minding their own business, gets their feelings crushed in a process that is already highly emotional.

What can be done to combat the discrimination in housing and lending?

If you feel you are being discriminated against, subtly or openly, based on the color of your skin, there are ways to fight back. If the home you want to purchase is listed for sale with a licensed broker who is a member of a local multiple listing service, you should report the broker both to the MLS and to the department that regulates brokers in your state. You may also report the discrimination to your state attorney general's office and to the Justice Department. When a broker lists a home on the MLS, he or she agrees to abide by the state and federal laws that prohibit discrimination against any buyer based on age, religion, race, sex, or disability.

If you have been turned down for a loan and the lender fails to give you a valid reason, and if you believe the reason could be because you are a member of a minority, a senior citizen, or a disabled person, consider reporting the lender to the department that regulates mortgage lenders in your state. You may also report the lender to HUD and the Justice Department.

In addition to racial discrimination in real estate, there is sexual discrimination against women; and other types of discrimination against gay and lesbian individuals or couples, against unmarried couples, and against couples with young children. Unfortunately, not all forms of discrimination are direct violations of existing laws.

The good news is that the vast majority of home buyers do not experience racial, sexual, age, or any other kind of illegal discrimination during their purchase process. For most, the process is difficult and full of obstacles, but these usually involve color-blind issues such as fixing credit problems or scraping together a down payment.

Those who do experience discrimination should fight back. Don't let someone else's ignorance tarnish your home buying experience. Your money is the same color as everyone else's. The only color the sellers should care about is green.

Problems with Family Lending

EMOTIONAL/
FAMILY ISSUE
2

Family lending can be wonderful for everyone involved. You know the lenders—you're related to them. They know you and what kind of a risk you are. You get a good rate of interest with no points and no fees. They get a better-than-average return on their investment.

But family lending can have its problems, and, before you accept a relative's offer, think carefully about whether problems might pop up. For example, in some families, there are strings attached to cash gifts and loans. Your relatives may insist, for example, on helping you select your home in exchange for their gift or loan. If you don't mind, then that's fine. But, for some folks, that string might feel like a noose. Even when there are no strings attached, you may not want your relatives knowing about your personal finances. If you're a private person, having a relative or in-law know how much you earn and what you spend it on might feel a little uncomfortable. Even though your lender says he or she will keep that information private, don't count on it. Finally, some family members who lend money can't keep their noses out of your business. That can be a problem, especially if, around the first of the month, they harass you about making your mortgage payment on time.

You may not encounter any of these problems with your relatives. But at least roll these possibilities over in your mind before you sign on the dotted line. If any of them are distasteful, stop the process and find a commercial lender to fund your house purchase.

The Closing

After all the work you've done, going to the closing (also known in some states as the settlement) on your home can be enormously satisfying. At the closing, you sign your loan documents, then exchange money for the deed. When the last papers are signed, and the funds have been distributed to all parties involved, the seller will hand you all the keys to the property, including those for the mailbox and toolshed. And you will be suddenly, magically, transformed from a home buyer into a home owner.

Closings can happen anywhere, but usually they occur in the title or escrow office, at the lender's, or at one of the attorneys' offices. With co-ops, the closing will sometimes take place in the building board room, to accommodate the building board member who may have to sign certain documents.

There is relatively little about the closing that you need to be concerned with this early in the game. If you haven't even begun looking for a home, the closing may seem miles off. But there are some basic issues you should be aware of, so that when the time comes to make decisions about the closing, you'll have a better handle on what issues are important.

FINANCIAL ISSUES

Scheduling the Closing

When you sit down to prepare your offer for purchase, your real estate agent will ask you when you want to close on your new home.

FINANCIAL
ISSUE
1

217

This is the first time you'll need to think about choosing a closing date. The timing is important. It relates to the closing date in the following ways:

1. *Your current rent obligation.* If you're currently renting a home, you might want to schedule your closing as close to the end of your lease as possible. In that way, you won't be paying rent and a mortgage at the same time. If you need to do some work on your new home that will take you beyond your current lease term, consider asking your landlord to extend your lease, or close a month or two before the end of your lease.

2. *Prepaid interest.* If you're buying your home with financing, the closing date you choose will directly affect how much cash you have to come up with at the closing. You pay interest on your loan *in arrears;* that is, you pay your mortgage on October 1st for the interest that became due on the money you borrowed in September. If you close in mid-September, the lender asks you to prepay the interest from the closing date through the end of September. Then your next mortgage payment will be November 1, for interest due on the money you borrowed in October. Another example: If you close on January 15, at the closing you would prepay the interest due on your loan from January 15 through January 31. On March 1, you would write your first mortgage check, for the interest for the month of February.

3. *This year or next year.* If you have the opportunity to schedule your closing on either side of New Year's Day, think carefully before you make your decision. If you schedule it on December 31 or before, and you pay points and prepay your first mortgage payment, you can deduct all of those costs on your tax return for the year of the closing. Consult with your tax adviser to see whether there is an advantage to closing in one year or another.

4. *Extra time for your move.* The first thing most folks like to do after a closing is go to their new home. When scheduling your closing, you may want to allow time, after the papers are signed, to take that first walk-through before you have to go back to work. Then there's the move. If you plan to move into your home on the same day that you close, take the entire day off and schedule the closing in the morning. If everything is in

order and both parties fulfill all their obligations, you'll still be able to greet your moving van at your door in the afternoon. Bear in mind that you cannot close on a Saturday, Sunday, or holiday. Lenders and title companies are not available, and most attorneys don't care to work weekends.

There are plenty of concerns to keep you busy before the closing takes place, including making your moving, decorating, repair, and renovation arrangements. You should also put in a change of address with the U.S. Post Office, end the telephone and utility service for your current residence, and set up new accounts for your new address. But your big pre-closing assignment is to do a final walk-through of your new home no more than 24 hours before closing. Make sure that everything the sellers agreed to leave has been left, and that the house is basically in no worse shape than on the day you signed your offer to purchase. (There will, of course, be wear and tear, but that's considered acceptable.) Ideally, you'll be able to do this after the sellers have moved out. If there is a problem, be sure you bring it to your attorney's or broker's attention *before* you close. Although you can pursue the seller later, it's best to resolve these issues before you hand over the money. Of course, make sure your contract includes a paragraph granting you the right to make this final inspection.

10 STEP TIP

FINANCIAL ISSUE 2

Closing Costs

Earlier in the book, we discussed what closing costs are and how much you can expect to pay. However, it's worth mentioning that closing costs can change during the course of your purchase, though they are not supposed to change much. Lenders are required to give you a good-faith estimate within 3 days of your submitting an application for a loan. But they can usually itemize all of your closing costs before you submit your application. That's what you should have them do. Lenders are supposed to tell you before the closing the exact amounts of your closing costs. If you are working with an attorney or escrow officer, he or she should be able to get you that information before the closing.

It's important that you keep track of your closing costs. Use the worksheet on pages 220–221 to keep tabs on them. In addition to the lender's closing costs, you may have extra title costs, attorney costs, and inspection fees that you haven't paid previously.

WORKSHEET
Closing Costs

Property address _____

_____

Closing date _____

Closing place _____

Lender's origination points   _____

Lender's loan service fee   _____

Loan underwriting fee   _____

Loan application fee   _____

Lender's credit report   _____

Lender's processing fee   _____

Lender's document preparation fee   _____

Lender's appraisal fee   _____

Lender's inspection fee (if required)   _____

Lender's reinspection fee (if required)   _____

Prepaid interest on loan   _____

Lender's insurance escrow   _____

Lender's real estate tax escrow   _____

Lender's tax and insurance escrow service fee   _____

Title insurance cost for lender's policy   _____

Title insurance for owner's policy (if applicable)   _____

Special endorsements to the title   _____

House inspection fees (if not paid)   _____

House reinspection fees (if required)   _____

Termite inspection fee   _____

WORKSHEET
Closing Costs, *continued*

Title or escrow company closing fee _____

Recording fees (of deed or mortgage) _____

Assignment of mortgage fee _____

City, town, or village transfer tax _____

County transfer tax _____

State transfer tax _____

Attorney's fee _____

PMI reserve _____

PMI up-front charges (if any) _____

Flood zone certification fee _____

Tax credit to seller for prepaid taxes _____

Assessment credit to seller for prepaid assessments _____

Other fees and charges:

_____ _____

_____ _____

_____ _____

_____ _____

_____ _____

_____ _____

Total Closing Costs _____

Although you may have to pay most of these closing costs, you may not have to pay all of them. Negotiate with the lender to pay as few of the lender's fees as possible. Remember, do all your negotiating with the lender *before* you apply for your loan. Also, you may be able to negotiate with the seller to pick up some of these closing costs. Whether he or she will agree to do so depends partly on your local customs. If you're not sure what local customs dictate, ask your real estate agent or your attorney.

EMOTIONAL/FAMILY ISSUES

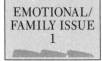

Scheduling Your Closing

Here's another real estate maxim: The longer the sellers have lived in their home, the harder it will be for them to move. As you're about to find out, owning a home has a strong emotional component for most people. In their heads, homeowners understand that their house is a piece of property, and perhaps even an investment vehicle. But in their hearts, many homeowners find themselves deeply attached to their homes. They contain memories and good feelings, not just furniture. If the sellers have raised children there, they may hear echoes of their footsteps even when the house is empty. They may have sunk roots into the community, been an active part of their neighbors' lives, and been involved with their children's school.

When the day comes to plan their move from a home they've lived in for 10, 20, or even 30 years, many sellers may shed some tears. As the buyer, be sensitive to these emotions, not only because it's a nice thing to do, but also because the seller's emotional state may be important to the way you structure your offer to purchase their home.

First-time home buyers sometimes mistakenly think that the only thing that matters in a transaction is how much money the sellers get for their home. Money may not be the key issue at all. Depending on whether the sellers have actually found another home, the closing date could be as important or far more important, to them. One Chicago seller nearly killed a deal because she had no place to move and worried that she and her son would be literally out on the street. She was willing to accept $5,000 less for her property simply so that she could postpone the closing date by 2 months. Another seller asked the home buyer if she and her husband could rent back their condominium after the closing. They sold faster than they'd anticipated and hadn't yet found a new home.

Keep in mind that if the closing date is a hot button for your seller, it could become a strategic part of your contract. Find out whether your city, county, or state has any statutes or customs regarding closing dates. For example, in New York, the seller is commonly given 30 days to get out of his or her home after closing, unless the issue is otherwise addressed in the contract. That means, by the 30th day after you own the home, the seller has to be out. This time frame is something you must consider from your perspective. Make sure you address, in writing, the issue of possession.

It's likely that the closing date you originally propose will not be the actual date you close; the date may change several times as you get closer to the closing. That's normal: You're trying to coordinate two attorneys, a lender's representative, a seller, a buyer, two brokers, and a closing agent (title or escrow officer)—a lot of schedules to work around.

Try to find out whether the closing date is important to your sellers. If it is, then offer to negotiate (sooner or later) for a lower price or better terms, or something that you want. But don't forsake the forest for the trees. You can agree to close earlier, say, in exchange for $5,000 off the purchase price. But if you'll be paying out the same $5,000, or more, in double rent and mortgage, the early closing won't be worth it. Make sure you run the numbers ahead of time.

Buyer's Remorse

EMOTIONAL/
FAMILY ISSUE
2

Buyer's remorse is that sinking feeling you get in the pit of your stomach when you realize you're in over your head. You've overstepped your limits. You've gone down the wrong path and don't know how to get back.

Buyer's remorse usually occurs in home buyers who don't know exactly how much they can truly afford, and don't have a clue whether their calculations have allowed them enough money to live comfortably. I'm all for making sacrifices to buy your first home. But you have to have enough cash at the end of the month to pay for food, electricity, gas, and your telephone bill.

Getting buyer's remorse over your home purchase is a little bit worse than spending too much on a new dress or suit. If you have to, you can return the suit. Once you've closed on your new home, you can't go back to the seller the next morning and ask him or her to rescind the contract. In fact, your only choice is to sell your home.

The best way to counteract buyer's remorse is to avoid it. If you've read this book thoroughly, followed its suggestions, and done your homework, you should be ready to start your home search. You'll know how much you can afford to buy, what you're really looking for, and the steps you need to take to fix your credit, save for a down payment, and cover your closing costs. In fact, you'll be ready to read my book for home buyers: *100 Questions Every First-Time Home Buyer Should Ask*, which picks up where this book leaves off. With both of these books, and plenty of other knowledge you'll gain from consulting with your real estate agent, reading your local newspaper, and talking to your friends and family about their home buying experiences, you shouldn't have to worry about buyer's remorse. You almost certainly won't get it.

Just to be certain you don't, sit down and think long and hard about any step you're going to take—*before* you take it. Before you contact any buyer's brokers, ask yourself whether you're ready to make this financial commitment. What will you have to give up to make it happen? Before you make your offer, ask yourself whether this is something you can really live with. Once your offer is accepted, unless the home doesn't pass muster with your home inspector, you're probably stuck with it.

The time to be certain you want to be a home buyer is before you buy, not the night after you signed the contract or the night after you closed on your new home. You don't want to spend that first night worried sick, wondering whether you'll be able to afford to take the kids to McDonald's ever again. The first night in your new home, when you and your loved ones are settling down, surrounded by unpacked boxes and cartons, look around and count your blessings. You're in your own home.

And that's a nice place to be.

The Top 5 Financial Mistakes and the Top 5 Emotional Mistakes First-Time Buyers Often Make

Everyone makes mistakes. The trick is to learn from yours. I also think it's enormously helpful to learn about the mistakes other people commonly make. Think of them as signposts on the journey. In other words, if you're driving from Manhattan to Los Angeles, it helps to know that you'll pass through Chicago, Kansas City, and Phoenix on the way. If you know where other folks have stumbled, you'll be on the lookout—and hopefully you'll be able to avoid the same potholes. That's not to say you won't find your own. You will. Everyone does.

Here are the top five financial mistakes and the top five emotional mistakes first-time buyers often make.

TOP 5 FINANCIAL MISTAKES FIRST-TIME BUYERS MAKE

1. *Blowing Your Budget—Spending More Than You Earn.* Here's an old cliché that still applies: If you carry money around, it'll burn a hole in your pocket. But having credit cards in your pocket is even more dangerous than carrying around a wad of cash. Since you probably have a credit limit of several thousand dollars, it wouldn't take much to do some serious damage to your budget in one fell swoop.

Many first-time buyers make the mistake of blowing their budget with consumer gizmos and gadgets that they really don't need. You may think you need the latest stereo equipment or CD, but how eager would you be to spend that cash if you realized it would delay your dream of homeownership by six more months? That's six months of paying rent when you could be building up equity in your very own house.

Another mistake is carrying too much credit for your level of income. If you've got 15 credit cards (check your wallet), you've probably got 11 to 13 too many. Pare down your credit cards, and the balance you're carrying on those cards, or you'll find that lenders may not be willing to lend you the amount of money you need to buy your home.

Creating a budget you can live with is an important part of preparing for homeownership. That doesn't mean you have to give up everything, forever. But you need to stay focused on the end goal. *See Step 3, Putting Together the Cash for Your Down Payment and Closing Costs for more information on putting together a winning budget.*

2. *Not Saving Enough for Your Down Payment and Closing Costs.* It isn't enough to get your budget in line if you forget to save enough for your down payments *and* closing costs. While some loans will allow you to purchase property with as little as 3 percent down in cash, you'll still need additional cash to pay closing costs and fees, which could run another 1 to 4 percent of the loan amount. On a $100,000 loan, that's an additional $1,000 to $4,000 that you'll need in cash at closing. *For a list of closing costs, see Step 3, Putting Together the Cash for Your Down Payment and Closing Costs and Step 9, Financing Your Home.*

3. *Underestimating the Costs of Owning and Maintaining a Home.* Renting is easy. You write one check a month to the landlord, who takes care of maintaining the property. Owning is more complicated, since you're now responsible for the maintenance and upkeep of your home.

One mistake first-time buyers often make is underestimating the costs of these types of homeownership expenses. You may not put aside enough cash for your property taxes. Or, you may not realize that tearing off your roof and replacing it will cost $5,000, not $3,000. If you're on a tight budget and you don't factor in the costs of replacing and repairing major mechanical or structural items, you could find yourself caught with an empty wallet just when you need cash the most. *For more information on how much it costs to own and maintain a home, see Step 2, How Much House Can I Afford? Step 8, Comparing Homes, Costs, and Finances might also be useful.*

4. *Mistaken Mortgage Assumptions.* One of the most costly mistakes home buyers make is not knowing enough about the various mortgage products on the market *before* applying for a loan. Start by looking through the real estate section of your local newspaper and seeing what kinds of loans and interest rates are being advertised. Then, think about how long you're going to live in your new home. If you're going to be there less than five years, you should consider an adjustable (ARM) rather than a fixed-rate loan. Next, call a few local lenders and ask a lot of questions about what types of loans they offer. Don't make the mistake of allowing your real estate agent to guide your mortgage process. Use a qualified, highly-recommended mortgage professional who is in the position of being able to lend you the money you need. *See Step 9, Financing Your Home for more information on choosing the right home loan for you.*

5. *Not Knowing When to Seek Professional Help.* There's a "can do" attitude in America today, a pride that stems from our ability to help ourselves. It's a wonderful thing to be able to fix up your own home, feed and clothe your family. But sometimes, our pride gets in the way, and we end up hurting, rather than helping, ourselves.

Although nearly five million Americans will buy a home this year, the path to homeownership is complex, filled with jargon that is confusing at best. There's nothing wrong with trying to solve your own financial problems, but there may come a time when they are too much to handle. Before you get yourself deeper in debt, or need to declare bankruptcy, seek professional help. There are financial counselors that can assist you in managing your cash flow and balancing your budget. They can guide you on how to improve your credit history, which can be so vulnerable. Don't let pride get in the way of your homeownership goals. *See Appendix III—Resources, for the names and telephone numbers of organizations that can assist you with your budgeting and credit problems.*

TOP 5 EMOTIONAL MISTAKES
FIRST-TIME BUYERS OFTEN MAKE

1. *Falling in Love with a House.* Buying a home is an incredibly emotional experience for many people, much more so than other

financial investments. That's because we're choosing the place we're going to call home: It should be safe and secure, and in some way touch our emotional core. But because the process calls upon us to reconcile our dreams with the realities of our checkbooks, it also plays upon our emotions. And once emotions are involved, it's difficult to inject the distance you need to make an objective choice.

Can you fall in love with a house? Certainly. You may also be encouraged down that path by a real estate agent who says things like, "Oh, this house was meant for you," and "It really suits you," and "I can tell this is the perfect house for you. Don't you just love it?" What you have to remember is this: love fades. After awhile, you'll start to see the flaws every home has. Nothing's perfect, and if you haven't based your choice on what you actually need, you may find yourself owning the wrong home. *For information on how to inject a little objectivity into your home search, see Step 6, Identifying Where You Want To Live.*

2. *Losing Control of Your Purchase.* Another mistake first-time buyers often make is losing control of the home-buying process. It can happen in any number of ways. You hire an assertive agent who puts you where she thinks you should be, which may or may not be where you actually want to live. Or perhaps your parents step in with a check and their two cents. Or, your children require more of the time you set aside as home-buying time.

Whichever way it happens, losing control of the home-buying process can result in a number of errors that can damage the end result. For example, if you and your spouse or partner want to be in a particular school district in time for the Fall semester and you let the Spring slip away, you could wind up having to transfer your kids sometime during mid-semester. Another way of losing control happens when you allow personality clashes (between you and the real estate agent, mortgage broker, or professional home inspector) to get the best of you.

Just remain focused on the end goal: A successful closing and move into your new home.

3. *Being Indecisive.* Do you want to buy a house? Or, do you want to start your own business? Or do you want to take a six-month sabbatical and travel the world? Buying a home means making plenty of tough decisions about budgets, neighborhoods, and even what you want in a house. Then you must reconcile your choices with those of your spouse or partner.

If you're indecisive about what you want and where you want it, it may indicate that you're not ready to make the emotional commitment to homeownership. If you're simply worried that the minute after you make your offer a better house at a better price will come along, remember this: There's more than one right house for you. There are countless anecdotes of people bidding on homes, losing them, and then finding a home that's a better choice the next time out. At some point in time, you'll have to make an offer or withdraw from the process. Of course, once you start looking for a home, your indecision may mean you'll lose a few homes before you decide you're really going to do what it takes to buy a home.

4. *Underestimating the Responsibilities of Homeownership.* As we've already discussed, renting is easy. You write one check a month and the landlord is supposed to take care of the rest. Owning a home is more complicated, and the responsibilities of homeownership can weigh heavily.

Here are some of the things you must do if you're a homeowner: You must remember to pay your mortgage, assessments (if any), and real estate property taxes. Here are some of the things you should do: If your tax bill seems unreasonably high in comparison to those your neighbors receive, you should fight to lower it with the tax collector. You should buy enough hazard insurance to protect you against loss or damage of your house and its belongings (underinsuring a home is one of the biggest mistakes home buyers make). If you don't keep your house and landscaping in wonderful condition your home may not appreciate in value as quickly as others. You should fight city hall for necessary street and sidewalk improvements and against unnecessary ones. You should work hard to be a good neighbor, and improve the neighborhood.

Yes, buying a home means you get to paint the walls any color you like. But if you're not prepared for the responsibilities—which may mean you'll have to spend the weekend puttering around the backyard instead of putting on the green—you may have bought before your time.

5. *Buying a Home Before You're Really Ready.* I started this book by saying that owning a home isn't for everyone—and it's the savvy home buyer who recognizes that he or she isn't really ready for the commitment.

How do you know whether or not you're ready to buy a home? It's different for everyone. If you find you're resisting any one particular path, you're probably trying to do something you're not ready for. Do your homework to give yourself a base of knowledge and comfort. For example, if you find yourself overwhelmed by the thought of choosing a neighborhood, start exploring neighborhoods slowly, one-by-one. Or, if you're concerned about being able to afford a home, sit down and work out a budget. You might find that you're living more cheaply than you could if you owned, though without the long-term financial benefits. If you're concerned that your quality of life will be compromised by a move, spend some time figuring out how you'll get to and from your job and what kind of time it will take. If you'll add two hours to your commute each day, you may indeed be better off renting until you can afford a home closer to your job.

Buying a home before you're really ready almost certainly will result in a heavy-duty case of buyer's remorse. That's the sinking feeling you get in the pit of your stomach when you've committed yourself beyond your financial or emotional resources. When you buy the right home at the right time, for the right amount of money, you won't have buyer's remorse. Instead, you'll have the pleasure of looking forward to your move as an exciting challenge rather than dreading it.

If you can't figure out why the thought of moving gives you the jitters, you should consult with a professional. Talk things over with your financial counselor, your real estate agent, and your mortgage professional. Remember that millions of first-time buyers have stood in your shoes, and taken the steps that you're about to take. Approximately two million first-time buyers successfully walk the path to homeownership every year. It is a path well-worn, with signposts along the way. You won't get lost. All you have to do is take it one step at a time.

Amortization Tables

The following amortization tables allow you to figure out exactly how much you'll be paying in interest and principal each month. Here's how to use them: First, find the table that reflects the interest rate you're being charged. Next, go to the column that corresponds with the length of your loan. Finally, add up the columns to find the amount of your loan.

For example, let's say you're borrowing $175,000 at 8.5 percent interest for 30 years. If you go to the 8.5 percent table and find the 30-year loan column, move down the column until you find $100,000. You'll see that borrowing $100,000 at 8.5 percent for 30 years will cost you $768.91 per month. Next, move your finger across the $70,000 column. It will cost you an additional $538.24 per month to borrow that $70,000. Finally, find the $5,000 row, and move across until you get to $38.45. Add these numbers up to get your monthly interest and principal payment:

$$\$768.91 + \$538.24 + \$38.45 = \$1,345.60$$

Your monthly amortized principal and interest payment for a 30-year $175,000 loan at 8.5 percent would be $1,345.60.

4.00% Rate

Amount	Term of Loan in Years					
	10	15	20	25	30	40
$ 50.00	$ 0.51	$ 0.37	$ 0.30	$ 0.26	$ 0.24	$ 0.21
100.00	1.01	0.74	0.61	0.53	0.48	0.42
200.00	2.02	1.48	1.21	1.06	0.95	0.84
300.00	3.04	2.22	1.82	1.58	1.43	1.25
400.00	4.05	2.96	2.42	2.11	1.91	1.67
500.00	5.06	3.70	3.03	2.64	2.39	2.09
600.00	6.07	4.44	3.64	3.17	2.86	2.51
700.00	7.09	5.18	4.24	3.69	3.34	2.93
800.00	8.10	5.92	4.85	4.22	3.82	3.34
900.00	9.11	6.66	5.45	4.75	4.30	3.76
1,000.00	10.12	7.40	6.06	5.28	4.77	4.18
2,000.00	20.25	14.79	12.12	10.56	9.55	8.36
3,000.00	30.37	22.19	18.18	15.84	14.32	12.54
4,000.00	40.50	29.59	24.24	21.11	19.10	16.72
5,000.00	50.62	36.98	30.30	26.39	23.87	20.90
6,000.00	60.75	44.38	36.36	31.67	28.64	25.08
7,000.00	70.87	51.78	42.42	36.95	33.42	29.26
8,000.00	81.00	59.18	48.48	42.23	38.19	33.44
9,000.00	91.12	66.57	54.54	47.51	42.97	37.61
10,000.00	101.25	73.97	60.60	52.78	47.74	41.79
20,000.00	202.49	147.94	121.20	105.57	95.48	83.59
30,000.00	303.74	221.91	181.79	158.35	143.22	125.38
40,000.00	404.98	295.88	242.39	211.13	190.97	167.18
50,000.00	506.23	369.84	302.99	263.92	238.71	208.97
60,000.00	607.47	443.81	363.59	316.70	286.45	250.76
70,000.00	708.72	517.78	424.19	369.49	334.19	292.56
80,000.00	809.96	591.75	484.78	422.27	381.93	334.35
90,000.00	911.21	665.72	545.38	475.05	429.67	376.14
100,000.00	1,012.45	739.69	605.98	527.84	477.42	417.94

4.125% Rate

Amount	Term of Loan in Years					
	10	15	20	25	30	40
$ 50.00	$ 0.51	$ 0.37	$ 0.31	$ 0.27	$ 0.24	$ 0.21
100.00	1.02	0.75	0.61	0.53	0.48	0.43
200.00	2.04	1.49	1.23	1.07	0.97	0.85
300.00	3.06	2.24	1.84	1.60	1.45	1.28
400.00	4.07	2.98	2.45	2.14	1.94	1.70
500.00	5.09	3.73	3.06	2.67	2.42	2.13
600.00	6.11	4.48	3.68	3.21	2.91	2.55
700.00	7.13	5.22	4.29	3.74	3.39	2.98
800.00	8.15	5.97	4.90	4.28	3.88	3.41
900.00	9.17	6.71	5.51	4.81	4.36	3.83
1,000.00	10.18	7.46	6.13	5.35	4.85	4.26
2,000.00	20.37	14.92	12.25	10.70	9.69	8.51
3,000.00	30.55	22.38	18.38	16.04	14.54	12.77
4,000.00	40.74	29.84	24.50	21.39	19.39	17.03
5,000.00	50.92	37.30	30.63	26.74	24.23	21.29
6,000.00	61.10	44.76	36.76	32.09	29.08	25.54
7,000.00	71.29	52.22	42.88	37.43	33.93	29.80
8,000.00	81.47	59.68	49.01	42.78	38.77	34.06
9,000.00	91.66	67.14	55.13	48.13	43.62	38.32
10,000.00	101.84	74.60	61.26	53.48	48.46	42.57
20,000.00	203.68	149.19	122.52	106.95	96.93	85.15
30,000.00	305.52	223.79	183.78	160.43	145.39	127.72
40,000.00	407.36	298.39	245.03	213.91	193.86	170.30
50,000.00	509.20	372.98	306.29	267.38	242.32	212.87
60,000.00	611.04	447.58	367.55	320.86	290.79	255.45
70,000.00	712.88	522.18	428.81	374.33	339.25	298.02
80,000.00	814.72	596.77	490.07	427.81	387.72	340.60
90,000.00	916.56	671.37	551.33	481.29	436.18	383.17
100,000.00	1,018.40	745.97	612.59	534.76	484.65	425.75

4.250% Rate

Amount	Term of Loan in Years					
	10	15	20	25	30	40
$ 50.00	$ 0.51	$ 0.38	$ 0.31	$ 0.27	$ 0.25	$ 0.22
100.00	1.02	0.75	0.62	0.54	0.49	0.43
200.00	2.05	1.50	1.24	1.08	0.98	0.87
300.00	3.07	2.26	1.86	1.63	1.48	1.30
400.00	4.10	3.01	2.48	2.17	1.97	1.73
500.00	5.12	3.76	3.10	2.71	2.46	2.17
600.00	6.15	4.51	3.72	3.25	2.95	2.60
700.00	7.17	5.27	4.33	3.79	3.44	3.04
800.00	8.20	6.02	4.95	4.33	3.94	3.47
900.00	9.22	6.77	5.57	4.88	4.43	3.90
1,000.00	10.24	7.52	6.19	5.42	4.92	4.34
2,000.00	20.49	15.05	12.38	10.83	9.84	8.67
3,000.00	30.73	22.57	18.58	16.25	14.76	13.01
4,000.00	40.98	30.09	24.77	21.67	19.68	17.34
5,000.00	51.22	37.61	30.96	27.09	24.60	21.68
6,000.00	61.46	45.14	37.15	32.50	29.52	26.02
7,000.00	71.71	52.66	43.35	37.92	34.44	30.35
8,000.00	81.95	60.18	49.54	43.34	39.36	34.69
9,000.00	92.19	67.71	55.73	48.76	44.27	39.03
10,000.00	102.44	75.23	61.92	54.17	49.19	43.36
20,000.00	204.88	150.46	123.85	108.35	98.39	86.72
30,000.00	307.31	225.68	185.77	162.52	147.58	130.09
40,000.00	409.75	300.91	247.69	216.70	196.78	173.45
50,000.00	512.19	376.14	309.62	270.87	245.97	216.81
60,000.00	614.63	451.37	371.54	325.04	295.16	260.17
70,000.00	717.06	526.59	433.46	379.22	344.36	303.53
80,000.00	819.50	601.82	495.39	433.39	393.55	346.90
90,000.00	921.94	677.05	557.31	487.56	442.75	390.26
100,000.00	1,024.38	752.28	619.23	541.74	491.94	433.62

4.375% Rate

Amount	Term of Loan in Years					
	10	15	20	25	30	40
$ 50.00	$ 0.52	$ 0.38	$ 0.31	$ 0.27	$ 0.25	$ 0.22
100.00	1.03	0.76	0.63	0.55	0.50	0.44
200.00	2.06	1.52	1.25	1.10	1.00	0.88
300.00	3.09	2.28	1.88	1.65	1.50	1.32
400.00	4.12	3.03	2.50	2.20	2.00	1.77
500.00	5.15	3.79	3.13	2.74	2.50	2.21
600.00	6.18	4.55	3.76	3.29	3.00	2.65
700.00	7.21	5.31	4.38	3.84	3.49	3.09
800.00	8.24	6.07	5.01	4.39	3.99	3.53
900.00	9.27	6.83	5.63	4.94	4.49	3.97
1,000.00	10.30	7.59	6.26	5.49	4.99	4.42
2,000.00	20.61	15.17	12.52	10.98	9.99	8.83
3,000.00	30.91	22.76	18.78	16.46	14.98	13.25
4,000.00	41.21	30.34	25.04	21.95	19.97	17.66
5,000.00	51.52	37.93	31.30	27.44	24.96	22.08
6,000.00	61.82	45.52	37.56	32.93	29.96	26.49
7,000.00	72.13	53.10	43.81	38.41	34.95	30.91
8,000.00	82.43	60.69	50.07	43.90	39.94	35.32
9,000.00	92.73	68.28	56.33	49.39	44.94	39.74
10,000.00	103.04	75.86	62.59	54.88	49.93	44.16
20,000.00	206.07	151.72	125.18	109.75	99.86	88.31
30,000.00	309.11	227.59	187.78	164.63	149.79	132.47
40,000.00	412.15	303.45	250.37	219.50	199.71	176.62
50,000.00	515.18	379.31	312.96	274.38	249.64	220.78
60,000.00	618.22	455.17	375.55	329.26	299.57	264.94
70,000.00	721.26	531.03	438.15	384.13	349.50	309.09
80,000.00	824.30	606.90	500.74	439.01	399.43	353.25
90,000.00	927.33	682.76	563.33	493.89	449.36	397.40
100,000.00	1,030.37	758.62	625.92	548.76	499.29	441.56

4.500% Rate

Amount	Term of Loan in Years					
	10	15	20	25	30	40
$ 50.00	$ 0.52	$ 0.38	$ 0.32	$ 0.28	$ 0.25	0.22
100.00	1.04	0.76	0.63	0.56	0.51	0.45
200.00	2.07	1.53	1.27	1.11	1.01	0.90
300.00	3.11	2.29	1.90	1.67	1.52	1.35
400.00	4.15	3.06	2.53	2.22	2.03	1.80
500.00	5.18	3.82	3.16	2.78	2.53	2.25
600.00	6.22	4.59	3.80	3.33	3.04	2.70
700.00	7.25	5.35	4.43	3.89	3.55	3.15
800.00	8.29	6.12	5.06	4.45	4.05	3.60
900.00	9.33	6.88	5.69	5.00	4.56	4.05
1,000.00	10.36	7.65	6.33	5.56	5.07	4.50
2,000.00	20.73	15.30	12.65	11.12	10.13	8.99
3,000.00	31.09	22.95	18.98	16.67	15.20	13.49
4,000.00	41.46	30.60	25.31	22.23	20.27	17.98
5,000.00	51.82	38.25	31.63	27.79	25.33	22.48
6,000.00	62.18	45.90	37.96	33.35	30.40	26.97
7,000.00	72.55	53.55	44.29	38.91	35.47	31.47
8,000.00	82.91	61.20	50.61	44.47	40.53	35.97
9,000.00	93.27	68.85	56.94	50.02	45.60	40.46
10,000.00	103.64	76.50	63.26	55.58	50.67	44.96
20,000.00	207.28	153.00	126.53	111.17	101.34	89.91
30,000.00	310.92	229.50	189.79	166.75	152.01	134.87
40,000.00	414.55	306.00	253.06	222.33	202.67	179.83
50,000.00	518.19	382.50	316.32	277.92	253.34	224.78
60,000.00	621.83	459.00	379.59	333.50	304.01	269.74
70,000.00	725.47	535.50	442.85	389.08	354.68	314.69
80,000.00	829.11	611.99	506.12	444.67	405.35	359.65
90,000.00	932.75	688.49	569.38	500.25	456.02	404.61
100,000.00	1,036.38	764.99	632.65	555.83	506.69	449.56

4.625% Rate

Amount	Term of Loan in Years					
	10	15	20	25	30	40
$ 50.00	0.52	$ 0.39	$ 0.32	$ 0.28	$ 0.26	$ 0.23
100.00	1.04	0.77	0.64	0.56	0.51	0.46
200.00	2.08	1.54	1.28	1.13	1.03	0.92
300.00	3.13	2.31	1.92	1.69	1.54	1.37
400.00	4.17	3.09	2.56	2.25	2.06	1.83
500.00	5.21	3.86	3.20	2.81	2.57	2.29
600.00	6.25	4.63	3.84	3.38	3.08	2.75
700.00	7.30	5.40	4.48	3.94	3.60	3.20
800.00	8.34	6.17	5.12	4.50	4.11	3.66
900.00	9.38	6.94	5.75	5.07	4.63	4.12
1,000.00	10.42	7.71	6.39	5.63	5.14	4.58
2,000.00	20.85	15.43	12.79	11.26	10.28	9.15
3,000.00	31.27	23.14	19.18	16.89	15.42	13.73
4,000.00	41.70	30.86	25.58	22.52	20.57	18.31
5,000.00	52.12	38.57	31.97	28.15	25.71	22.88
6,000.00	62.55	46.28	38.37	33.78	30.85	27.46
7,000.00	72.97	54.00	44.76	39.41	35.99	32.03
8,000.00	83.39	61.71	51.15	45.04	41.13	36.61
9,000.00	93.82	69.43	57.55	50.67	46.27	41.19
10,000.00	104.24	77.14	63.94	56.30	51.41	45.76
20,000.00	208.48	154.28	127.88	112.59	102.83	91.53
30,000.00	312.73	231.42	191.83	168.89	154.24	137.29
40,000.00	416.97	308.56	255.77	225.18	205.66	183.05
50,000.00	521.21	385.70	319.71	281.48	257.07	228.81
60,000.00	625.45	462.84	383.65	337.77	308.48	274.58
70,000.00	729.69	539.98	447.59	394.07	359.90	320.34
80,000.00	833.94	617.12	511.53	450.36	411.31	366.10
90,000.00	938.18	694.26	575.48	506.66	462.73	411.87
100,000.00	1,042.42	771.40	639.42	562.95	514.14	457.63

4.750% Rate

Amount	Term of Loan in Years					
	10	15	20	25	30	40
$ 50.00	$ 0.52	$ 0.39	$ 0.32	$ 0.29	$ 0.26	$ 0.23
100.00	1.05	0.78	0.65	0.57	0.52	0.47
200.00	2.10	1.56	1.29	1.14	1.04	0.93
300.00	3.15	2.33	1.94	1.71	1.56	1.40
400.00	4.19	3.11	2.58	2.28	2.09	1.86
500.00	5.24	3.89	3.23	2.85	2.61	2.33
600.00	6.29	4.67	3.88	3.42	3.13	2.79
700.00	7.34	5.44	4.52	3.99	3.65	3.26
800.00	8.39	6.22	5.17	4.56	4.17	3.73
900.00	9.44	7.00	5.82	5.13	4.69	4.19
1,000.00	10.48	7.78	6.46	5.70	5.22	4.66
2,000.00	20.97	15.56	12.92	11.40	10.43	9.32
3,000.00	31.45	23.33	19.39	17.10	15.65	13.97
4,000.00	41.94	31.11	25.85	22.80	20.87	18.63
5,000.00	52.42	38.89	32.31	28.51	26.08	23.29
6,000.00	62.91	46.67	38.77	34.21	31.30	27.95
7,000.00	73.39	54.45	45.24	39.91	36.52	32.60
8,000.00	83.88	62.23	51.70	45.61	41.73	37.26
9,000.00	94.36	70.00	58.16	51.31	46.95	41.92
10,000.00	104.85	77.78	64.62	57.01	52.16	46.58
20,000.00	209.70	155.57	129.24	114.02	104.33	93.15
30,000.00	314.54	233.35	193.87	171.04	156.49	139.73
40,000.00	419.39	311.13	258.49	228.05	208.66	186.30
50,000.00	524.24	388.92	323.11	285.06	260.82	232.88
60,000.00	629.09	466.70	387.73	342.07	312.99	279.45
70,000.00	733.93	544.48	452.36	399.08	365.15	326.03
80,000.00	838.78	622.27	516.98	456.09	417.32	372.61
90,000.00	943.63	700.05	581.60	513.11	469.48	419.18
100,000.00	1,048.48	777.83	646.22	570.12	521.65	465.76

4.875% Rate

Amount	Term of Loan in Years					
	10	15	20	25	30	40
$ 50.00	$ 0.53	$ 0.39	$ 0.33	$ 0.29	$ 0.26	$ 0.24
100.00	1.05	0.78	0.65	0.58	0.53	0.47
200.00	2.11	1.57	1.31	1.15	1.06	0.95
300.00	3.16	2.35	1.96	1.73	1.59	1.42
400.00	4.22	3.14	2.61	2.31	2.12	1.90
500.00	5.27	3.92	3.27	2.89	2.65	2.37
600.00	6.33	4.71	3.92	3.46	3.18	2.84
700.00	7.38	5.49	4.57	4.04	3.70	3.32
800.00	8.44	6.27	5.22	4.62	4.23	3.79
900.00	9.49	7.06	5.88	5.20	4.76	4.27
1,000.00	10.55	7.84	6.53	5.77	5.29	4.74
2,000.00	21.09	15.69	13.06	11.55	10.58	9.48
3,000.00	31.64	23.53	19.59	17.32	15.88	14.22
4,000.00	42.18	31.37	26.12	23.09	21.17	18.96
5,000.00	52.73	39.21	32.65	28.87	26.46	23.70
6,000.00	63.27	47.06	39.18	34.64	31.75	28.44
7,000.00	73.82	54.90	45.71	40.41	37.04	33.18
8,000.00	84.36	62.74	52.25	46.19	42.34	37.92
9,000.00	94.91	70.59	58.78	51.96	47.63	42.66
10,000.00	105.46	78.43	65.31	57.73	52.92	47.39
20,000.00	210.91	156.86	130.61	115.47	105.84	94.79
30,000.00	316.37	235.29	195.92	173.20	158.76	142.18
40,000.00	421.82	313.72	261.23	230.93	211.68	189.58
50,000.00	527.28	392.15	326.54	288.67	264.60	236.97
60,000.00	632.73	470.58	391.84	346.40	317.52	284.37
70,000.00	738.19	549.01	457.15	404.13	370.45	331.76
80,000.00	843.64	627.44	522.46	461.86	423.37	379.16
90,000.00	949.10	705.87	587.76	519.60	476.29	426.55
100,000.00	1,054.56	784.30	653.07	577.33	529.21	473.95

5.000% Rate

Amount		Term of Loan in Years					
		10	15	20	25	30	40
$	50.00	$ 0.53	$ 0.40	$ 0.33	$ 0.29	$ 0.27	$ 0.24
	100.00	1.06	0.79	0.66	0.58	0.54	0.48
	200.00	2.12	1.58	1.32	1.17	1.07	0.96
	300.00	3.18	2.37	1.98	1.75	1.61	1.45
	400.00	4.24	3.16	2.64	2.34	2.15	1.93
	500.00	5.30	3.95	3.30	2.92	2.68	2.41
	600.00	6.36	4.74	3.96	3.51	3.22	2.89
	700.00	7.42	5.54	4.62	4.09	3.76	3.38
	800.00	8.49	6.33	5.28	4.68	4.29	3.86
	900.00	9.55	7.12	5.94	5.26	4.83	4.34
	1,000.00	10.61	7.91	6.60	5.85	5.37	4.82
	2,000.00	21.21	15.82	13.20	11.69	10.74	9.64
	3,000.00	31.82	23.72	19.80	17.54	16.10	14.47
	4,000.00	42.43	31.63	26.40	23.38	21.47	19.29
	5,000.00	53.03	39.54	33.00	29.23	26.84	24.11
	6,000.00	63.64	47.45	39.60	35.08	32.21	28.93
	7,000.00	74.25	55.36	46.20	40.92	37.58	33.75
	8,000.00	84.85	63.26	52.80	46.77	42.95	38.58
	9,000.00	95.46	71.17	59.40	52.61	48.31	43.40
	10,000.00	106.07	79.08	66.00	58.46	53.68	48.22
	20,000.00	212.13	158.16	131.99	116.92	107.36	96.44
	30,000.00	318.20	237.24	197.99	175.38	161.05	144.66
	40,000.00	424.26	316.32	263.98	233.84	214.73	192.88
	50,000.00	530.33	395.40	329.98	292.30	268.41	241.10
	60,000.00	636.39	474.48	395.97	350.75	322.09	289.32
	70,000.00	742.46	553.56	461.97	409.21	375.78	337.54
	80,000.00	848.52	632.63	527.96	467.67	429.46	385.76
	90,000.00	954.59	711.71	593.96	526.13	483.14	433.98
	100,000.00	1,060.66	790.79	659.96	584.59	536.82	482.20

5.125% Rate

Amount	Term of Loan in Years					
	10	15	20	25	30	40
$ 50.00	$ 0.53	$ 0.40	$ 0.33	$ 0.30	$ 0.27	$ 0.25
100.00	1.07	0.80	0.67	0.59	0.54	0.49
200.00	2.13	1.59	1.33	1.18	1.09	0.98
300.00	3.20	2.39	2.00	1.78	1.63	1.47
400.00	4.27	3.19	2.67	2.37	2.18	1.96
500.00	5.33	3.99	3.33	2.96	2.72	2.45
600.00	6.40	4.78	4.00	3.55	3.27	2.94
700.00	7.47	5.58	4.67	4.14	3.81	3.43
800.00	8.53	6.38	5.34	4.74	4.36	3.92
900.00	9.60	7.18	6.00	5.33	4.90	4.41
1,000.00	10.67	7.97	6.67	5.92	5.44	4.91
2,000.00	21.34	15.95	13.34	11.84	10.89	9.81
3,000.00	32.00	23.92	20.01	17.76	16.33	14.72
4,000.00	42.67	31.89	26.68	23.68	21.78	19.62
5,000.00	53.34	39.87	33.34	29.59	27.22	24.53
6,000.00	64.01	47.84	40.01	35.51	32.67	29.43
7,000.00	74.67	55.81	46.68	41.43	38.11	34.34
8,000.00	85.34	63.79	53.35	47.35	43.56	39.24
9,000.00	96.01	71.76	60.02	53.27	49.00	44.15
10,000.00	106.68	79.73	66.69	59.19	54.45	49.05
20,000.00	213.36	159.46	133.38	118.38	108.90	98.10
30,000.00	320.03	239.20	200.06	177.57	163.35	147.15
40,000.00	426.71	318.93	266.75	236.76	217.79	196.20
50,000.00	533.39	398.66	333.44	295.95	272.24	245.25
60,000.00	640.07	478.39	400.13	355.14	326.69	294.30
70,000.00	746.74	558.12	466.82	414.33	381.14	343.35
80,000.00	853.42	637.86	533.50	473.52	435.59	392.40
90,000.00	960.10	717.59	600.19	532.71	490.04	441.45
100,000.00	1,066.78	797.32	666.88	591.90	544.49	490.50

5.250% Rate

Amount	Term of Loan in Years					
	10	15	20	25	30	40
$ 50.00	$ 0.54	$ 0.40	$ 0.34	$ 0.30	$ 0.28	$ 0.25
100.00	1.07	0.80	0.67	0.60	0.55	0.50
200.00	2.15	1.61	1.35	1.20	1.10	1.00
300.00	3.22	2.41	2.02	1.80	1.66	1.50
400.00	4.29	3.22	2.70	2.40	2.21	2.00
500.00	5.36	4.02	3.37	3.00	2.76	2.49
600.00	6.44	4.82	4.04	3.60	3.31	2.99
700.00	7.51	5.63	4.72	4.19	3.87	3.49
800.00	8.58	6.43	5.39	4.79	4.42	3.99
900.00	9.66	7.23	6.06	5.39	4.97	4.49
1,000.00	10.73	8.04	6.74	5.99	5.52	4.99
2,000.00	21.46	16.08	13.48	11.98	11.04	9.98
3,000.00	32.19	24.12	20.22	17.98	16.57	14.97
4,000.00	42.92	32.16	26.95	23.97	22.09	19.95
5,000.00	53.65	40.19	33.69	29.96	27.61	24.94
6,000.00	64.38	48.23	40.43	35.95	33.13	29.93
7,000.00	75.10	56.27	47.17	41.95	38.65	34.92
8,000.00	85.83	64.31	53.91	47.94	44.18	39.91
9,000.00	96.56	72.35	60.65	53.93	49.70	44.90
10,000.00	107.29	80.39	67.38	59.92	55.22	49.89
20,000.00	214.58	160.78	134.77	119.85	110.44	99.77
30,000.00	321.88	241.16	202.15	179.77	165.66	149.66
40,000.00	429.17	321.55	269.54	239.70	220.88	199.55
50,000.00	536.46	401.94	336.92	299.62	276.10	249.44
60,000.00	643.75	482.33	404.31	359.55	331.32	299.32
70,000.00	751.04	562.71	471.69	419.47	386.54	349.21
80,000.00	858.33	643.10	539.08	479.40	441.76	399.10
90,000.00	965.63	723.49	606.46	539.32	496.98	448.98
100,000.00	1,072.92	803.88	673.84	599.25	552.20	498.87

5.375% Rate

Amount	Term of Loan in Years					
	10	15	20	25	30	40
$ 50.00	$ 0.54	$ 0.41	$ 0.34	$ 0.30	$ 0.28	$ 0.25
100.00	1.08	0.81	0.68	0.61	0.56	0.51
200.00	2.16	1.62	1.36	1.21	1.12	1.01
300.00	3.24	2.43	2.04	1.82	1.68	1.52
400.00	4.32	3.24	2.72	2.43	2.24	2.03
500.00	5.40	4.05	3.40	3.03	2.80	2.54
600.00	6.47	4.86	4.09	3.64	3.36	3.04
700.00	7.55	5.67	4.77	4.25	3.92	3.55
800.00	8.63	6.48	5.45	4.85	4.48	4.06
900.00	9.71	7.29	6.13	5.46	5.04	4.57
1,000.00	10.79	8.10	6.81	6.07	5.60	5.07
2,000.00	21.58	16.21	13.62	12.13	11.20	10.15
3,000.00	32.37	24.31	20.43	18.20	16.80	15.22
4,000.00	43.16	32.42	27.23	24.27	22.40	20.29
5,000.00	53.95	40.52	34.04	30.33	28.00	25.36
6,000.00	64.74	48.63	40.85	36.40	33.60	30.44
7,000.00	75.54	56.73	47.66	42.47	39.20	35.51
8,000.00	86.33	64.84	54.47	48.53	44.80	40.58
9,000.00	97.12	72.94	61.28	54.60	50.40	45.66
10,000.00	107.91	81.05	68.08	60.66	56.00	50.73
20,000.00	215.82	162.09	136.17	121.33	111.99	101.46
30,000.00	323.72	243.14	204.25	181.99	167.99	152.19
40,000.00	431.63	324.19	272.34	242.66	223.99	202.92
50,000.00	539.54	405.23	340.42	303.32	279.99	253.65
60,000.00	647.45	486.28	408.51	363.99	335.98	304.38
70,000.00	755.36	567.33	476.59	424.65	391.98	355.10
80,000.00	863.26	648.37	544.68	485.32	447.98	405.83
90,000.00	971.17	729.42	612.76	545.98	503.97	456.56
100,000.00	1,079.08	810.47	680.85	606.65	559.97	507.29

5.500% Rate

Amount	Term of Loan in Years					
	10	15	20	25	30	40
$ 50.00	$ 0.54	$ 0.41	$ 0.34	$ 0.31	$ 0.28	$ 0.26
100.00	1.09	0.82	0.69	0.61	0.57	0.52
200.00	2.17	1.63	1.38	1.23	1.14	1.03
300.00	3.26	2.45	2.06	1.84	1.70	1.55
400.00	4.34	3.27	2.75	2.46	2.27	2.06
500.00	5.43	4.09	3.44	3.07	2.84	2.58
600.00	6.51	4.90	4.13	3.68	3.41	3.09
700.00	7.60	5.72	4.82	4.30	3.97	3.61
800.00	8.68	6.54	5.50	4.91	4.54	4.13
900.00	9.77	7.35	6.19	5.53	5.11	4.64
1,000.00	10.85	8.17	6.88	6.14	5.68	5.16
2,000.00	21.71	16.34	13.76	12.28	11.36	10.32
3,000.00	32.56	24.51	20.64	18.42	17.03	15.47
4,000.00	43.41	32.68	27.52	24.56	22.71	20.63
5,000.00	54.26	40.85	34.39	30.70	28.39	25.79
6,000.00	65.12	49.03	41.27	36.85	34.07	30.95
7,000.00	75.97	57.20	48.15	42.99	39.75	36.10
8,000.00	86.82	65.37	55.03	49.13	45.42	41.26
9,000.00	97.67	73.54	61.91	55.27	51.10	46.42
10,000.00	108.53	81.71	68.79	61.41	56.78	51.58
20,000.00	217.05	163.42	137.58	122.82	113.56	103.15
30,000.00	325.58	245.13	206.37	184.23	170.34	154.73
40,000.00	434.11	326.83	275.15	245.63	227.12	206.31
50,000.00	542.63	408.54	343.94	307.04	283.89	257.89
60,000.00	651.16	490.25	412.73	368.45	340.67	309.46
70,000.00	759.68	571.96	481.52	429.86	397.45	361.04
80,000.00	868.21	653.67	550.31	491.27	454.23	412.62
90,000.00	976.74	735.38	619.10	552.68	511.01	464.19
100,000.00	1,085.26	817.08	687.89	614.09	567.79	515.77

5.625% Rate

Amount	Term of Loan in Years					
	10	15	20	25	30	40
$ 50.00	$ 0.55	$ 0.41	$ 0.35	$ 0.31	$ 0.29	$ 0.26
100.00	1.09	0.82	0.69	0.62	0.58	0.52
200.00	2.18	1.65	1.39	1.24	1.15	1.05
300.00	3.27	2.47	2.08	1.86	1.73	1.57
400.00	4.37	3.29	2.78	2.49	2.30	2.10
500.00	5.46	4.12	3.47	3.11	2.88	2.62
600.00	6.55	4.94	4.17	3.73	3.45	3.15
700.00	7.64	5.77	4.86	4.35	4.03	3.67
800.00	8.73	6.59	5.56	4.97	4.61	4.19
900.00	9.82	7.41	6.25	5.59	5.18	4.72
1,000.00	10.91	8.24	6.95	6.22	5.76	5.24
2,000.00	21.83	16.47	13.90	12.43	11.51	10.49
3,000.00	32.74	24.71	20.85	18.65	17.27	15.73
4,000.00	43.66	32.95	27.80	24.86	23.03	20.97
5,000.00	54.57	41.19	34.75	31.08	28.78	26.22
6,000.00	65.49	49.42	41.70	37.29	34.54	31.46
7,000.00	76.40	57.66	48.65	43.51	40.30	36.70
8,000.00	87.32	65.90	55.60	49.73	46.05	41.94
9,000.00	98.23	74.14	62.55	55.94	51.81	47.19
10,000.00	109.15	82.37	69.50	62.16	57.57	52.43
20,000.00	218.29	164.75	138.99	124.31	115.13	104.86
30,000.00	327.44	247.12	208.49	186.47	172.70	157.29
40,000.00	436.59	329.49	277.99	248.63	230.26	209.72
50,000.00	545.73	411.87	347.48	310.79	287.83	262.15
60,000.00	654.88	494.24	416.98	372.94	345.39	314.58
70,000.00	764.03	576.61	486.48	435.10	402.96	367.01
80,000.00	873.17	658.99	555.97	497.26	460.53	419.44
90,000.00	982.32	741.36	625.47	559.42	518.09	471.87
100,000.00	1,091.47	823.73	694.97	621.57	575.66	524.30

5.750% Rate

Amount	Term of Loan in Years					
	10	15	20	25	30	40
$ 50.00	$ 0.55	$ 0.42	$ 0.35	$ 0.31	$ 0.29	$ 0.27
100.00	1.10	0.83	0.70	0.63	0.58	0.53
200.00	2.20	1.66	1.40	1.26	1.17	1.07
300.00	3.29	2.49	2.11	1.89	1.75	1.60
400.00	4.39	3.32	2.81	2.52	2.33	2.13
500.00	5.49	4.15	3.51	3.15	2.92	2.66
600.00	6.59	4.98	4.21	3.77	3.50	3.20
700.00	7.68	5.81	4.91	4.40	4.09	3.73
800.00	8.78	6.64	5.62	5.03	4.67	4.26
900.00	9.88	7.47	6.32	5.66	5.25	4.80
1,000.00	10.98	8.30	7.02	6.29	5.84	5.33
2,000.00	21.95	16.61	14.04	12.58	11.67	10.66
3,000.00	32.93	24.91	21.06	18.87	17.51	15.99
4,000.00	43.91	33.22	28.08	25.16	23.34	21.32
5,000.00	54.88	41.52	35.10	31.46	29.18	26.64
6,000.00	65.86	49.82	42.13	37.75	35.01	31.97
7,000.00	76.84	58.13	49.15	44.04	40.85	37.30
8,000.00	87.82	66.43	56.17	50.33	46.69	42.63
9,000.00	98.79	74.74	63.19	56.62	52.52	47.96
10,000.00	109.77	83.04	70.21	62.91	58.36	53.29
20,000.00	219.54	166.08	140.42	125.82	116.71	106.58
30,000.00	329.31	249.12	210.63	188.73	175.07	159.87
40,000.00	439.08	332.16	280.83	251.64	233.43	213.16
50,000.00	548.85	415.21	351.04	314.55	291.79	266.44
60,000.00	658.62	498.25	421.25	377.46	350.14	319.73
70,000.00	768.38	581.29	491.46	440.37	408.50	373.02
80,000.00	878.15	664.33	561.67	503.29	466.86	426.31
90,000.00	987.92	747.37	631.88	566.20	525.22	479.60
100,000.00	1,097.69	830.41	702.08	629.11	583.57	532.89

5.875% Rate

Amount	Term of Loan in Years					
	10	15	20	25	30	40
$ 50.00	$ 0.55	$ 0.42	$ 0.35	$ 0.32	$ 0.30	$ 0.27
100.00	1.10	0.84	0.71	0.64	0.59	0.54
200.00	2.21	1.67	1.42	1.27	1.18	1.08
300.00	3.31	2.51	2.13	1.91	1.77	1.62
400.00	4.42	3.35	2.84	2.55	2.37	2.17
500.00	5.52	4.19	3.55	3.18	2.96	2.71
600.00	6.62	5.02	4.26	3.82	3.55	3.25
700.00	7.73	5.86	4.96	4.46	4.14	3.79
800.00	8.83	6.70	5.67	5.09	4.73	4.33
900.00	9.94	7.53	6.38	5.73	5.32	4.87
1,000.00	11.04	8.37	7.09	6.37	5.92	5.42
2,000.00	22.08	16.74	14.18	12.73	11.83	10.83
3,000.00	33.12	25.11	21.28	19.10	17.75	16.25
4,000.00	44.16	33.48	28.37	25.47	23.66	21.66
5,000.00	55.20	41.86	35.46	31.83	29.58	27.08
6,000.00	66.24	50.23	42.55	38.20	35.49	32.49
7,000.00	77.28	58.60	49.65	44.57	41.41	37.91
8,000.00	88.32	66.97	56.74	50.93	47.32	43.32
9,000.00	99.35	75.34	63.83	57.30	53.24	48.74
10,000.00	110.39	83.71	70.92	63.67	59.15	54.15
20,000.00	220.79	167.42	141.85	127.34	118.31	108.31
30,000.00	331.18	251.14	212.77	191.00	177.46	162.46
40,000.00	441.58	334.85	283.70	254.67	236.62	216.61
50,000.00	551.97	418.56	354.62	318.34	295.77	270.76
60,000.00	662.36	502.27	425.54	382.01	354.92	324.92
70,000.00	772.76	585.98	496.47	445.68	414.08	379.07
80,000.00	883.15	669.69	567.39	509.35	473.23	433.22
90,000.00	993.54	753.41	638.31	573.01	532.38	487.37
100,000.00	1,103.94	837.12	709.24	636.68	591.54	541.53

6.000% Rate

Amount	Term of Loan in Years					
	10	15	20	25	30	40
$ 50.00	$ 0.56	$ 0.42	$ 0.36	$ 0.32	$ 0.30	$ 0.28
100.00	1.11	0.84	0.72	0.64	0.60	0.55
200.00	2.22	1.69	1.43	1.29	1.20	1.10
300.00	3.33	2.53	2.15	1.93	1.80	1.65
400.00	4.44	3.38	2.87	2.58	2.40	2.20
500.00	5.55	4.22	3.58	3.22	3.00	2.75
600.00	6.66	5.06	4.30	3.87	3.60	3.30
700.00	7.77	5.91	5.02	4.51	4.20	3.85
800.00	8.88	6.75	5.73	5.15	4.80	4.40
900.00	9.99	7.59	6.45	5.80	5.40	4.95
1,000.00	11.10	8.44	7.16	6.44	6.00	5.50
2,000.00	22.20	16.88	14.33	12.89	11.99	11.00
3,000.00	33.31	25.32	21.49	19.33	17.99	16.51
4,000.00	44.41	33.75	28.66	25.77	23.98	22.01
5,000.00	55.51	42.19	35.82	32.22	29.98	27.51
6,000.00	66.61	50.63	42.99	38.66	35.97	33.01
7,000.00	77.71	59.07	50.15	45.10	41.97	38.51
8,000.00	88.82	67.51	57.31	51.54	47.96	44.02
9,000.00	99.92	75.95	64.48	57.99	53.96	49.52
10,000.00	111.02	84.39	71.64	64.43	59.96	55.02
20,000.00	222.04	168.77	143.29	128.86	119.91	110.04
30,000.00	333.06	253.16	214.93	193.29	179.87	165.06
40,000.00	444.08	337.54	286.57	257.72	239.82	220.09
50,000.00	555.10	421.93	358.22	322.15	299.78	275.11
60,000.00	666.12	506.31	429.86	386.58	359.73	330.13
70,000.00	777.14	590.70	501.50	451.01	419.69	385.15
80,000.00	888.16	675.09	573.14	515.44	479.64	440.17
90,000.00	999.18	759.47	644.79	579.87	539.60	495.19
100,000.00	1,110.21	843.86	716.43	644.30	599.55	550.21

6.125% Rate

Amount	Term of Loan in Years					
	10	15	20	25	30	40
$ 50.00	$ 0.56	$ 0.43	$ 0.36	$ 0.33	$ 0.30	$ 0.28
100.00	1.12	0.85	0.72	0.65	0.61	0.56
200.00	2.23	1.70	1.45	1.30	1.22	1.12
300.00	3.35	2.55	2.17	1.96	1.82	1.68
400.00	4.47	3.40	2.89	2.61	2.43	2.24
500.00	5.58	4.25	3.62	3.26	3.04	2.79
600.00	6.70	5.10	4.34	3.91	3.65	3.35
700.00	7.82	5.95	5.07	4.56	4.25	3.91
800.00	8.93	6.80	5.79	5.22	4.86	4.47
900.00	10.05	7.66	6.51	5.87	5.47	5.03
1,000.00	11.16	8.51	7.24	6.52	6.08	5.59
2,000.00	22.33	17.01	14.47	13.04	12.15	11.18
3,000.00	33.49	25.52	21.71	19.56	18.23	16.77
4,000.00	44.66	34.02	28.95	26.08	24.30	22.36
5,000.00	55.82	42.53	36.18	32.60	30.38	27.95
6,000.00	66.99	51.04	43.42	39.12	36.46	33.54
7,000.00	78.15	59.54	50.66	45.64	42.53	39.13
8,000.00	89.32	68.05	57.89	52.16	48.61	44.72
9,000.00	100.48	76.56	65.13	58.68	54.68	50.31
10,000.00	111.65	85.06	72.37	65.20	60.76	55.90
20,000.00	223.30	170.12	144.73	130.39	121.52	111.79
30,000.00	334.95	255.19	217.10	195.59	182.28	167.69
40,000.00	446.60	340.25	289.46	260.79	243.04	223.58
50,000.00	558.25	425.31	361.83	325.98	303.81	279.48
60,000.00	669.90	510.37	434.20	391.18	364.57	335.37
70,000.00	781.54	595.44	506.56	456.37	425.33	391.27
80,000.00	893.19	680.50	578.93	521.57	486.09	447.16
90,000.00	1,004.84	765.56	651.29	586.77	546.85	503.06
100,000.00	1,116.49	850.62	723.66	651.96	607.61	558.95

6.250% Rate

Amount	Term of Loan in Years					
	10	15	20	25	30	40
$ 50.00	$ 0.56	$ 0.43	$ 0.37	$ 0.33	$ 0.31	$ 0.28
100.00	1.12	0.86	0.73	0.66	0.62	0.57
200.00	2.25	1.71	1.46	1.32	1.23	1.14
300.00	3.37	2.57	2.19	1.98	1.85	1.70
400.00	4.49	3.43	2.92	2.64	2.46	2.27
500.00	5.61	4.29	3.65	3.30	3.08	2.84
600.00	6.74	5.14	4.39	3.96	3.69	3.41
700.00	7.86	6.00	5.12	4.62	4.31	3.97
800.00	8.98	6.86	5.85	5.28	4.93	4.54
900.00	10.11	7.72	6.58	5.94	5.54	5.11
1,000.00	11.23	8.57	7.31	6.60	6.16	5.68
2,000.00	22.46	17.15	14.62	13.19	12.31	11.35
3,000.00	33.68	25.72	21.93	19.79	18.47	17.03
4,000.00	44.91	34.30	29.24	26.39	24.63	22.71
5,000.00	56.14	42.87	36.55	32.98	30.79	28.39
6,000.00	67.37	51.45	43.86	39.58	36.94	34.06
7,000.00	78.60	60.02	51.16	46.18	43.10	39.74
8,000.00	89.82	68.59	58.47	52.77	49.26	45.42
9,000.00	101.05	77.17	65.78	59.37	55.41	51.10
10,000.00	112.28	85.74	73.09	65.97	61.57	56.77
20,000.00	224.56	171.48	146.19	131.93	123.14	113.55
30,000.00	336.84	257.23	219.28	197.90	184.72	170.32
40,000.00	449.12	342.97	292.37	263.87	246.29	227.10
50,000.00	561.40	428.71	365.46	329.83	307.86	283.87
60,000.00	673.68	514.45	438.56	395.80	369.43	340.64
70,000.00	785.96	600.20	511.65	461.77	431.00	397.42
80,000.00	898.24	685.94	584.74	527.74	492.57	454.19
90,000.00	1,010.52	771.68	657.84	593.70	554.15	510.97
100,000.00	1,122.80	857.42	730.93	659.67	615.72	567.74

6.375% Rate

Amount	Term of Loan in Years					
	10	15	20	25	30	40
$ 50.00	$ 0.56	$ 0.43	$ 0.37	$ 0.33	$ 0.31	$ 0.29
100.00	1.13	0.86	0.74	0.67	0.62	0.58
200.00	2.26	1.73	1.48	1.33	1.25	1.15
300.00	3.39	2.59	2.21	2.00	1.87	1.73
400.00	4.52	3.46	2.95	2.67	2.50	2.31
500.00	5.65	4.32	3.69	3.34	3.12	2.88
600.00	6.77	5.19	4.43	4.00	3.74	3.46
700.00	7.90	6.05	5.17	4.67	4.37	4.04
800.00	9.03	6.91	5.91	5.34	4.99	4.61
900.00	10.16	7.78	6.64	6.01	5.61	5.19
1,000.00	11.29	8.64	7.38	6.67	6.24	5.77
2,000.00	22.58	17.29	14.76	13.35	12.48	11.53
3,000.00	33.87	25.93	22.15	20.02	18.72	17.30
4,000.00	45.17	34.57	29.53	26.70	24.95	23.06
5,000.00	56.46	43.21	36.91	33.37	31.19	28.83
6,000.00	67.75	51.86	44.29	40.05	37.43	34.59
7,000.00	79.04	60.50	51.68	46.72	43.67	40.36
8,000.00	90.33	69.14	59.06	53.39	49.91	46.13
9,000.00	101.62	77.78	66.44	60.07	56.15	51.89
10,000.00	112.91	86.43	73.82	66.74	62.39	57.66
20,000.00	225.83	172.85	147.65	133.48	124.77	115.31
30,000.00	338.74	259.28	221.47	200.23	187.16	172.97
40,000.00	451.65	345.70	295.29	266.97	249.55	230.63
50,000.00	564.57	432.13	369.12	333.71	311.93	288.29
60,000.00	677.48	518.55	442.94	400.45	374.32	345.94
70,000.00	790.39	604.98	516.76	467.19	436.71	403.60
80,000.00	903.30	691.40	590.59	533.93	499.10	461.26
90,000.00	1,016.22	777.83	664.41	600.68	561.48	518.92
100,000.00	1,129.13	864.25	738.23	667.42	623.87	576.57

6.500% Rate

Amount	Term of Loan in Years					
	10	15	20	25	30	40
$ 50.00	$ 0.57	$ 0.44	$ 0.37	$ 0.34	$ 0.32	$ 0.29
100.00	1.14	0.87	0.75	0.68	0.63	0.59
200.00	2.27	1.74	1.49	1.35	1.26	1.17
300.00	3.41	2.61	2.24	2.03	1.90	1.76
400.00	4.54	3.48	2.98	2.70	2.53	2.34
500.00	5.68	4.36	3.73	3.38	3.16	2.93
600.00	6.81	5.23	4.47	4.05	3.79	3.51
700.00	7.95	6.10	5.22	4.73	4.42	4.10
800.00	9.08	6.97	5.96	5.40	5.06	4.68
900.00	10.22	7.84	6.71	6.08	5.69	5.27
1,000.00	11.35	8.71	7.46	6.75	6.32	5.85
2,000.00	22.71	17.42	14.91	13.50	12.64	11.71
3,000.00	34.06	26.13	22.37	20.26	18.96	17.56
4,000.00	45.42	34.84	29.82	27.01	25.28	23.42
5,000.00	56.77	43.56	37.28	33.76	31.60	29.27
6,000.00	68.13	52.27	44.73	40.51	37.92	35.13
7,000.00	79.48	60.98	52.19	47.26	44.24	40.98
8,000.00	90.84	69.69	59.65	54.02	50.57	46.84
9,000.00	102.19	78.40	67.10	60.77	56.89	52.69
10,000.00	113.55	87.11	74.56	67.52	63.21	58.55
20,000.00	227.10	174.22	149.11	135.04	126.41	117.09
30,000.00	340.64	261.33	223.67	202.56	189.62	175.64
40,000.00	454.19	348.44	298.23	270.08	252.83	234.18
50,000.00	567.74	435.55	372.79	337.60	316.03	292.73
60,000.00	681.29	522.66	447.34	405.12	379.24	351.27
70,000.00	794.84	609.78	521.90	472.65	442.45	409.82
80,000.00	908.38	696.89	596.46	540.17	505.65	468.37
90,000.00	1,021.93	784.00	671.02	607.69	568.86	526.91
100,000.00	1,135.48	871.11	745.57	675.21	632.07	585.46

6.625% Rate

Amount	Term of Loan in Years					
	10	15	20	25	30	40
$ 50.00	$ 0.57	$ 0.44	$ 0.38	$ 0.34	$ 0.32	$ 0.30
100.00	1.14	0.88	0.75	0.68	0.64	0.59
200.00	2.28	1.76	1.51	1.37	1.28	1.19
300.00	3.43	2.63	2.26	2.05	1.92	1.78
400.00	4.57	3.51	3.01	2.73	2.56	2.38
500.00	5.71	4.39	3.76	3.42	3.20	2.97
600.00	6.85	5.27	4.52	4.10	3.84	3.57
700.00	7.99	6.15	5.27	4.78	4.48	4.16
800.00	9.13	7.02	6.02	5.46	5.12	4.76
900.00	10.28	7.90	6.78	6.15	5.76	5.35
1,000.00	11.42	8.78	7.53	6.83	6.40	5.94
2,000.00	22.84	17.56	15.06	13.66	12.81	11.89
3,000.00	34.26	26.34	22.59	20.49	19.21	17.83
4,000.00	45.67	35.12	30.12	27.32	25.61	23.78
5,000.00	57.09	43.90	37.65	34.15	32.02	29.72
6,000.00	68.51	52.68	45.18	40.98	38.42	35.66
7,000.00	79.93	61.46	52.71	47.81	44.82	41.61
8,000.00	91.35	70.24	60.24	54.64	51.22	47.55
9,000.00	102.77	79.02	67.77	61.47	57.63	53.49
10,000.00	114.19	87.80	75.30	68.30	64.03	59.44
20,000.00	228.37	175.60	150.59	136.61	128.06	118.88
30,000.00	342.56	263.40	225.89	204.91	192.09	178.32
40,000.00	456.74	351.20	301.18	273.22	256.12	237.75
50,000.00	570.93	439.00	376.48	341.52	320.16	297.19
60,000.00	685.11	526.80	451.77	409.82	384.19	356.63
70,000.00	799.30	614.60	527.07	478.13	448.22	416.07
80,000.00	913.48	702.40	602.36	546.43	512.25	475.51
90,000.00	1,027.67	790.19	677.66	614.73	576.28	534.95
100,000.00	1,141.85	877.99	752.95	683.04	640.31	594.38

6.750% Rate

Amount	Term of Loan in Years					
	10	15	20	25	30	40
$ 50.00	$ 0.57	$ 0.44	$ 0.38	$ 0.35	$ 0.32	$ 0.30
100.00	1.15	0.88	0.76	0.69	0.65	0.60
200.00	2.30	1.77	1.52	1.38	1.30	1.21
300.00	3.44	2.65	2.28	2.07	1.95	1.81
400.00	4.59	3.54	3.04	2.76	2.59	2.41
500.00	5.74	4.42	3.80	3.45	3.24	3.02
600.00	6.89	5.31	4.56	4.15	3.89	3.62
700.00	8.04	6.19	5.32	4.84	4.54	4.22
800.00	9.19	7.08	6.08	5.53	5.19	4.83
900.00	10.33	7.96	6.84	6.22	5.84	5.43
1,000.00	11.48	8.85	7.60	6.91	6.49	6.03
2,000.00	22.96	17.70	15.21	13.82	12.97	12.07
3,000.00	34.45	26.55	22.81	20.73	19.46	18.10
4,000.00	45.93	35.40	30.41	27.64	25.94	24.13
5,000.00	57.41	44.25	38.02	34.55	32.43	30.17
6,000.00	68.89	53.09	45.62	41.45	38.92	36.20
7,000.00	80.38	61.94	53.23	48.36	45.40	42.23
8,000.00	91.86	70.79	60.83	55.27	51.89	48.27
9,000.00	103.34	79.64	68.43	62.18	58.37	54.30
10,000.00	114.82	88.49	76.04	69.09	64.86	60.34
20,000.00	229.65	176.98	152.07	138.18	129.72	120.67
30,000.00	344.47	265.47	228.11	207.27	194.58	181.01
40,000.00	459.30	353.96	304.15	276.36	259.44	241.34
50,000.00	574.12	442.45	380.18	345.46	324.30	301.68
60,000.00	688.94	530.95	456.22	414.55	389.16	362.01
70,000.00	803.77	619.44	532.25	483.64	454.02	422.35
80,000.00	918.59	707.93	608.29	552.73	518.88	482.69
90,000.00	1,033.42	796.42	684.33	621.82	583.74	543.02
100,000.00	1,148.24	884.91	760.36	690.91	648.60	603.36

6.875% Rate

Amount	Term of Loan in Years					
	10	15	20	25	30	40
$ 50.00	$ 0.58	$ 0.45	$ 0.38	$ 0.35	$ 0.33	$ 0.31
100.00	1.15	0.89	0.77	0.70	0.66	0.61
200.00	2.31	1.78	1.54	1.40	1.31	1.22
300.00	3.46	2.68	2.30	2.10	1.97	1.84
400.00	4.62	3.57	3.07	2.80	2.63	2.45
500.00	5.77	4.46	3.84	3.49	3.28	3.06
600.00	6.93	5.35	4.61	4.19	3.94	3.67
700.00	8.08	6.24	5.37	4.89	4.60	4.29
800.00	9.24	7.13	6.14	5.59	5.26	4.90
900.00	10.39	8.03	6.91	6.29	5.91	5.51
1,000.00	11.55	8.92	7.68	6.99	6.57	6.12
2,000.00	23.09	17.84	15.36	13.98	13.14	12.25
3,000.00	34.64	26.76	23.03	20.96	19.71	18.37
4,000.00	46.19	35.67	30.71	27.95	26.28	24.49
5,000.00	57.73	44.59	38.39	34.94	32.85	30.62
6,000.00	69.28	53.51	46.07	41.93	39.42	36.74
7,000.00	80.83	62.43	53.75	48.92	45.99	42.87
8,000.00	92.37	71.35	61.43	55.91	52.55	48.99
9,000.00	103.92	80.27	69.10	62.89	59.12	55.11
10,000.00	115.47	89.19	76.78	69.88	65.69	61.24
20,000.00	230.93	178.37	153.56	139.77	131.39	122.47
30,000.00	346.40	267.56	230.34	209.65	197.08	183.71
40,000.00	461.86	356.74	307.13	279.53	262.77	244.95
50,000.00	577.33	445.93	383.91	349.41	328.46	306.19
60,000.00	692.79	535.11	460.69	419.30	394.16	367.42
70,000.00	808.26	624.30	537.47	489.18	459.85	428.66
80,000.00	923.72	713.48	614.25	559.06	525.54	489.90
90,000.00	1,039.19	802.67	691.03	628.94	591.24	551.14
100,000.00	1,154.65	891.85	767.81	698.83	656.93	612.37

7.000% Rate

Amount	Term of Loan in Years					
	10	15	20	25	30	40
$ 50.00	$ 0.58	$ 0.45	$ 0.39	$ 0.35	$ 0.33	$ 0.31
100.00	1.16	0.90	0.78	0.71	0.67	0.62
200.00	2.32	1.80	1.55	1.41	1.33	1.24
300.00	3.48	2.70	2.33	2.12	2.00	1.86
400.00	4.64	3.60	3.10	2.83	2.66	2.49
500.00	5.81	4.49	3.88	3.53	3.33	3.11
600.00	6.97	5.39	4.65	4.24	3.99	3.73
700.00	8.13	6.29	5.43	4.95	4.66	4.35
800.00	9.29	7.19	6.20	5.65	5.32	4.97
900.00	10.45	8.09	6.98	6.36	5.99	5.59
1,000.00	11.61	8.99	7.75	7.07	6.65	6.21
2,000.00	23.22	17.98	15.51	14.14	13.31	12.43
3,000.00	34.83	26.96	23.26	21.20	19.96	18.64
4,000.00	46.44	35.95	31.01	28.27	26.61	24.86
5,000.00	58.05	44.94	38.76	35.34	33.27	31.07
6,000.00	69.67	53.93	46.52	42.41	39.92	37.29
7,000.00	81.28	62.92	54.27	49.47	46.57	43.50
8,000.00	92.89	71.91	62.02	56.54	53.22	49.71
9,000.00	104.50	80.89	69.78	63.61	59.88	55.93
10,000.00	116.11	89.88	77.53	70.68	66.53	62.14
20,000.00	232.22	179.77	155.06	141.36	133.06	124.29
30,000.00	348.33	269.65	232.59	212.03	199.59	186.43
40,000.00	464.43	359.53	310.12	282.71	266.12	248.57
50,000.00	580.54	449.41	387.65	353.39	332.65	310.72
60,000.00	696.65	539.30	465.18	424.07	399.18	372.86
70,000.00	812.76	629.18	542.71	494.75	465.71	435.00
80,000.00	928.87	719.06	620.24	565.42	532.24	497.15
90,000.00	1,044.98	808.95	697.77	636.10	598.77	559.29
100,000.00	1,161.08	898.83	775.30	706.78	665.30	621.43

7.125% Rate

Amount	Term of Loan in Years					
	10	15	20	25	30	40
$ 50.00	$ 0.58	$ 0.45	$ 0.39	$ 0.36	$ 0.34	$ 0.32
100.00	1.17	0.91	0.78	0.71	0.67	0.63
200.00	2.34	1.81	1.57	1.43	1.35	1.26
300.00	3.50	2.72	2.35	2.14	2.02	1.89
400.00	4.67	3.62	3.13	2.86	2.69	2.52
500.00	5.84	4.53	3.91	3.57	3.37	3.15
600.00	7.01	5.43	4.70	4.29	4.04	3.78
700.00	8.17	6.34	5.48	5.00	4.72	4.41
800.00	9.34	7.25	6.26	5.72	5.39	5.04
900.00	10.51	8.15	7.05	6.43	6.06	5.67
1,000.00	11.68	9.06	7.83	7.15	6.74	6.31
2,000.00	23.35	18.12	15.66	14.30	13.47	12.61
3,000.00	35.03	27.17	23.48	21.44	20.21	18.92
4,000.00	46.70	36.23	31.31	28.59	26.95	25.22
5,000.00	58.38	45.29	39.14	35.74	33.69	31.53
6,000.00	70.05	54.35	46.97	42.89	40.42	37.83
7,000.00	81.73	63.41	54.80	50.03	47.16	44.14
8,000.00	93.40	72.47	62.63	57.18	53.90	50.44
9,000.00	105.08	81.52	70.45	64.33	60.63	56.75
10,000.00	116.75	90.58	78.28	71.48	67.37	63.05
20,000.00	233.51	181.17	156.56	142.95	134.74	126.11
30,000.00	350.26	271.75	234.85	214.43	202.12	189.16
40,000.00	467.01	362.33	313.13	285.91	269.49	252.21
50,000.00	583.77	452.92	391.41	357.39	336.86	315.27
60,000.00	700.52	543.50	469.69	428.86	404.23	378.32
70,000.00	817.28	634.08	547.97	500.34	471.60	441.37
80,000.00	934.03	724.66	626.26	571.82	538.97	504.43
90,000.00	1,050.78	815.25	704.54	643.30	606.35	567.48
100,000.00	1,167.54	905.83	782.82	714.77	673.72	630.53

7.250% Rate

Amount	Term of Loan in Years					
	10	15	20	25	30	40
$ 50.00	$ 0.59	$ 0.46	$ 0.40	$ 0.36	$ 0.34	$ 0.32
100.00	1.17	0.91	0.79	0.72	0.68	0.64
200.00	2.35	1.83	1.58	1.45	1.36	1.28
300.00	3.52	2.74	2.37	2.17	2.05	1.92
400.00	4.70	3.65	3.16	2.89	2.73	2.56
500.00	5.87	4.56	3.95	3.61	3.41	3.20
600.00	7.04	5.48	4.74	4.34	4.09	3.84
700.00	8.22	6.39	5.53	5.06	4.78	4.48
800.00	9.39	7.30	6.32	5.78	5.46	5.12
900.00	10.57	8.22	7.11	6.51	6.14	5.76
1,000.00	11.74	9.13	7.90	7.23	6.82	6.40
2,000.00	23.48	18.26	15.81	14.46	13.64	12.79
3,000.00	35.22	27.39	23.71	21.68	20.47	19.19
4,000.00	46.96	36.51	31.62	28.91	27.29	25.59
5,000.00	58.70	45.64	39.52	36.14	34.11	31.98
6,000.00	70.44	54.77	47.42	43.37	40.93	38.38
7,000.00	82.18	63.90	55.33	50.60	47.75	44.78
8,000.00	93.92	73.03	63.23	57.82	54.57	51.17
9,000.00	105.66	82.16	71.13	65.05	61.40	57.57
10,000.00	117.40	91.29	79.04	72.28	68.22	63.97
20,000.00	234.80	182.57	158.08	144.56	136.44	127.93
30,000.00	352.20	273.86	237.11	216.84	204.65	191.90
40,000.00	469.60	365.15	316.15	289.12	272.87	255.87
50,000.00	587.01	456.43	395.19	361.40	341.09	319.84
60,000.00	704.41	547.72	474.23	433.68	409.31	383.80
70,000.00	821.81	639.00	553.26	505.96	477.52	447.77
80,000.00	939.21	730.29	632.30	578.25	545.74	511.74
90,000.00	1,056.61	821.58	711.34	650.53	613.96	575.70
100,000.00	1,174.01	912.86	790.38	722.81	682.18	639.67

7.375% Rate

Amount	Term of Loan in Years					
	10	15	20	25	30	40
$ 50.00	$ 0.59	$ 0.46	$ 0.40	$ 0.37	$ 0.35	$ 0.32
100.00	1.18	0.92	0.80	0.73	0.69	0.65
200.00	2.36	1.84	1.60	1.46	1.38	1.30
300.00	3.54	2.76	2.39	2.19	2.07	1.95
400.00	4.72	3.68	3.19	2.92	2.76	2.60
500.00	5.90	4.60	3.99	3.65	3.45	3.24
600.00	7.08	5.52	4.79	4.39	4.14	3.89
700.00	8.26	6.44	5.59	5.12	4.83	4.54
800.00	9.44	7.36	6.38	5.85	5.53	5.19
900.00	10.62	8.28	7.18	6.58	6.22	5.84
1,000.00	11.81	9.20	7.98	7.31	6.91	6.49
2,000.00	23.61	18.40	15.96	14.62	13.81	12.98
3,000.00	35.42	27.60	23.94	21.93	20.72	19.47
4,000.00	47.22	36.80	31.92	29.24	27.63	25.95
5,000.00	59.03	46.00	39.90	36.54	34.53	32.44
6,000.00	70.83	55.20	47.88	43.85	41.44	38.93
7,000.00	82.64	64.39	55.86	51.16	48.35	45.42
8,000.00	94.44	73.59	63.84	58.47	55.25	51.91
9,000.00	106.25	82.79	71.82	65.78	62.16	58.40
10,000.00	118.05	91.99	79.80	73.09	69.07	64.89
20,000.00	236.10	183.98	159.59	146.18	138.14	129.77
30,000.00	354.15	275.98	239.39	219.26	207.20	194.66
40,000.00	472.20	367.97	319.19	292.35	276.27	259.54
50,000.00	590.25	459.96	398.98	365.44	345.34	324.43
60,000.00	708.30	551.95	478.78	438.53	414.41	389.31
70,000.00	826.35	643.95	558.58	511.62	483.47	454.20
80,000.00	944.40	735.94	638.37	584.70	552.54	519.08
90,000.00	1,062.45	827.93	718.17	657.79	621.61	583.97
100,000.00	1,180.50	919.92	797.97	730.88	690.68	648.85

7.500% Rate

Amount		Term of Loan in Years					
	10	15	20	25	30	40
$ 50.00	$ 0.59	$ 0.46	$ 0.40	$ 0.37	$ 0.35	$ 0.33
100.00	1.19	0.93	0.81	0.74	0.70	0.66
200.00	2.37	1.85	1.61	1.48	1.40	1.32
300.00	3.56	2.78	2.42	2.22	2.10	1.97
400.00	4.75	3.71	3.22	2.96	2.80	2.63
500.00	5.94	4.64	4.03	3.69	3.50	3.29
600.00	7.12	5.56	4.83	4.43	4.20	3.95
700.00	8.31	6.49	5.64	5.17	4.89	4.61
800.00	9.50	7.42	6.44	5.91	5.59	5.26
900.00	10.68	8.34	7.25	6.65	6.29	5.92
1,000.00	11.87	9.27	8.06	7.39	6.99	6.58
2,000.00	23.74	18.54	16.11	14.78	13.98	13.16
3,000.00	35.61	27.81	24.17	22.17	20.98	19.74
4,000.00	47.48	37.08	32.22	29.56	27.97	26.32
5,000.00	59.35	46.35	40.28	36.95	34.96	32.90
6,000.00	71.22	55.62	48.34	44.34	41.95	39.48
7,000.00	83.09	64.89	56.39	51.73	48.95	46.06
8,000.00	94.96	74.16	64.45	59.12	55.94	52.65
9,000.00	106.83	83.43	72.50	66.51	62.93	59.23
10,000.00	118.70	92.70	80.56	73.90	69.92	65.81
20,000.00	237.40	185.40	161.12	147.80	139.84	131.61
30,000.00	356.11	278.10	241.68	221.70	209.76	197.42
40,000.00	474.81	370.80	322.24	295.60	279.69	263.23
50,000.00	593.51	463.51	402.80	369.50	349.61	329.04
60,000.00	712.21	556.21	483.36	443.39	419.53	394.84
70,000.00	830.91	648.91	563.92	517.29	489.45	460.65
80,000.00	949.61	741.61	644.47	591.19	559.37	526.46
90,000.00	1,068.32	834.31	725.03	665.09	629.29	592.26
100,000.00	1,187.02	927.01	805.59	738.99	699.21	658.07

7.625% Rate

Amount	Term of Loan in Years					
	10	15	20	25	30	40
$ 50.00	$ 0.60	$ 0.47	$ 0.41	$ 0.37	$ 0.35	$ 0.33
100.00	1.19	0.93	0.81	0.75	0.71	0.67
200.00	2.39	1.87	1.63	1.49	1.42	1.33
300.00	3.58	2.80	2.44	2.24	2.12	2.00
400.00	4.77	3.74	3.25	2.99	2.83	2.67
500.00	5.97	4.67	4.07	3.74	3.54	3.34
600.00	7.16	5.60	4.88	4.48	4.25	4.00
700.00	8.35	6.54	5.69	5.23	4.95	4.67
800.00	9.55	7.47	6.51	5.98	5.66	5.34
900.00	10.74	8.41	7.32	6.72	6.37	6.01
1,000.00	11.94	9.34	8.13	7.47	7.08	6.67
2,000.00	23.87	18.68	16.27	14.94	14.16	13.35
3,000.00	35.81	28.02	24.40	22.41	21.23	20.02
4,000.00	47.74	37.37	32.53	29.89	28.31	26.69
5,000.00	59.68	46.71	40.66	37.36	35.39	33.37
6,000.00	71.61	56.05	48.80	44.83	42.47	40.04
7,000.00	83.55	65.39	56.93	52.30	49.55	46.71
8,000.00	95.48	74.73	65.06	59.77	56.62	53.39
9,000.00	107.42	84.07	73.19	67.24	63.70	60.06
10,000.00	119.36	93.41	81.33	74.71	70.78	66.73
20,000.00	238.71	186.83	162.65	149.43	141.56	133.47
30,000.00	358.07	280.24	243.98	224.14	212.34	200.20
40,000.00	477.42	373.65	325.30	298.86	283.12	266.93
50,000.00	596.78	467.06	406.63	373.57	353.90	333.66
60,000.00	716.13	560.48	487.95	448.28	424.68	400.40
70,000.00	835.49	653.89	569.28	523.00	495.46	467.13
80,000.00	954.84	747.30	650.60	597.71	566.23	533.86
90,000.00	1,074.20	840.72	731.93	672.43	637.01	600.59
100,000.00	1,193.55	934.13	813.25	747.14	707.79	667.33

7.750% Rate

Amount	Term of Loan in Years					
	10	15	20	25	30	40
$ 50.00	$ 0.60	$ 0.47	$ 0.41	$ 0.38	$ 0.36	$ 0.34
100.00	1.20	0.94	0.82	0.76	0.72	0.68
200.00	2.40	1.88	1.64	1.51	1.43	1.35
300.00	3.60	2.82	2.46	2.27	2.15	2.03
400.00	4.80	3.77	3.28	3.02	2.87	2.71
500.00	6.00	4.71	4.10	3.78	3.58	3.38
600.00	7.20	5.65	4.93	4.53	4.30	4.06
700.00	8.40	6.59	5.75	5.29	5.01	4.74
800.00	9.60	7.53	6.57	6.04	5.73	5.41
900.00	10.80	8.47	7.39	6.80	6.45	6.09
1,000.00	12.00	9.41	8.21	7.55	7.16	6.77
2,000.00	24.00	18.83	16.42	15.11	14.33	13.53
3,000.00	36.00	28.24	24.63	22.66	21.49	20.30
4,000.00	48.00	37.65	32.84	30.21	28.66	27.06
5,000.00	60.01	47.06	41.05	37.77	35.82	33.83
6,000.00	72.01	56.48	49.26	45.32	42.98	40.60
7,000.00	84.01	65.89	57.47	52.87	50.15	47.36
8,000.00	96.01	75.30	65.68	60.43	57.31	54.13
9,000.00	108.01	84.71	73.89	67.98	64.48	60.90
10,000.00	120.01	94.13	82.09	75.53	71.64	67.66
20,000.00	240.02	188.26	164.19	151.07	143.28	135.32
30,000.00	360.03	282.38	246.28	226.60	214.92	202.99
40,000.00	480.04	376.51	328.38	302.13	286.56	270.65
50,000.00	600.05	470.64	410.47	377.66	358.21	338.31
60,000.00	720.06	564.77	492.57	453.20	429.85	405.97
70,000.00	840.07	658.89	574.66	528.73	501.49	473.63
80,000.00	960.09	753.02	656.76	604.26	573.13	541.30
90,000.00	1,080.10	847.15	738.85	679.80	644.77	608.96
100,000.00	1,200.11	941.28	820.95	755.33	716.41	676.62

7.875% Rate

Amount	Term of Loan in Years					
	10	15	20	25	30	40
$ 50.00	$ 0.60	$ 0.47	$ 0.41	$ 0.38	$ 0.36	$ 0.34
100.00	1.21	0.95	0.83	0.76	0.73	0.69
200.00	2.41	1.90	1.66	1.53	1.45	1.37
300.00	3.62	2.85	2.49	2.29	2.18	2.06
400.00	4.83	3.79	3.31	3.05	2.90	2.74
500.00	6.03	4.74	4.14	3.82	3.63	3.43
600.00	7.24	5.69	4.97	4.58	4.35	4.12
700.00	8.45	6.64	5.80	5.34	5.08	4.80
800.00	9.65	7.59	6.63	6.11	5.80	5.49
900.00	10.86	8.54	7.46	6.87	6.53	6.17
1,000.00	12.07	9.48	8.29	7.64	7.25	6.86
2,000.00	24.13	18.97	16.57	15.27	14.50	13.72
3,000.00	36.20	28.45	24.86	22.91	21.75	20.58
4,000.00	48.27	37.94	33.15	30.54	29.00	27.44
5,000.00	60.33	47.42	41.43	38.18	36.25	34.30
6,000.00	72.40	56.91	49.72	45.81	43.50	41.16
7,000.00	84.47	66.39	58.01	53.45	50.75	48.02
8,000.00	96.53	75.88	66.29	61.08	58.01	54.88
9,000.00	108.60	85.36	74.58	68.72	65.26	61.74
10,000.00	120.67	94.84	82.87	76.36	72.51	68.59
20,000.00	241.34	189.69	165.74	152.71	145.01	137.19
30,000.00	362.00	284.53	248.60	229.07	217.52	205.78
40,000.00	482.67	379.38	331.47	305.42	290.03	274.38
50,000.00	603.34	474.22	414.34	381.78	362.53	342.97
60,000.00	724.01	569.07	497.21	458.13	435.04	411.57
70,000.00	844.68	663.91	580.07	534.49	507.55	480.16
80,000.00	965.34	758.76	662.94	610.84	580.06	548.76
90,000.00	1,086.01	853.60	745.81	687.20	652.56	617.35
100,000.00	1,206.68	948.45	828.68	763.55	725.07	685.95

8.000% Rate

Amount	Term of Loan in Years					
	10	15	20	25	30	40
$ 50.00	$ 0.61	$ 0.48	$ 0.42	$ 0.39	$ 0.37	$ 0.35
100.00	1.21	0.96	0.84	0.77	0.73	0.70
200.00	2.43	1.91	1.67	1.54	1.47	1.39
300.00	3.64	2.87	2.51	2.32	2.20	2.09
400.00	4.85	3.82	3.35	3.09	2.94	2.78
500.00	6.07	4.78	4.18	3.86	3.67	3.48
600.00	7.28	5.73	5.02	4.63	4.40	4.17
700.00	8.49	6.69	5.86	5.40	5.14	4.87
800.00	9.71	7.65	6.69	6.17	5.87	5.56
900.00	10.92	8.60	7.53	6.95	6.60	6.26
1,000.00	12.13	9.56	8.36	7.72	7.34	6.95
2,000.00	24.27	19.11	16.73	15.44	14.68	13.91
3,000.00	36.40	28.67	25.09	23.15	22.01	20.86
4,000.00	48.53	38.23	33.46	30.87	29.35	27.81
5,000.00	60.66	47.78	41.82	38.59	36.69	34.77
6,000.00	72.80	57.34	50.19	46.31	44.03	41.72
7,000.00	84.93	66.90	58.55	54.03	51.36	48.67
8,000.00	97.06	76.45	66.92	61.75	58.70	55.62
9,000.00	109.19	86.01	75.28	69.46	66.04	62.58
10,000.00	121.33	95.57	83.64	77.18	73.38	69.53
20,000.00	242.66	191.13	167.29	154.36	146.75	139.06
30,000.00	363.98	286.70	250.93	231.54	220.13	208.59
40,000.00	485.31	382.26	334.58	308.73	293.51	278.12
50,000.00	606.64	477.83	418.22	385.91	366.88	347.66
60,000.00	727.97	573.39	501.86	463.09	440.26	417.19
70,000.00	849.29	668.96	585.51	540.27	513.64	486.72
80,000.00	970.62	764.52	669.15	617.45	587.01	556.25
90,000.00	1,091.95	860.09	752.80	694.63	660.39	625.78
100,000.00	1,213.28	955.65	836.44	771.82	733.76	695.31

8.125% Rate

Amount	Term of Loan in Years					
	10	15	20	25	30	40
$ 50.00	$ 0.61	$ 0.48	$ 0.42	$ 0.39	$ 0.37	$ 0.35
100.00	1.22	0.96	0.84	0.78	0.74	0.70
200.00	2.44	1.93	1.69	1.56	1.48	1.41
300.00	3.66	2.89	2.53	2.34	2.23	2.11
400.00	4.88	3.85	3.38	3.12	2.97	2.82
500.00	6.10	4.81	4.22	3.90	3.71	3.52
600.00	7.32	5.78	5.07	4.68	4.45	4.23
700.00	8.54	6.74	5.91	5.46	5.20	4.93
800.00	9.76	7.70	6.75	6.24	5.94	5.64
900.00	10.98	8.67	7.60	7.02	6.68	6.34
1,000.00	12.20	9.63	8.44	7.80	7.42	7.05
2,000.00	24.40	19.26	16.88	15.60	14.85	14.09
3,000.00	36.60	28.89	25.33	23.40	22.27	21.14
4,000.00	48.80	38.52	33.77	31.20	29.70	28.19
5,000.00	60.99	48.14	42.21	39.01	37.12	35.24
6,000.00	73.19	57.77	50.65	46.81	44.55	42.28
7,000.00	85.39	67.40	59.10	54.61	51.97	49.33
8,000.00	97.59	77.03	67.54	62.41	59.40	56.38
9,000.00	109.79	86.66	75.98	70.21	66.82	63.42
10,000.00	121.99	96.29	84.42	78.01	74.25	70.47
20,000.00	243.98	192.58	168.85	156.02	148.50	140.94
30,000.00	365.97	288.86	253.27	234.03	222.75	211.41
40,000.00	487.96	385.15	337.69	312.05	297.00	281.88
50,000.00	609.95	481.44	422.12	390.06	371.25	352.35
60,000.00	731.93	577.73	506.54	468.07	445.50	422.83
70,000.00	853.92	674.02	590.97	546.08	519.75	493.30
80,000.00	975.91	770.31	675.39	624.09	594.00	563.77
90,000.00	1,097.90	866.59	759.81	702.10	668.25	634.24
100,000.00	1,219.89	962.88	844.24	780.12	742.50	704.71

8.250% Rate

Amount	Term of Loan in Years					
	10	15	20	25	30	40
$ 50.00	$ 0.61	$ 0.49	$ 0.43	$ 0.39	$ 0.38	$ 0.36
100.00	1.23	0.97	0.85	0.79	0.75	0.71
200.00	2.45	1.94	1.70	1.58	1.50	1.43
300.00	3.68	2.91	2.56	2.37	2.25	2.14
400.00	4.91	3.88	3.41	3.15	3.01	2.86
500.00	6.13	4.85	4.26	3.94	3.76	3.57
600.00	7.36	5.82	5.11	4.73	4.51	4.28
700.00	8.59	6.79	5.96	5.52	5.26	5.00
800.00	9.81	7.76	6.82	6.31	6.01	5.71
900.00	11.04	8.73	7.67	7.10	6.76	6.43
1,000.00	12.27	9.70	8.52	7.88	7.51	7.14
2,000.00	24.53	19.40	17.04	15.77	15.03	14.28
3,000.00	36.80	29.10	25.56	23.65	22.54	21.42
4,000.00	49.06	38.81	34.08	31.54	30.05	28.57
5,000.00	61.33	48.51	42.60	39.42	37.56	35.71
6,000.00	73.59	58.21	51.12	47.31	45.08	42.85
7,000.00	85.86	67.91	59.64	55.19	52.59	49.99
8,000.00	98.12	77.61	68.17	63.08	60.10	57.13
9,000.00	110.39	87.31	76.69	70.96	67.61	64.27
10,000.00	122.65	97.01	85.21	78.85	75.13	71.41
20,000.00	245.31	194.03	170.41	157.69	150.25	142.83
30,000.00	367.96	291.04	255.62	236.54	225.38	214.24
40,000.00	490.61	388.06	340.83	315.38	300.51	285.66
50,000.00	613.26	485.07	426.03	394.23	375.63	357.07
60,000.00	735.92	582.08	511.24	473.07	450.76	428.48
70,000.00	858.57	679.10	596.45	551.92	525.89	499.90
80,000.00	981.22	776.11	681.65	630.76	601.01	571.31
90,000.00	1,103.87	873.13	766.86	709.61	676.14	642.72
100,000.00	1,226.53	970.14	852.07	788.45	751.27	714.14

8.375% Rate

Amount	10	15	20	25	30	40
	\$	\$	\$	\$	\$	\$
$ 50.00	0.62	0.49	0.43	0.40	0.38	0.36
100.00	1.23	0.98	0.86	0.80	0.76	0.72
200.00	2.47	1.95	1.72	1.59	1.52	1.45
300.00	3.70	2.93	2.58	2.39	2.28	2.17
400.00	4.93	3.91	3.44	3.19	3.04	2.89
500.00	6.17	4.89	4.30	3.98	3.80	3.62
600.00	7.40	5.86	5.16	4.78	4.56	4.34
700.00	8.63	6.84	6.02	5.58	5.32	5.07
800.00	9.87	7.82	6.88	6.37	6.08	5.79
900.00	11.10	8.80	7.74	7.17	6.84	6.51
1,000.00	12.33	9.77	8.60	7.97	7.60	7.24
2,000.00	24.66	19.55	17.20	15.94	15.20	14.47
3,000.00	37.00	29.32	25.80	23.90	22.80	21.71
4,000.00	49.33	39.10	34.40	31.87	30.40	28.94
5,000.00	61.66	48.87	43.00	39.84	38.00	36.18
6,000.00	73.99	58.65	51.60	47.81	45.60	43.42
7,000.00	86.32	68.42	60.19	55.78	53.21	50.65
8,000.00	98.65	78.19	68.79	63.75	60.81	57.89
9,000.00	110.99	87.97	77.39	71.71	68.41	65.12
10,000.00	123.32	97.74	85.99	79.68	76.01	72.36
20,000.00	246.64	195.49	171.99	159.36	152.01	144.72
30,000.00	369.95	293.23	257.98	239.05	228.02	217.08
40,000.00	493.27	390.97	343.97	318.73	304.03	289.44
50,000.00	616.59	488.71	429.96	398.41	380.04	361.80
60,000.00	739.91	586.46	515.96	478.09	456.04	434.16
70,000.00	863.23	684.20	601.95	557.77	532.05	506.52
80,000.00	986.55	781.94	687.94	637.46	608.06	578.88
90,000.00	1,109.86	879.68	773.94	717.14	684.07	651.24
100,000.00	1,233.18	977.43	859.93	796.82	760.07	723.60

8.500% Rate

Amount	Term of Loan in Years					
	10	15	20	25	30	40
$ 50.00	$ 0.62	$ 0.49	$ 0.43	$ 0.40	$ 0.38	$ 0.37
100.00	1.24	0.98	0.87	0.81	0.77	0.73
200.00	2.48	1.97	1.74	1.61	1.54	1.47
300.00	3.72	2.95	2.60	2.42	2.31	2.20
400.00	4.96	3.94	3.47	3.22	3.08	2.93
500.00	6.20	4.92	4.34	4.03	3.84	3.67
600.00	7.44	5.91	5.21	4.83	4.61	4.40
700.00	8.68	6.89	6.07	5.64	5.38	5.13
800.00	9.92	7.88	6.94	6.44	6.15	5.86
900.00	11.16	8.86	7.81	7.25	6.92	6.60
1,000.00	12.40	9.85	8.68	8.05	7.69	7.33
2,000.00	24.80	19.69	17.36	16.10	15.38	14.66
3,000.00	37.20	29.54	26.03	24.16	23.07	21.99
4,000.00	49.59	39.39	34.71	32.21	30.76	29.32
5,000.00	61.99	49.24	43.39	40.26	38.45	36.65
6,000.00	74.39	59.08	52.07	48.31	46.13	43.99
7,000.00	86.79	68.93	60.75	56.37	53.82	51.32
8,000.00	99.19	78.78	69.43	64.42	61.51	58.65
9,000.00	111.59	88.63	78.10	72.47	69.20	65.98
10,000.00	123.99	98.47	86.78	80.52	76.89	73.31
20,000.00	247.97	196.95	173.56	161.05	153.78	146.62
30,000.00	371.96	295.42	260.35	241.57	230.67	219.93
40,000.00	495.94	393.90	347.13	322.09	307.57	293.24
50,000.00	619.93	492.37	433.91	402.61	384.46	366.55
60,000.00	743.91	590.84	520.69	483.14	461.35	439.86
70,000.00	867.90	689.32	607.48	563.66	538.24	513.17
80,000.00	991.89	787.79	694.26	644.18	615.13	586.48
90,000.00	1,115.87	886.27	781.04	724.70	692.02	659.78
100,000.00	1,239.86	984.74	867.82	805.23	768.91	733.09

8.625% Rate

Amount	Term of Loan in Years					
	10	15	20	25	30	40
$ 50.00	$ 0.62	$ 0.50	$ 0.44	$ 0.41	$ 0.39	$ 0.37
100.00	1.25	0.99	0.88	0.81	0.78	0.74
200.00	2.49	1.98	1.75	1.63	1.56	1.49
300.00	3.74	2.98	2.63	2.44	2.33	2.23
400.00	4.99	3.97	3.50	3.25	3.11	2.97
500.00	6.23	4.96	4.38	4.07	3.89	3.71
600.00	7.48	5.95	5.25	4.88	4.67	4.46
700.00	8.73	6.94	6.13	5.70	5.44	5.20
800.00	9.97	7.94	7.01	6.51	6.22	5.94
900.00	11.22	8.93	7.88	7.32	7.00	6.68
1,000.00	12.47	9.92	8.76	8.14	7.78	7.43
2,000.00	24.93	19.84	17.52	16.27	15.56	14.85
3,000.00	37.40	29.76	26.27	24.41	23.33	22.28
4,000.00	49.86	39.68	35.03	32.55	31.11	29.70
5,000.00	62.33	49.60	43.79	40.68	38.89	37.13
6,000.00	74.79	59.52	52.55	48.82	46.67	44.56
7,000.00	87.26	69.45	61.30	56.96	54.45	51.98
8,000.00	99.72	79.37	70.06	65.09	62.22	59.41
9,000.00	112.19	89.29	78.82	73.23	70.00	66.84
10,000.00	124.66	99.21	87.58	81.37	77.78	74.26
20,000.00	249.31	198.42	175.15	162.73	155.56	148.52
30,000.00	373.97	297.62	262.73	244.10	233.34	222.79
40,000.00	498.62	396.83	350.30	325.47	311.12	297.05
50,000.00	623.28	496.04	437.88	406.83	388.89	371.31
60,000.00	747.93	595.25	525.45	488.20	466.67	445.57
70,000.00	872.59	694.46	613.03	569.57	544.45	519.83
80,000.00	997.24	793.66	700.60	650.93	622.23	594.09
90,000.00	1,121.90	892.87	788.18	732.30	700.01	668.36
100,000.00	1,246.55	992.08	875.75	813.67	777.79	742.62

8.750% Rate

Amount	Term of Loan in Years					
	10	15	20	25	30	40
$ 50.00	$ 0.63	$ 0.50	$ 0.44	$ 0.41	$ 0.39	$ 0.38
100.00	1.25	1.00	0.88	0.82	0.79	0.75
200.00	2.51	2.00	1.77	1.64	1.57	1.50
300.00	3.76	3.00	2.65	2.47	2.36	2.26
400.00	5.01	4.00	3.53	3.29	3.15	3.01
500.00	6.27	5.00	4.42	4.11	3.93	3.76
600.00	7.52	6.00	5.30	4.93	4.72	4.51
700.00	8.77	7.00	6.19	5.76	5.51	5.27
800.00	10.03	8.00	7.07	6.58	6.29	6.02
900.00	11.28	9.00	7.95	7.40	7.08	6.77
1,000.00	12.53	9.99	8.84	8.22	7.87	7.52
2,000.00	25.07	19.99	17.67	16.44	15.73	15.04
3,000.00	37.60	29.98	26.51	24.66	23.60	22.57
4,000.00	50.13	39.98	35.35	32.89	31.47	30.09
5,000.00	62.66	49.97	44.19	41.11	39.34	37.61
6,000.00	75.20	59.97	53.02	49.33	47.20	45.13
7,000.00	87.73	69.96	61.86	57.55	55.07	52.65
8,000.00	100.26	79.96	70.70	65.77	62.94	60.17
9,000.00	112.79	89.95	79.53	73.99	70.80	67.70
10,000.00	125.33	99.94	88.37	82.21	78.67	75.22
20,000.00	250.65	199.89	176.74	164.43	157.34	150.43
30,000.00	375.98	299.83	265.11	246.64	236.01	225.65
40,000.00	501.31	399.78	353.48	328.86	314.68	300.87
50,000.00	626.63	499.72	441.86	411.07	393.35	376.09
60,000.00	751.96	599.67	530.23	493.29	472.02	451.30
70,000.00	877.29	699.61	618.60	575.50	550.69	526.52
80,000.00	1,002.61	799.56	706.97	657.71	629.36	601.74
90,000.00	1,127.94	899.50	795.34	739.93	708.03	676.95
100,000.00	1,253.27	999.45	883.71	822.14	786.70	752.17

8.875% Rate

Amount	Term of Loan in Years					
	10	15	20	25	30	40
$ 50.00	$ 0.63	$ 0.50	$ 0.45	$ 0.42	$ 0.40	$ 0.38
100.00	1.26	1.01	0.89	0.83	0.80	0.76
200.00	2.52	2.01	1.78	1.66	1.59	1.52
300.00	3.78	3.02	2.68	2.49	2.39	2.29
400.00	5.04	4.03	3.57	3.32	3.18	3.05
500.00	6.30	5.03	4.46	4.15	3.98	3.81
600.00	7.56	6.04	5.35	4.98	4.77	4.57
700.00	8.82	7.05	6.24	5.81	5.57	5.33
800.00	10.08	8.05	7.13	6.65	6.37	6.09
900.00	11.34	9.06	8.03	7.48	7.16	6.86
1,000.00	12.60	10.07	8.92	8.31	7.96	7.62
2,000.00	25.20	20.14	17.83	16.61	15.91	15.24
3,000.00	37.80	30.21	26.75	24.92	23.87	22.85
4,000.00	50.40	40.27	35.67	33.23	31.83	30.47
5,000.00	63.00	50.34	44.59	41.53	39.78	38.09
6,000.00	75.60	60.41	53.50	49.84	47.74	45.71
7,000.00	88.20	70.48	62.42	58.15	55.70	53.32
8,000.00	100.80	80.55	71.34	66.45	63.65	60.94
9,000.00	113.40	90.62	80.25	74.76	71.61	68.56
10,000.00	126.00	100.68	89.17	83.07	79.56	76.18
20,000.00	252.00	201.37	178.34	166.13	159.13	152.35
30,000.00	378.00	302.05	267.51	249.20	238.69	228.53
40,000.00	504.00	402.74	356.68	332.26	318.26	304.70
50,000.00	630.00	503.42	445.85	415.33	397.82	380.88
60,000.00	756.00	604.11	535.02	498.39	477.39	457.05
70,000.00	882.00	704.79	624.19	581.46	556.95	533.23
80,000.00	1,008.00	805.48	713.36	664.52	636.52	609.40
90,000.00	1,134.00	906.16	802.53	747.59	716.08	685.58
100,000.00	1,260.00	1,006.84	891.70	830.65	795.64	761.75

9.000% Rate

Amount	Term of Loan in Years					
	10	15	20	25	30	40
$ 50.00	$ 0.63	$ 0.51	$ 0.45	$ 0.42	$ 0.40	$ 0.39
100.00	1.27	1.01	0.90	0.84	0.80	0.77
200.00	2.53	2.03	1.80	1.68	1.61	1.54
300.00	3.80	3.04	2.70	2.52	2.41	2.31
400.00	5.07	4.06	3.60	3.36	3.22	3.09
500.00	6.33	5.07	4.50	4.20	4.02	3.86
600.00	7.60	6.09	5.40	5.04	4.83	4.63
700.00	8.87	7.10	6.30	5.87	5.63	5.40
800.00	10.13	8.11	7.20	6.71	6.44	6.17
900.00	11.40	9.13	8.10	7.55	7.24	6.94
1,000.00	12.67	10.14	9.00	8.39	8.05	7.71
2,000.00	25.34	20.29	17.99	16.78	16.09	15.43
3,000.00	38.00	30.43	26.99	25.18	24.14	23.14
4,000.00	50.67	40.57	35.99	33.57	32.18	30.85
5,000.00	63.34	50.71	44.99	41.96	40.23	38.57
6,000.00	76.01	60.86	53.98	50.35	48.28	46.28
7,000.00	88.67	71.00	62.98	58.74	56.32	54.00
8,000.00	101.34	81.14	71.98	67.14	64.37	61.71
9,000.00	114.01	91.28	80.98	75.53	72.42	69.42
10,000.00	126.68	101.43	89.97	83.92	80.46	77.14
20,000.00	253.35	202.85	179.95	167.84	160.92	154.27
30,000.00	380.03	304.28	269.92	251.76	241.39	231.41
40,000.00	506.70	405.71	359.89	335.68	321.85	308.54
50,000.00	633.38	507.13	449.86	419.60	402.31	385.68
60,000.00	760.05	608.56	539.84	503.52	482.77	462.82
70,000.00	886.73	709.99	629.81	587.44	563.24	539.95
80,000.00	1,013.41	811.41	719.78	671.36	643.70	617.09
90,000.00	1,140.08	912.84	809.75	755.28	724.16	694.23
100,000.00	1,266.76	1,014.27	899.73	839.20	804.62	771.36

9.125% Rate

Amount	Term of Loan in Years					
	10	15	20	25	30	40
$ 50.00	$ 0.64	$ 0.51	$ 0.45	$ 0.42	$ 0.41	$ 0.39
100.00	1.27	1.02	0.91	0.85	0.81	0.78
200.00	2.55	2.04	1.82	1.70	1.63	1.56
300.00	3.82	3.07	2.72	2.54	2.44	2.34
400.00	5.09	4.09	3.63	3.39	3.25	3.12
500.00	6.37	5.11	4.54	4.24	4.07	3.90
600.00	7.64	6.13	5.45	5.09	4.88	4.69
700.00	8.91	7.15	6.35	5.93	5.70	5.47
800.00	10.19	8.17	7.26	6.78	6.51	6.25
900.00	11.46	9.20	8.17	7.63	7.32	7.03
1,000.00	12.74	10.22	9.08	8.48	8.14	7.81
2,000.00	25.47	20.43	18.16	16.96	16.27	15.62
3,000.00	38.21	30.65	27.23	25.43	24.41	23.43
4,000.00	50.94	40.87	36.31	33.91	32.55	31.24
5,000.00	63.68	51.09	45.39	42.39	40.68	39.05
6,000.00	76.41	61.30	54.47	50.87	48.82	46.86
7,000.00	89.15	71.52	63.54	59.34	56.95	54.67
8,000.00	101.88	81.74	72.62	67.82	65.09	62.48
9,000.00	114.62	91.95	81.70	76.30	73.23	70.29
10,000.00	127.35	102.17	90.78	84.78	81.36	78.10
20,000.00	254.71	204.34	181.56	169.55	162.73	156.20
30,000.00	382.06	306.51	272.33	254.33	244.09	234.30
40,000.00	509.41	408.69	363.11	339.11	325.45	312.40
50,000.00	636.77	510.86	453.89	423.89	406.82	390.50
60,000.00	764.12	613.03	544.67	508.66	488.18	468.60
70,000.00	891.47	715.20	635.45	593.44	569.54	546.70
80,000.00	1,018.83	817.37	726.22	678.22	650.91	624.80
90,000.00	1,146.18	919.54	817.00	763.00	732.27	702.90
100,000.00	1,273.53	1,021.72	907.78	847.77	813.63	781.00

9.250% Rate

Amount	Term of Loan in Years					
	10	15	20	25	30	40
$ 50.00	$ 0.64	$ 0.51	$ 0.46	$ 0.43	$ 0.41	$ 0.40
100.00	1.28	1.03	0.92	0.86	0.82	0.79
200.00	2.56	2.06	1.83	1.71	1.65	1.58
300.00	3.84	3.09	2.75	2.57	2.47	2.37
400.00	5.12	4.12	3.66	3.43	3.29	3.16
500.00	6.40	5.15	4.58	4.28	4.11	3.95
600.00	7.68	6.18	5.50	5.14	4.94	4.74
700.00	8.96	7.20	6.41	5.99	5.76	5.53
800.00	10.24	8.23	7.33	6.85	6.58	6.33
900.00	11.52	9.26	8.24	7.71	7.40	7.12
1,000.00	12.80	10.29	9.16	8.56	8.23	7.91
2,000.00	25.61	20.58	18.32	17.13	16.45	15.81
3,000.00	38.41	30.88	27.48	25.69	24.68	23.72
4,000.00	51.21	41.17	36.63	34.26	32.91	31.63
5,000.00	64.02	51.46	45.79	42.82	41.13	39.53
6,000.00	76.82	61.75	54.95	51.38	49.36	47.44
7,000.00	89.62	72.04	64.11	59.95	57.59	55.35
8,000.00	102.43	82.34	73.27	68.51	65.81	63.25
9,000.00	115.23	92.63	82.43	77.07	74.04	71.16
10,000.00	128.03	102.92	91.59	85.64	82.27	79.07
20,000.00	256.07	205.84	183.17	171.28	164.54	158.13
30,000.00	384.10	308.76	274.76	256.91	246.80	237.20
40,000.00	512.13	411.68	366.35	342.55	329.07	316.26
50,000.00	640.16	514.60	457.93	428.19	411.34	395.33
60,000.00	768.20	617.52	549.52	513.83	493.61	474.40
70,000.00	896.23	720.43	641.11	599.47	575.87	553.46
80,000.00	1,024.26	823.35	732.69	685.11	658.14	632.53
90,000.00	1,152.29	926.27	824.28	770.74	740.41	711.59
100,000.00	1,280.33	1,029.19	915.87	856.38	822.68	790.66

9.375% Rate

Amount	Term of Loan in Years					
	10	15	20	25	30	40
$ 50.00	$ 0.64	$ 0.52	$ 0.46	$ 0.43	$ 0.42	$ 0.40
100.00	1.29	1.04	0.92	0.87	0.83	0.80
200.00	2.57	2.07	1.85	1.73	1.66	1.60
300.00	3.86	3.11	2.77	2.60	2.50	2.40
400.00	5.15	4.15	3.70	3.46	3.33	3.20
500.00	6.44	5.18	4.62	4.33	4.16	4.00
600.00	7.72	6.22	5.54	5.19	4.99	4.80
700.00	9.01	7.26	6.47	6.06	5.82	5.60
800.00	10.30	8.29	7.39	6.92	6.65	6.40
900.00	11.58	9.33	8.32	7.79	7.49	7.20
1,000.00	12.87	10.37	9.24	8.65	8.32	8.00
2,000.00	25.74	20.73	18.48	17.30	16.63	16.01
3,000.00	38.61	31.10	27.72	25.95	24.95	24.01
4,000.00	51.49	41.47	36.96	34.60	33.27	32.01
5,000.00	64.36	51.83	46.20	43.25	41.59	40.02
6,000.00	77.23	62.20	55.44	51.90	49.90	48.02
7,000.00	90.10	72.57	64.68	60.55	58.22	56.02
8,000.00	102.97	82.94	73.92	69.20	66.54	64.03
9,000.00	115.84	93.30	83.16	77.85	74.86	72.03
10,000.00	128.71	103.67	92.40	86.50	83.17	80.03
20,000.00	257.43	207.34	184.80	173.00	166.35	160.07
30,000.00	386.14	311.01	277.20	259.51	249.52	240.10
40,000.00	514.86	414.68	369.59	346.01	332.70	320.14
50,000.00	643.57	518.35	461.99	432.51	415.87	400.17
60,000.00	772.28	622.02	554.39	519.01	499.05	480.21
70,000.00	901.00	725.69	646.79	605.52	582.22	560.24
80,000.00	1,029.71	829.36	739.19	692.02	665.40	640.28
90,000.00	1,158.43	933.03	831.59	778.52	748.57	720.31
100,000.00	1,287.14	1,036.70	923.98	865.02	831.75	800.35

9.500% Rate

Amount	Term of Loan in Years					
	10	15	20	25	30	40
$ 50.00	$ 0.65	$ 0.52	$ 0.47	$ 0.44	$ 0.42	$ 0.41
100.00	1.29	1.04	0.93	0.87	0.84	0.81
200.00	2.59	2.09	1.86	1.75	1.68	1.62
300.00	3.88	3.13	2.80	2.62	2.52	2.43
400.00	5.18	4.18	3.73	3.49	3.36	3.24
500.00	6.47	5.22	4.66	4.37	4.20	4.05
600.00	7.76	6.27	5.59	5.24	5.05	4.86
700.00	9.06	7.31	6.52	6.12	5.89	5.67
800.00	10.35	8.35	7.46	6.99	6.73	6.48
900.00	11.65	9.40	8.39	7.86	7.57	7.29
1,000.00	12.94	10.44	9.32	8.74	8.41	8.10
2,000.00	25.88	20.88	18.64	17.47	16.82	16.20
3,000.00	38.82	31.33	27.96	26.21	25.23	24.30
4,000.00	51.76	41.77	37.29	34.95	33.63	32.40
5,000.00	64.70	52.21	46.61	43.68	42.04	40.50
6,000.00	77.64	62.65	55.93	52.42	50.45	48.60
7,000.00	90.58	73.10	65.25	61.16	58.86	56.70
8,000.00	103.52	83.54	74.57	69.90	67.27	64.80
9,000.00	116.46	93.98	83.89	78.63	75.68	72.91
10,000.00	129.40	104.42	93.21	87.37	84.09	81.01
20,000.00	258.80	208.84	186.43	174.74	168.17	162.01
30,000.00	388.19	313.27	279.64	262.11	252.26	243.02
40,000.00	517.59	417.69	372.85	349.48	336.34	324.02
50,000.00	646.99	522.11	466.07	436.85	420.43	405.03
60,000.00	776.39	626.53	559.28	524.22	504.51	486.04
70,000.00	905.78	730.96	652.49	611.59	588.60	567.04
80,000.00	1,035.18	835.38	745.70	698.96	672.68	648.05
90,000.00	1,164.58	939.80	838.92	786.33	756.77	729.06
100,000.00	1,293.98	1,044.22	932.13	873.70	840.85	810.06

9.625% Rate

Amount	Term of Loan in Years					
	10	15	20	25	30	40
$ 50.00	$ 0.65	$ 0.53	$ 0.47	$ 0.44	$ 0.42	$ 0.41
100.00	1.30	1.05	0.94	0.88	0.85	0.82
200.00	2.60	2.10	1.88	1.76	1.70	1.64
300.00	3.90	3.16	2.82	2.65	2.55	2.46
400.00	5.20	4.21	3.76	3.53	3.40	3.28
500.00	6.50	5.26	4.70	4.41	4.25	4.10
600.00	7.80	6.31	5.64	5.29	5.10	4.92
700.00	9.11	7.36	6.58	6.18	5.95	5.74
800.00	10.41	8.41	7.52	7.06	6.80	6.56
900.00	11.71	9.47	8.46	7.94	7.65	7.38
1,000.00	13.01	10.52	9.40	8.82	8.50	8.20
2,000.00	26.02	21.04	18.81	17.65	17.00	16.40
3,000.00	39.02	31.55	28.21	26.47	25.50	24.59
4,000.00	52.03	42.07	37.61	35.30	34.00	32.79
5,000.00	65.04	52.59	47.02	44.12	42.50	40.99
6,000.00	78.05	63.11	56.42	52.94	51.00	49.19
7,000.00	91.06	73.62	65.82	61.77	59.50	57.39
8,000.00	104.07	84.14	75.22	70.59	68.00	65.58
9,000.00	117.07	94.66	84.63	79.42	76.50	73.78
10,000.00	130.08	105.18	94.03	88.24	85.00	81.98
20,000.00	260.17	210.36	188.06	176.48	170.00	163.96
30,000.00	390.25	315.53	282.09	264.72	255.00	245.94
40,000.00	520.33	420.71	376.12	352.96	340.00	327.92
50,000.00	650.41	525.89	470.15	441.20	424.99	409.90
60,000.00	780.50	631.07	564.19	529.44	509.99	491.88
70,000.00	910.58	736.25	658.22	617.68	594.99	573.86
80,000.00	1,040.66	841.42	752.25	705.92	679.99	655.84
90,000.00	1,170.75	946.60	846.28	794.16	764.99	737.82
100,000.00	1,300.83	1,051.78	940.31	882.40	849.99	819.80

9.750% Rate

Amount	Term of Loan in Years					
	10	15	20	25	30	40
$ 50.00	$ 0.65	$ 0.53	$ 0.47	$ 0.45	$ 0.43	$ 0.41
100.00	1.31	1.06	0.95	0.89	0.86	0.83
200.00	2.62	2.12	1.90	1.78	1.72	1.66
300.00	3.92	3.18	2.85	2.67	2.58	2.49
400.00	5.23	4.24	3.79	3.56	3.44	3.32
500.00	6.54	5.30	4.74	4.46	4.30	4.15
600.00	7.85	6.36	5.69	5.35	5.15	4.98
700.00	9.15	7.42	6.64	6.24	6.01	5.81
800.00	10.46	8.47	7.59	7.13	6.87	6.64
900.00	11.77	9.53	8.54	8.02	7.73	7.47
1,000.00	13.08	10.59	9.49	8.91	8.59	8.30
2,000.00	26.15	21.19	18.97	17.82	17.18	16.59
3,000.00	39.23	31.78	28.46	26.73	25.77	24.89
4,000.00	52.31	42.37	37.94	35.65	34.37	33.18
5,000.00	65.39	52.97	47.43	44.56	42.96	41.48
6,000.00	78.46	63.56	56.91	53.47	51.55	49.77
7,000.00	91.54	74.16	66.40	62.38	60.14	58.07
8,000.00	104.62	84.75	75.88	71.29	68.73	66.36
9,000.00	117.69	95.34	85.37	80.20	77.32	74.66
10,000.00	130.77	105.94	94.85	89.11	85.92	82.96
20,000.00	261.54	211.87	189.70	178.23	171.83	165.91
30,000.00	392.31	317.81	284.56	267.34	257.75	248.87
40,000.00	523.08	423.75	379.41	356.45	343.66	331.82
50,000.00	653.85	529.68	474.26	445.57	429.58	414.78
60,000.00	784.62	635.62	569.11	534.68	515.49	497.74
70,000.00	915.39	741.55	663.96	623.80	601.41	580.69
80,000.00	1,046.16	847.49	758.81	712.91	687.32	663.65
90,000.00	1,176.93	953.43	853.67	802.02	773.24	746.60
100,000.00	1,307.70	1,059.36	948.52	891.14	859.15	829.56

9.875% Rate

Amount	Term of Loan in Years					
	10	15	20	25	30	40
$ 50.00	$ 0.66	$ 0.53	$ 0.48	$ 0.45	$ 0.43	$ 0.42
100.00	1.31	1.07	0.96	0.90	0.87	0.84
200.00	2.63	2.13	1.91	1.80	1.74	1.68
300.00	3.94	3.20	2.87	2.70	2.61	2.52
400.00	5.26	4.27	3.83	3.60	3.47	3.36
500.00	6.57	5.33	4.78	4.50	4.34	4.20
600.00	7.89	6.40	5.74	5.40	5.21	5.04
700.00	9.20	7.47	6.70	6.30	6.08	5.88
800.00	10.52	8.54	7.65	7.20	6.95	6.71
900.00	11.83	9.60	8.61	8.10	7.82	7.55
1,000.00	13.15	10.67	9.57	9.00	8.68	8.39
2,000.00	26.29	21.34	19.14	18.00	17.37	16.79
3,000.00	39.44	32.01	28.70	27.00	26.05	25.18
4,000.00	52.58	42.68	38.27	36.00	34.73	33.57
5,000.00	65.73	53.35	47.84	45.00	43.42	41.97
6,000.00	78.88	64.02	57.41	53.99	52.10	50.36
7,000.00	92.02	74.69	66.97	62.99	60.78	58.75
8,000.00	105.17	85.36	76.54	71.99	69.47	67.15
9,000.00	118.31	96.03	86.11	80.99	78.15	75.54
10,000.00	131.46	106.70	95.68	89.99	86.83	83.93
20,000.00	262.92	213.39	191.35	179.98	173.67	167.87
30,000.00	394.38	320.09	287.03	269.97	260.50	251.80
40,000.00	525.84	426.79	382.70	359.96	347.34	335.74
50,000.00	657.30	533.49	478.38	449.95	434.17	419.67
60,000.00	788.76	640.18	574.05	539.94	521.01	503.60
70,000.00	920.22	746.88	669.73	629.93	607.84	587.54
80,000.00	1,051.68	853.58	765.40	719.92	694.68	671.47
90,000.00	1,183.14	960.27	861.08	809.91	781.51	755.41
100,000.00	1,314.60	1,066.97	956.75	899.90	868.35	839.34

10.000% Rate

Amount	Term of Loan in Years					
	10	15	20	25	30	40
$ 50.00	$ 0.66	$ 0.54	$ 0.48	$ 0.45	$ 0.44	$ 0.42
100.00	1.32	1.07	0.97	0.91	0.88	0.85
200.00	2.64	2.15	1.93	1.82	1.76	1.70
300.00	3.96	3.22	2.90	2.73	2.63	2.55
400.00	5.29	4.30	3.86	3.63	3.51	3.40
500.00	6.61	5.37	4.83	4.54	4.39	4.25
600.00	7.93	6.45	5.79	5.45	5.27	5.09
700.00	9.25	7.52	6.76	6.36	6.14	5.94
800.00	10.57	8.60	7.72	7.27	7.02	6.79
900.00	11.89	9.67	8.69	8.18	7.90	7.64
1,000.00	13.22	10.75	9.65	9.09	8.78	8.49
2,000.00	26.43	21.49	19.30	18.17	17.55	16.98
3,000.00	39.65	32.24	28.95	27.26	26.33	25.47
4,000.00	52.86	42.98	38.60	36.35	35.10	33.97
5,000.00	66.08	53.73	48.25	45.44	43.88	42.46
6,000.00	79.29	64.48	57.90	54.52	52.65	50.95
7,000.00	92.51	75.22	67.55	63.61	61.43	59.44
8,000.00	105.72	85.97	77.20	72.70	70.21	67.93
9,000.00	118.94	96.71	86.85	81.78	78.98	76.42
10,000.00	132.15	107.46	96.50	90.87	87.76	84.91
20,000.00	264.30	214.92	193.00	181.74	175.51	169.83
30,000.00	396.45	322.38	289.51	272.61	263.27	254.74
40,000.00	528.60	429.84	386.01	363.48	351.03	339.66
50,000.00	660.75	537.30	482.51	454.35	438.79	424.57
60,000.00	792.90	644.76	579.01	545.22	526.54	509.49
70,000.00	925.06	752.22	675.52	636.09	614.30	594.40
80,000.00	1,057.21	859.68	772.02	726.96	702.06	679.32
90,000.00	1,189.36	967.14	868.52	817.83	789.81	764.23
100,000.00	1,321.51	1,074.61	965.02	908.70	877.57	849.15

10.125% Rate

Amount	Term of Loan in Years					
	10	15	20	25	30	40
$ 50.00	$ 0.66	$ 0.54	$ 0.49	$ 0.46	$ 0.44	$ 0.43
100.00	1.33	1.08	0.97	0.92	0.89	0.86
200.00	2.66	2.16	1.95	1.84	1.77	1.72
300.00	3.99	3.25	2.92	2.75	2.66	2.58
400.00	5.31	4.33	3.89	3.67	3.55	3.44
500.00	6.64	5.41	4.87	4.59	4.43	4.29
600.00	7.97	6.49	5.84	5.51	5.32	5.15
700.00	9.30	7.58	6.81	6.42	6.21	6.01
800.00	10.63	8.66	7.79	7.34	7.09	6.87
900.00	11.96	9.74	8.76	8.26	7.98	7.73
1,000.00	13.28	10.82	9.73	9.18	8.87	8.59
2,000.00	26.57	21.65	19.47	18.35	17.74	17.18
3,000.00	39.85	32.47	29.20	27.53	26.60	25.77
4,000.00	53.14	43.29	38.93	36.70	35.47	34.36
5,000.00	66.42	54.11	48.67	45.88	44.34	42.95
6,000.00	79.71	64.94	58.40	55.05	53.21	51.54
7,000.00	92.99	75.76	68.13	64.23	62.08	60.13
8,000.00	106.28	86.58	77.87	73.40	70.95	68.72
9,000.00	119.56	97.40	87.60	82.58	79.81	77.31
10,000.00	132.84	108.23	97.33	91.75	88.68	85.90
20,000.00	265.69	216.45	194.66	183.51	177.36	171.79
30,000.00	398.53	324.68	292.00	275.26	266.05	257.69
40,000.00	531.38	432.91	389.33	367.01	354.73	343.59
50,000.00	664.22	541.13	486.66	458.76	443.41	429.49
60,000.00	797.06	649.36	583.99	550.52	532.09	515.38
70,000.00	929.91	757.59	681.32	642.27	620.78	601.28
80,000.00	1,062.75	865.81	778.65	734.02	709.46	687.18
90,000.00	1,195.60	974.04	875.99	825.77	798.14	773.07
100,000.00	1,328.44	1,082.27	973.32	917.53	886.82	858.97

10.250% Rate

Amount	Term of Loan in Years					
	10	15	20	25	30	40
$ 50.00	$ 0.67	$ 0.54	$ 0.49	$ 0.46	$ 0.45	$ 0.43
100.00	1.34	1.09	0.98	0.93	0.90	0.87
200.00	2.67	2.18	1.96	1.85	1.79	1.74
300.00	4.01	3.27	2.94	2.78	2.69	2.61
400.00	5.34	4.36	3.93	3.71	3.58	3.48
500.00	6.68	5.45	4.91	4.63	4.48	4.34
600.00	8.01	6.54	5.89	5.56	5.38	5.21
700.00	9.35	7.63	6.87	6.48	6.27	6.08
800.00	10.68	8.72	7.85	7.41	7.17	6.95
900.00	12.02	9.81	8.83	8.34	8.06	7.82
1,000.00	13.35	10.90	9.82	9.26	8.96	8.69
2,000.00	26.71	21.80	19.63	18.53	17.92	17.38
3,000.00	40.06	32.70	29.45	27.79	26.88	26.06
4,000.00	53.42	43.60	39.27	37.06	35.84	34.75
5,000.00	66.77	54.50	49.08	46.32	44.81	43.44
6,000.00	80.12	65.40	58.90	55.58	53.77	52.13
7,000.00	93.48	76.30	68.72	64.85	62.73	60.82
8,000.00	106.83	87.20	78.53	74.11	71.69	69.51
9,000.00	120.19	98.10	88.35	83.37	80.65	78.19
10,000.00	133.54	109.00	98.16	92.64	89.61	86.88
20,000.00	267.08	217.99	196.33	185.28	179.22	173.76
30,000.00	400.62	326.99	294.49	277.91	268.83	260.65
40,000.00	534.16	435.98	392.66	370.55	358.44	347.53
50,000.00	667.70	544.98	490.82	463.19	448.05	434.41
60,000.00	801.23	653.97	588.99	555.83	537.66	521.29
70,000.00	934.77	762.97	687.15	648.47	627.27	608.17
80,000.00	1,068.31	871.96	785.31	741.11	716.88	695.05
90,000.00	1,201.85	980.96	883.48	833.74	806.49	781.94
100,000.00	1,335.39	1,089.95	981.64	926.38	896.10	868.82

10.375% Rate

Amount	Term of Loan in Years					
	10	15	20	25	30	40
$ 50.00	$ 0.67	$ 0.55	$ 0.49	$ 0.47	$ 0.45	$ 0.44
100.00	1.34	1.10	0.99	0.94	0.91	0.88
200.00	2.68	2.20	1.98	1.87	1.81	1.76
300.00	4.03	3.29	2.97	2.81	2.72	2.64
400.00	5.37	4.39	3.96	3.74	3.62	3.51
500.00	6.71	5.49	4.95	4.68	4.53	4.39
600.00	8.05	6.59	5.94	5.61	5.43	5.27
700.00	9.40	7.68	6.93	6.55	6.34	6.15
800.00	10.74	8.78	7.92	7.48	7.24	7.03
900.00	12.08	9.88	8.91	8.42	8.15	7.91
1,000.00	13.42	10.98	9.90	9.35	9.05	8.79
2,000.00	26.85	21.95	19.80	18.71	18.11	17.57
3,000.00	40.27	32.93	29.70	28.06	27.16	26.36
4,000.00	53.69	43.91	39.60	37.41	36.22	35.15
5,000.00	67.12	54.88	49.50	46.76	45.27	43.93
6,000.00	80.54	65.86	59.40	56.12	54.32	52.72
7,000.00	93.97	76.84	69.30	65.47	63.38	61.51
8,000.00	107.39	87.81	79.20	74.82	72.43	70.29
9,000.00	120.81	98.79	89.10	84.17	81.49	79.08
10,000.00	134.24	109.77	99.00	93.53	90.54	87.87
20,000.00	268.47	219.53	198.00	187.05	181.08	175.74
30,000.00	402.71	329.30	297.00	280.58	271.62	263.61
40,000.00	536.94	439.06	396.00	374.11	362.16	351.47
50,000.00	671.18	548.83	495.00	467.63	452.70	439.34
60,000.00	805.42	658.60	594.00	561.16	543.24	527.21
70,000.00	939.65	768.36	693.00	654.69	633.78	615.08
80,000.00	1,073.89	878.13	792.00	748.21	724.33	702.95
90,000.00	1,208.12	987.90	891.00	841.74	814.87	790.82
100,000.00	1,342.36	1,097.66	990.00	935.27	905.41	878.68

10.500% Rate

Amount	Term of Loan in Years					
	10	15	20	25	30	40
$ 50.00	$ 0.67	$ 0.55	$ 0.50	$ 0.47	$ 0.46	$ 0.44
100.00	1.35	1.11	1.00	0.94	0.91	0.89
200.00	2.70	2.21	2.00	1.89	1.83	1.78
300.00	4.05	3.32	3.00	2.83	2.74	2.67
400.00	5.40	4.42	3.99	3.78	3.66	3.55
500.00	6.75	5.53	4.99	4.72	4.57	4.44
600.00	8.10	6.63	5.99	5.67	5.49	5.33
700.00	9.45	7.74	6.99	6.61	6.40	6.22
800.00	10.79	8.84	7.99	7.55	7.32	7.11
900.00	12.14	9.95	8.99	8.50	8.23	8.00
1,000.00	13.49	11.05	9.98	9.44	9.15	8.89
2,000.00	26.99	22.11	19.97	18.88	18.29	17.77
3,000.00	40.48	33.16	29.95	28.33	27.44	26.66
4,000.00	53.97	44.22	39.94	37.77	36.59	35.54
5,000.00	67.47	55.27	49.92	47.21	45.74	44.43
6,000.00	80.96	66.32	59.90	56.65	54.88	53.31
7,000.00	94.45	77.38	69.89	66.09	64.03	62.20
8,000.00	107.95	88.43	79.87	75.53	73.18	71.09
9,000.00	121.44	99.49	89.85	84.98	82.33	79.97
10,000.00	134.93	110.54	99.84	94.42	91.47	88.86
20,000.00	269.87	221.08	199.68	188.84	182.95	177.71
30,000.00	404.80	331.62	299.51	283.25	274.42	266.57
40,000.00	539.74	442.16	399.35	377.67	365.90	355.43
50,000.00	674.67	552.70	499.19	472.09	457.37	444.29
60,000.00	809.61	663.24	599.03	566.51	548.84	533.14
70,000.00	944.54	773.78	698.87	660.93	640.32	622.00
80,000.00	1,079.48	884.32	798.70	755.35	731.79	710.86
90,000.00	1,214.41	994.86	898.54	849.76	823.27	799.71
100,000.00	1,349.35	1,105.40	998.38	944.18	914.74	888.57

10.625% Rate

Amount	Term of Loan in Years					
	10	15	20	25	30	40
$ 50.00	$ 0.68	$ 0.56	$ 0.50	$ 0.48	$ 0.46	$ 0.45
100.00	1.36	1.11	1.01	0.95	0.92	0.90
200.00	2.71	2.23	2.01	1.91	1.85	1.80
300.00	4.07	3.34	3.02	2.86	2.77	2.70
400.00	5.43	4.45	4.03	3.81	3.70	3.59
500.00	6.78	5.57	5.03	4.77	4.62	4.49
600.00	8.14	6.68	6.04	5.72	5.54	5.39
700.00	9.49	7.79	7.05	6.67	6.47	6.29
800.00	10.85	8.91	8.05	7.62	7.39	7.19
900.00	12.21	10.02	9.06	8.58	8.32	8.09
1,000.00	13.56	11.13	10.07	9.53	9.24	8.98
2,000.00	27.13	22.26	20.14	19.06	18.48	17.97
3,000.00	40.69	33.39	30.20	28.59	27.72	26.95
4,000.00	54.25	44.53	40.27	38.12	36.96	35.94
5,000.00	67.82	55.66	50.34	47.66	46.20	44.92
6,000.00	81.38	66.79	60.41	57.19	55.45	53.91
7,000.00	94.95	77.92	70.48	66.72	64.69	62.89
8,000.00	108.51	89.05	80.54	76.25	73.93	71.88
9,000.00	122.07	100.18	90.61	85.78	83.17	80.86
10,000.00	135.64	111.32	100.68	95.31	92.41	89.85
20,000.00	271.27	222.63	201.36	190.62	184.82	179.69
30,000.00	406.91	333.95	302.04	285.94	277.23	269.54
40,000.00	542.54	445.26	402.72	381.25	369.64	359.39
50,000.00	678.18	556.58	503.40	476.56	462.05	449.24
60,000.00	813.82	667.90	604.07	571.87	554.46	539.08
70,000.00	949.45	779.21	704.75	667.19	646.87	628.93
80,000.00	1,085.09	890.53	805.43	762.50	739.28	718.78
90,000.00	1,220.72	1,001.84	906.11	857.81	831.69	808.63
100,000.00	1,356.36	1,113.16	1,006.79	953.12	924.10	898.47

10.750% Rate

Amount	Term of Loan in Years					
	10	15	20	25	30	40
$ 50.00	$ 0.68	$ 0.56	$ 0.51	$ 0.48	$ 0.47	$ 0.45
100.00	1.36	1.12	1.02	0.96	0.93	0.91
200.00	2.73	2.24	2.03	1.92	1.87	1.82
300.00	4.09	3.36	3.05	2.89	2.80	2.73
400.00	5.45	4.48	4.06	3.85	3.73	3.63
500.00	6.82	5.60	5.08	4.81	4.67	4.54
600.00	8.18	6.73	6.09	5.77	5.60	5.45
700.00	9.54	7.85	7.11	6.73	6.53	6.36
800.00	10.91	8.97	8.12	7.70	7.47	7.27
900.00	12.27	10.09	9.14	8.66	8.40	8.18
1,000.00	13.63	11.21	10.15	9.62	9.33	9.08
2,000.00	27.27	22.42	20.30	19.24	18.67	18.17
3,000.00	40.90	33.63	30.46	28.86	28.00	27.25
4,000.00	54.54	44.84	40.61	38.48	37.34	36.34
5,000.00	68.17	56.05	50.76	48.10	46.67	45.42
6,000.00	81.80	67.26	60.91	57.73	56.01	54.50
7,000.00	95.44	78.47	71.07	67.35	65.34	63.59
8,000.00	109.07	89.68	81.22	76.97	74.68	72.67
9,000.00	122.70	100.89	91.37	86.59	84.01	81.76
10,000.00	136.34	112.09	101.52	96.21	93.35	90.84
20,000.00	272.68	224.19	203.05	192.42	186.70	181.68
30,000.00	409.02	336.28	304.57	288.63	280.04	272.52
40,000.00	545.35	448.38	406.09	384.84	373.39	363.36
50,000.00	681.69	560.47	507.61	481.05	466.74	454.20
60,000.00	818.03	672.57	609.14	577.26	560.09	545.04
70,000.00	954.37	784.66	710.66	673.46	653.44	635.88
80,000.00	1,090.71	896.76	812.18	769.67	746.79	726.72
90,000.00	1,227.05	1,008.85	913.71	865.88	840.13	817.56
100,000.00	1,363.39	1,120.95	1,015.23	962.09	933.48	908.40

10.875% Rate

Amount	Term of Loan in Years					
	10	15	20	25	30	40
$ 50.00	$ 0.69	$ 0.56	$ 0.51	$ 0.49	$ 0.47	$ 0.46
100.00	1.37	1.13	1.02	0.97	0.94	0.92
200.00	2.74	2.26	2.05	1.94	1.89	1.84
300.00	4.11	3.39	3.07	2.91	2.83	2.76
400.00	5.48	4.52	4.09	3.88	3.77	3.67
500.00	6.85	5.64	5.12	4.86	4.71	4.59
600.00	8.22	6.77	6.14	5.83	5.66	5.51
700.00	9.59	7.90	7.17	6.80	6.60	6.43
800.00	10.96	9.03	8.19	7.77	7.54	7.35
900.00	12.33	10.16	9.21	8.74	8.49	8.27
1,000.00	13.70	11.29	10.24	9.71	9.43	9.18
2,000.00	27.41	22.58	20.47	19.42	18.86	18.37
3,000.00	41.11	33.86	30.71	29.13	28.29	27.55
4,000.00	54.82	45.15	40.95	38.84	37.72	36.73
5,000.00	68.52	56.44	51.18	48.55	47.14	45.92
6,000.00	82.23	67.73	61.42	58.27	56.57	55.10
7,000.00	95.93	79.01	71.66	67.98	66.00	64.28
8,000.00	109.63	90.30	81.90	77.69	75.43	73.47
9,000.00	123.34	101.59	92.13	87.40	84.86	82.65
10,000.00	137.04	112.88	102.37	97.11	94.29	91.83
20,000.00	274.09	225.75	204.74	194.22	188.58	183.67
30,000.00	411.13	338.63	307.11	291.33	282.87	275.50
40,000.00	548.17	451.50	409.48	388.44	377.16	367.33
50,000.00	685.22	564.38	511.85	485.54	471.45	459.17
60,000.00	822.26	677.26	614.22	582.65	565.73	551.00
70,000.00	959.30	790.13	716.59	679.76	660.02	642.84
80,000.00	1,096.35	903.01	818.96	776.87	754.31	734.67
90,000.00	1,233.39	1,015.88	921.33	873.98	848.60	826.50
100,000.00	1,370.43	1,128.76	1,023.70	971.09	942.89	918.34

11.000% Rate

Amount	Term of Loan in Years					
	10	15	20	25	30	40
$ 50.00	$ 0.69	$ 0.57	$ 0.52	$ 0.49	$ 0.48	$ 0.46
100.00	1.38	1.14	1.03	0.98	0.95	0.93
200.00	2.76	2.27	2.06	1.96	1.90	1.86
300.00	4.13	3.41	3.10	2.94	2.86	2.78
400.00	5.51	4.55	4.13	3.92	3.81	3.71
500.00	6.89	5.68	5.16	4.90	4.76	4.64
600.00	8.27	6.82	6.19	5.88	5.71	5.57
700.00	9.64	7.96	7.23	6.86	6.67	6.50
800.00	11.02	9.09	8.26	7.84	7.62	7.43
900.00	12.40	10.23	9.29	8.82	8.57	8.35
1,000.00	13.78	11.37	10.32	9.80	9.52	9.28
2,000.00	27.55	22.73	20.64	19.60	19.05	18.57
3,000.00	41.33	34.10	30.97	29.40	28.57	27.85
4,000.00	55.10	45.46	41.29	39.20	38.09	37.13
5,000.00	68.88	56.83	51.61	49.01	47.62	46.41
6,000.00	82.65	68.20	61.93	58.81	57.14	55.70
7,000.00	96.43	79.56	72.25	68.61	66.66	64.98
8,000.00	110.20	90.93	82.58	78.41	76.19	74.26
9,000.00	123.98	102.29	92.90	88.21	85.71	83.55
10,000.00	137.75	113.66	103.22	98.01	95.23	92.83
20,000.00	275.50	227.32	206.44	196.02	190.46	185.66
30,000.00	413.25	340.98	309.66	294.03	285.70	278.49
40,000.00	551.00	454.64	412.88	392.05	380.93	371.32
50,000.00	688.75	568.30	516.09	490.06	476.16	464.15
60,000.00	826.50	681.96	619.31	588.07	571.39	556.98
70,000.00	964.25	795.62	722.53	686.08	666.63	649.81
80,000.00	1,102.00	909.28	825.75	784.09	761.86	742.64
90,000.00	1,239.75	1,022.94	928.97	882.10	857.09	835.46
100,000.00	1,377.50	1,136.60	1,032.19	980.11	952.32	928.29

11.125% Rate

Amount	Term of Loan in Years					
	10	15	20	25	30	40
$ 50.00	$ 0.69	$ 0.57	$ 0.52	$ 0.49	$ 0.48	$ 0.47
100.00	1.38	1.14	1.04	0.99	0.96	0.94
200.00	2.77	2.29	2.08	1.98	1.92	1.88
300.00	4.15	3.43	3.12	2.97	2.89	2.81
400.00	5.54	4.58	4.16	3.96	3.85	3.75
500.00	6.92	5.72	5.20	4.95	4.81	4.69
600.00	8.31	6.87	6.24	5.93	5.77	5.63
700.00	9.69	8.01	7.28	6.92	6.73	6.57
800.00	11.08	9.16	8.33	7.91	7.69	7.51
900.00	12.46	10.30	9.37	8.90	8.66	8.44
1,000.00	13.85	11.44	10.41	9.89	9.62	9.38
2,000.00	27.69	22.89	20.81	19.78	19.24	18.77
3,000.00	41.54	34.33	31.22	29.67	28.85	28.15
4,000.00	55.38	45.78	41.63	39.57	38.47	37.53
5,000.00	69.23	57.22	52.04	49.46	48.09	46.91
6,000.00	83.08	68.67	62.44	59.35	57.71	56.30
7,000.00	96.92	80.11	72.85	69.24	67.32	65.68
8,000.00	110.77	91.56	83.26	79.13	76.94	75.06
9,000.00	124.61	103.00	93.66	89.02	86.56	84.44
10,000.00	138.46	114.45	104.07	98.92	96.18	93.83
20,000.00	276.92	228.89	208.14	197.83	192.36	187.65
30,000.00	415.38	343.34	312.21	296.75	288.53	281.48
40,000.00	553.83	457.78	416.28	395.67	384.71	375.31
50,000.00	692.29	572.23	520.35	494.58	480.89	469.13
60,000.00	830.75	686.68	624.43	593.50	577.07	562.96
70,000.00	969.21	801.12	728.50	692.41	673.25	656.79
80,000.00	1,107.67	915.57	832.57	791.33	769.42	750.61
90,000.00	1,246.13	1,030.01	936.64	890.25	865.60	844.44
100,000.00	1,384.59	1,144.46	1,040.71	989.16	961.78	938.27

11.250% Rate

Amount	Term of Loan in Years					
	10	15	20	25	30	40
$ 50.00	$ 0.70	$ 0.58	$ 0.52	$ 0.50	$ 0.49	$ 0.47
100.00	1.39	1.15	1.05	1.00	0.97	0.95
200.00	2.78	2.30	2.10	2.00	1.94	1.90
300.00	4.18	3.46	3.15	2.99	2.91	2.84
400.00	5.57	4.61	4.20	3.99	3.89	3.79
500.00	6.96	5.76	5.25	4.99	4.86	4.74
600.00	8.35	6.91	6.30	5.99	5.83	5.69
700.00	9.74	8.07	7.34	6.99	6.80	6.64
800.00	11.13	9.22	8.39	7.99	7.77	7.59
900.00	12.53	10.37	9.44	8.98	8.74	8.53
1,000.00	13.92	11.52	10.49	9.98	9.71	9.48
2,000.00	27.83	23.05	20.99	19.96	19.43	18.97
3,000.00	41.75	34.57	31.48	29.95	29.14	28.45
4,000.00	55.67	46.09	41.97	39.93	38.85	37.93
5,000.00	69.58	57.62	52.46	49.91	48.56	47.41
6,000.00	83.50	69.14	62.96	59.89	58.28	56.90
7,000.00	97.42	80.66	73.45	69.88	67.99	66.38
8,000.00	111.34	92.19	83.94	79.86	77.70	75.86
9,000.00	125.25	103.71	94.43	89.84	87.41	85.34
10,000.00	139.17	115.23	104.93	99.82	97.13	94.83
20,000.00	278.34	230.47	209.85	199.65	194.25	189.65
30,000.00	417.51	345.70	314.78	299.47	291.38	284.48
40,000.00	556.68	460.94	419.70	399.30	388.50	379.30
50,000.00	695.84	576.17	524.63	499.12	485.63	474.13
60,000.00	835.01	691.41	629.55	598.94	582.76	568.95
70,000.00	974.18	806.64	734.48	698.77	679.88	663.78
80,000.00	1,113.35	921.88	839.40	798.59	777.01	758.61
90,000.00	1,252.52	1,037.11	944.33	898.42	874.14	853.43
100,000.00	1,391.69	1,152.34	1,049.26	998.24	971.26	948.26

11.375% Rate

Amount	Term of Loan in Years					
	10	15	20	25	30	40
$ 50.00	$ 0.70	$ 0.58	$ 0.53	$ 0.50	$ 0.49	$ 0.48
100.00	1.40	1.16	1.06	1.01	0.98	0.96
200.00	2.80	2.32	2.12	2.01	1.96	1.92
300.00	4.20	3.48	3.17	3.02	2.94	2.87
400.00	5.60	4.64	4.23	4.03	3.92	3.83
500.00	6.99	5.80	5.29	5.04	4.90	4.79
600.00	8.39	6.96	6.35	6.04	5.88	5.75
700.00	9.79	8.12	7.40	7.05	6.87	6.71
800.00	11.19	9.28	8.46	8.06	7.85	7.67
900.00	12.59	10.44	9.52	9.07	8.83	8.62
1,000.00	13.99	11.60	10.58	10.07	9.81	9.58
2,000.00	27.98	23.21	21.16	20.15	19.62	19.17
3,000.00	41.96	34.81	31.73	30.22	29.42	28.75
4,000.00	55.95	46.41	42.31	40.29	39.23	38.33
5,000.00	69.94	58.01	52.89	50.37	49.04	47.91
6,000.00	83.93	69.62	63.47	60.44	58.85	57.50
7,000.00	97.92	81.22	74.05	70.51	68.65	67.08
8,000.00	111.91	92.82	84.63	80.59	78.46	76.66
9,000.00	125.89	104.42	95.20	90.66	88.27	86.24
10,000.00	139.88	116.03	105.78	100.73	98.08	95.83
20,000.00	279.76	232.05	211.57	201.47	196.15	191.65
30,000.00	419.64	348.08	317.35	302.20	294.23	287.48
40,000.00	559.53	464.10	423.13	402.94	392.31	383.30
50,000.00	699.41	580.13	528.91	503.67	490.38	479.13
60,000.00	839.29	696.15	634.70	604.40	588.46	574.96
70,000.00	979.17	812.18	740.48	705.14	686.54	670.78
80,000.00	1,119.05	928.20	846.26	805.87	784.61	766.61
90,000.00	1,258.93	1,044.23	952.05	906.61	882.69	862.44
100,000.00	1,398.81	1,160.26	1,057.83	1,007.34	980.77	958.26

11.500% Rate

Amount	Term of Loan in Years					
	10	15	20	25	30	40
$ 50.00	$ 0.70	$ 0.58	$ 0.53	$ 0.51	$ 0.50	$ 0.48
100.00	1.41	1.17	1.07	1.02	0.99	0.97
200.00	2.81	2.34	2.13	2.03	1.98	1.94
300.00	4.22	3.50	3.20	3.05	2.97	2.90
400.00	5.62	4.67	4.27	4.07	3.96	3.87
500.00	7.03	5.84	5.33	5.08	4.95	4.84
600.00	8.44	7.01	6.40	6.10	5.94	5.81
700.00	9.84	8.18	7.47	7.12	6.93	6.78
800.00	11.25	9.35	8.53	8.13	7.92	7.75
900.00	12.65	10.51	9.60	9.15	8.91	8.71
1,000.00	14.06	11.68	10.66	10.16	9.90	9.68
2,000.00	28.12	23.36	21.33	20.33	19.81	19.37
3,000.00	42.18	35.05	31.99	30.49	29.71	29.05
4,000.00	56.24	46.73	42.66	40.66	39.61	38.73
5,000.00	70.30	58.41	53.32	50.82	49.51	48.41
6,000.00	84.36	70.09	63.99	60.99	59.42	58.10
7,000.00	98.42	81.77	74.65	71.15	69.32	67.78
8,000.00	112.48	93.46	85.31	81.32	79.22	77.46
9,000.00	126.54	105.14	95.98	91.48	89.13	87.15
10,000.00	140.60	116.82	106.64	101.65	99.03	96.83
20,000.00	281.19	233.64	213.29	203.29	198.06	193.66
30,000.00	421.79	350.46	319.93	304.94	297.09	290.48
40,000.00	562.38	467.28	426.57	406.59	396.12	387.31
50,000.00	702.98	584.09	533.21	508.23	495.15	484.14
60,000.00	843.57	700.91	639.86	609.88	594.17	580.97
70,000.00	984.17	817.73	746.50	711.53	693.20	677.80
80,000.00	1,124.76	934.55	853.14	813.18	792.23	774.63
90,000.00	1,265.36	1,051.37	959.79	914.82	891.26	871.45
100,000.00	1,405.95	1,168.19	1,066.43	1,016.47	990.29	968.28

11.625% Rate

Amount	Term of Loan in Years					
	10	15	20	25	30	40
$ 50.00	$ 0.71	$ 0.59	$ 0.54	$ 0.51	$ 0.50	$ 0.49
100.00	1.41	1.18	1.08	1.03	1.00	0.98
200.00	2.83	2.35	2.15	2.05	2.00	1.96
300.00	4.24	3.53	3.23	3.08	3.00	2.93
400.00	5.65	4.70	4.30	4.10	4.00	3.91
500.00	7.07	5.88	5.38	5.13	5.00	4.89
600.00	8.48	7.06	6.45	6.15	6.00	5.87
700.00	9.89	8.23	7.53	7.18	7.00	6.85
800.00	11.30	9.41	8.60	8.20	8.00	7.83
900.00	12.72	10.59	9.68	9.23	9.00	8.80
1,000.00	14.13	11.76	10.75	10.26	10.00	9.78
2,000.00	28.26	23.52	21.50	20.51	20.00	19.57
3,000.00	42.39	35.28	32.25	30.77	30.00	29.35
4,000.00	56.52	47.05	43.00	41.02	39.99	39.13
5,000.00	70.66	58.81	53.75	51.28	49.99	48.92
6,000.00	84.79	70.57	64.50	61.54	59.99	58.70
7,000.00	98.92	82.33	75.25	71.79	69.99	68.48
8,000.00	113.05	94.09	86.00	82.05	79.99	78.27
9,000.00	127.18	105.85	96.75	92.31	89.99	88.05
10,000.00	141.31	117.61	107.51	102.56	99.98	97.83
20,000.00	282.62	235.23	215.01	205.12	199.97	195.66
30,000.00	423.93	352.84	322.52	307.69	299.95	293.49
40,000.00	565.25	470.46	430.02	410.25	399.94	391.33
50,000.00	706.56	588.07	537.53	512.81	499.92	489.16
60,000.00	847.87	705.69	645.03	615.37	599.90	586.99
70,000.00	989.18	823.30	752.54	717.93	699.89	684.82
80,000.00	1,130.49	940.92	860.04	820.50	799.87	782.65
90,000.00	1,271.80	1,058.53	967.55	923.06	899.86	880.48
100,000.00	1,413.12	1,176.15	1,075.06	1,025.62	999.84	978.32

11.750% Rate

Amount	Term of Loan in Years					
	10	15	20	25	30	40
$ 50.00	$ 0.71	$ 0.59	$ 0.54	$ 0.52	$ 0.50	$ 0.49
100.00	1.42	1.18	1.08	1.03	1.01	0.99
200.00	2.84	2.37	2.17	2.07	2.02	1.98
300.00	4.26	3.55	3.25	3.10	3.03	2.97
400.00	5.68	4.74	4.33	4.14	4.04	3.95
500.00	7.10	5.92	5.42	5.17	5.05	4.94
600.00	8.52	7.10	6.50	6.21	6.06	5.93
700.00	9.94	8.29	7.59	7.24	7.07	6.92
800.00	11.36	9.47	8.67	8.28	8.08	7.91
900.00	12.78	10.66	9.75	9.31	9.08	8.90
1,000.00	14.20	11.84	10.84	10.35	10.09	9.88
2,000.00	28.41	23.68	21.67	20.70	20.19	19.77
3,000.00	42.61	35.52	32.51	31.04	30.28	29.65
4,000.00	56.81	47.37	43.35	41.39	40.38	39.53
5,000.00	71.01	59.21	54.19	51.74	50.47	49.42
6,000.00	85.22	71.05	65.02	62.09	60.56	59.30
7,000.00	99.42	82.89	75.86	72.44	70.66	69.19
8,000.00	113.62	94.73	86.70	82.78	80.75	79.07
9,000.00	127.83	106.57	97.53	93.13	90.85	88.95
10,000.00	142.03	118.41	108.37	103.48	100.94	98.84
20,000.00	284.06	236.83	216.74	206.96	201.88	197.67
30,000.00	426.09	355.24	325.11	310.44	302.82	296.51
40,000.00	568.12	473.65	433.48	413.92	403.76	395.35
50,000.00	710.15	592.07	541.85	517.40	504.70	494.18
60,000.00	852.18	710.48	650.22	620.88	605.65	593.02
70,000.00	994.21	828.89	758.59	724.36	706.59	691.85
80,000.00	1,136.24	947.31	866.97	827.84	807.53	790.69
90,000.00	1,278.27	1,065.72	975.34	931.32	908.47	889.53
100,000.00	1,420.29	1,184.13	1,083.71	1,034.80	1,009.41	988.36

11.875% Rate

Amount	Term of Loan in Years					
	10	15	20	25	30	40
$ 50.00	$ 0.71	$ 0.60	$ 0.55	$ 0.52	$ 0.51	$ 0.50
100.00	1.43	1.19	1.09	1.04	1.02	1.00
200.00	2.85	2.38	2.18	2.09	2.04	2.00
300.00	4.28	3.58	3.28	3.13	3.06	3.00
400.00	5.71	4.77	4.37	4.18	4.08	3.99
500.00	7.14	5.96	5.46	5.22	5.10	4.99
600.00	8.56	7.15	6.55	6.26	6.11	5.99
700.00	9.99	8.34	7.65	7.31	7.13	6.99
800.00	11.42	9.54	8.74	8.35	8.15	7.99
900.00	12.85	10.73	9.83	9.40	9.17	8.99
1,000.00	14.27	11.92	10.92	10.44	10.19	9.98
2,000.00	28.55	23.84	21.85	20.88	20.38	19.97
3,000.00	42.82	35.76	32.77	31.32	30.57	29.95
4,000.00	57.10	47.69	43.70	41.76	40.76	39.94
5,000.00	71.37	59.61	54.62	52.20	50.95	49.92
6,000.00	85.65	71.53	65.54	62.64	61.14	59.91
7,000.00	99.92	83.45	76.47	73.08	71.33	69.89
8,000.00	114.20	95.37	87.39	83.52	81.52	79.87
9,000.00	128.47	107.29	98.31	93.96	91.71	89.86
10,000.00	142.75	119.21	109.24	104.40	101.90	99.84
20,000.00	285.50	238.43	218.48	208.80	203.80	199.69
30,000.00	428.25	357.64	327.72	313.20	305.70	299.53
40,000.00	571.00	476.86	436.95	417.60	407.60	399.37
50,000.00	713.75	596.07	546.19	522.00	509.50	499.21
60,000.00	856.50	715.28	655.43	626.40	611.40	599.06
70,000.00	999.24	834.50	764.67	730.80	713.30	698.90
80,000.00	1,141.99	953.71	873.91	835.20	815.20	798.74
90,000.00	1,284.74	1,072.92	983.15	939.60	917.10	898.58
100,000.00	1,427.49	1,192.14	1,092.38	1,044.00	1,019.00	998.43

12.000% Rate

Amount	Term of Loan in Years					
	10	15	20	25	30	40
$ 50.00	$ 0.72	$ 0.60	$ 0.55	$ 0.53	$ 0.51	$ 0.50
100.00	1.43	1.20	1.10	1.05	1.03	1.01
200.00	2.87	2.40	2.20	2.11	2.06	2.02
300.00	4.30	3.60	3.30	3.16	3.09	3.03
400.00	5.74	4.80	4.40	4.21	4.11	4.03
500.00	7.17	6.00	5.51	5.27	5.14	5.04
600.00	8.61	7.20	6.61	6.32	6.17	6.05
700.00	10.04	8.40	7.71	7.37	7.20	7.06
800.00	11.48	9.60	8.81	8.43	8.23	8.07
900.00	12.91	10.80	9.91	9.48	9.26	9.08
1,000.00	14.35	12.00	11.01	10.53	10.29	10.08
2,000.00	28.69	24.00	22.02	21.06	20.57	20.17
3,000.00	43.04	36.01	33.03	31.60	30.86	30.25
4,000.00	57.39	48.01	44.04	42.13	41.14	40.34
5,000.00	71.74	60.01	55.05	52.66	51.43	50.42
6,000.00	86.08	72.01	66.07	63.19	61.72	60.51
7,000.00	100.43	84.01	77.08	73.73	72.00	70.59
8,000.00	114.78	96.01	88.09	84.26	82.29	80.68
9,000.00	129.12	108.02	99.10	94.79	92.58	90.76
10,000.00	143.47	120.02	110.11	105.32	102.86	100.85
20,000.00	286.94	240.03	220.22	210.64	205.72	201.70
30,000.00	430.41	360.05	330.33	315.97	308.58	302.55
40,000.00	573.88	480.07	440.43	421.29	411.45	403.40
50,000.00	717.35	600.08	550.54	526.61	514.31	504.25
60,000.00	860.83	720.10	660.65	631.93	617.17	605.10
70,000.00	1,004.30	840.12	770.76	737.26	720.03	705.95
80,000.00	1,147.77	960.13	880.87	842.58	822.89	806.80
90,000.00	1,291.24	1,080.15	990.98	947.90	925.75	907.65
100,000.00	1,434.71	1,200.17	1,101.09	1,053.22	1,028.61	1,008.50

12.125% Rate

Amount	Term of Loan in Years					
	10	15	20	25	30	40
$ 50.00	$ 0.72	$ 0.60	$ 0.55	$ 0.53	$ 0.52	$ 0.51
100.00	1.44	1.21	1.11	1.06	1.04	1.02
200.00	2.88	2.42	2.22	2.12	2.08	2.04
300.00	4.33	3.62	3.33	3.19	3.11	3.06
400.00	5.77	4.83	4.44	4.25	4.15	4.07
500.00	7.21	6.04	5.55	5.31	5.19	5.09
600.00	8.65	7.25	6.66	6.37	6.23	6.11
700.00	10.09	8.46	7.77	7.44	7.27	7.13
800.00	11.54	9.67	8.88	8.50	8.31	8.15
900.00	12.98	10.87	9.99	9.56	9.34	9.17
1,000.00	14.42	12.08	11.10	10.62	10.38	10.19
2,000.00	28.84	24.16	22.20	21.25	20.76	20.37
3,000.00	43.26	36.25	33.29	31.87	31.15	30.56
4,000.00	57.68	48.33	44.39	42.50	41.53	40.74
5,000.00	72.10	60.41	55.49	53.12	51.91	50.93
6,000.00	86.52	72.49	66.59	63.75	62.29	61.12
7,000.00	100.94	84.58	77.69	74.37	72.68	71.30
8,000.00	115.36	96.66	88.79	85.00	83.06	81.49
9,000.00	129.78	108.74	99.88	95.62	93.44	91.67
10,000.00	144.19	120.82	110.98	106.25	103.82	101.86
20,000.00	288.39	241.64	221.96	212.49	207.65	203.72
30,000.00	432.58	362.47	332.94	318.74	311.47	305.58
40,000.00	576.78	483.29	443.93	424.99	415.30	407.43
50,000.00	720.97	604.11	554.91	531.24	519.12	509.29
60,000.00	865.17	724.93	665.89	637.48	622.95	611.15
70,000.00	1,009.36	845.76	776.87	743.73	726.77	713.01
80,000.00	1,153.56	966.58	887.85	849.98	830.60	814.87
90,000.00	1,297.75	1,087.40	998.83	956.23	934.42	916.73
100,000.00	1,441.94	1,208.22	1,109.81	1,062.47	1,038.24	1,018.59

12.250% Rate

Amount	Term of Loan in Years					
	10	15	20	25	30	40
$ 50.00	$ 0.72	$ 0.61	$ 0.56	$ 0.54	$ 0.52	$ 0.51
100.00	1.45	1.22	1.12	1.07	1.05	1.03
200.00	2.90	2.43	2.24	2.14	2.10	2.06
300.00	4.35	3.65	3.36	3.22	3.14	3.09
400.00	5.80	4.87	4.47	4.29	4.19	4.11
500.00	7.25	6.08	5.59	5.36	5.24	5.14
600.00	8.70	7.30	6.71	6.43	6.29	6.17
700.00	10.14	8.51	7.83	7.50	7.34	7.20
800.00	11.59	9.73	8.95	8.57	8.38	8.23
900.00	13.04	10.95	10.07	9.65	9.43	9.26
1,000.00	14.49	12.16	11.19	10.72	10.48	10.29
2,000.00	28.98	24.33	22.37	21.43	20.96	20.57
3,000.00	43.48	36.49	33.56	32.15	31.44	30.86
4,000.00	57.97	48.65	44.74	42.87	41.92	41.15
5,000.00	72.46	60.81	55.93	53.59	52.39	51.43
6,000.00	86.95	72.98	67.11	64.30	62.87	61.72
7,000.00	101.44	85.14	78.30	75.02	73.35	72.01
8,000.00	115.94	97.30	89.49	85.74	83.83	82.29
9,000.00	130.43	109.47	100.67	96.46	94.31	92.58
10,000.00	144.92	121.63	111.86	107.17	104.79	102.87
20,000.00	289.84	243.26	223.71	214.35	209.58	205.74
30,000.00	434.76	364.89	335.57	321.52	314.37	308.61
40,000.00	579.68	486.52	447.43	428.70	419.16	411.47
50,000.00	724.60	608.15	559.28	535.87	523.95	514.34
60,000.00	869.52	729.78	671.14	643.05	628.74	617.21
70,000.00	1,014.44	851.41	783.00	750.22	733.53	720.08
80,000.00	1,159.36	973.04	894.85	857.40	838.32	822.95
90,000.00	1,304.28	1,094.67	1,006.71	964.57	943.11	925.82
100,000.00	1,449.20	1,216.30	1,118.56	1,071.74	1,047.90	1,028.69

12.375% Rate

Amount	Term of Loan in Years					
	10	15	20	25	30	40
$ 50.00	$ 0.73	$ 0.61	$ 0.56	$ 0.54	$ 0.53	$ 0.52
100.00	1.46	1.22	1.13	1.08	1.06	1.04
200.00	2.91	2.45	2.25	2.16	2.12	2.08
300.00	4.37	3.67	3.38	3.24	3.17	3.12
400.00	5.83	4.90	4.51	4.32	4.23	4.16
500.00	7.28	6.12	5.64	5.41	5.29	5.19
600.00	8.74	7.35	6.76	6.49	6.35	6.23
700.00	10.20	8.57	7.89	7.57	7.40	7.27
800.00	11.65	9.80	9.02	8.65	8.46	8.31
900.00	13.11	11.02	10.15	9.73	9.52	9.35
1,000.00	14.56	12.24	11.27	10.81	10.58	10.39
2,000.00	29.13	24.49	22.55	21.62	21.15	20.78
3,000.00	43.69	36.73	33.82	32.43	31.73	31.16
4,000.00	58.26	48.98	45.09	43.24	42.30	41.55
5,000.00	72.82	61.22	56.37	54.05	52.88	51.94
6,000.00	87.39	73.46	67.64	64.86	63.45	62.33
7,000.00	101.95	85.71	78.91	75.67	74.03	72.72
8,000.00	116.52	97.95	90.19	86.48	84.61	83.10
9,000.00	131.08	110.20	101.46	97.29	95.18	93.49
10,000.00	145.65	122.44	112.73	108.10	105.76	103.88
20,000.00	291.29	244.88	225.47	216.21	211.51	207.76
30,000.00	436.94	367.32	338.20	324.31	317.27	311.64
40,000.00	582.59	489.76	450.94	432.42	423.03	415.52
50,000.00	728.24	612.20	563.67	540.52	528.78	519.40
60,000.00	873.88	734.64	676.40	648.62	634.54	623.28
70,000.00	1,019.53	857.08	789.14	756.73	740.30	727.16
80,000.00	1,165.18	979.52	901.87	864.83	846.05	831.04
90,000.00	1,310.82	1,101.96	1,014.61	972.93	951.81	934.92
100,000.00	1,456.47	1,224.40	1,127.34	1,081.04	1,057.57	1,038.80

12.500% Rate

Amount	Term of Loan in Years					
	10	15	20	25	30	40
$ 50.00	$ 0.73	$ 0.62	$ 0.57	$ 0.55	$ 0.53	$ 0.52
100.00	1.46	1.23	1.14	1.09	1.07	1.05
200.00	2.93	2.47	2.27	2.18	2.13	2.10
300.00	4.39	3.70	3.41	3.27	3.20	3.15
400.00	5.86	4.93	4.54	4.36	4.27	4.20
500.00	7.32	6.16	5.68	5.45	5.34	5.24
600.00	8.78	7.40	6.82	6.54	6.40	6.29
700.00	10.25	8.63	7.95	7.63	7.47	7.34
800.00	11.71	9.86	9.09	8.72	8.54	8.39
900.00	13.17	11.09	10.23	9.81	9.61	9.44
1,000.00	14.64	12.33	11.36	10.90	10.67	10.49
2,000.00	29.28	24.65	22.72	21.81	21.35	20.98
3,000.00	43.91	36.98	34.08	32.71	32.02	31.47
4,000.00	58.55	49.30	45.45	43.61	42.69	41.96
5,000.00	73.19	61.63	56.81	54.52	53.36	52.45
6,000.00	87.83	73.95	68.17	65.42	64.04	62.94
7,000.00	102.46	86.28	79.53	76.32	74.71	73.42
8,000.00	117.10	98.60	90.89	87.23	85.38	83.91
9,000.00	131.74	110.93	102.25	98.13	96.05	94.40
10,000.00	146.38	123.25	113.61	109.04	106.73	104.89
20,000.00	292.75	246.50	227.23	218.07	213.45	209.78
30,000.00	439.13	369.76	340.84	327.11	320.18	314.68
40,000.00	585.50	493.01	454.46	436.14	426.90	419.57
50,000.00	731.88	616.26	568.07	545.18	533.63	524.46
60,000.00	878.26	739.51	681.68	654.21	640.35	629.35
70,000.00	1,024.63	862.77	795.30	763.25	747.08	734.24
80,000.00	1,171.01	986.02	908.91	872.28	853.81	839.14
90,000.00	1,317.39	1,109.27	1,022.53	981.32	960.53	944.03
100,000.00	1,463.76	1,232.52	1,136.14	1,090.35	1,067.26	1,048.92

12.625% Rate

Amount	Term of Loan in Years					
	10	15	20	25	30	40
$ 50.00	$ 0.74	$ 0.62	$ 0.57	$ 0.55	$ 0.54	$ 0.53
100.00	1.47	1.24	1.14	1.10	1.08	1.06
200.00	2.94	2.48	2.29	2.20	2.15	2.12
300.00	4.41	3.72	3.43	3.30	3.23	3.18
400.00	5.88	4.96	4.58	4.40	4.31	4.24
500.00	7.36	6.20	5.72	5.50	5.38	5.30
600.00	8.83	7.44	6.87	6.60	6.46	6.35
700.00	10.30	8.68	8.01	7.70	7.54	7.41
800.00	11.77	9.93	9.16	8.80	8.62	8.47
900.00	13.24	11.17	10.30	9.90	9.69	9.53
1,000.00	14.71	12.41	11.45	11.00	10.77	10.59
2,000.00	29.42	24.81	22.90	21.99	21.54	21.18
3,000.00	44.13	37.22	34.35	32.99	32.31	31.77
4,000.00	58.84	49.63	45.80	43.99	43.08	42.36
5,000.00	73.55	62.03	57.25	54.98	53.85	52.95
6,000.00	88.26	74.44	68.70	65.98	64.62	63.54
7,000.00	102.97	86.85	80.15	76.98	75.39	74.13
8,000.00	117.69	99.25	91.60	87.98	86.16	84.72
9,000.00	132.40	111.66	103.05	98.97	96.93	95.31
10,000.00	147.11	124.07	114.50	109.97	107.70	105.91
20,000.00	294.21	248.13	228.99	219.94	215.39	211.81
30,000.00	441.32	372.20	343.49	329.91	323.09	317.72
40,000.00	588.43	496.27	457.99	439.88	430.79	423.62
50,000.00	735.54	620.33	572.48	549.85	538.48	529.53
60,000.00	882.64	744.40	686.98	659.82	646.18	635.43
70,000.00	1,029.75	868.47	801.48	769.78	753.88	741.34
80,000.00	1,176.86	992.53	915.97	879.75	861.57	847.24
90,000.00	1,323.96	1,116.60	1,030.47	989.72	969.27	953.15
100,000.00	1,471.07	1,240.67	1,144.96	1,099.69	1,076.97	1,059.05

12.750% Rate

Amount	Term of Loan in Years					
	10	15	20	25	30	40
$ 50.00	$ 0.74	$ 0.62	$ 0.58	$ 0.55	$ 0.54	$ 0.53
100.00	1.48	1.25	1.15	1.11	1.09	1.07
200.00	2.96	2.50	2.31	2.22	2.17	2.14
300.00	4.44	3.75	3.46	3.33	3.26	3.21
400.00	5.91	5.00	4.62	4.44	4.35	4.28
500.00	7.39	6.24	5.77	5.55	5.43	5.35
600.00	8.87	7.49	6.92	6.65	6.52	6.42
700.00	10.35	8.74	8.08	7.76	7.61	7.48
800.00	11.83	9.99	9.23	8.87	8.69	8.55
900.00	13.31	11.24	10.38	9.98	9.78	9.62
1,000.00	14.78	12.49	11.54	11.09	10.87	10.69
2,000.00	29.57	24.98	23.08	22.18	21.73	21.38
3,000.00	44.35	37.47	34.61	33.27	32.60	32.08
4,000.00	59.14	49.95	46.15	44.36	43.47	42.77
5,000.00	73.92	62.44	57.69	55.45	54.33	53.46
6,000.00	88.70	74.93	69.23	66.54	65.20	64.15
7,000.00	103.49	87.42	80.77	77.63	76.07	74.84
8,000.00	118.27	99.91	92.30	88.72	86.94	85.54
9,000.00	133.06	112.40	103.84	99.81	97.80	96.23
10,000.00	147.84	124.88	115.38	110.91	108.67	106.92
20,000.00	295.68	249.77	230.76	221.81	217.34	213.84
30,000.00	443.52	374.65	346.14	332.72	326.01	320.76
40,000.00	591.36	499.53	461.52	443.62	434.68	427.68
50,000.00	739.20	624.42	576.91	554.53	543.35	534.60
60,000.00	887.04	749.30	692.29	665.43	652.02	641.52
70,000.00	1,034.88	874.19	807.67	776.34	760.69	748.44
80,000.00	1,182.72	999.07	923.05	887.24	869.35	855.36
90,000.00	1,330.56	1,123.95	1,038.43	998.15	978.02	962.28
100,000.00	1,478.40	1,248.84	1,153.81	1,109.05	1,086.69	1,069.20

12.875% Rate

Amount	Term of Loan in Years					
	10	15	20	25	30	40
$ 50.00	$ 0.74	$ 0.63	$ 0.58	$ 0.56	$ 0.55	$ 0.54
100.00	1.49	1.26	1.16	1.12	1.10	1.08
200.00	2.97	2.51	2.33	2.24	2.19	2.16
300.00	4.46	3.77	3.49	3.36	3.29	3.24
400.00	5.94	5.03	4.65	4.47	4.39	4.32
500.00	7.43	6.29	5.81	5.59	5.48	5.40
600.00	8.91	7.54	6.98	6.71	6.58	6.48
700.00	10.40	8.80	8.14	7.83	7.68	7.56
800.00	11.89	10.06	9.30	8.95	8.77	8.63
900.00	13.37	11.31	10.46	10.07	9.87	9.71
1,000.00	14.86	12.57	11.63	11.18	10.96	10.79
2,000.00	29.71	25.14	23.25	22.37	21.93	21.59
3,000.00	44.57	37.71	34.88	33.55	32.89	32.38
4,000.00	59.43	50.28	46.51	44.74	43.86	43.17
5,000.00	74.29	62.85	58.13	55.92	54.82	53.97
6,000.00	89.14	75.42	69.76	67.11	65.79	64.76
7,000.00	104.00	87.99	81.39	78.29	76.75	75.55
8,000.00	118.86	100.56	93.01	89.47	87.72	86.35
9,000.00	133.72	113.13	104.64	100.66	98.68	97.14
10,000.00	148.57	125.70	116.27	111.84	109.64	107.94
20,000.00	297.15	251.41	232.54	223.69	219.29	215.87
30,000.00	445.72	377.11	348.80	335.53	328.93	323.81
40,000.00	594.30	502.81	465.07	447.37	438.58	431.74
50,000.00	742.87	628.51	581.34	559.22	548.22	539.68
60,000.00	891.45	754.22	697.61	671.06	657.86	647.61
70,000.00	1,040.02	879.92	813.88	782.90	767.51	755.55
80,000.00	1,188.59	1,005.62	930.15	894.75	877.15	863.48
90,000.00	1,337.17	1,131.33	1,046.41	1,006.59	986.79	971.42
100,000.00	1,485.74	1,257.03	1,162.68	1,118.43	1,096.44	1,079.35

13.000% Rate

Amount		Term of Loan in Years					
		10	15	20	25	30	40
$	50.00	$ 0.75	$ 0.63	$ 0.59	$ 0.56	$ 0.55	$ 0.54
	100.00	1.49	1.27	1.17	1.13	1.11	1.09
	200.00	2.99	2.53	2.34	2.26	2.21	2.18
	300.00	4.48	3.80	3.51	3.38	3.32	3.27
	400.00	5.97	5.06	4.69	4.51	4.42	4.36
	500.00	7.47	6.33	5.86	5.64	5.53	5.45
	600.00	8.96	7.59	7.03	6.77	6.64	6.54
	700.00	10.45	8.86	8.20	7.89	7.74	7.63
	800.00	11.94	10.12	9.37	9.02	8.85	8.72
	900.00	13.44	11.39	10.54	10.15	9.96	9.81
	1,000.00	14.93	12.65	11.72	11.28	11.06	10.90
	2,000.00	29.86	25.30	23.43	22.56	22.12	21.79
	3,000.00	44.79	37.96	35.15	33.84	33.19	32.69
	4,000.00	59.72	50.61	46.86	45.11	44.25	43.58
	5,000.00	74.66	63.26	58.58	56.39	55.31	54.48
	6,000.00	89.59	75.91	70.29	67.67	66.37	65.37
	7,000.00	104.52	88.57	82.01	78.95	77.43	76.27
	8,000.00	119.45	101.22	93.73	90.23	88.50	87.16
	9,000.00	134.38	113.87	105.44	101.51	99.56	98.06
	10,000.00	149.31	126.52	117.16	112.78	110.62	108.95
	20,000.00	298.62	253.05	234.32	225.57	221.24	217.90
	30,000.00	447.93	379.57	351.47	338.35	331.86	326.85
	40,000.00	597.24	506.10	468.63	451.13	442.48	435.81
	50,000.00	746.55	632.62	585.79	563.92	553.10	544.76
	60,000.00	895.86	759.15	702.95	676.70	663.72	653.71
	70,000.00	1,045.18	885.67	820.10	789.48	774.34	762.66
	80,000.00	1,194.49	1,012.19	937.26	902.27	884.96	871.61
	90,000.00	1,343.80	1,138.72	1,054.42	1,015.05	995.58	980.56
	100,000.00	1,493.11	1,265.24	1,171.58	1,127.84	1,106.20	1,089.51

13.125% Rate

Amount	Term of Loan in Years					
	10	15	20	25	30	40
$ 50.00	$ 0.75	$ 0.64	$ 0.59	$ 0.57	$ 0.56	$ 0.55
100.00	1.50	1.27	1.18	1.14	1.12	1.10
200.00	3.00	2.55	2.36	2.27	2.23	2.20
300.00	4.50	3.82	3.54	3.41	3.35	3.30
400.00	6.00	5.09	4.72	4.55	4.46	4.40
500.00	7.50	6.37	5.90	5.69	5.58	5.50
600.00	9.00	7.64	7.08	6.82	6.70	6.60
700.00	10.50	8.91	8.26	7.96	7.81	7.70
800.00	12.00	10.19	9.44	9.10	8.93	8.80
900.00	13.50	11.46	10.62	10.24	10.04	9.90
1,000.00	15.00	12.73	11.80	11.37	11.16	11.00
2,000.00	30.01	25.47	23.61	22.75	22.32	21.99
3,000.00	45.01	38.20	35.41	34.12	33.48	32.99
4,000.00	60.02	50.94	47.22	45.49	44.64	43.99
5,000.00	75.02	63.67	59.02	56.86	55.80	54.98
6,000.00	90.03	76.41	70.83	68.24	66.96	65.98
7,000.00	105.03	89.14	82.63	79.61	78.12	76.98
8,000.00	120.04	101.88	94.44	90.98	89.28	87.97
9,000.00	135.04	114.61	106.24	102.35	100.44	98.97
10,000.00	150.05	127.35	118.05	113.73	111.60	109.97
20,000.00	300.10	254.70	236.10	227.45	223.20	219.94
30,000.00	450.15	382.04	354.15	341.18	334.79	329.91
40,000.00	600.20	509.39	472.20	454.90	446.39	439.87
50,000.00	750.24	636.74	590.25	568.63	557.99	549.84
60,000.00	900.29	764.09	708.30	682.35	669.59	659.81
70,000.00	1,050.34	891.43	826.34	796.08	781.18	769.78
80,000.00	1,200.39	1,018.78	944.39	909.81	892.78	879.75
90,000.00	1,350.44	1,146.13	1,062.44	1,023.53	1,004.38	989.72
100,000.00	1,500.49	1,273.48	1,180.49	1,137.26	1,115.98	1,099.69

13.250% Rate

Amount	Term of Loan in Years					
	10	15	20	25	30	40
$ 50.00	$ 0.75	$ 0.64	$ 0.59	$ 0.57	$ 0.56	$ 0.55
100.00	1.51	1.28	1.19	1.15	1.13	1.11
200.00	3.02	2.56	2.38	2.29	2.25	2.22
300.00	4.52	3.85	3.57	3.44	3.38	3.33
400.00	6.03	5.13	4.76	4.59	4.50	4.44
500.00	7.54	6.41	5.95	5.73	5.63	5.55
600.00	9.05	7.69	7.14	6.88	6.75	6.66
700.00	10.56	8.97	8.33	8.03	7.88	7.77
800.00	12.06	10.25	9.52	9.17	9.01	8.88
900.00	13.57	11.54	10.70	10.32	10.13	9.99
1,000.00	15.08	12.82	11.89	11.47	11.26	11.10
2,000.00	30.16	25.63	23.79	22.93	22.52	22.20
3,000.00	45.24	38.45	35.68	34.40	33.77	33.30
4,000.00	60.32	51.27	47.58	45.87	45.03	44.39
5,000.00	75.39	64.09	59.47	57.34	56.29	55.49
6,000.00	90.47	76.90	71.37	68.80	67.55	66.59
7,000.00	105.55	89.72	83.26	80.27	78.80	77.69
8,000.00	120.63	102.54	95.15	91.74	90.06	88.79
9,000.00	135.71	115.36	107.05	103.20	101.32	99.89
10,000.00	150.79	128.17	118.94	114.67	112.58	110.99
20,000.00	301.58	256.35	237.89	229.34	225.15	221.97
30,000.00	452.37	384.52	356.83	344.01	337.73	332.96
40,000.00	603.16	512.69	475.77	458.68	450.31	443.95
50,000.00	753.94	640.87	594.72	573.35	562.89	554.93
60,000.00	904.73	769.04	713.66	688.02	675.46	665.92
70,000.00	1,055.52	897.22	832.60	802.69	788.04	776.91
80,000.00	1,206.31	1,025.39	951.54	917.36	900.62	887.90
90,000.00	1,357.10	1,153.56	1,070.49	1,032.03	1,013.20	998.88
100,000.00	1,507.89	1,281.74	1,189.43	1,146.70	1,125.77	1,109.87

13.375% Rate

Amount	Term of Loan in Years					
	10	15	20	25	30	40
$ 50.00	$ 0.76	$ 0.65	$ 0.60	$ 0.58	$ 0.57	$ 0.56
100.00	1.52	1.29	1.20	1.16	1.14	1.12
200.00	3.03	2.58	2.40	2.31	2.27	2.24
300.00	4.55	3.87	3.60	3.47	3.41	3.36
400.00	6.06	5.16	4.79	4.62	4.54	4.48
500.00	7.58	6.45	5.99	5.78	5.68	5.60
600.00	9.09	7.74	7.19	6.94	6.81	6.72
700.00	10.61	9.03	8.39	8.09	7.95	7.84
800.00	12.12	10.32	9.59	9.25	9.08	8.96
900.00	13.64	11.61	10.79	10.41	10.22	10.08
1,000.00	15.15	12.90	11.98	11.56	11.36	11.20
2,000.00	30.31	25.80	23.97	23.12	22.71	22.40
3,000.00	45.46	38.70	35.95	34.68	34.07	33.60
4,000.00	60.61	51.60	47.94	46.25	45.42	44.80
5,000.00	75.77	64.50	59.92	57.81	56.78	56.00
6,000.00	90.92	77.40	71.90	69.37	68.14	67.20
7,000.00	106.07	90.30	83.89	80.93	79.49	78.40
8,000.00	121.22	103.20	95.87	92.49	90.85	89.60
9,000.00	136.38	116.10	107.86	104.05	102.20	100.81
10,000.00	151.53	129.00	119.84	115.62	113.56	112.01
20,000.00	303.06	258.00	239.68	231.23	227.12	224.01
30,000.00	454.59	387.00	359.52	346.85	340.68	336.02
40,000.00	606.12	516.01	479.36	462.47	454.23	448.02
50,000.00	757.65	645.01	599.20	578.08	567.79	560.03
60,000.00	909.18	774.01	719.04	693.70	681.35	672.04
70,000.00	1,060.71	903.01	838.87	809.31	794.91	784.04
80,000.00	1,212.25	1,032.01	958.71	924.93	908.47	896.05
90,000.00	1,363.78	1,161.01	1,078.55	1,040.55	1,022.03	1,008.06
100,000.00	1,515.31	1,290.02	1,198.39	1,156.16	1,135.58	1,120.06

13.500% Rate

Amount	Term of Loan in Years					
	10	15	20	25	30	40
$ 50.00	$ 0.76	$ 0.65	$ 0.60	$ 0.58	$ 0.57	$ 0.57
100.00	1.52	1.30	1.21	1.17	1.15	1.13
200.00	3.05	2.60	2.41	2.33	2.29	2.26
300.00	4.57	3.89	3.62	3.50	3.44	3.39
400.00	6.09	5.19	4.83	4.66	4.58	4.52
500.00	7.61	6.49	6.04	5.83	5.73	5.65
600.00	9.14	7.79	7.24	6.99	6.87	6.78
700.00	10.66	9.09	8.45	8.16	8.02	7.91
800.00	12.18	10.39	9.66	9.33	9.16	9.04
900.00	13.70	11.68	10.87	10.49	10.31	10.17
1,000.00	15.23	12.98	12.07	11.66	11.45	11.30
2,000.00	30.45	25.97	24.15	23.31	22.91	22.61
3,000.00	45.68	38.95	36.22	34.97	34.36	33.91
4,000.00	60.91	51.93	48.29	46.63	45.82	45.21
5,000.00	76.14	64.92	60.37	58.28	57.27	56.51
6,000.00	91.36	77.90	72.44	69.94	68.72	67.82
7,000.00	106.59	90.88	84.52	81.60	80.18	79.12
8,000.00	121.82	103.87	96.59	93.25	91.63	90.42
9,000.00	137.05	116.85	108.66	104.91	103.09	101.72
10,000.00	152.27	129.83	120.74	116.56	114.54	113.03
20,000.00	304.55	259.66	241.47	233.13	229.08	226.05
30,000.00	456.82	389.50	362.21	349.69	343.62	339.08
40,000.00	609.10	519.33	482.95	466.26	458.16	452.10
50,000.00	761.37	649.16	603.69	582.82	572.71	565.13
60,000.00	913.65	778.99	724.42	699.39	687.25	678.16
70,000.00	1,065.92	908.82	845.16	815.95	801.79	791.18
80,000.00	1,218.19	1,038.65	965.90	932.52	916.33	904.21
90,000.00	1,370.47	1,168.49	1,086.64	1,049.08	1,030.87	1,017.24
100,000.00	1,522.74	1,298.32	1,207.37	1,165.64	1,145.41	1,130.26

13.625% Rate

Amount	Term of Loan in Years					
	10	15	20	25	30	40
$ 50.00	$ 0.77	$ 0.65	$ 0.61	$ 0.59	$ 0.58	$ 0.57
100.00	1.53	1.31	1.22	1.18	1.16	1.14
200.00	3.06	2.61	2.43	2.35	2.31	2.28
300.00	4.59	3.92	3.65	3.53	3.47	3.42
400.00	6.12	5.23	4.87	4.70	4.62	4.56
500.00	7.65	6.53	6.08	5.88	5.78	5.70
600.00	9.18	7.84	7.30	7.05	6.93	6.84
700.00	10.71	9.15	8.51	8.23	8.09	7.98
800.00	12.24	10.45	9.73	9.40	9.24	9.12
900.00	13.77	11.76	10.95	10.58	10.40	10.26
1,000.00	15.30	13.07	12.16	11.75	11.55	11.40
2,000.00	30.60	26.13	24.33	23.50	23.11	22.81
3,000.00	45.91	39.20	36.49	35.25	34.66	34.21
4,000.00	61.21	52.27	48.66	47.01	46.21	45.62
5,000.00	76.51	65.33	60.82	58.76	57.76	57.02
6,000.00	91.81	78.40	72.98	70.51	69.32	68.43
7,000.00	107.11	91.46	85.15	82.26	80.87	79.83
8,000.00	122.42	104.53	97.31	94.01	92.42	91.24
9,000.00	137.72	117.60	109.47	105.76	103.97	102.64
10,000.00	153.02	130.66	121.64	117.51	115.53	114.05
20,000.00	306.04	261.33	243.28	235.03	231.05	228.09
30,000.00	459.06	391.99	364.91	352.54	346.58	342.14
40,000.00	612.08	522.66	486.55	470.06	462.10	456.19
50,000.00	765.10	653.32	608.19	587.57	577.63	570.23
60,000.00	918.12	783.99	729.83	705.09	693.15	684.28
70,000.00	1,071.14	914.65	851.47	822.60	808.68	798.33
80,000.00	1,224.16	1,045.31	973.10	940.12	924.20	912.38
90,000.00	1,377.18	1,175.98	1,094.74	1,057.63	1,039.73	1,026.42
100,000.00	1,530.20	1,306.64	1,216.38	1,175.15	1,155.25	1,140.47

13.750% Rate

Amount	Term of Loan in Years					
	10	15	20	25	30	40
$ 50.00	$ 0.77	$ 0.66	$ 0.61	$ 0.59	$ 0.58	$ 0.58
100.00	1.54	1.31	1.23	1.18	1.17	1.15
200.00	3.08	2.63	2.45	2.37	2.33	2.30
300.00	4.61	3.94	3.68	3.55	3.50	3.45
400.00	6.15	5.26	4.90	4.74	4.66	4.60
500.00	7.69	6.57	6.13	5.92	5.83	5.75
600.00	9.23	7.89	7.35	7.11	6.99	6.90
700.00	10.76	9.20	8.58	8.29	8.16	8.05
800.00	12.30	10.52	9.80	9.48	9.32	9.21
900.00	13.84	11.83	11.03	10.66	10.49	10.36
1,000.00	15.38	13.15	12.25	11.85	11.65	11.51
2,000.00	30.75	26.30	24.51	23.69	23.30	23.01
3,000.00	46.13	39.45	36.76	35.54	34.95	34.52
4,000.00	61.51	52.60	49.02	47.39	46.60	46.03
5,000.00	76.88	65.75	61.27	59.23	58.26	57.53
6,000.00	92.26	78.90	73.52	71.08	69.91	69.04
7,000.00	107.64	92.05	85.78	82.93	81.56	80.55
8,000.00	123.01	105.20	98.03	94.77	93.21	92.05
9,000.00	138.39	118.35	110.29	106.62	104.86	103.56
10,000.00	153.77	131.50	122.54	118.47	116.51	115.07
20,000.00	307.53	263.00	245.08	236.93	233.02	230.14
30,000.00	461.30	394.50	367.62	355.40	349.53	345.21
40,000.00	615.07	525.99	490.16	473.87	466.05	460.27
50,000.00	768.83	657.49	612.70	592.33	582.56	575.34
60,000.00	922.60	788.99	735.24	710.80	699.07	690.41
70,000.00	1,076.37	920.49	857.78	829.27	815.58	805.48
80,000.00	1,230.13	1,051.99	980.32	947.73	932.09	920.55
90,000.00	1,383.90	1,183.49	1,102.86	1,066.20	1,048.60	1,035.62
100,000.00	1,537.67	1,314.99	1,225.41	1,184.67	1,165.11	1,150.69

13.875% Rate

Amount	Term of Loan in Years					
	10	15	20	25	30	40
$ 50.00	$ 0.77	$ 0.66	$ 0.62	$ 0.60	$ 0.59	$ 0.58
100.00	1.55	1.32	1.23	1.19	1.17	1.16
200.00	3.09	2.65	2.47	2.39	2.35	2.32
300.00	4.64	3.97	3.70	3.58	3.52	3.48
400.00	6.18	5.29	4.94	4.78	4.70	4.64
500.00	7.73	6.62	6.17	5.97	5.87	5.80
600.00	9.27	7.94	7.41	7.17	7.05	6.97
700.00	10.82	9.26	8.64	8.36	8.22	8.13
800.00	12.36	10.59	9.88	9.55	9.40	9.29
900.00	13.91	11.91	11.11	10.75	10.57	10.45
1,000.00	15.45	13.23	12.34	11.94	11.75	11.61
2,000.00	30.90	26.47	24.69	23.88	23.50	23.22
3,000.00	46.35	39.70	37.03	35.83	35.25	34.83
4,000.00	61.81	52.93	49.38	47.77	47.00	46.44
5,000.00	77.26	66.17	61.72	59.71	58.75	58.05
6,000.00	92.71	79.40	74.07	71.65	70.50	69.65
7,000.00	108.16	92.63	86.41	83.59	82.25	81.26
8,000.00	123.61	105.87	98.76	95.54	94.00	92.87
9,000.00	139.06	119.10	111.10	107.48	105.75	104.48
10,000.00	154.52	132.34	123.45	119.42	117.50	116.09
20,000.00	309.03	264.67	246.89	238.84	235.00	232.18
30,000.00	463.55	397.01	370.34	358.26	352.50	348.27
40,000.00	618.06	529.34	493.78	477.68	469.99	464.36
50,000.00	772.58	661.68	617.23	597.10	587.49	580.45
60,000.00	927.09	794.01	740.67	716.52	704.99	696.55
70,000.00	1,081.61	926.35	864.12	835.94	822.49	812.64
80,000.00	1,236.13	1,058.68	987.56	955.36	939.99	928.73
90,000.00	1,390.64	1,191.02	1,111.01	1,074.78	1,057.49	1,044.82
100,000.00	1,545.16	1,323.35	1,234.45	1,194.20	1,174.98	1,160.91

APPENDIX III

Resources

When it comes to buying a home, it's difficult to do everything yourself. A first-time buyer may find the whole process a bit overwhelming. Here are some resources that you may find helpful.

CREDIT BUREAUS

Trans Union

Consumer Relations Center
760 Sproul Road
PO Box 390
Springfield, PA 19064-0390
(312) 408-1400

Trans Union charges up to $8 for a copy of your credit report, except in Maryland and Vermont, where state law requires that a credit report be given to an individual for free, and in Maine, where the fee is capped at $3. Trans Union will also give you a free copy of your credit report if you were denied credit.

T.R.W.

Woodfield Corporate Center
Suite 600
425 N. Martingale Road
Schaumburg, IL 60173
(800) 831-5614

Will give you one free copy of your credit report each year, whether or not your credit was denied.

Equifax

Credit Information Services
PO Box 105873
5505 Peachtree Dunwoody Road
Suite 600
Atlanta, GA 30348
(770) 612-2585

Equifax charges up to $8 for a copy of your credit report (except in Maryland and Vermont, where by law it's free, or in Maine, where it's capped at $3).

GOVERNMENTAL AND QUASI-GOVERNMENTAL ORGANIZATIONS

Federal Trade Commission

Correspondence Branch
Washington, DC 20580

The Federal Trade Commission enforces a number of federal credit laws and provides consumers with free information about them. The following comes from "Building A Better Credit Record," a free publication produced by the Federal Trade Commission in cooperation with the Associated Credit Bureaus, Inc., National Foundation for Consumer Credit, U.S. Office of Consumer Affairs, and the Consumer Information Center:

- *The Equal Credit Opportunity Act* prohibits the denial of credit because of your sex, race, marital status, religion, national origin, age, or because you receive public assistance.
- *The Fair Credit Reporting Act* gives you the right to learn what information is being distributed about you by credit bureaus.
- *The Truth in Lending Act* requires lenders to give you written disclosures of the cost of credit and terms of repayment before you enter into a credit transaction.
- *The Fair Credit Billing Act* establishes procedures for resolving billing errors on your credit-card accounts.

313

• *The Fair Debt Collection Practices Act* prohibits debt collectors from using unfair or deceptive practices to collect overdue bills that your creditor has forwarded for collection.

For brochures on these laws, or related publications, including "Credit Billing Blues," "Credit and Older Americans," "Scoring For Credit," "Solving Credit Problems," "Women and Credit Histories," and "Building A Better Credit Record: What To Do and What To Avoid," write to Public Reference, Federal Trade Commission, Washington, DC 20580.

Department of Housing and Urban Development (HUD)

451 7th Street, SW
Washington, DC 20410
To locate the HUD office nearest to you: (202) 708-1112
To get program information: (202) 708-4374
HUD-User, a clearinghouse of information: (800) 245-2691

This agency provides programs for low-income housing, including public housing and privately owned rental housing. It supports housing-related site development and housing rehabilitation through Community Development Block Grants to state and local governments. It also provides support for the residential mortgage market through the Federal Housing Administration (FHA) mortgage insurance program and Government National Mortgage Association (Ginnie Mae) mortgage-backed securities guarantee program.

There is a local HUD office in nearly every major urban area. If you are located outside of an urban area call the HUD office in your state capital or in Washington, DC to find the office located closest to you.

Consumer Product Safety Division

Washington, DC 20207
(800) 638-2772

Call this toll-free number to lodge a complaint about the safety of houses and buildings, including smoke alarms, electrical systems, indoor air quality, and home insulation. You can also get recall information and safety tips. If you negotiate the options successfully, an operator will eventually come on the line to take your complaint.

Department of Veterans Affairs (VA)

Loan Guarantee Service
Department of Veterans Affairs
810 Vermont Avenue, NW
Washington, DC 20420
General number: (800) 827-1000

The federal agency that guarantees a portion of home loans to veterans and regulates their distribution. The Department of Veterans Affairs publishes a pamphlet about guaranteed home loans for veterans that's free for the writing. Contact your local VA office (you can call the general number for information) for additional information.

The Department of Veterans Affairs also runs a Vendee Financing program, which provides inexpensive financing (with little or no down payment required, and a discount for a cash purchase) of VA-acquired homes. You need not be a veteran to qualify. Check with the Loan Guarantee Service for more information and current qualification.

Consumer Publications

For a list of consumer publications that may be useful to you as a first-time (or repeat) home buyer, write to Consumer Publications, Pueblo, Colorado 81003. Especially useful is the "Consumer Credit Handbook."

National Council for State Housing Agencies

444 N. Capital Street, NW
Suite 438
Washington, DC 20001
(202) 624-7710

NCSHA is an advocacy group for low-income housing in Washington. It represents state housing finance agencies in all fifty states, plus Puerto Rico and the Virgin Islands. If you are unable to find your state housing finance agency, write to this organization.

As of 1990, there were more than 180 public agencies that provide financial assistance to first-time buyers. Generally, there are home price and family income limitations. Your state housing agency or real estate agent should be able to point you in the right direction.

Federal National Mortgage Association (Fannie Mae)

Headquarters
3900 Wisconsin Avenue, NW
Washington, DC 20016
(800) 7-FANNIE

Fannie Mae, the nation's largest investor in home mortgages, is a private corporation, federally chartered to provide financial products and services that increase the availability and affordability of housing for low-, moderate-, and middle-income Americans. Fannie Mae buys residential mortgages for its investment portfolio. If you call the 800 number, you'll get the public information office, and will be able to order information packets on Community Homebuyers programs, as well as other first-time buyer information.

Consumer Credit Counseling Service

CCCS National Referral Number: (800) 388-2227

A nationwide, non-profit service with local representatives in every major city across the country, this organization provides many services to first-time buyers, including credit and comprehensive housing counseling. These services are confidential and typically free of charge or available at an extremely low cost. CCCS offices can prequalify buyers and talk about various mortgage types and may be able to tap you into affordable housing programs.

Be aware that CCCS is funded by national credit institutions, and while their advice to pay off your debt rather than declare bankruptcy will help your personal credit, it may not be the best financial decision for you. Consult an outside source, such as your accountant or tax advisor, before agreeing to any long-term debt workout schemes.

For more information, look in your telephone book for the nearest CCCS offices to you.

Council of Better Business Bureaus

Headquarters
4200 Wilson Boulevard, Suite 800
Arlington, VA 22203
(703) 276-0100

This organization is dedicated to consumers and attempts to be an effective national self-regulation force for business. The headquarters can help you find the bureau nearest you.

Home Information Center, Part of the Office of Affordable Housing

PO Box 7189
Gaithersburg, MD 20898-7189
(800) 998-9999

This organization works with two programs: The Home Program and Hope 3. The Home Program gives grant money to nonprofit associations. Hope 3 is a single family home buyer program using government help properties. For more information on Hope 3, call the 800 number.

CONSUMER INFORMATION

Good Advice Press

(800) 255-0899

Sells "The Banker's Secret" book, cassette, and software which helps readers calculate the benefits of prepaying mortgages or credit card debt. Good Advice Press also publishes a quarterly newsletter with information on how to cut down debt and save money.

Cardtrak

RAM Research Corp.
PO Box 1700
Frederick, MD 21702

A monthly survey that tracks low-rate credit cards, no-annual-fee credit cards, gold cards, reward credit cards, and secured credit cards and their interest rates. To get a copy, send $5 to the above address.

Consumer Federation of America (CFA)

Headquarters
1424 16th Street, NW
Suite 604
Washington, DC 20036
(202) 387-6121

The Consumer Federation of America has 240 pro-consumer organizations with 50 million individual members. It is a lobbying group that represents consumer interests on Capitol Hill. It publishes CFANews eight times each year. Occasionally, it will copublish a booklet on residential real estate with a related organization.

Insurance Information Institute

110 William Street
New York, NY 10038

The Insurance Information Institute is a nonprofit communications, educational, and fact-finding organization dedicated to improving the public's understanding of the property/casualty insurance business.

SchoolMatch

5027 Pine Creek Drive
Westerville, Ohio 43081
(800) 992-5323

SchoolMatch is a company that develops reports on schools and school districts all over the country. They currently sell tens of thousands of reports each year, usually for home buyers who want an independent evaluation of a school or school district. SchoolMatch reports list all kinds of information, from test scores to special programs. The company also offers a program that will search for the right school district for your children, matching their needs to specific programs.

National Association of Mortgage Planners (NAMP)

Headquarters
3001 LBJ Freeway
Suite 105
Dallas, TX 75234
(800) 724-2004

Established in 1994, NAMP members work on the borrower's behalf to find a mortgage that meets their financial needs. In addition, they disclose upfront all fees they will receive for making the loan. NAMP also takes calls from consumers who don't understand the mortgage process or are unhappy with their own mortgage brokers. The organization fields all mortgage-related calls from the Texas Real Estate Commission. Consumers who have questions should call the 800 number.

Glossary of
Real Estate Terms

Abstract (of Title)   A summary of the public records affecting the title to a particular piece of land. An attorney or title insurance company officer creates the abstract of title by examining all recorded instruments (documents) relating to a specific piece of property, such as easements, liens, mortgages, etc.

Acceleration Clause   A provision in a loan agreement that allows the lender to require the balance of the loan to become due immediately if mortgage payments are not made or there is a breach in your obligation under your mortgage or note.

Addendum   Any addition to, or modification of, a contract. Also called an amendment or rider.

Adjustable-Rate Mortgage (ARM)   A type of loan whose prevailing interest rate is tied to an economic index (like one-year Treasury Bills), which fluctuates with the market. There are three types of ARMs, including one-year ARMs, which adjust every year; three-year ARMs, which adjust every three years; and five-year ARMs, which adjust every five years. When the loan adjusts, the lender tacks a margin onto the economic index rate to come up with your loan's new rate. ARMs are considered far riskier than fixed-rate mortgages, but their starting interest rates are extremely low, and in the past five to ten years, people have done very well with them.

Agency   A term used to describe the relationship between a seller and a broker, or a buyer and a broker.

Agency Closing   The lender's use of a title company or other party to act on the lender's behalf for the purposes of closing on the purchase of a home or refinancing of a loan.

Agent An individual who represents a buyer or a seller in the purchase or sale of a home. Licensed by the state, an agent must work for a broker or a brokerage firm.

Agreement of Sale This document is also known as the contract of purchase, purchase agreement, or sales agreement. It is the agreement by which the seller agrees to sell you his or her property if you pay a certain price. It contains all the provisions and conditions for the purchase, must be written, and is signed by both parties.

Amortization A payment plan which enables the borrower to reduce his debt gradually through monthly payments of principal and interest. Amortization tables allow you to see exactly how much you would pay each month in interest and how much you repay in principal, depending on the amount of money borrowed at a specific interest rate.

Annual Percentage Rate (APR) The total cost of your loan, expressed as a percentage rate of interest, which includes not only the loan's interest rate, but factors in all the costs associated with making that loan, including closing costs and fees. The costs are then amortized over the life of the loan. Banks are required by the federal Truth-in-Lending statutes to disclose the APR of a loan, which allows borrowers a common ground for comparing various loans from different lenders.

Application A series of documents you must fill out when you apply for a loan.

Application Fee A one-time fee charged by the mortgage company for processing your application for a loan. Sometimes the application fee is applied toward certain costs, including the appraisal and credit report.

Appraisal The opinion of an appraiser, who estimates the value of a home at a specific point in time.

Articles-of-Agreement Mortgage A type of seller financing which allows the buyer to purchase the home in installments over a specified period of time. The seller keeps legal title to the home until the loan is paid off. The buyer receives an interest in the property—called equitable title—but does not own it. However, because the buyer is paying the real estate taxes and paying interest to the seller, it is the buyer who receives the tax benefits of home ownership.

Assumption of Mortgage If you assume a mortgage when you purchase a home, you undertake to fulfill the obligations of the existing loan agreement the seller made with the lender. The obligations are similar to those that you would incur if you took out a new mortgage. When assuming a mortgage, you become personally liable for the payment of principal and interest. The seller, or original mortgagor, is released from the liability, and should get that release in writing. Otherwise, he or she could be liable if you don't make the monthly payments.

Balloon Mortgage   A type of mortgage which is generally short in length, but is amortized over twenty-five or thirty years so that the borrower pays a combination of interest and principal each month. At the end of the loan term, the entire balance of the loan must be repaid at once.

Broker   An individual who acts as the agent of the seller or buyer. A real estate broker must be licensed by the state.

Building Line or Setback   The distance from the front, back, or side of a lot beyond which construction or improvements may not extend without permission by the proper governmental authority. The building line may be established by a filed plat of subdivision, by restrictive covenants in deeds, by building codes, or by zoning ordinances.

Buy Down   An incentive offered by a developer or seller that allows the buyer to lower his or her initial interest rate by putting up a certain amount of money. A buy down also refers to the process of paying extra points up front at the closing of your loan in order to have a lower interest rate over the life of the loan.

Buyer Broker   A buyer broker is a real estate broker who specializes in representing buyers. Unlike a seller broker or conventional broker, the buyer broker has a fiduciary duty to the buyer, because the buyer accepts the legal obligation of paying the broker. The buyer broker is obligated to find the best property for a client, and then negotiate the best possible purchase price and terms. Buyer brokerage has gained a significant amount of respect in recent years, since the National Association of Realtors has changed its code of ethics to accept this designation.

Buyer's Market   Market conditions that favor the buyer. A buyer's market is usually expressed when there are too many homes for sale, and a home can be bought for less money.

Certificate of Title   A document or instrument issued by a local government agency to a homeowner, naming the homeowner as the owner of a specific piece of property. At the sale of the property, the certificate of title is transferred to the buyer. The agency then issues a new certificate of title to the buyer.

Chain of Title   The lineage of ownership of a particular property.

Closing   The day when buyers and sellers sign the papers and actually swap money for title to the new home. The closing finalizes the agreements reached in the sales agreement.

Closing Costs   This phrase can refer to a lender's costs for closing on a loan, or it can mean all the costs associated with closing on a piece of property. Considering all closing costs, it's easy to see that closing can be expensive for both buyers and sellers. A home buyer's closing costs might include: lender's points, loan origination or loan service fees; loan application fee; lender's credit report; lender's processing fee; lender's document preparation fee; lender's appraisal fee; prepaid interest on the loan; lender's insurance escrow; lender's real estate tax escrow; lender's tax escrow service fee; cost for the lender's title policy; special endorsements to the lender's title policy; house inspection fees; title company closing fee; deed or mortgage recording fees; local municipal, county, and state taxes; and the attorney's fee. A seller's closing costs might include: survey (which in some parts of the country is paid for by the buyer); title insurance; recorded release of mortgage; broker's commission; state, county, and local municipality transfer taxes; credit to the buyer for unpaid real estate taxes and other bills; attorney's fees; FHA fees and costs.

Cloud (on Title)   An outstanding claim or encumbrance that adversely affects the marketability of a property.

Commission   The amount of money paid to the broker by the seller (or, in some cases, the buyer), as compensation for selling the home. Usually, the commission is a percentage of the sales price of the home, and generally hovers in the 5 to 7 percent range. There is no "set" commission rate. It is always and entirely negotiable.

Condemnation   The government holds the right to "condemn" land for public use, even against the will of the owner. The government, however, must pay fair market price for the land. Condemnation may also mean that the government has decided a particular piece of land, or a dwelling, is unsafe for human habitation.

Condominium   A dwelling of two or more units in which you individually own the interior space of your unit and jointly own common areas such as the lobby, roof, parking, plumbing, and recreational areas.

Contingency   A provision in a contract that sets forth one or more conditions that must be met prior to the closing. If the contingency is not met, usually the party who is benefitting from the contingency can terminate the contract. Some common contingencies include financing, inspection, attorney approval, and toxic substances.

Contract to Purchase   Another name for Agreement of Sale.

Contractor   In the building industry, the contractor is the individual who contracts to build the property. He or she erects the structure and manages the subcontracting (to the electrician, plumber, etc.) until the project is finished.

Conventional Mortgage A conventional mortgage means that the loan is underwritten by banks, savings and loans, or other types of mortgage companies. There are also certain limitations imposed on conventional mortgages that allow them to be sold to private institutional investors (like pension funds) on the secondary market. For example, as of 1993, the loan must be less than $203,500, otherwise it is considered a "jumbo" loan. Also, if you are buying a condominium, conventional financing decrees that the condo building be more than 70 percent owner-occupied.

Co-op Cooperative housing refers to a building, or a group of buildings, that is owned by a corporation. The shareholders of the corporation are the people who live in the building. They own shares—which gives them the right to lease a specific unit within the building—in the corporation that owns their building and pay "rent" or monthly maintenance assessments for the expenses associated with living in the building. Co-ops are relatively unknown outside of New York, Chicago, and a few other cities. Since the 1970s, condominiums have become much more popular.

Counteroffer When the seller or buyer responds to a bid. If you decide to offer $100,000 for a home listed at $150,000, the seller might counter your offer and propose that you purchase the home for $140,000. That new proposal, and any subsequent offer, is called a counteroffer.

Covenant Assurances or promises set out in the deed or a legally binding contract, or implied in the law. For example, when you obtain title to a property by warranty, there is the Covenant of Quiet Enjoyment, which gives you the right to enjoy your property without disturbances.

Credit Report A lender will decide whether or not to give you a loan based on your credit history. A credit report lists all of your credit accounts (such as charge cards), and any debts or late payments that have been reported to the credit company.

Cul de Sac A street that ends in a U-shape, leading the driver or pedestrian back to the beginning. The cul de sac has become exceptionally popular with modern subdivision developers, who use the design technique to create quiet streets and give the development a nonlinear feel.

Custom Builder A home builder who builds houses for individual owners to the owners' specification. The home builder may either own a piece of property or build a home on someone else's land.

Debt Service The total amount of debt (credit cards, mortgage, car loan) that an individual is carrying at any one time.

Declaration of Restrictions   Developers of condominiums (or any other type of housing unit that functions as a condo) are required to file a condominium declaration, which sets out the rules and restrictions for the property, the division of ownership, and the rights and privileges of the owners. The "condo dec" or "home owner's dec," as it is commonly called, reflects the developer's original intent, and may only be changed by unit-owner vote. There are other types of declarations, including homeowners' association and town house association. Co-op dwellers are governed by a similar type of document.

Deed   The document used to transfer ownership in a property from seller to buyer.

Deed of Trust   A deed of trust or trust deed is an instrument similar to a mortgage that gives the lender the right to foreclose on the property if there is a default under the trust deed or note by the borrower.

Deposit   Money given by the buyer to the seller with a signed contract to purchase or offer to purchase, as a show of good faith. Also called the earnest money.

Down Payment   The cash put into a purchase by the borrower. Lenders like to see the borrower put at least 20 percent down in cash, because lenders generally believe that if you have a higher cash down payment, it is less likely the home will go into foreclosure. In recent years, however, lenders have become more flexible about cash down payments; recently, lenders have begun accepting cash down payments of as little as 5 percent.

Dual Agency   When a real estate broker represents both the buyer and the seller in a single transaction it creates a situation known as dual agency. In most states, brokers must disclose to the buyer and to the seller whom they are representing. Even with disclosure, dual agency presents a conflict of interest for the broker in the transaction. If the broker is acting as the seller broker and the subagent for the seller (by bringing the buyer), then anything the buyer tells the broker must by law be brought to the seller's attention. If the broker represents the seller as a seller broker and the buyer as a buyer broker in the same transaction, the broker will receive money from both the buyer and the seller, an obvious conflict of interest.

Due on Sale Clause   Nearly every mortgage has this clause, which states that the mortgage must be paid off in full upon the sale of the home.

Earnest Money   The money the buyer gives the seller up front as a show of good faith. It can be as much as 10 percent of the purchase price. Earnest money is sometimes called a deposit.

Easement   A right given by a landowner to a third party to make use of the land in a specific way. There may be several easements on your property, including for passage of utility lines or poles, sewer or water mains, and even a driveway. Once the right is given, it continues indefinitely, or until released by the party who received it.

Eminent Domain   The right of the government to condemn private land for public use. The government must, however, pay full market value for the property.

Encroachment   When your neighbor builds a garage or a fence, and it occupies your land, it is said to "encroach on" your property.

Encumbrance   A claim or lien or interest in a property by another party. An encumbrance hinders the seller's ability to pass good, marketable, and unencumbered title to you.

Escrow Closing   A third party, usually a title company, acts as the neutral party for the receipt of documents for the exchange of the deed by the sellers for the buyer's money. The final exchange is completed when the third party determines that certain preset requirements have been satisfied.

Escrow (for Earnest Money)   The document that creates the arrangement whereby a third party or broker holds the earnest money for the benefit of the buyer and seller.

Escrow (for Real Estate Taxes and Insurance)   An account in which monthly installments for real estate taxes and property insurance are held—usually in the name of the home buyer's lender.

Fee Simple   The most basic type of ownership, under which the owner has the right to use and dispose of the property at will.

Fiduciary Duty   A relationship of trust between a broker and a seller or a buyer broker and a buyer, or an attorney and a client.

First Mortgage   A mortgage that takes priority over all other voluntary liens.

Fixture   Personal property, such as a built-in bookcase, furnace, hot water heater, and recessed lights, that becomes "affixed" because it has been permanently attached to the home.

Foreclosure   The legal action taken to extinguish a home owner's right and interest in a property, so that the property can be sold in a foreclosure sale to satisfy a debt.

Gift Letter   A letter to the lender indicating that a gift of cash has been made to the buyer and that it is not expected to be repaid. The letter must detail the amount of the gift, and the name of the giver.

327

Good Faith Estimate (GFE)   Under RESPA, lenders are required to give potential borrowers a written Good Faith Estimate of closing costs within three days of an application submission.

Grace Period   The period of time after a loan payment due date in which a mortgage payment may be made and not be considered delinquent.

Graduated Payment Mortgage   A mortgage in which the payments increase over the life of the mortgage, allowing the borrower to make very low payments at the beginning of the loan.

Hazard Insurance   Insurance that covers the property from damages that might materially affect its value. Also known as homeowner's insurance.

Holdback   An amount of money held back at closing by the lender or the escrow agent until a particular condition has been met. If the problem is a repair, the money is kept until the repair is made. If the repair is not made, the lender or escrow agent uses the money to make the repair. Buyers and sellers may also have holdbacks between them, to ensure that specific conditions of the sale are met.

Homeowner's Association   A group of home owners in a particular subdivision or area who band together to take care of common property and common interests.

Homeowner's Insurance   Coverage that includes hazard insurance, as well as personal liability and theft.

Home Warranty   A service contract that covers appliances (with exclusions) in working condition in the home for a certain period of time, usually one year. Home owners are responsible for a per-call service fee. There is a home owner's warranty for new construction. Some developers will purchase a warranty from a company specializing in new construction for the homes they sell. A home owner's warranty will warrant the good working order of the appliances and workmanship of a new home for between one and ten years; for example, appliances might be covered for one year while the roof may be covered for several years.

Housing and Urban Development, Department of   Also known as HUD, this is the federal department responsible for the nation's housing programs. It also regulates RESPA, the Real Estate Settlement Procedures Act, which governs how lenders must deal with their customers.

Inspection   The service an inspector performs when he or she is hired to scrutinize the home for any possible structural defects. May also be done in order to check for the presence of toxic substances, such as leaded paint or water, asbestos, radon, or pests, including termites.

Installment Contract   The purchase of property in installments. Title to the property is given to the purchaser when all installments are made.

Institutional Investors or Lenders   Private or public companies, corporations, or funds (such as pension funds) that purchase loans on the secondary market from commercial lenders such as banks and savings and loans. Or, they are sources of funds for mortgages through mortgage brokers.

Interest   Money charged for the use of borrowed funds. Usually expressed as an interest rate, it is the percentage of the total loan charged annually for the use of the funds.

Interest-Only Mortgage   A loan in which only the interest is paid on a regular basis (usually monthly), and the principal is owed in full at the end of the loan term.

Interest Rate Cap   The total number of percentage points that an adjustable-rate mortgage (ARM) might rise over the life of the loan.

Joint Tenancy   An equal, undivided ownership in a property taken by two or more owners. Under joint tenancy there are rights of survivorship, which means that if one of the owners dies, the surviving owner rather than the heirs of the estate inherits the other's total interest in the property.

Landscape   The trees, flowers, planting, lawn, and shrubbery that surround the exterior of a dwelling.

Late Charge   A penalty applied to a mortgage payment that arrives after the grace period (usually the 10th or 15th of a month).

Lease with an Option to Buy   When the renter or lessee of a piece of property has the right to purchase the property for a specific period of time at a specific price. Usually, a lease with an option to buy allows a first-time buyer to accumulate a down payment by applying a portion of the monthly rent toward the down payment.

Lender   A person, company, corporation, or entity that lends money for the purchase of real estate.

Letter of Intent   A formal statement, usually in letter form, from the buyer to the seller stating that the buyer intends to purchase a specific piece of property for a specific price on a specific date.

Leverage   Using a small amount of cash, say a 10 or 20 percent down payment, to purchase a piece of property.

Lien   An encumbrance against the property, which may be voluntary or involuntary. There are many different kinds of liens, including a tax lien (for unpaid federal, state, or real estate taxes), a judgment lien (for

329

monetary judgments by a court of law), a mortgage lien (when you take out a mortgage), and a mechanic's lien (for work done by a contractor on the property that has not been paid for). For a lien to be attached to the property's title, it must be filed or recorded with local county government.

Listing   A property that a broker agrees to list for sale in return for a commission.

Loan   An amount of money that is lent to a borrower, who agrees to repay it plus interest.

Loan Commitment   A written document that states that a mortgage company has agreed to lend a buyer a certain amount of money at a certain rate of interest for a specific period of time, which may contain sets of conditions and a date by which the loan must close.

Loan Origination Fee   A one-time fee charged by the mortgage company to arrange the financing for the loan.

Loan-to-Value Ratio   The ratio of the amount of money you wish to borrow compared to the value of the property you wish to purchase. Institutional investors (who buy loans on the secondary market from your mortgage company) set up certain ratios that guide lending practices. For example, the mortgage company might only lend you 80 percent of a property's value.

Location   Where property is geographically situated. "Location, location, location" is a broker's maxim that states that where the property is located is its most important feature, because you can change everything about a house, except its location.

Lock-In   When a borrower signals to a mortgage company that he or she has decided to lock in, or take, a particular interest rate for a specific amount of time. The mechanism by which a borrower locks in the interest rate that will be charged on a particular loan. Usually, the lock lasts for a certain time period, such as thirty, forty-five, or sixty days. On a new construction, the lock may be much longer.

Maintenance Fee   The monthly or annual fee charged to condo, co-op, or townhouse owners, and paid to the homeowner's association, for the maintenance of common property. Also called an assessment.

Mortgage   A document granting a lien on a home in exchange for financing granted by a lender. The mortgage is the means by which the lender secures the loan and has the ability to foreclose on the home.

330

Mortgage Banker   A company or a corporation, like a bank, that lends its own funds to borrowers in addition to bringing together lenders and borrowers. A mortgage banker may also service the loan (i.e., collect the monthly payments).

Mortgage Broker   A company or individual that brings together lenders and borrowers and processes mortgage applications.

Mortgagee   A legal term for the lender.

Mortgagor   A legal term for the borrower.

Multiple Listing Service (MLS)   A computerized listing of all properties offered for sale by member brokers. Buyers may only gain access to the MLS by working with a member broker.

Negative Amortization   A condition created when the monthly mortgage payment is less than the amount necessary to pay off the loan over the period of time set forth in the note. Because you're paying less than the amount necessary, the actual loan amount increases over time. That's how you end up with negative equity. To pay off the loan, a lump-sum payment must be made.

Option   When a buyer pays for the right or option to purchase property for a given length of time, without having the obligation to actually purchase the property.

Origination Fee   A fee charged by the lender for allowing you to borrow money to purchase property. The fee—which is also referred to as points—is usually expressed as a percentage of the total loan amount.

Ownership   The absolute right to use, enjoy, and dispose of property. You own it!

Package Mortgage   A mortgage that uses both real and personal property to secure a loan.

Paper   Slang usage that refers to the mortgage, trust deed, installment, and land contract.

Personal Property   Moveable property, such as appliances, furniture, clothing, and artwork.

PITI   An acronym for Principal-Interest-Taxes-and-Insurance. These are usually the four parts of your monthly mortgage payment.

Pledged Account   Borrowers who do not want to have a real estate tax or insurance escrow administered by the mortgage servicer can, in some circumstances, pledge a savings account into which enough money to cover real estate taxes and the insurance premium must be deposited. You must then make the payments for your real estate taxes and insurance premiums from a separate account. If you fail to pay your taxes or premiums, the lender is allowed to use the funds in the pledged account to make those payments.

Point   A point is one percent of the loan amount.

Possession   Being in control of a piece of property, and having the right to use it to the exclusion of all others.

Power of Attorney   The legal authorization given to an individual to act on behalf of another individual.

Prepaid Interest   Interest paid at closing for the number of days left in the month after closing. For example, if you close on the 15th, you would prepay the interest for the 16th through the end of the month.

Prepayment Penalty   A fine imposed when a loan is paid off before it comes due. Many states now have laws against prepayment penalties, although banks with federal charters are exempt from state laws. If possible, do not use a mortgage that has a prepayment penalty, or you will be charged a fine if you sell your property before your mortgage has been paid off.

Prequalifying for a Loan   When a mortgage company tells a buyer in advance of the formal application approximately how much money the buyer can afford to borrow.

Principal   The amount of money you borrow.

Private Mortgage Insurance (PMI)   Special insurance that specifically protects the top 20 percent of a loan, allowing the lender to lend more than 80 percent of the value of the property. PMI is paid in monthly installments by the borrower.

Property Tax   A tax levied by a county or local authority on the value of real estate.

Proration   The proportional division of certain costs of home ownership. Usually used at closing to figure out how much the buyer and seller each owe for certain expenditures, including real estate taxes, assessments, and water bills.

Purchase Agreement   An agreement between the buyer and seller for the purchase of property.

Purchase Money Mortgage   An instrument used in seller financing, a purchase money mortgage is signed by a buyer and given to the seller in exchange for a portion of the purchase price.

Quitclaim Deed   A deed that operates to release any interest in a property that a person may have, *without a representation that he or she actually has* *a right in that property.* For example, Sally may use a quit-claim deed to grant Bill her interest in the White House, in Washington, D.C., although she may not actually own, or have any rights to, that particular house.

Real Estate   Land, and anything permanently attached to it, such as buildings and improvements.

Real Estate Agent   An individual licensed by the state, who acts on behalf of the seller or buyer. For his or her services, the agent receives a commission, which is usually expressed as a percentage of the sales price of a home and is split with his or her real estate firm. A real estate agent must either be a real estate broker or work for one.

Real Estate Attorney   An attorney who specializes in the purchase and sale of real estate.

Real Estate Broker   An individual who is licensed by the state to act as an agent on behalf of the seller or buyer. For his or her services, the broker receives a commission, which is usually expressed as a percentage of the sales price of a home.

Real Estate Settlement Procedures Act (RESPA)   This federal statute was originally passed in 1974, and contains provisions that govern the way companies involved with a real estate closing must treat each other and the consumer. For example, one section of RESPA requires lenders to give consumers a written Good Faith Estimate within three days of making an application for a loan. Another section of RESPA prohibits title companies from giving referral fees to brokers for steering business to them.

Realtist   A designation given to an agent or broker who is a member of the National Association of Real Estate Brokers.

Realtor   A designation given to a real estate agent or broker who is a member of the National Association of Realtors.

Recording   The process of filing documents at a specific government office. Upon such recording, the document becomes part of the public record.

Redlining   The slang term used to describe an illegal practice of discrimination against a particular racial group by real estate lenders. Redlining occurs when lenders decide certain areas of a community are too high risk and refuse to lend to buyers who want to purchase property in those areas, regardless of their qualifications or creditworthiness.

Regulation Z   Also known as the Truth in Lending Act. Congress determined that lenders must provide a written good faith estimate of closing costs to all borrowers and provide them with other written information about the loan.

Reserve   The amount of money set aside by a condo, co-op, or homeowners' association for future capital improvements.

Sale-Leaseback   A transaction in which the seller sells property to a buyer, who then leases the property back to the seller. This is accomplished within the same transaction.

Sales Contract   The document by which a buyer contracts to purchase property. Also known as the purchase contract or a Contract to Purchase.

Second Mortgage   A mortgage that is obtained after the primary mortgage, and whose rights for repayment are secondary to the first mortgage.

Seller Broker   A broker who has a fiduciary responsibility to the seller. Most brokers are seller brokers, although an increasing number are buyer brokers, who have a fiduciary responsibility to the buyer.

Settlement Statement   A statement that details the monies paid out and received by the buyer and seller at closing.

Shared Appreciation Mortgage   A relatively new mortgage used to help first-time buyers who might not qualify for conventional financing. In a shared appreciation mortgage, the lender offers a below-market interest rate in return for a portion of the profits made by the home owner when the property is sold. Before entering into a shared appreciation mortgage, be sure to have your real estate attorney review the documentation.

Special Assessment   An additional charge levied by a condo or co-op board in order to pay for capital improvements, or other unforeseen expenses.

Subagent   A broker who brings the buyer to the property. Although subagents would appear to be working for the buyer (a subagent usually ferries around the buyer, showing him or her properties), they are paid by the seller and have a fiduciary responsibility to the seller. Subagency is often confusing to first-time buyers, who think that because the subagent shows them property, the subagent is "their" agent, rather than the seller's.

Subdivision   The division of a large piece of property into several smaller pieces. Usually a developer or a group of developers will build single family or duplex homes of a similar design and cost within one subdivision.

Tax Lien   A lien that is attached to property if the owner does not pay his or her real estate taxes or federal income taxes. If overdue property taxes are not paid, the owner's property might be sold at auction for the amount owed in back taxes.

Tenancy by the Entirety   A type of ownership whereby both the husband and wife each own the complete property. Each spouse has an ownership interest in the property as their marital residence and, as a result, creditors cannot force the sale of the home to pay back the debts of one spouse without the other spouse's consent. There are rights of survivorship whereby upon the death of one spouse, the other spouse would immediately inherit the entire property.

Tenants in Common A type of ownership in which two or more parties have an undivided interest in the property. The owners may or may not have equal shares of ownership, and there are no rights of survivorship. However, each owner retains the right to sell his or her share in the property as he or she sees fit.

Title Refers to the ownership of a particular piece of property.

Title Company The corporation or company that insures the status of title (title insurance) through the closing, and may handle other aspects of the closing.

Title Insurance Insurance that protects the lender and the property owner against losses arising from defects or problems with the title to property.

Torrens Title A system of recording the chain of ownership for property, which takes its name from the man who created it in Australia in 1858, Sir Robert Torrens. While that system was popular in the nineteenth century, most cities have converted to other, less cumbersome, systems of recording.

Trust Account An account used by brokers and escrow agents, in which funds for another individual are held separately, and not commingled with other funds.

Underwriter One who underwrites a loan for another. Your lender will have an investor underwrite your loan.

Variable Interest Rate An interest rate that rises and falls according to a particular economic indicator, such as Treasury Bills.

Void A contract or document that is not enforceable.

Voluntary Lien A lien, such as a mortgage, that a homeowner elects to grant to a lender.

Waiver The surrender or relinquishment of a particular right, claim, or privilege.

Warranty A legally binding promise given to the buyer at closing by the seller, generally regarding the condition of the home, property, or other matter.

Zoning The right of the local municipal government to decide how different areas of the municipality will be used. Zoning ordinances are the laws that govern the use of the land.

Acknowledgments

Whoever said God works in mysterious ways must have been a writer. As I wrote this book, I met some wonderful folks who shared their experiences—the good, the bad, and the ugly. I am particularly grateful to the dozens of real estate professionals, who allowed me to tag along behind closed doors and see how their clients really struggled with many of the issues discussed in this book. And, I am equally grateful to the dozens of first-time buyers, who openly discussed their experiences in the hopes that the path to homeownership would be somehow smoother for those who follow.

In the real estate industry, there are spokespeople and public relations folk who have the power to make my job easier or much more difficult. Those who continue to go "above and beyond" include Sharon McHale, Freddie Mac; Liz Johnson, National Association of Realtors; Jeff Hershberger, California Association of Realtors; Sherry Fishman, Fishman Public Relations; Todd Cooley, Cooley & Co.; and Roger Cruzan, Fleishman Hillard. Sources you can trust are hard to find and harder to keep. My thanks to Phil Ravid, of the Chicago accounting firm Ravid & Berstein, for double-checking my numbers and providing easy-to-understand explanations to some complicated personal finance and home-buying quandaries.

A book might have one author, but there are literally dozens of people who help create it, starting with my agent and friend, Alice Martell, whose instincts, tenacity, and patience are treasured. Also, thanks to my attorney, Ralph Martire, for his unchecked wit and wisdom, and his friendship. I continue to be amazed by the quality of the Times Books and Random House staff. Without the help of these wonderful folks, this book wouldn't exist. I am particularly grateful to my publicists, Mary Beth Roche and Diane Henry, who are always looking for new opportunities. Alison Rivers, John Groton, Jennifer Goodall, James Powell, and Paula Schuster are equally talented, helpful, and nice. They, and others, work hard to make all of my books successful, and I am grateful to have them on my team. Olga Sehan's sharp vision helped rein in the manuscript and keep it focused. My brilliant editor and good friend, Carie Freimuth, Associate Publisher of Times Books, made astute suggestions, offered tremendous encouragement, then helped me nurture this book from start to finish, through production, and beyond.

Other friends have offered tremendous support and insights, including Wendy Miller, Maureen O'Grady, Laurie Scheer, Janet Bunn, Pamela Sherrod, Karen Egolf, Ann Hagedorn Auerbach, Henry Ferris, Lisa Kitei, Steve Rynkiewicz, Greg Langer, Jason Klarman, Bob Pisani, Thea Flaum, Sue St. Laurent, Dick Barnes, Malka Margolies, Brad Saul, Janet Franz, Pat Clinton, and Ellen Shubart.

My family continues to be incredibly supportive, offering love and encouragement. I'd like to thank my in-laws, Stan and Margo, Mitch and Alice, Brad and Maru, Linda and Simon, Kiki and Mike, Marya and Tim, Judy, and Alvin and Jackie, for dinners eaten, guest rooms occupied, and for always asking how the real estate market is doing; my mother-in-law, Marilyn, for calling at just the right moment; Grandma Betty and Irving, for sending ruggelah and grapefruit; Aunt Jeanne and Uncle Meyer, for never forgetting to check in; Uncle Richard, for his insights and advice; my sisters, Phyllis and Shona, and my brother-in-law, Jonathan, for their open ears and understanding hearts; my mother, Susanne Glink, who continues to be one of Chicago's top real estate agents, for sharing her stories and suggestions, and for being a wonderful grandma.

Finally, I would never have finished this book without the unstinting help of my husband and best friend, Samuel J. Tamkin, the world's best real estate attorney and one hell of an editor, who continues to believe all my wildest dreams will come true.

Index

339

About the Author

ILYCE R. GLINK is an award-winning, nationally syndicated journalist who writes about real estate, personal finance, business, television, and film. Her work has been published by *Worth* magazine, the *Chicago Sun-Times*, *Chicago Tribune*, *Washington Post*, *Los Angeles Times*, *Working Woman* magazine, *Chicago* magazine, *San Diego Union-Tribune*, *San Francisco Chronicle*, *Electronic Media*, *Crain's New York Business*, *Crain's Chicago Business*, and other publications. Her weekly column, "Real Estate Matters," is read by millions of readers in newspapers published from coast to coast. She hosts *Century 21 REAL ESTATE USA*, a live, nationally-syndicated weekly radio show. She is the author of two books, including the best-selling *100 Questions Every First-Time Home Buyer Should Ask*, which was named Best Consumer Reference Book of 1994 by Chicago Women In Publishing and *100 Questions Every Home Seller Should Ask*. In 1992, Glink was named Best Consumer Reporter by the National Association of Real Estate Editors, and was previously honored by the National Association of Real Estate Editors for an article on Chicago's building boom of the 1980s. She is currently writing a book about personal finance.